LIFE AND WORK
ON THE MISSION FIELD

LIFE AND WORK
ON THE MISSION FIELD

J. HERBERT KANE
Professor Emeritus
School of World Mission and Evangelism
Trinity Evangelical Divinity School
Deerfield, Illinois

BAKER BOOK HOUSE
Grand Rapids, Michigan

Copyright 1980 by
Baker Book House Company

Cloth edition, six printings
Paperback edition, March 1989

ISBN: 0-8010-5282-3

Library of Congress
Catalog Card Number: 80-65010

Printed in the United States of America

The following chapters, with adapations taken from the author's earlier
volume, *The Making of a Missionary,* © 1975 by Baker Book House:
"Getting a Call," "Meeting the Qualifications," and "Overcoming
Obstacles."

Scripture quotations from the Revised Standard Version, copyright 1946,
1952, 1971, 1973.

To
WINNIE
For fifty years
My one and only sweetheart

FOREWORD

God has chosen to use people in accomplishing His purpose of man's redemption. Missions is the most serious work in which a person can possibly be involved. Dr. Kane stated that it is doubtful that any other Christian worker has to meet the rigid requirements as those demanded of missionaries.

Often, however, a commitment to missionary service is made with little or no consideration given to the overall preparation for missions, the demands of missionary life, and the involvement of missionary work. Dr. Kane has in this volume brought all three aspects together. The book is unique and timely. It clears up much of the fog that surrounds missions and provides deeper and fuller understanding of what an effective missionary is and does. It is a valuable resource for the candidate, the missionary, the mission executive, the professor, the pastor, the laity.

The author is eminently qualified to deal with the issues. He is a former missionary to China, a noted missiologist, and a gifted professor and scholar. His own rich life, dedicated to missions, gives authenticity to this work and enhances its usefulness.

Life and Work on the Mission Field deals primarily with areas of concern to the young missionary. Dr. Kane offers an interesting presentation of current missiological theory and practice interspersed with illustrations drawn from daily missionary life. His interpretation of the "missionary call" is biblically sound. He is right on target when he discusses qualifications, other aspects of preparation, and missionary life and work.

All missionaries, whether young or veteran, career or short-term, would benefit greatly from studying this book. I am convinced that thorough study and application would largely weed out those who should not be on the mission field, decrease missionary mistakes and frustrations, and cut down significantly the number of missionary dropouts.

This is a classic textbook, both for training prospective missionaries and for training pastors. Pastoral staff and local church missions committees will find it helpful in understanding missionaries, their preparation, life and work. It will be a useful tool for church education programs on missions. Mission agencies will want to use it in missionary orientation and furlough sessions.

Missionary life and work often is complex; it is not easy. We are indebted to Dr. Kane for this contribution to missions. I heartily commend it to all who are committed to world evangelization.

February 29, 1980   *Edwin L. Frizen, Jr.*
Wheaton, Illinois   Executive Director
                                              Interdenominational Foreign
                                                     Mission Association

PREFACE

Missionary work is not child's play. It has always been difficult. At times it has even been dangerous, especially since the collapse of the colonial system which, in spite of all its evils, provided an umbrella under which the missionary could work in comparative safety.

Stephen Neill has said: "Christian missionary work is the most difficult thing in the world. It is surprising that it should ever have been attempted. It is surprising that it should have been attended by such a measure of success. And it is not at all surprising that an immense number of mistakes should have been made."[1]

Many of the mistakes occurred because would-be missionaries didn't take the time to acquaint themselves with the basic features of life and work on the field. As a result, they didn't know what to expect once they got there.

Missionary life and work are not getting any easier. In some respects they are becoming more difficult and complex. It is imperative that the young missionary have a good understanding of missions before venturing forth to do battle with the powers of darkness.

Even the short-term missionary should take a course or two in missions. This would enable him to avoid having to learn by trial-and-error, a method which can be rather painful to himself, his colleagues, and those to whom he has pledged to minister.

The cost of missionary support is now so high—in some countries $30,000 a year for a family of four—that we can no longer afford to send out and

1. Stephen Neill, *Call to Mission* (Philadelphia, Fortress Press, 1970), p. 24.

support mediocre missionaries who for lack of proper preparation cannot hack it on the mission field.

This book is an attempt to discuss some of the areas of concern to the young missionary. It is written with the hope that it might serve to make missionary life more pleasant and missionary work more effective.

Once again my wife has helped in the writing of a book. After each book is completed she vows that she will not be party to another, but when the time comes she changes her mind and gives unstintingly of her time, thought, and effort. I shudder to think what this book would be like if she had not done so. Any literary merit it may have is due to her untiring efforts to track down every error in spelling, grammar, sentence structure, and paragraph arrangement. She has ruthlessly expunged most if not all of my clichés and substituted more felicitous clichés of her own! I am deeply grateful.

Deerfield, Illinois   *J. Herbert Kane*
Feb. 1, 1980

CONTENTS

Contents

PART THREE
Missionary Work

PART ONE

MISSIONARY PREPARATION

1

Getting a Call

No aspect of the Christian mission is more puzzling than the problem of a call. It is the biggest hang-up that young people encounter as they face the claims of the mission field. At every panel discussion on missions the questions fly thick and fast: "What exactly is a missionary call?" "How can I know that I have a call?" "Can I be a missionary without a call?" These questions are asked by dedicated Christians who take the Great Commission seriously and genuinely desire to know and do God's will. They are fair questions; they deserve honest answers.

In dealing with this most important subject we must avoid two extreme positions. On the one hand there are those who insist that everyone must have what is known as a "Macedonian call" such as Paul experienced at Troas (Acts 16: 9–10). This is usually associated with voices, visions, dreams, and other mysterious happenings whereby a clear knowledge of God's will is directly and infallibly imparted to the consciousness of the seeking soul. According to this viewpoint, without this esoteric experience it is impossible to receive a missionary call. Therefore everyone ought to seek such an experience and wait patiently until it comes.

At the other end of the spectrum are those who maintain that because all Christians are missionaries no call of any kind is required. Missionary work is no different from any other Christian service. Indeed, there is no essential difference between a missionary and a butcher or a baker or a candlestick maker. If you want to be a missionary, catch the next plane, go where you like, and do your own thing when you get there. Don't worry about such

trivial matters as time, call, place, board, or ministry. Just hang loose and
assume that the Lord will guide.

Needless to say, both positions are wrong. Those who advocate the first
frequently end up staying at home. Those who practice the second often do
more harm than good on the mission field and come home with feelings of
failure and frustration. The truth lies somewhere between the two extremes.
This leads us to the first question.

IS A CALL NECESSARY?

Much depends on the kind of call one has in mind. The word *call* is used
in many different ways in the New Testament. In most instances it refers to
Christian life, not service. There is a general call of God (Ro 9: 24–26) which
became articulate in Christ (Lk 5:32). All believers are called to be saints (Ro
1:7), and the ultimate purpose of such a call is that they might be conformed
to the image of Jesus Christ (Ro 8:30). In the meantime, *all* believers are
called to grace (Ga 1:6), peace (1 Co 7:15), light (1 Pe 2:9), hope (Eph 4:4),
glory (1 Th 2:12), holiness (1 Th 4:7), liberty (Ga 5:13), and suffering (1 Pe
2:20–21).

There is, however, a second kind of call—a call to Christian service. This
is not addressed to all, but only to those who are called upon to leave their
ordinary occupation and devote themselves full time to what Peter called
"prayer and the ministry of the Word" (Acts 6:4, KJV). All are called to be
saints (Ro 1:7); not all are called to be apostles (1 Co 12:29). Paul is careful to
point out that he was a genuine apostle (1 Co 9). Moreover he insisted that
he was an apostle by the will (1 Co 1:1) and calling (Ro 1:1) of God. He did
not choose this high calling (1 Co 9:16–18), nor was it conferred on him by
others (Ga 1:1).

He was an apostle "by the will of God," and he described himself as
having been made a minister of the gospel (Eph 3:7). He was appointed to be
a preacher, apostle, and teacher (2 Ti 1:11). It is true, of course, that he
labored with his hands to support himself and his colleagues (Acts 20:34), but
he did not regard tent-making as his vocation. He never referred to himself
as "tent-maker by the will of God," though he certainly did not take himself
out of the will of God by resorting now and then to his old trade. He was an
apostle; he made tents simply to pay the bills. To his dying day Paul could
never adequately express his utter amazement at the grace of God which
made him a preacher and an apostle (1 Co 15:9–10; 1 Ti 1:12–14).

There is a call, a very definite call, to the service of God on a full-time
basis. Jesus "called" Peter and Andrew to follow Him. "Immediately they
left their nets and followed him" (Mt 4:20, RSV). Later He "called" James
and John. "Immediately they left the boat and their father, and followed
him" (Mt 4:22, RSV). When Luke describes the same event he says: "And
when they had brought their boats to land, they left everything and followed
him" (Lk 5:11, KJV).

It seems clear from the passage that this "call" involved a clean break from their work as fishermen and launched them into a brand new occupation, that of "fishers of men." Apparently it was not possible for them to be fishers of fish and fishers of men at the same time. This does not mean that there was anything wrong with their previous occupation or that their new positions were to be regarded as "higher" or "holier." It was a completely different work that would require all of their time and energy. In present-day parlance it would be "full-time Christian service." It is worth noting that these four men and the other apostles never went back to their old occupations.

This idea of a call to Christian service is further strengthened by our Lord's attitude toward those who took it upon themselves to volunteer for His service. One fellow in a moment of enthusiasm said: "I will follow you wherever you go." Jesus replied: "Foxes have holes, and birds of the air have nests; but the Son of man has nowhere to lay his head" (Lk 9:57–58, RSV). Apparently the man withdrew his offer at this point.

Another person volunteered, "I will follow you, Lord; but let me first say farewell to those at my home." Jesus replied: "No one who puts his hand to the plow and looks back is fit for the kingdom of God" (Lk 9:61–62, RSV).

There are those who object to the terms *secular* and *sacred* as applied to the vocational life of the Christian. To the dedicated Christian, all vocations are sacred because whatever he does, he does it unto the Lord (Co 3:23). This does not, however, invalidate the distinction that the New Testament seems to make between secular and sacred ministries.

In several passages of his epistles Paul seems to make a distinction between the "spiritual" and the "secular" or "material" (Ro 15:27; 1 Co 9:11). In his own case Paul was conscious of having been appointed to a special ministry (1 Ti 1:12), that of teaching and preaching the Word (2 Ti 1:11). Moreover, he recognized the possibility that he might fail in the ministry (1 Co 9:27) and expressed the hope that he would be able to complete it (Acts 20:24), which he seems to have done (2 Ti 4:7).

He spoke of Epaphras as a "faithful minister of Christ" (Co 1:7; 4:12), a description he obviously did not apply to everyone. He reminded Timothy of his consecration to the gospel ministry when the elders laid their hands on him (1 Ti 4:14). There is nothing in the New Testament to suggest that men in secular employment were ever set apart for their work by the laying on of hands. This seems to have been reserved for those whose lifework was directly connected with the preaching of the gospel and the life of the church.

Apparently the apostles felt that there was something "sacred" or "special" about their ministry, for when the daily distribution of food threatened the unity of the church in Jerusalem they refused to get involved in "serving tables." They said, "It is not right that we should give up preaching the Word of God to serve tables" (Acts 6:2, RSV). Instead they decided that they would continue to devote themselves to "prayer and the ministry of the Word."

It is difficult to escape the conviction that the early church regarded "prayer and the ministry of the Word" as being the equivalent of what we now call "full-time Christian service." All Christians are expected to work and witness for Christ regardless of their vocation, but only a few are called to leave everything and follow Christ in order to give themselves unreservedly to prayer and the ministry of the Word. It is important to preserve this distinction in a day when egalitarianism threatens to do away with all distinctions between the clergy and the laity in the Christian church.

WHAT ABOUT THE MACEDONIAN CALL?

The so-called Macedonian call (Acts 16:9–10) was not a missionary call at all. Paul had been a missionary for years. His call to missionary service coincided with his conversion, when God said to Ananias, "He is a chosen instrument of mine to carry my name before the Gentiles and kings and the sons of Israel" (Acts 9:15, RSV). Paul's call was later confirmed by the Holy Spirit when He said to the leaders of the church in Antioch: "Set apart for me Barnabas and Saul for the work to which I have called them" (Acts 13:2, RSV).

What then was the nature of the Macedonian call? It was not a divine call; it was simply a human call for help. The call came not from God but from a "man of Macedonia." The plea was, "Come over to Macedonia and help us." This episode had nothing whatsoever to do with a missionary call. It was a matter of guidance to a man already in full-time missionary service. Paul had reached the extreme western end of the continent of Asia and there were several options open to him. Apparently he had not given any thought to crossing over into Europe. He attempted to turn eastward again, first into the Roman province of Asia and then into Bithynia, but the Holy Spirit prevented him in both instances. Where should he go? Obviously he was in need of special guidance if he were to take the gospel for the first time into Europe. The decision he was about to make was of such momentous importance that he required unusual guidance. This God gave him in the vision of the man from Macedonia. It is regrettable that this Macedonian call should have ever been equated with a missionary call.

The term *missionary call* should never have been coined. It is not scriptural and therefore can be harmful. Thousands of youths desiring to serve the Lord have waited for some mysterious "missionary call" that never came. After a time they became weary of waiting and gave up the idea of going to the mission field.

A clear distinction must be made between a call to full-time Christian service and guidance. We have already stated that the "Macedonian call" in Acts 16 was not a missionary call but simply a matter of guidance. The call comes once in a lifetime, and once it is understood and obeyed it need not be repeated. Guidance is something that is required throughout the whole of life.

Where does the Lord want His servant to serve: at home or overseas? A person can't be in both places at the same time, so guidance is necessary. And even when he knows he will be serving overseas he still needs guidance regarding the country to which he will go and the mission under which he will serve. These important considerations are not left to chance or even to the choice of the individual. God deploys His servants according to His own wisdom. He sent Paul to the Gentiles and Peter to the Jews (Ga 2:7–8). He directed William Carey to India, David Livingstone to Africa, and Hudson Taylor to China.

The missionary is not the only one who needs guidance. Those who serve at home need it just as much. Does the Christian worker become a pastor, an evangelist, or a Christian education director? Should he teach in a Bible college or a seminary? If he goes into the pastorate, where will he minister? In Maine or California or Colorado? And how long will he remain in any one church? Five years? Ten years? Thirty years? In all these momentous decisions the Christian worker is dependent on God for guidance. This kind of guidance, however, should not be mistaken for a call.

FACTORS UNDERLYING A CALL

The call to full-time Christian service seldom occurs in a spiritual vacuum. It is based on certain well-defined principles laid down in the Word of God. As one walks with the Lord in the light of His Word, he discovers that step by step he is led to the place where he hears the still small voice behind him saying, "This is the way, walk in it" (Is 30:21, RSV).

1. **Acknowledgment of the claims of Christ.** The first step in the process is the recognition of the lordship of Christ. "Jesus Christ is Lord" was the great affirmation of the early church. That one fact ought to settle everything. He created me for His glory. He redeemed me with His blood. He saved me by His grace. He keeps me by His power. Therefore He has first claim on my life. I am His personal property. Body, mind, and soul I belong to Him. I am His obedient servant. When He speaks, I listen. When He calls, I answer. When He commands, I obey. I have only one question to ask of Him: "Lord, what wilt Thou have me to do?" If He wants me in Christian service I have no option but to obey.

2. **Understanding the will of God.** God's will is twofold, general and specific. His general will embraces His plan and purpose for the whole creation. This is spelled out in broad outlines in the Scriptures. There is no mystery about it. It is plain for all to see. For instance, we know that God is not willing that any should perish, but that all should come to repentance (2 Pe 3:9). When we pray for the salvation of our loved ones and add, "If it be Thy will," we weaken our prayer. God has already told us that it *is* His will. We know that it is His will that *all* of His children should be holy in character and conduct (1 Th 4:3). There can be no doubt about this.

God also has His specific will which differs with each individual Christian. "We are his workmanship, created in Christ Jesus for good works, which God prepared beforehand, that we should walk in them" (Eph 2:10, RSV). God has a tailor-made plan for the life of every believer. The details, of course, are not indicated in the Scriptures. To ascertain the specific will of God, the mind of the believer must be renewed day by day by an act of continual consecration (Ro 12:1–2). When discovered, that will will prove to be "good and acceptable and perfect."

It is not easy, however, to ascertain God's specific will. It takes time and discipline. Moreover, it is impossible to know God's specific will unless we are willing to bring our lives into conformity with His general will. Only when we do His general will, which we do know, will He give us direction regarding His specific will, which we do not know. It is at this point that many Christians go wrong. They pay little attention to what God has revealed regarding His general will but spend much time and thought trying to ascertain His specific will.

3. Susceptibility to the leading of the Holy Spirit. What constitutes a call to Christian service? It is easier to ask that question than to answer it. Indeed, it is probably impossible to answer it to the satisfaction of everyone, for the simple reason that the call is communicated to the soul by the Holy Spirit, who works in different ways with different people. Speaking of the regenerating work of the Holy Spirit, Jesus said, "The wind blows where it wills, and you hear the sound of it, but you do not know whence it comes or whither it goes; so it is with everyone who is born of the Spirit" (Jn 3:8, RSV). The same element of mystery accompanies the consecrating work of the Holy Spirit. He works, moves, directs, and controls in His own sovereign way, and no one can be sure just when, where, or what His next move will be. For this reason it is dangerous to compare one Christian's experience with another's.

No two Christians are alike, either in their conversion experience or in the matter of the guidance that comes later. The Holy Spirit deals with each believer in a manner best suited to his needs and interests, his attitudes and aptitudes. It is therefore difficult to tell another person how the Holy Spirit is likely to lead him.

To most serious-minded Christians Jesus Christ is a "living, bright reality." Not so the Holy Spirit. He seems to be so distant, so ethereal, so unreal, that many Christians aren't even on speaking terms with Him. John E. Skoglund calls Him "the missing person."[1] That is precisely what He is to many Christians. Some of them would have to confess with the believers in Ephesus: "We have never even heard that there is a Holy Spirit" (Acts 19:2, RSV).

To the early church the Holy Spirit was not only a power to be employed

---

1. John E. Skoglund, *To the Whole Creation* (Valley Forge: Judson Press, 1962), chap. 5.

but a person to be loved, trusted, consulted, and obeyed. When the first church council wrote up its final report, it said: "It has seemed good to the Holy Spirit and to us" (Acts 15:28, RSV). Imagine any church council talking like that today!

The Holy Spirit was as real to the early church as Jesus was to His disciples in the days of His flesh. He was indeed the "other comforter" sent to take the place of the risen, ascended Lord (Jn 14:16). The early Christians had little difficulty in getting guidance. They lived on such a high spiritual plane that communion with the Holy Spirit was a matter of course. They confided in Him and He spoke to them. Their ears were attuned to the sound of His voice. When He spoke they listened and obeyed. One problem with present-day Christians is that we have failed to develop our spiritual faculties. We are so busy running here and there to get counsel and advice from pastors, teachers, and guidance counselors that we have neglected to listen for the still small voice of the Holy Spirit. He speaks, but we are not listening. And all the while we wonder why we don't get a call to Christian service.

4. Confirmation by the local church. This is an aspect of the call to Christian service that is prominent in the New Testament but is almost completely missing in church life today. The classic example is the command of the Holy Spirit to the church in Antioch: "Set apart for me Barnabas and Saul for the work to which I have called them" (Acts 13:2, RSV). If the Holy Spirit has already called them, is that not enough? Why does the church have to get in on the act?

The reason is that the church is the pillar and ground of the truth (1 Ti 3:15). It is the channel through which God's saving grace flows out to a needy world (Acts 1:8). The evangelization of the world is not the work of a few individuals but the responsibility of the church as a whole. Paul and Barnabas were sent out by the Holy Spirit *and* the local church, and when they returned they made their report to that church.

All of Paul's coworkers mentioned in the Acts of the Apostles were identified with local churches. Timothy was "well spoken of by the brethren at Lystra and Iconium" (Acts 16:2, RSV). Epaphras hailed from Colossae (Co 1:7), Gaius from Derbe, and Sopater from Berea (Acts 20:4). When the fledgling church in Antioch was just getting under way, the church in Jerusalem sent Barnabas to help the believers there to get established (Acts 11:22). In the early church there were no "independent" missionaries. Each one was a member of a local church, approved by that church, and sent out and supported by that church.

The call to Christian service can come only from the Holy Spirit, but there should be some kind of confirmation on the part of the local church of which the individual is a member. That church will know him best, and if its leadership is what it ought to be, it will be in a position to give its blessing to those going into full-time Christian service. If this were done it would greatly strengthen the hands and encourage the hearts of young candidates for the Christian ministry. It would help to confirm the leading of the Lord.

PREREQUISITES FOR RECEIVING A CALL

God is sovereign in the choice of the servants who will serve Him. This does not mean that we sit down with folded hands and wait for some miraculous event to catapult us into the service of Jesus Christ. There must be on our part an attitude of receptivity and readiness so that when the call comes we will be in a position to hear and answer. The chances of our getting a call will be greatly enhanced if we meet certain conditions. Among these are the following:

1. **An open mind.** Everybody prides himself on having an open mind but few actually achieve it. Man's capacity for self-deception is enormous. We think we have an open mind while in fact we are the victims of our own prejudices and predilections. We have long ago decided that there are certain things we will not do. We wouldn't dare say it to God, but in our own minds we have decided, "Anything but Christian service," or "Anywhere but the foreign field." So long as we harbor preconceived negative notions about the will of God or the work of the church, we shall wait in vain for a call.

It is incumbent on every young Christian to be absolutely honest in his dealings with God, to keep his options open, and to allow the Holy Spirit to take full control of his mental faculties. This is by no means easy. J. B. Phillips expresses it well: "Our battle is to bring down every deceptive fantasy and every imposing defense that men erect against the true knowledge of God. We even fight to capture every thought until it acknowledges the authority of Christ" (2 Co 10:5).

2. **An attentive ear.** An open mind is a great achievement, but it may still fall short unless it is accompanied by an attentive ear. It is not enough to rid one's mind of all "deceptive fantasies." We must also have our ear open to the voice of the Holy Spirit.

We know all too well that the hearing faculty can be turned on or off almost at will. It doesn't take much practice to sharpen one's sense of hearing provided there is sufficient motivation. In the dead of night the young mother can hear the cry of her young child and is instantly on her feet to prepare the two o'clock feeding, while the father in the same room sleeps blissfully through the entire operation. What makes the difference? Do not both parents have the same hearing faculty? The maternal instinct in the mother sharpened her sense of hearing to the point where the slightest cry from the little one in the crib brought her out of bed. She slept, as we say, "with one ear open," while her husband slept with both ears closed.

The same thing can happen in the spiritual realm. With a little practice we can train ourselves to detect the slightest whisper of the Holy Spirit when He speaks to us. On the other hand we can turn a deaf ear to His entreaties. We need do this only two or three times and our hearing faculty will be so impaired that we will be beyond the reach of His voice.

Christians have been known to complain: "How is it that God speaks to others, but never to me?" It may be that God did speak, not once but many times, but they were not listening. Effective communication is possible only when the speaker and the listener are in direct contact. If only one is operating there can be no communication.

3. A pure heart. Understanding God's truth, or ascertaining God's will, is not a purely intellectual exercise. It has a moral dimension. God does not reveal Himself to every Tom, Dick, or Harry whose interest in His truth takes the form of intellectual curiosity. God reveals His truth not to those who want to *know* it but to those who are prepared to *do* it. The Jews of Jesus' day had difficulty in deciding the true origin of His teaching, whether it was from God or from man. Jesus said to them, "If any man's will is to *do* his [God's] will, he shall know whether the teaching is from God or whether I am speaking on my own authority" (Jn 7:17, RSV).

In the Hall of Science at the Century of Progress World's Fair in Chicago in 1933–34, there was a huge motto which read: "Nature reveals her secrets only to those who obey her laws." Every scientist knows the truth of those words. This truth, however, is not confined to the physical realm of science. It is also true in the metaphysical realm of theology. God reveals His truths only to those who obey His laws. One of His laws is that since He is holy (Ps 99:5) all who wish to have fellowship with Him must likewise be holy (He 12:14). King David asked: "Who shall ascend the hill of the Lord? And who shall stand in his holy place?" And the answer came back: "He who has clean hands and a pure heart, who does not lift up his soul to what is false, and does not swear deceitfully" (Ps 24:3–4, RSV). A pure heart is absolutely essential to communication between God and man. The psalmist said: "If I had cherished iniquity in my heart, the Lord would not have listened" (Ps 66:18, RSV).

The person with unconfessed sin in his life will wait in vain for any call from the Lord other than the call to repent (Is 55:7). For the Christian waiting for God's call it is not enough to have an open mind and an attentive ear; he must also have a pure heart.

4. Busy hands. There is a common saying that Satan is sure to find work for idle hands. Doubtless there is some truth in the statement. If Satan prefers idle hands, God certainly does not. If the Scriptures are any criterion, God's call comes to those who are busy, not those who are idle. Moses, David, Peter, Matthew, and Paul were all engaged in some demanding work when the call of God came. He wants workers, not loafers, in His vineyard. Jesus Himself was the great Worker. He said: "My Father is working still, and I am working" (Jn 5:17, RSV). Again He said: "We must work the works of him who sent me while it is day; night comes when no man can work" (Jn 9:4, RSV).

Any person contemplating even the possibility of a call should begin by getting involved in some kind of work for the Lord. How is God going to call a person into full-time service if he has never engaged in any kind of Christian work? One could begin by teaching a Sunday school class, home visitation, tract distribution, or rescue mission work, or leading a youth group, helping in a vacation Bible school, or doing any one of the many things that need to be done in the local church.

In this connection it is instructive to observe that the vast majority of missionary candidates come from the Bible colleges, not from the Christian liberal arts colleges or the secular universities. Why is this? Probably the most important reason is that the Bible colleges require all students to engage in practical Christian work during their four years. During that time they gain courage, experience, and expertise. As a result they acquire a taste for Christian service which they might never have received under different circumstances.

It is tragically possible for a student to spend four years in a Christian liberal arts college and never accept a single Christian service assignment, attend a single missionary prayer meeting, read a single missionary biography or periodical, or even give his testimony in a class meeting. It is fair to ask: How is the Holy Spirit to reach that student with a call to Christian service?

5. Ready feet. The psalmist said: "I will run in the way of thy commandments" (Ps 119:32, RSV). Isaiah said: "How beautiful on the mountains are the feet of him who brings good tidings, who publishes peace" (Is 52:7, RSV). The time is short (1 Co 7:29, RSV) and the king's business requires haste (1 Sa 21:8, RSV). Indecision and procrastination have more than once played havoc with a call to Christian service.

Young people facing Christian service encounter two temptations. One is to run before the Lord; the other is to lag behind. For every one who succumbs to the first temptation there are ten who fall before the second. There are people who can't bring themselves to make a major decision such as that required to enter full-time Christian service. They examine all aspects of the situation; they pray about it; they discuss it with others; they do everything but come to a conclusion.

One problem is that they don't understand the true nature of divine guidance; consequently, they are not prepared to step out in faith. They want to wait until their guidance is 100 percent certain, and that, of course, never happens. Guidance as granted by God is always perfect, but once it has filtered through the human mind it is no longer so. If one waits until he is *absolutely* sure of the Lord's leading, he will wait forever. Divine guidance is never 100 percent certain; if it were, where would faith come in? We must remember that the Christian walks by faith and not by sight (2 Co 5:7), which means that he must be willing to act on the guidance God has given and expect Him to take care of the consequences.

Even Paul, when giving instructions on Christian marriage, was obliged to say, "I *think* that I have the Spirit of God" (1 Co 7:40, RSV). And after he received the so-called Macedonian call, Paul says, "Immediately we sought to go into Macedonia, *concluding* that God had called us to preach the gospel to them" (Acts 16:10, RSV).

Somewhere along the line the individual must make up his mind to act. It is always easier to steer a moving vehicle than a stationary one. Some would-be missionaries give the impression that they are waiting for God to pack their trunks, buy their tickets, and see them off at the airport.

RECOGNIZING THE CALL

This is probably the most crucial question of all, at least as far as young people are concerned. Just how does a call come? What should I look for? Is it a matter of knowledge or feeling? Should I wait for a vision or a voice? Will I recognize it when I get it?

The truth of the matter is that the call to full-time Christian service seldom comes like a meteor out of the blue. The dramatic experience of Saul of Tarsus on the Damascus road is not to be considered the norm for present-day Christians.

Timothy, Titus, Silas and others did not share Paul's sensational call to the Lord's service. More often, a call is a developing process that may take months, even years, to come to full fruition, and along the way some rather well-defined stages can be traced.

The first step is *curiosity*. This may come about in a variety of ways—a casual remark by a friend, a letter from a missionary, a chapter in a book, a hymn in church on Sunday morning, a bull session in the college dorm, an article in the newspaper, or any one of a hundred other ways. Nothing is more unpredictable than the moving of the Holy Spirit. Under His leadership the first step is often taken and the person involved remains completely unaware of it.

In no time at all curiosity leads to *interest*. The person will find himself turning again and again to the subject that has caught his attention. For the first time in his life he thinks and talks about missions, and he can hardly wait for the annual missionary conference to come.

But curiosity and interest are not enough. Something deeper is required, namely, *understanding*. This is not achieved in a hurry. It will take time and study. As he reads missionary literature and studies the Scriptures, a person gradually comes to understand something of the nature, scope, meaning, and mandate of the Christian world mission, the lostness of man, the magnitude of the unfinished task, and the unprecedented opportunities for Christian service. Missionary work is certainly a viable option in the last quarter of the twentieth century.

As one continues to read, study, meditate, and pray, understanding leads to *assurance*. His heart is "strangely warmed" and he begins to get a feel for full-time Christian service. What time and again he vowed he would never do, now begins to look downright attractive. The thought of being a missionary, once intolerable has now a warm and pleasant glow about it. He really *could* be a missionary!

At this point he will probably want to share his secret with others—his parents, his wife (if he has one), his pastor, or his close friends. If they are sympathetic they will help to confirm the leading he has already received from the Holy Spirit. If they are apathetic or opposed—and sometimes they are—he must tell them anyway because his heart is beginning to stir and he cannot keep the matter to himself.

As he continues to search the Scriptures and the Holy Spirit continues to work in his heart, assurance grows stronger and stronger until it becomes *conviction*. He *must* be a missionary. Anything else would be unthinkable. He can now appreciate the words of another:

> *The uniqueness of the missionary vocation lies in the fact that the Holy Spirit brings to certain members of the Church a compelling conviction that they have been set apart as apostles and commissioned to give their whole lives to the gospel and to build the Church of the Lord Jesus Christ.* [2]

Once this stage is reached there is no turning back. He knows beyond a doubt that Jesus Christ has called him into His glorious service. At that point conviction leads to *commitment*. He is ready to sign the Princeton Pledge of the Student Volunteer Movement: "I *purpose*, God willing, to be a foreign missionary." No disappointment, no discouragement, no opposition of friends or relatives can turn him aside. He is convinced of his personal call to full-time Christian service.

Finally, commitment culminates in *action*. He gets moving. He makes plans to prepare for the mission field because that is where he is going. That's where the action is. That's where his heart is. And where his heart is, his feet soon follow. So he resigns his job and goes off to seminary or Bible college to begin preparation for a missionary career.

It is worth noting that these seven steps involve the whole man. The first three—curiosity, interest, and understanding—involve the mind. The next three—assurance, conviction, and commitment—involve the heart. The last one—action—involves the will. That missionary is blessed indeed whose mind, heart, and will are all involved in his high calling. He is not likely to fail, nor will he become a dropout. He is a missionary by the will of God, by the call of Christ, and by the leading of the Holy Spirit.

2. David Adeney, *The Unchanging Commission* (Chicago: InterVarsity Press, 1955), p. 79.

2

Overcoming Obstacles

It has been estimated that for every hundred persons who dedicate their lives for missionary work only one actually gets to the field. It is impossible to say how accurate that figure is, for there is no possible way to check it. It is true, however, that only a fraction of those who declare their willingness to go to the mission field ever get there.

There are many reasons for this. In the first place, time is always a factor. Many come to a decision in their teens before they realize what it is all about. Such a decision may not have been of the Lord to begin with. Others make the decision in good faith but find it fading with the passage of time. Still others drift along with the crowd and eventually end up in secular work. The reasons are legion. We shall discuss only some of the more common obstacles.

ADVANCED EDUCATION

Education is a splendid thing and every prospective missionary should get as much as he possibly can before going to the field. Most Americans contemplating missionary service should have a college degree. Up to this point they are fairly safe, but for every year after that that they remain in this country, their chances of getting to the field are correspondingly diminished. Why?

It usually requires two full years to get an M.A. During that time many things may happen to the prospective missionary. He may become so absorbed in his studies that he loses sight of the mission field and takes a teaching position at home. If he goes to seminary it will take him three years to graduate. During his seminary years he will be exposed more to the opportunities of the pastorate than to the challenges of the mission field. He may decide that the Lord has called him to be a pastor, not a missionary.

If he stays around long enough to get a Ph. D. his chances of getting to the mission field are drastically reduced. By this time he will have become a scholar, more interested in the pursuit of knowledge than in the propagation of the gospel. It need not be that way, but in fact it oftens happens. Most evangelists are not scholars; most scholars are not evangelists. The ideal missionary is one who has the mind of a scholar and the heart of an evangelist. That combination is very rare.

The person with advanced degrees may assume that the mission field does not offer sufficient scope for his many talents. He may think that to make the best use of his education he should remain at home, where he can teach in a prestigious university.

This does not mean that all of these persons are out of the will of God. The Lord may have called some of them to teach in a university or to pastor a church. If so, there can be no quarrel with them. The fact remains that they are lost to the mission field.

ACCUMULATION OF DEBTS

"Buy now and pay later" is the foundation stone of the American free enterprise system. With every passing year it becomes easier to do just that. The only exception to this rule is the funeral service!

The cost of higher education has risen so much in the last decade that tens of thousands of college students have been obliged to borrow money to put themselves through school. Uncle Sam doesn't charge any interest on his loans until after graduation, and if the borrower goes into public school teaching his loan is reduced by 10 percent each year. With our rampant inflation it pays the student to borrow money rather than to work for it.

This arrangement is excellent for the average student. His college degree will enable him to earn a good salary and repay his loan in two or three years. But what about the prospective missionary who majors in Bible or missions? When he graduates he goes into Christian service where the salary scale is much lower than in business or the professions. If he has accumulated a sizable debt it may take him five or six years to liquidate it. By that time he may have settled down in the pastorate and decided to stay.

No reputable mission board will accept a candidate who has an outstanding debt. He must be free of all debts before he is permitted to proceed to the field. One candidate secretary has gone on record saying that he personally does not know of a single missionary candidate with a large debt who ever got to the mission field.

LOVE AND MARRIAGE

Only the Lord knows exactly how many people have fallen by the way on this account, but the number must be very high. According to several recent studies a significant number of those who opt for the mission field make their decision before they go to college. While in college they make many friends and in the process they may fall in love. The other partner may be a good Christian but may be one who has no call to full-time Christian work and certainly no intention of going to the mission field.

Occasionally the missionary-minded student will win the other partner to his or her point of view and together they prepare for missionary service. They may even get married before leaving for the field. That is the exception, however, not the rule. More often than not the missionary-minded one gradually loses his missionary vision and never gets to the field.

There are, of course, some shining exceptions. I am personally acquainted with a number of persons whose dedication to the Lord and His service was strong enough to overcome every other consideration. Some of them went to the mission field at great sacrifice to themselves and found that the Lord had someone waiting for them when they got there. Others have waited patiently for years until the Holy Spirit spoke to the reluctant partner and he or she eventually joined them on the field.

Others get married when they are quite young and by the time they are ready to go to the field they have two or three children. This may pose a problem, depending on the policy of the mission one is interested in. A generation ago this problem did not exist. At that time the majority of candidates were young and single. Today's youth are marrying at a younger age, however, and many of them wed while still in college. Moreover, more of them are remaining at home for an extra year or two to earn an advanced degree. Consequently, it is not uncommon for candidates to have one or two children by the time they apply to the mission.

Policy on this matter differs from mission to mission. There are not more than one or two boards that will accept a couple regardless of the number of children they have. Most boards draw the line at two; some reduce it to one. There are a few boards that refuse to accept a couple with even one child. In this, as in most other things, the mission boards have good reasons for the policies they adopt. Experience has taught them that adjustment to a different culture and the learning of a foreign language are achieved with greater facility and success if the persons involved can give all their time and thought to the business at hand. Young mothers with children seldom achieve either accuracy or fluency in a foreign tongue, and this hampers their efficiency throughout their missionary career.

PARENTAL OPPOSITION

This is a greater obstacle than most people think. There are two kinds of opposition. One kind comes from non-Christian parents who have no use for religion, much less missions. The other comes from Christian parents, some of them evangelical, who believe in missions but are unhappy when *their* children become involved.

In the case of non-Christian parents, the opposition sometimes assumes violent, almost paranoiac, proportions. I know young people who have been locked out of their homes for no other offense than announcing their intention to become missionaries. Some have been completely disowned by their families. Others have had their names removed from their father's will.

One mother was so sick at the thought of her daughter going to the mission field that when it came time for her to leave, the mother went to bed, turned her face to the wall, and refused to say good-bye. For seven years the daughter wrote regularly to her mother, but she didn't get so much as a postcard in reply. It was not until she returned on furlough that the mother relented and was reconciled to her daughter. This is by no means an unusual case.

The opposition that comes from Christian parents is more silent and more subtle but none the less damaging. Such parents are in favor of Christian missions and give generously to the cause, but they are less than happy when their *own* son or daughter decides on a missionary career. That brings the matter a little too close to home. Missions are all right for the other fellow's children but not for theirs. They have grand plans for their child's future and these *don't* include the mission field. The father may want his son to succeed him in the family business. The pressure generated by this kind of situation is sometimes harder to resist than the outright opposition of non-Christian parents.

What should young people do when they find themselves in this predicament? Filial piety is a Christian virtue, and under ordinary circumstances children are obliged to obey their parents, especially when they are Christians. But nowhere does the Bible suggest that parents, Christian or non-Christian, have the right to come between their children and the will of God. From a purely humanistic point of view it is wrong for parents to force their plans on their children. It is doubly wrong when those plans run contrary to the will of God.

If the parents are old, or ill, or poor, or for some other reason are absolutely dependent on their son or daughter for their livelihood, then the young person should give serious consideration to what Paul had to say to Timothy: "If any one does not provide for his relatives, and especially for his own family, he has disowned the faith and is worse than an unbeliever" (1 Ti 5:8, RSV). After much prayer and soul searching he may decide that the Lord would have him remain at home, at least for the time being, to fulfill his Christian duty to his parents. Some missionaries in mid-career have remained at home for five or ten years to minister to the needs of aging parents. But I Timothy 5:8 should not be applied to self-centered parents who are unwilling to give their children to the Lord for His service.

In that case the young person should be guided by the words of Christ:

"He who loves father or mother more than me is not worthy of me; and he who loves son or daughter more than me is not worthy of me" (Mt 10:37, RSV).

It should be borne in mind, however, that when we obey the teaching of Scripture, the Lord has a way of working on our behalf and giving us the desire of our hearts (Ps 37:4). In the case of those who have left family and loved ones, He has given His word of promise: "Truly, I say to you, there is no one who has left house or brothers or sisters or mother or father or children or lands, for my sake and for the gospel, who will not receive a hundredfold now in this time . . . and in the age to come eternal life" (Mk 10:29–30, RSV).

God is no man's debtor. He has said: "Those who honor me I will honor" (1 Sam 2:30, RSV). Missionaries have given their children to the Lord only to find that He took better care of them than they themselves could possibly have done. There are missionaries who have given up parents and found that He made ample provision for them, far exceeding anything they could have asked or thought (Eph 3:20). On the other hand, some parents have refused to allow their children to go to the mission field only to have them become a sorrow to them in their old age.

HEALTH PROBLEMS

Most mission boards maintain high health standards and anyone who falls below them is rejected. The health standards of the Peace Corps are considerably lower than those of the average mission board. The Peace Corps volunteer spends only twenty-one months overseas, whereas the missionary usually serves for life. This makes a big difference.

Mission boards have been criticized for rejecting people on health grounds, but experience has taught them that a poor risk can be very costly, for the mission as well as for the missionary. Missions are supported by the churches, and boards feel an obligation to be faithful in their stewardship.

The average missionary doesn't reach his full potential until his second term of service. To send a family to the field and keep them there for four years is an expensive undertaking. The cost might run as high as $100,000, depending on the field to which they go. If for any reason the family doesn't return for a second term that huge investment is lost. Little wonder that the mission boards are reluctant to take the risk of accepting a person with a health problem.

Mission boards are not infallible. They do make mistakes. One man from Scotland was turned down by the China Inland Mission but accepted by the British and Foreign Bible Society with whom he served for thirty years in Singapore. Missions have, however, accepted some candidates who seemed to be in good health but who were physically disabled within a year.

It is always disappointing for a young person to pass all the other tests and then to be rejected on health grounds. More than one candidate has dissolved into tears when the final verdict was made known. It is equally disappointing for the mission. Good candidates are not so plentiful that mission boards can afford to turn them down. It is an agonizing decision to make.

The candidate who has offered himself for overseas service and has been rejected at least has the satisfaction of knowing that he followed the Lord to the end of the trail and gave up only when the door was closed. Such persons usually find their way into some form of full-time Christian service at home. They never lose their interest in missions and quite frequently are instrumental in sending others to the field. So the venture is by no means in vain and the Lord will say to them, as He said to David: "You did well that it was in your heart" (1 Kg 8:18, RSV).

LACK OF DIRECTION

Modern youth is restive, uncertain, confused, and sometimes frightened. Human problems are so enormous that they defy solution. Career options are so numerous that they cause confusion. Today's young people are caught between the problems and the options and they hardly know how to relate the one to the other. In such a complex situation it is difficult to make up one's mind. It is not uncommon for students to reach their senior year in college and still not know what they are going to do. By the time June rolls around, they are in the throes of "senior panic."

One problem is that today's students, with their knowledge of psychology, anthropology, sociology, etc., are tempted to rely on their own resources (Pr 3:5) rather than look to the Lord for His direction and guidance. Some years ago a student of mine was approaching graduation and was still uncertain about his future. He was a fine Christian who, when he entered college, had definite plans to go into the ministry. Now he was not so sure. I asked him, "Jim, do you ever pray about this matter? Have you ever asked the Lord to guide you with regard to your lifework?"

He replied, "Oh, I take God for granted. He is always in the back of my mind. I make my decisions as best I can in the light of what I know about myself, and I trust Him to keep me from going wrong."

Then there is the problem of understanding what Christian missions are all about. There are many fine Christian students today who have a passing interest in missions and from time to time have an urge to participate, but they don't have sufficient information to enable them to make an intelligent decision one way or the other. Their knowledge of missions is derived largely from missionary speakers in church or chapel whose messages tend to center around their own local work. Seldom do students hear a message that deals with the major issues of Christian missions on anything like a global scale. Consequently their knowledge of missions is fragmentary and superficial. What they do know seems intriguing, but they don't know enough to enable them to make a definite commitment.

There is no substitute for knowledge. The best form of inspiration is information. It is sad but true that it is possible for students to attend a Christian liberal arts college for four years and never be required to read a single book on church history or world missions. In what sense is a college Christian if it does not include in its offerings those courses which might conceivably lead the graduates into full-time Christian service, either at home or overseas? This is usually left to the inspiration provided by chapel services, prayer meetings, and spiritual emphasis week. These are good, to be sure, but they hardly afford a solid foundation upon which to build a missionary vocation.

LACK OF BIBLE TRAINING

The conservative mission boards require their candidates to have a working knowledge of the Bible. The absolute minimum is one year of formal Bible training. Some Bible colleges have a special one-year program designed to meet this particular need. Several seminaries now have a two-year program in Biblical studies leading to a Master of Arts in Religion degree. The ideal preparation for missionary service is four years of liberal arts and three years of seminary with a concentration in missions. In this way the candidate gets a good foundation in all three major areas: liberal arts, theological studies, and missiology. Another acceptable program is that offered by the four-year Bible colleges.

Even specialists such as doctors and nurses are required to have some Bible training. The rationale for this requirement is that the candidate is first a missionary and only secondarily a doctor, nurse, or some other specialist. Consequently he is expected to have a good grasp of the major doctrines of the Christian faith and to be able to explain them to others. The extra year of study will also give him the opportunity to take some courses in personal evangelism, non-Christian religions, and cross-cultural communications, all designed to help him articulate his faith when he gets to the mission field. Without this additional training he may be a competent doctor, but he will be a poor communicator. To be a *missionary* doctor he should be good at both.

The problem arises when a graduate of a secular university offers himself for missionary service. His academic record may be impeccable, but because he lacks Bible courses and theology he is disqualified. Even a person from a Christian liberal arts college will run into trouble at this point. Unless he has majored in Bible, he will have only two or three Bible survey courses to his credit and that is not enough. So the mission board says to the candidate: "Fine, you have a good, sound liberal arts education; now you must to back to school to get at least one year of concentrated Bible study and theology."

With some people this is no great problem. They understand the reason for the requirement and are quite willing to cooperate. They are still young and therefore not averse to returning to school for another year. With others it may be a problem, depending on age, finances, and family circumstances. Some have been in school so long that the thought of another year of the academic rat race is not a pleasant prospect. Others simply balk at the requirement and withdraw their offer for missionary service.

LACK OF PRACTICAL EXPERIENCE

There is a growing recognition on the part of educators of the importance of in-service training. The American Association of Theological Schools is now insisting that all its member schools strengthen their field education program. The minimum requirement is nine hours of field education under qualified supervision. To put teeth into the program, academic credit is given.

One of the outstanding features of the Bible college movement has been the insistence on Christian service. Every student is required to engage in some form of Christian service during his entire course of study. Up to this point such service has not carried academic credit but it has been required right across the board. The theories learned in the classroom are tested in the laboratory of experience. In this way the student gains valuable experience while he is learning. In fact, learning by doing is now an accepted principle of modern pedagogy. The student with three or four years of experience in Christian service makes a better missionary candidate.

Most Christian liberal arts colleges have a Christian service department. While Christian service is not required, it is definitely encouraged. It is estimated that about 50 percent of the students engage in some form of Christian service during the course of the academic year.

It goes without saying that the secular colleges and universities have no such program. Christian students in these institutions can, if they wish, find their own Christian service but not many go to the trouble.

The missionary candidate who has had little or no practical experience will encounter grave difficulty when he meets the mission board. Even if he is qualified in all other respects he will not be accepted without sufficient practical experience. What usually happens is that the board will accept him tentatively on condition that he spend eight or nine months at Missionary Internship in Detroit. There he will be placed in a church where he will work closely with the pastor and engage in the various kinds of ministry usually connected with the local church. During this time he will be under the supervision of Missionary Internship personnel. When the internship is over, MI will evaluate his work and send a report to the mission. If the report is favorable his tentative acceptance will be changed to total acceptance; if not, he will be turned down. It is important that young people looking forward to missionary service get as much practical training as possible during their college career.

So important is Christian service training that some mission boards now require all candidates, regardless of their background or experience, to spend two years in the pastorate before going overseas. This is particularly true of missionaries looking forward to church planting work.

ATTRACTIVE OFFERS AT HOME

This is the final hurdle and many a candidate has failed to clear it successfully.

It is an excellent idea to get two years of experience in some form of ministry in the homeland before proceeding to the field but during that time many things can happen. Some candidates get married to a person who does not share their missionary vision. Others become so absorbed in the work they are doing that they lose contact with the mission and their missionary burden evaporates. Still others are so successful that the churches are reluctant to release them when the two years are up. Not all churches are as magnanimous as the one at Antioch, which was willing to part with its best teachers, Barnabas and Saul, when the Holy Spirit called them into missionary service (Acts 13:1–3).

Not a few missionary candidates have ended up in homeland pastorates because of the pressure brought to bear on them by well-meaning but shortsighted churches. I know of one large church which offered its youth director a substantial increase in salary if he would give up the idea of going to Africa. Fortunately he had the fortitude to stick to his guns and do what he believed the Lord wanted him to do.

The longer the missionary candidate remains in Christian work at home and the more successful he is, the greater is the temptation to remain in this country.

3

Meeting the Qualifications

In the nineteenth century the missionary was regarded as a hero. It was assumed that he was an intellectual and spiritual giant, more dedicated, more courageous, and more spiritual than his counterpart, the pastor at home. Today the pendulum has swung in the opposite direction, and now the missionary is in danger of being reduced to the status of a "humdrum worker in the vineyard of the Lord." Students returning from a summer of missionary work overseas report that their greatest discovery was that missionaries are human after all. In our reaction against the adulation of the past we may be underestimating the qualities of today's missionary.

Stephen Neill, himself a missionary of no mean stature, wrote:

> *I may place on record my conviction that the needs of the mission field are always far greater than the needs of the Church at home, that no human qualifications, however high, render a man or woman more than adequate for missionary work, that there is no career that affords such scope for enterprise and creative work, and that in comparison with the slight sacrifice demanded, the reward is great beyond all measuring.*[1]

Most mission societies screen their candidates very carefully. They do this for two reasons. First, they want to reduce as far as possible the number of dropouts. Second, they want to be sure that they get the highest caliber of missionary. The best is none too good for the mission field.

1. Stephen Neill, *Builders of the Indian Church* (London: Edinburgh House Press, 1934), p. 4.

It is doubtful if any other Christian worker has to meet the rigid requirements demanded of missionaries. Certainly pastors in the homeland are not expected to. Medical and psychological tests are now routine with most mission boards. Besides being asked to subscribe to the mission's statement of faith, each candidate must prepare his own statement. References are required from pastors, educators, employers, and others who have had first-hand contact with the candidate. Original references are asked to submit the names of additional references. In this way the mission gets twelve to fifteen recommendations. Each of these persons is asked to fill out a lengthy and exhaustive questionnaire relating to all phases of the candidate's life, character, temperament, and experience. By the time all this information is collected, digested, and evaluated, the mission authorities have a pretty good idea of the candidate's strengths and weaknesses.

There are 714 missionary agencies based in North America. Naturally they don't all have the same standards. Some accept only seminary graduates. Others will accept college graduates while still others may accept only Bible school graduates. Some insist on very high academic qualifications but don't worry too much about spiritual qualifications. Others are very particular about spiritual qualifications but don't quibble over academic qualifications. There are others that do their best to maintain high standards in both areas.

The perfect missionary has not yet appeared on the scene and it would be foolish and futile to set standards bordering on perfection. On the other hand, it would be a grave mistake to suggest that any Tom, Dick, or Harry, without any special training or any particular qualifications, can make an acceptable missionary. He need not be a genius, but he had better not be a dunce.

The qualifications of a good missionary break down into several categories.

PHYSICAL QUALIFICATIONS

Colleges, the Peace Corps, and the United States Army require a physical examination before accepting the applicant. The reasons for this are obvious. Mission boards have additional reasons to be careful about the health of their applicants. Life on the mission field, with few exceptions, is harder on one's health than life here at home. Contributing factors include hot, humid climate, poor food, contagious diseases, and lack of public sanitation. Medical facilities are woefully inadequate. Some families live in isolated areas where the nearest doctor or hospital may be a three-day journey away. When casualties occur they are very costly to both the missionary and the mission.

For this reason all missions require a complete medical checkup. They are particularly wary of any signs of high blood pressure, impaired sight or hearing, nervous disorders, or allergies. Some physical defects can be cor-

rected by surgery, after which the applicant will be accepted. He doesn't
have to be a physical giant or have a near-perfect physique, but he must have
a good, consistent health record. Any chronic ailment, however slight, is apt
to be aggravated on the mission field. It is always a tragedy when an otherwise fully qualified candidate is rejected for health reasons.

ACADEMIC QUALIFICATIONS

For the most part the mainline denominations have maintained fairly
high academic standards. Even in the nineteenth century most of their
missionaries were college or seminary graduates. When Hudson Taylor
started the faith missions movement, he appealed for those "of little formal
education." When the Bible schools got under way on this continent in the
last decades of the nineteenth century, they too accepted those of little
formal education and gave them enough Bible training to enable them to
become effective lay workers in the Christian church. It comes as no surprise
to learn that most of the Bible school graduates who went overseas joined the
faith missions. In recent decades both the faith missions and the Bible
schools have raised their academic standards. Most of the larger schools are
now degree-granting institutions.

Most missions prefer their candidates to have at least a college education.
Beyond that, the higher they go the better. The demands on today's missionary are so great that he should get as much education as he possibly can
before going to the field. Only then will he be able to cope with the intellectual, social, political, and religious problems he is likely to encounter in
the course of his missionary career. This is especially true if he plans to work
among students and other intellectuals.

At the same time it should be recognized that a college or seminary
education is no guarantee of genuine intellectual prowess—at least not here
in the U.S., where higher education is accessible to all. On the mission field
there are hundreds of older missionaries who never had the chance to go to
college. They have, however, something that no college can impart: intellectual capacity. They are largely self-educated, but they can hold their
own with the best. The real test of a person's intellectual prowess is whether
he keeps on growing after his formal education has ceased.

VOCATIONAL QUALIFICATIONS

We hear a great deal today about specialization, not only at home but also
on the mission field. Most missionaries need some technical or vocational
training in addition to their liberal arts and theological education. All missionaries, regardless of their area of specialization, should have a thorough
understanding of missiology, including the history, theology, philosophy,
and methodology of missions, non-Christian religions, cross-cultural communications, missionary anthropology, church planting, etc. Those going

into Bible translation work should have a mastery of Greek and Hebrew and be completely conversant with the language and culture of the host country. This has not always been the case.

> Out of some 1,500 evangelical missionaries in Japan recently not one could be found who was competent enough in both languages to check a new Japanese translation against the original Hebrew. Liberals and Roman Catholics could have done it—but not the evangelicals.[2]

Much depends, of course, on the kind of work into which the specialist goes. The larger missions have room for all kinds of specialists in the areas of theology, teaching, medicine, evangelism, radio and television, literature, journalism, youth work, business, finance, accounting, secretarial work, linguistics, and aviation. There is a crying need for specialists in all of these areas. The tragedy is that in many instances these roles are now being filled by persons without the special or technical training essential for the tasks they are performing. They mean well, they work long and hard, and they are doing a tolerably good job, but they lack professional competence and the work suffers accordingly. The time is long past when we can do a second-rate job and get away with it.

Topflight theologians are desperately needed on the mission field. Until such time as they are forthcoming it will be necessary for church leaders in the Third World to come to the West for their theological training. It would be much better, and certainly much cheaper, to educate them in their own countries.

PSYCHOLOGICAL QUALIFICATIONS

By psychological qualifications we really mean personality traits. Personality traits are more important in some roles than in others.

> A bookkeeper doesn't have to worry about the impression he makes on anybody but the boss. The main thing is to have his records neat and accurate. That's not true of the salesperson, however. The volume of his sales and the commission he gets may depend on such impressions. A research scientist may be a very disagreeable person to meet, at the same time that he is highly regarded for his contribution to science. But a minister of the Gospel can't even get a hearing for his message if he continually rubs people the wrong way.[3]

Rubbing people the wrong way is more likely to happen on the mission field than here at home, for the simple reason that missionaries have to live in close quarters. If one person in the group is abrasive he can make life

2. Michael Griffiths, *Give Up Your Small Ambitions* (London: Inter-Varsity Press, 1970), p. 50.
3. Harold C. Cook, *An Introduction to the Study of Christian Missions* (Chicago: Moody Press, 1954), p. 112.

miserable for the others. Nowhere are interpersonal relations more important.

No matter how hard we try we will not be able to achieve the perfectly integrated personality, but human relations are greatly facilitated if the persons involved possess certain desirable personality traits.

1. Emotional stability. Life on the mission field is considerably more difficult than here at home. The problem lies not in the nervous breakdowns but in the scores of irritations that are part of everyday life. Over the long haul these can completely upset one's emotional equilibrium. Persons who are given to introspection, who have an inferiority complex, or who are afflicted with phobias and frustrations of various kinds usually have a difficult time adjusting to the kind of communal life found in some parts of the mission field. Poor mental health and emotional immaturity account for almost 11 percent of all the dropouts in missionary work.

2. Adaptability. Confucius once said, "When you enter a new territory, be sure to inquire concerning its customs." The Western counterpart of that is, "When in Rome do as the Romans do." When the missionary from the West arrives in the East he finds himself in an entirely new world. Everything is different—climate, food, dress, language, religion, and customs. In a word, the entire culture is radically different from anything he has known up to that point.

Obviously if he is going to be a success he must adapt to the customs of the host country. This is absolutely necessary if he wants to make friends and influence people. Otherwise he will be just another "ugly American." The person who is unable to change his ways will probably not last more than a year or two on the mission field.

3. Versatility. One of the greatest single virtues any missionary can possess is the ability to do half-a-dozen things and do them well. Nowhere is versatility more necessary than on the mission field where, in many cases, the Christian worker is required to be a jack, if not a master, of all trades. Theological professors are expected to teach every course in the catalog. Doctors are expected to be physicians, surgeons, administrators, building inspectors, and general repairmen. In some instances doctors have been known to build their own hospitals. As for the general missionary, he must be able to preach sermons, pull teeth, repair cars, teach school, set bones, build houses, fight fires, deliver babies, keep books, and do a host of other things usually performed by specialists here at home.

When the Anglican Mission in Polynesia advertised for missionaries it listed the following qualifications:

Ability to mix people, mix concrete, wade rivers, write articles, love one's neighbor, deliver babies, sit cross-legged, conduct meetings, drain swamps, digest questionable dishes, patch human weaknesses, suffer as fools gladly, and burn the midnight oil.

Persons allergic to ants, babies, beggars, chop suey, cockroaches, curried crabs, duplicators, guitars, humidity, indifference, itches, jungles, mildew, minority groups, mud, poverty, sweat, and unmarried mothers, had better think twice before applying. [4]

4. Sense of humor. Missionary work is serious business, but the missionary himself must not be *too* serious. He must not take his fellow missionaries too seriously either. Above all he ought to be able to laugh at himself. Many a tense and potentially explosive situation can be avoided if he sees the humorous side.

Particularly irksome to some missionaries is the universal practice of "talking price." On one occasion I was at the mercy of a group of ricksha coolies in Nanking. I was escorting four children with all their baggage back to school after the Christmas break. We needed nine rickshas to take us from the ferry to the railway station, a distance of about three miles. To make matters worse it was raining. Knowing my predicament, they began by asking an exorbitant price. We haggled back and forth for several minutes, but they refused to come down to a reasonable figure. Finally I said to the leader, "Venerable brother, you misunderstand me. I don't want to *buy* the rickshas, I just want to *hire* them!" The other coolies burst into laughter, and the leader said, "Okay. Okay. Let's go." And away we went to the railway station.

5. Ability to get along with others. The leaders of a mission with almost a hundred years of experience have said: "More missionary failures are due to personal incompatibility than to any other cause. Working with others is a prime essential."[5] The same is true of life here in the U.S. A recent study has shown that incompatibility is responsible for one-third of all the job changes in this country.

The missionary's lifestyle only accentuates the problem. On the mission field there are many more frustrations to try one's patience. Heat, humidity, isolation, overwork—these tend to make the missionary irritable. Add to that the fact that in the more primitive parts of the world, missionaries still live in compounds with other missionaries as their nearest neighbors. They live, work, worship, and play with the same people seven days a week. Unfortunately, they do not choose their fellow workers. To make matters worse, missionaries as a rule tend to be strong willed characters who do not find it easy to play second fiddle. All these features combine to make the situation potentially combustible.

It is absolutely essential, therefore, that the young missionary heading for the field know how to get along with others.

4. *Standard*, September 28, 1964, p. 13.
5. North Africa Mission, *Qualifications for a Missionary to North Africa*, p. 4.

6. Willingness to take orders. Much of the paternalism has gone out of the missionary movement, and that is a good thing. But so long as there is a structured organization with a chain of command, somebody has to give the orders and others must accept them. Major decisions and policies must be made at the top and carried out by those below. This does not preclude the desirability of input at all levels, but the final decision must be made by the leaders, after which the rank and file are expected to fall into line.

In all well-ordered missions, every effort is made to canvass the opinions of the membership. Annual conferences are held on the various fields where the missionaries are given ample opportunity to air their grievances and present their points of view. The responsibility for policy making, however, rests with the leadership. Above the field council is the home council or, in some missions, the international council, which is responsible for the total operation of the entire mission at home and overseas. The field council members must be willing to implement the policies laid down by the international council, and the missionaries must be prepared to abide by the decisions of the field council. There is no other way to operate an international organization.

7. Ability to endure hardship. The Chinese call it "eating bitterness." There is no doubt that the affluent society in which we live has produced in all of us a love of ease and comfort that is the hallmark of the American way of life. We have central heating in the winter, air conditioning in the summer and 31 flavors of ice cream the year round. Physical well-being, financial security, material prosperity—these are the main ingredients that make up the affluent society that is America. The individual is pampered and protected from the cradle to the grave. Dentistry, surgery, and even childbirth, are all rendered painless. Even band-aids must be "ouchless." The energy crisis that now threatens to drastically change the American lifestyle is perhaps the best thing that has happened to us since Thomas Edison invented the incandescent lamp.

The American missionary more than any other finds it difficult to knuckle down to the simple lifestyle of most parts of the Third World. Like the Children of Israel who hankered after the "leeks and onions of Egypt," he wants to retain as much as possible of the American standard of living. That is why some of them take tons of household stuff when they leave for the field. In this respect the Peace Corps volunteers put the missionaries to shame. They live at the level of the people they serve. They are not allowed to own jeeps, cars, or even bicycles. They use public transportation, second class where available.

Most missionaries are married and have families, so they cannot be expected to compete with the Peace Corps, but they must be prepared to endure hardship as good soldiers of Jesus Christ in order to identify with the people they are seeking to win. The gap between the "have" nations and the "have not" nations is altogether too great. The Christian missionary cannot close that gap by himself no matter what he does, but he can help to bridge it at the local level if he is willing to "eat bitterness."

8. Patience and perseverance. The missionary is not going to change the world overnight. The East is agonizingly slow. The West is ridiculously fast. A man's whole day can be spoiled if the elevator in the office building takes him one floor beyond where he wants to go.

One of the most difficult adjustments for the missionary is to s-l-o-w d-o-w-n. In thirty-six hours he goes from the jet age to the ox age, and the sudden change can be traumatic. In all aspects of his life and work he will have need of patience and perseverance. Without these virtues he is almost sure to crack up. He may try to circumvent the problem by operating his own jeep, but he will still need patience when it bogs down in two feet of mire or when he comes to a river that has no bridge and the ferry is not operating. If he decides to go by bus he may find that the bus driver has decided to take the day off.

Government officials, church leaders, and the people in general are in no great rush to get things done. The missionary may have to wait nine months to get his car through Customs and another two years to get his driver's license. Church leaders also take their time in making decisions, and once having made them they are often slow in executing them. They see no need for haste and can't understand why the missionary should be upset by the delay. What isn't accomplished today can always be done tomorrow—or the next day, or the day after that. In the meantime they may discover that the decision wasn't a wise one to begin with and therefore need not be implemented at all. And all the while the American missionary is fussing and fuming and sometimes fulminating.

9. Without a superiority complex. In the words of Kenneth Scott Latourette, the nineteenth-century missionary was "serenely convinced of the superiority of Western culture." In the missionary literature of that period the words "Christianity" and "civilization" were used almost interchangeably. The missionaries conceived of themselves as playing a civilizing as well as a Christianizing role. That day is gone. No missionary today would entertain such naive notions. We know better.

That does not mean that we have licked the problem. It is still with us, albeit in more subtle forms. By his attitudes and mannerisms the missionary may unconsciously reveal his superiority complex. There is an almost irresistible temptation to compare local products with their counterparts in the U.S. Quite frequently they appear to be inferior in quality and craftsmanship. They don't work as well. They don't last as long. The missionary tosses them aside with some remark about "these crazy gadgets that don't work." His remarks may be heard only by his household servants, but that is enough. The word soon spreads through the community that he doesn't like native products.

The very fact that he arrives from the U.S. with nineteen drums of personal effects conveys the impression that American goods are superior to all others, or why would he go to all the trouble and expense?

The peoples of the Third World are doing their best to catch up to the technology of the West and they are very self-conscious about the gap that still exists. Understandably they are touchy on these points and appreciate the missionary who has a genuine appreciation of them and their culture.

In most parts of the world the missionary is still treated with a certain degree of deference, partly as a carryover from the past and partly because the Third World culture has always shown kindness and hospitality to strangers. It is very easy for the missionary to come to expect this kind of treatment and take offense if he does not receive it.

The missionary, with his advanced degrees and his expertise, may easily get a swollen head and think that he has all the answers and that the national leaders should listen to him and follow his advice. An attitude of superiority is something the missionary must guard against all the days of his life. It was bad enough in the nineteenth century; it is quite intolerable now.

10. Without racial prejudice. The white race has no monopoly on racial prejudice. The ancient Greeks divided the world into Greeks and barbarians. The Chinese called their country the "Middle Kingdom" and referred to all foreigners as barbarians. There is hardly a country in the world that does not have some form of racial prejudice.

On one occasion when riding the subway in New York City I saw an ad which contained only one word printed in large black letters on a white background—ECIDUJERP. For several minutes I could not figure out what it was all about. Then at the bottom of the ad, in small letters barely discernible, I read: "This word is PREJUDICE spelled backwards. Whichever way you spell it, it doesn't make sense." But sense or nonsense, it still persists in almost every society.

Problems of racism in the U.S. have been published in all the major newspapers of the world. There are people in the Third World who have never heard of Chicago or San Francisco but are well acquainted with Little Rock and Birmingham. Martin Luther King is almost as well known as John F. Kennedy.

It wouldn't be so bad if racism were confined to American secular society, but it has infected the churches as well. The eleven o'clock hour on Sunday morning is the most segregated hour of the week. This sad fact has not gone unnoticed by foreign nationals in this country. Racism in America is a millstone around the neck of the missionary.

In its more blatant forms racism has disappeared from the mission field, but there are many subtle ways in which it can still be seen. It comes out not so much in the conduct of the missionary's work as in various aspects of his social life. It is one thing to work with the nationals on a basis of equality; it is another to socialize with them on the same basis. There is still a tendency for missionaries to seek the company of fellow missionaries or other Americans. The real test of a missionary's love for the people is his choice of friends with whom he shares his leisure time.

Racial prejudice is particularly unfortunate in the Christian missionary for two reasons. First, it is a denial of the teachings of Christ. Second, it alienates the very people he is trying to win.

SPIRITUAL QUALIFICATIONS

If the missionary is not in every respect a godly man, he might as well remain at home. "It cannot be too positively asserted that missionary work is a spiritual enterprise, undertaken for spiritual results to be achieved only by spiritual means. It follows, therefore, that the essential qualifications are spiritual."[6]

1. **A genuine conversion experience.** It is hardly necessary to belabor this point. To be a missionary a person must have an evangelical fervor growing out of a conversion experience. This is very important in a so-called Christian society where everyone whose name appears on a church roll is assumed to be a Christian. Some of the most zealous missionaries are those from a "pagan" background who were converted to Christ through various campus ministries after they reached college. The missionary who is not sure of his own salvation is not likely to lead others to a saving knowledge of Christ.

2. **Knowledge of the Scriptures.** The missionary's chief task is to share Jesus Christ with the non-Christian world. All he knows about Christ was learned from the Bible. He should, therefore, have a thorough working knowledge of the Scriptures, which are able to make men wise unto salvation (2 Ti 3:15). No amount of worldly wisdom can substitute for a knowledge of the Scriptures. The missionary should not only know their content but should also have a thorough understanding of the major doctrines concerning God, man, sin, and salvation.

Moreover, the Scriptures are the source from which he gets the sustenance for his spiritual life. They provide him with his message and his mandate. They are his chart and compass. They are his trustworthy guide in all matters pertaining to faith and morals. From them he derives wisdom, counsel, comfort, encouragement, and cleansing. In short, the Bible is the foundation on which he builds both his life and his work. If the missionary does not know it thoroughly he is at a serious disadvantage.

3. **Assurance of divine guidance.** A. Jack Dain, veteran missionary to India, has some wise words of counsel for young people about to rush into missionary service.

6. Rowland Hogben, *In Training* (Chicago: Inter-Varsity Christian Fellowship, 1946), p. 30.

It seems to me that in these days when so much emphasis is put upon missionary service, we need to guard against pressuring our young people into missionary work when they do not have a real call from God. It is not a question of doubting their integrity, or their discipleship, or their love for God, but are they called of God? If they are not, they are doomed to failure, and the result will be serious for all concerned.[7]

Missionary work is not getting any easier. Some of the physical hardships have been eliminated, but a host of other difficulties—psychological, ideological, and interpersonal—have taken their place. The short-termer may be able to get along fairly well with no great "sense of call," but the career missionary will find it mighty handy when the going gets rough. It will help him immensely if he can say, "I am a missionary by the will of God."

Two journalists, both agnostics, spent three months with missionaries in East Africa to find out what makes them tick. In their report they made this observation: "It is obvious when you talk to missionaries, and still more obvious on reflection, that the phenomenon of missionary work really makes sense only if their belief in a calling is taken at its face value . . . . Virtually everyone we met really did feel that in some deep sense they had surrendered their own will for that of another way of life—for their Lord, as they would put it."[8]

If a missionary has a deep, abiding conviction that he is in Brazil, Borneo, or Burundi by the will of God, he will not turn and run at the first sight or sound of danger, nor will he give up when the difficulties multiply and the frustrations almost drive him crazy. He will go the second mile and stay on the job long after the sun has gone down if he is sure that he is in the will of the Lord.

4. Strong devotional life. The devotional life of the missionary is all-important. He will be a man of God only if his spiritual life is systematically developed by daily Bible study, prayer, meditation, and worship.

Here at home, especially in seminary or Bible college, the student is buoyed up and carried along by the spiritual support provided by the Christian community of which he is a part: prayer meetings, chapel services, dorm fellowships, and rap sessions. On the mission field these props are missing. The missionary is on his own. He can't depend on others for fellowship or growth. He must know how to cultivate his own spiritual life without any outside help. His roots must go down deep; otherwise his spiritual life will wither and die

Hudson Taylor was one of the missionary giants of the nineteenth century whose name is a household word in evangelical circles. It was said of

7. A. Jack Dain, *The Screening of Missionary Candidates* (Washington, D.C.: Evangelical Foreign Missions Association, 1956), pp. 15–16.
8. Helen and Richard Exley, *In Search of the Missionary* (London: Highway Press, 1970), p. 38.

him that never once in fifty years did the sun rise in China without finding Hudson Taylor on his knees.

Most missionaries would have to confess that this is one of their greatest problems. They are constantly ministering to others but nobody ministers to them. If they don't set aside the "quiet time" and observe it each morning, they will soon find themselves robbed of their joy as well as their power.

5. Self-discipline. Discipline seems to be necessary to the perpetuation of human society. Without it, community life tends to disintegrate. There are two kinds of discipline. One is imposed from without; the other is cultivated from within. Most people have to rely on the first because they possess so little of the second. This is why we hear so much talk about "law and order." Apparently it is impossible to achieve the one without the other.

The missionary more than anyone else is dependent on self-discipline. Even the pastor at home is not in the same boat as the missionary. The pastor is constantly under the surveillance of the people who pay his salary. If he falls down on the job he will be called before the church board to give an account of himself. More than one pastor has been asked to terminate his service for that reason. What about the missionary? Who is to check on him? He may not see the field director more than once a year. If he loafs on the job or becomes lazy in body or mind he can easily get away with it.

Self-discipline is listed by Paul as one of the fruits of the Spirit in Galatians 5:23, where it is called "self-control." Even the great apostle had problems along this line. He said, "Every athlete exercises self-control in all things. They do it to receive a perishable wreath, but we an imperishable. Well, I do not run aimlessly, I do not box as one beating the air; but I pommel my body and subdue it, lest after preaching to others I myself should be disqualified" (1 Co 9:25–27, RSV).

6. A heart of love. Love is the hallmark of the Christian life (Jn 13:34–35) and the *sine qua non* of Christian service (1 Co 13:1–3). Jesus Christ, as the first and chief Missionary, came into the world to express the Father's love (Jn 3:16). The missionary goes into the world to express Christ's love. Paul and the other apostles were so controlled by the love of Christ (2 Co 5:14) that they were willing to risk their lives for His sake (Acts 15:26).

Writing to the little mission church in Thessalonica, Paul said, "So, being affectionately desirous of you, we were ready to share with you not only the gospel of God but also our own selves, because you had become very dear to us" (1 Th 2:8, RSV). Missionaries don't have to be bright or brave to be successful (though both are very desirable qualities), but they *must* be loving. The nationals will overlook many weaknesses and forgive many blunders if they are persuaded that the missionary has a heart of love.

7. Some success in Christian service. Important as the above-mentioned qualifications are, they are not sufficient by themselves. In addition there should be some evidence of fruitfulness in Christian service here at home. Before setting out for distant shores the missionary should have proved himself in church or mission work at home. If he can't win souls in his own culture, what reason is there to believe he will do better in a foreign culture? He should have given evidence that he has the gift of evangelism. Does he hope to be a Bible teacher? Then he should have demonstrated that he possesses the gift of teaching.

There should be some evidence of God's blessing in his life and some proof of the power of the Holy Spirit in his ministry before he ventures overseas. Of one thing he can be sure: success will not come more easily on the mission field.

4

Choosing a Mission

Most missionaries serve under the auspices of a mission board. There are a few, however, who, for one reason or another, have elected to "go it alone." They are known as independent missionaries. Most of them tend to be "lone eagles" who prefer to go their own way and do their own thing without being responsible to any human organization; they would rather take their orders directly from God. Others are obliged to follow an independent career through no fault of their own. They applied to one or more missions but were not accepted. So strong was their sense of call, however, and so clear their guidance, that they proceeded to the field without the support of a mission, looking solely to the Lord for the supply of their needs.

Gladys Aylward, whose life story was written in *The Small Woman* and later made into a film called *The Inn of the Sixth Happiness,* was one of these independent missionaries. She was rejected by the China Inland Mission (now the Overseas Missionary Fellowship) for academic reasons, but her dedication and sense of call were so strong that she went to China on her own, arriving in Peking with only a few dollars in her purse. God honored her faith and gave her an unusual ministry with war orphans during the Sino-Japanese War. In her case all went well, but for every one in that category who succeeds, scores of others fail. It is certainly not recommended for the rank and file of missionaries. One requires a *very* special call for that kind of career.

It is taken for granted, then, that most missionaries will serve in connection with a mission board. Persons belonging to the mainline denominations usually find it convenient to apply to their own denominational board of foreign missions. This is right and proper and is usually a happy arrangement.

In some instances, however, the candidate prefers to serve under an interdenominational board, commonly called a "faith" mission. There are several reasons for this, the main one being theological orientation. Not a few evangelicals are unhappy with the liberal theology and the social programs of their denominational board and prefer to work under a mission whose conservative theological position is closer to their own. In this way they are more likely to have a happy and successful missionary career.

Theology, however, is not always the issue. Even candidates from conservative denominations, such as the Evangelical Free Church, Conservative Baptists, Baptist General Conference, and others, prefer to serve with a faith mission rather than with their own board. In that case, theology does not enter the picture. It is purely a matter of divine guidance. They believe they are led of the Lord to join a faith mission, and their own denominational churches are happy to support them in their plans.

Before considering the factors that enter into the choice of a mission, it might be well to enumerate the advantages of belonging to a mission, especially in these days when there is a tendency on the part of some to do their own thing.

ADVANTAGES OF SERVING WITH A MISSION

There are many solid advantages to membership in a reputable mission. In fact, they are so many and so attractive that one wonders why anyone would prefer to work independently.

1. **Family solidarity.** Man by nature is a gregarious creature who has certain personal and social needs that can be met only in concert with others. He has an innate desire to "belong." He functions more happily and more effectively in a group than by himself. He needs to feel that he is part of a team. He prefers to do things with others who share his world view and his value system. He soon develops a sense of loyalty to the group. As a result he enjoys a sense of solidarity. The moral support he derives from being a member of a team stands him in good stead when difficulties arise. This is extremely important on the mission field where the missionary, especially the newcomer, is a stranger in a strange land which often results in feelings of insecurity and rootlessness that may disturb his peace of mind.

2. **Financial security.** In the mainline denominations the missionary is given a fixed salary sufficient to enable him and his family to maintain a fairly high standard of living in the host country. In some instances the missionaries, with a retinue of servants, manage to live quite comfortably even by Western standards. This is particularly true of American missionaries, whose salaries may be two or three times those of their British and European counterparts.

With the evangelical missions, the arrangements are somewhat different. Each missionary is expected to look to the Lord for the supply of his personal and family needs. Each member brings his quota of faith and prayer to the mission family, and together they trust the Lord to supply all their needs. At the same time, however, the mission does stand behind the individual worker. In some missions they all share alike from a common fund. In others each missionary is expected to raise his own support before going to the field. If during the course of the term of service the support level drops, or the cost of living rises, the mission takes up the slack and sees to it that his allowance does not fall below the level regarded as essential to health and well being. This is done by dipping into the general fund or borrowing from the emergency account.

The mission helps in other ways. Special gifts (birthday, Christmas, etc.) are transmitted through the mission to the individual without charge. When the cost-of-living index rises, the mission notifies all donors and churches and suggests that their missionary support be increased. This is a very important service that the mission renders on behalf of its members, who would naturally be embarrassed to write themselves.

3. Christian fellowship. The missionary is often a lonely figure. Some missionaries living in isolated communities may go for months without seeing a fellow worker. If they are in pioneer work they may have to live without any Christian fellowship apart from that provided by the mission. Most missions arrange for a field conference once a year when all the workers in a given country or region get together for a week of fellowship, inspiration, discussion, and mutual encouragement.

The Greater Europe Mission has such a conference every summer and all their missionaries throughout Europe are expected to attend. Travel and other expenses in connection with the conference are written into the missionary's regular support so money is no problem. Conferences of this kind are like a blood transfusion to the weary missionary who may have been slugging it out alone for eleven months.

If sickness or tragedy strikes, the entire mission family is notified and prayer support is forthcoming immediately. This kind of fellowship is a very precious asset which the free-lance missionary does not have.

4. Counsel and guidance. Elisabeth Elliott in her book, *No Graven Image*, graphically portrays the horrendous problems encountered by a young missionary who found herself alone in a strange environment with no one to turn to for help. Fortunately, new missionaries are seldom if ever placed by themselves and told to "sink or swim." Usually they are sent to a center where there is an existing mission, preferably a flourishing one, and where, with the help and guidance of older missionaries, they are gradually initiated into the work. In some cases they spend the first year or two in a school where they devote all their time and energy to learning the native language. Even in those cases they usually end up with older missionaries whose experience and expertise are at their disposal. Those new missionaries are fortunate who can count on the sympathy and support of older and wiser workers who will take the time and trouble to tutor them, as Paul tutored Timothy.

No amount of academic training in the homeland can adequately prepare the missionary for foreign service. Some things can be learned only after he gets to the field. He can learn them in one of two ways: the hard way, by the trial-and-error method; or the easier way, with the help of a good-natured, kind-hearted, experienced older worker who still remembers what it was like to be a novice. Try as he may, the young missionary is bound to make mistakes, but these will be greatly reduced in number and severity if a senior missionary is available for counsel and prayer. Should a problem arise that cannot be solved by the senior missionary, the matter can be referred to the district superintendent. In either case the young missionary has the moral support of godly men and women at various levels of administration who will do their best to help him achieve success.

5. Continuity in the work. Continuity is an important element in any form of Christian work; it is absolutely essential in missionary work. One of the biggest problems on the mission field is filling the gaps left by missionaries going on furlough. A generation ago furloughs came every seven years. Now, with faster travel, the average term of service has been reduced to four years. In some instances missionaries are permitted to take a mini-furlough every two years.

When the free-lance missionary goes on furlough, what becomes of his work? If it does not come to a standstill it will at least suffer some deterioration. Worse still, what happens if ill health obliges him to leave the field permanently? What provision is made for his ultimate retirement after forty years of service? In many cases the work either grinds to a halt or is turned over to some nearby mission. Missionary annals are filled with problems of this kind.

6. Education of children. The free-lance missionary is in real trouble when it comes to educating his children. Without a mission school of his own it will be necessary for him either to educate his children at home or to send them to a private American school, where the fees are so high as to be prohibitive. On the other hand, the team missionary can look to his mission to solve the problem for him. Some of the larger missions have their own school for MKs (Missionary Kids). Smaller missions sometimes form a consortium which supports a school. In either case the team missionary is sure of having a good school with reasonable fees at his disposal. The peace of mind that comes from such an arrangement can be appreciated only by those who have lived abroad.

7. Fringe benefits. These vary from mission to mission. The larger the mission, the more numerous the fringe benefits. All missions, however, both large and small, provide certain facilities and services free of charge for their workers at home and on the field. These include taking care of all the red tape involved in securing passports and visas, purchasing tickets, making reservations, meeting planes, arranging meetings, mailing prayer letters, sending cablegrams, and a host of other little things which, when put together, have a way of looming large in the life of the missionary. In the homelands, missions often provide hostels for school children, homes for retired workers, and centers where transients can secure meals and room at greatly reduced rates, with all kinds of Christian fellowship thrown in for good measure.

There is, of course, one disadvantage. The team missionary is not 100 percent free to come and go as he pleases. There is of necessity a restriction placed on his freedom of movement and action. He is a member of a team and is expected to shoulder the responsibilities as well as to enjoy the privileges of the Christian community to which he belongs. This is a small price to pay, however, for all the benefits of collegiality.

MAKING THE CHOICE

Assuming that the advantages far outweigh the disadvantages, we are now ready to discuss how one goes about the task of choosing a mission. The latest edition of *Mission Handbook: North American Ministries Overseas* lists no fewer than 714 sending and supporting agencies engaged in overseas operations. How can the candidate ever reduce his choice to one? At first glance it looks like a formidable task fraught with all kinds of difficulties and pitfalls, but the problem is greatly simplified if one remembers that there are four avenues of approach: mission, country, people, and vocation. The candidate may start with any one of the four and gradually work out the other three. The order to be followed will differ with the individual.

1. The mission. The Lord guides His servants in different ways. Sometimes it is the mission rather than the field that becomes the first point of clarity. As the prospective missionary prays he is strangely drawn to one particular mission, and the more he prays the more persuaded he is that the Lord is leading him to apply to that mission. So far, so good. He should get all the information he can on that mission. After reading all the material and satisfying himself that his leading is of the Lord he should make preliminary application.

Once the matter of the mission is settled, it automatically restricts to some extent the remaining three options. The smaller the mission, the easier it is to decide on a field of service. If the mission selected has work only in Japan, India, and Nigeria, the choice is immediately reduced from 182 (the number of countries in which missionary work is carried on) to three.

Some of the larger missions have work in over 90 countries in all six continents. In that case the candidate will still have some deciding to do, but he will have the counsel and advice of the mission leaders. The average

mission, with 100 to 200 members, usually has work in ten to twenty countries. That still calls for much thought and prayer—again in consultation with
the mission.

2. The country. The first point of clarity may be the country, not the
mission. The young person finds his attention turning again and again to
Japan. He hears missionaries from Africa and Latin America and he rejoices
in what the Lord is doing in those parts of the world, but he feels no great
urge to serve there. But let a missionary from Japan come to his church or
college and immediately his heart is strangely warmed. He begins to pray for
guidance, and the more he prays the more his heart is drawn to Japan.
Somebody gives him a book on Japan which he reads avidly. Geography,
history, culture, people, religion—he is fascinated by it all. After reading
several books on Japan he is practically convinced that God wants him in that
country.

With the matter of the country settled, he will turn his attention to the
question of a mission. Under which mission should he serve? Many missions
will be automatically ruled out; they have no work in Japan. He can readily
find out which missions are working in Japan by going to the *Mission Handbook*. There he will find 137 agencies listed. After further thought and
prayer, five or six will appeal to him, so he writes for information concerning
them. With more thought, counsel, and prayer those half dozen will be
reduced to one—the mission of God's choice. He is then ready to send in his
application.

3. The people. Suppose one's interest is first aroused by the people, not
the country or mission. The Lord may have given him a special love for the
Indians or the Eskimos or the Muslims or the Jews or the Arabs. This, then,
is the place to begin. If he knows he has been called by God to work among
the Eskimos, the choice of both field and mission is greatly restricted. Eskimos are found in Alaska and Northern Canada, and only a handful of
missions are working in those parts. To choose a mission there ought to be a
rather simple procedure.

4. The vocation. By temperament and training a person may be cut out
for a career in music, literature, medicine, agriculture, radio, or some other
field. He feels God wants him to be a radio technician or a medical missionary. Once this is clear, other factors will soon fall into place. Many missions
will be ruled out because they have no radio or medical work. The same is
true of certain countries. There is no need for doctors in Japan; India has no
Christian broadcasting stations. With the vocational problem solved, the
question of country and mission can be more readily decided.

The secret is to zero in on one of these four factors and get clear guidance, then wait on the Lord for His leading on the other three. Of one thing

we may be sure; His way is perfect and He can make our way perfect (Ps 18:30, 32).

WHAT SHOULD ONE LOOK FOR IN A MISSION?

It is of the utmost importance that the career missionary select a mission in which he can be genuinely happy, for no one can do his best work over a long period of time unless his working conditions are satisfactory and his colleagues congenial. A short-term missionary can live with disillusionment and survive, but this is not so with a career missionary. For this reason it is essential that the candidate have a thorough understanding of the mission and that the mission have an equally thorough understanding of him. It is better not to go to the field than to go and then drop out after a year or two.

The candidate will have many questions to ask about the mission of his choice. Most of these will fall into one of the four main categories.

1. Its theological position. We are living in a day of vast confusion. The theological spectrum includes liberals, neo-orthodox, liberal evangelicals, conservative evangelicals, neo-evangelicals, fundamentalists, neo-fundamentalists, Pentecostals, and neo-Pentecostals. Fully two-thirds of all missionaries from North America regard themselves as evangelicals of one sort or another, and the majority of them belong to the Interdenominational Foreign Mission Association, the Evangelical Foreign Missions Association, or the Fellowship of Missions.

These missions are in complete agreement with the basic fundamentals of the faith and their missionaries would wish to be known as conservative evangelicals. This does not, however, rule out minor differences. Most of these missions have a statement of faith which all members are required to sign. Some are short, concise statements; others are more detailed. Some include certain eschatological items which are unimportant to others. Some practice second-degree separation and refuse to cooperate with equally conservative missions that practice only first-degree separation. Some missions hold distinct view on sanctification, healing, miracles, etc. Some are hyper-dispensational; others are mildly dispensational; still others are non-dispensational. Some are charismatic but not Pentecostal; others are both. Some are Calvinistic, others Arminian; still others welcome persons of either persuasion.

Most conservatives pay lip service to the maxim: "In essentials unity; in non-essentials liberty; in all things charity." The problem arises when we attempt to define the term "essential." It means one thing to one person and something else to another.

For this reason it is not enough to choose a "conservative" mission. One must be sure to choose a mission in which he will feel at home. If certain distinctive views regarding eschatology, sanctification, eternal security, pre-

destination, baptism, etc., are so important that he could not work happily
with a mission espousing slightly different views, he should make doubly
sure that the mission he chooses is in complete agreement with him on all
these finer points of doctrine. Otherwise both mission and missionary will be
unhappy.

At the moment the most vexing question has to do with the charismatic
movement. Some missions will not have anything to do with a charismatic.
Others will accept him on the understanding that he exercise the gift of
tongues only in his private devotions and promise not to proselytize.

Some mainline mission boards, conservative as well as liberal, will not
accept graduates from such seminaries as Dallas, Fuller, and Trinity. They
prefer graduates from their own denominational schools. In that case the
candidate has no choice; he must settle for a faith mission.

2. Its administrative policies. All mission boards have a handbook or
manual in which their principles and practices are spelled out in detail. This
document should be studied carefully, for policies vary quite widely from
mission to mission. Some are progressive; others are paternalistic. Some are
inclined to be autocratic in their treatment of their workers while others are
more democratic in their approach. In some the final authority is vested in
the home council; in others it rests with the field council. In a few the
general director is the final court of appeal and he can override both field and
home councils. In some missions the young missionary is on probation during his first term and cannot vote. In others he is accepted as a full voting
member from the day he joins. In most faith missions women do not hold
high office, even though they usually outnumber the men.

What about such matters as qualifications for service, the education of
children, marriage, voting rights, language requirements, working conditions, length of service, furlough, and retirement? Some missions admit
blacks; others do not. Some accept Third World nationals as full members;
others do not. Some insist that the children be sent to boarding school;
others leave the choice to the parents. Some arrange for full furloughs every
four years; others permit short furloughs every two years. Some require the
wife and mother to carry a full program of missionary work while others
expect her to give most of her time to her children, at least while they are
young.

It may come as a surprise to some that such "carnal" considerations
should be of importance to people as spiritual as missionaries are supposed to
be. For all their spirituality, however, they are human beings just like the
rest of us. Touch them and they get touchy. Cross them and they get cross. It
would be naive to expect them to be anything else. For this reason it is
highly important that the missionary candidate go through the mission
handbook with a fine comb lest he get to the field and discover that he has
made a mistake. If he is going to be disappointed with mission policy he
might as well find this out before he gets to the field.

The candidate should feel free to probe into all areas of mission policy and ask any questions pertaining to life and work that concern him. The mission should be willing to give full and frank answers to all such questions, regardless of how probing they may be. Only in this way will the missionary be able to avoid the heartache of disillusionment later on.

3. Its financial policies. It is often assumed that all missions have the same financial policies. This is not so. Here again the candidate should take nothing for granted. No matter how "unspiritual" it may sound, he should inquire into the financial arrangements he will be expected to live with on the mission field. This is especially true of the career missionary, who may serve 40 or 50 years with the mission.

Here the questions come thick and fast. Does the mission operate on sound fiscal policies? Are the books audited? Is an annual statement published? How does the mission raise funds? Does it appeal for funds or look to the Lord alone to supply its needs? Does it go into debt? Does it encourage individualized giving? Does each missionary have his own account or do all share alike from a general pool?

Is the candidate required to raise his own support before going to the field? Can he be sure of an adequate standard of living when he gets there? What provision is made for children? Does their support cease when they go to college? Does the missionary have his own work account? What about housing? Is that furnished by the mission or does the missionary have the right to buy a house?

What responsibility does the mission assume for outfit, travel, and language study? What about emergencies involving sick leave, early furlough, extended furlough? What provision is made for health insurance, social security payments, income tax, continuing education, etc.? What happens when pledged support drops off or the cost of living soars? Does a car bought with support money belong to the mission or the missionary? What financial obligations does the missionary incur if he resigns in the middle of a term of service? Finally, does the mission have a pension plan?

These are all legitimate questions that should be answered before the candidate joins the mission. It has often been said that to touch a man's pocketbook is to touch the apple of his eye. That is true. Few things demoralize an employee more quickly than inequities in the salary scale. While the missionary is not in any sense an "employee" of the mission, the principle still pertains. Our Lord himself has told us that the laborer is worthy of his hire. The candidate therefore should not be embarrassed to ask questions which so closely affect his well being and that of his family.

4. Opportunities for service. Many a missionary has resigned from the mission and returned to the homeland, not because his salary was inadequate or the living conditions were poor, nor because he could not get along with his colleagues, but because he failed to find his niche in the program. He fully expected to be doing one thing but ended up doing something entirely different. As a result, he felt like a square peg in a round hole.

This stems in large part from the fact that college students today are much more vocation conscious than their forbears a generation or two ago. They have majored in certain disciplines and naturally expect to use the knowledge, expertise, and skills they acquired in college, seminary, or graduate school. It is, therefore, exceedingly important that they have some idea beforehand of the kind of work they can expect to do when they reach the field. To be highly trained for one kind of ministry and have one's heart set on it, and then to be forced into another kind of ministry, is a very frustrating experience. A highly competent surgeon will naturally want a hospital, not a clinic, in which to work. A seminary professor with a Ph. D. in Old Testament will prefer to teach in a seminary rather than a Bible school. A person with an advanced degree in agriculture will want to use his expertise in that area.

Every effort, therefore, should be made by the candidate to ascertain exactly what opportunities he can expect in the mission under consideration. The mission, on the other hand, should not accept a highly trained candidate without making clear to him the opportunities available on the field. Not to do so is to mislead him, and that can be bad for both the missionary and the mission.

It goes without saying that the larger and older the mission the more varied are the opportunities for service. The Interdenominational Foreign Mission Association publishes an annual list of overseas opportunities, usually indexed by mission and by country. Intercristo (International Christian Organization) operates a computer retrieval system which lists some 5,000 separate job descriptions, both long and short term. It functions as an information link between the potential missionary and the sending agency.

It is not a good idea for the candidate to go to the field without this kind of information. He will have to exert a determined effort to acquire it, but it will be abundantly worthwhile.

A WORD OF CAUTION

Having chosen a mission the missionary is expected to live with his choice. This involves, among other things. a sense of loyalty and belonging. He should recognize that he now belongs to a team; he is a member of a family. He joins the mission; he is not *hired* by it. He is a member, not an employee. The mission is not just another organization whose members remain in good standing only as long as they pull their weight and pay their dues. He has joined a family—a very intimate and precious family where he will find sympathy, compassion, understanding, good will, and, above all, love.

This being so, he will want to cultivate and maintain a deep sense of loyalty to the family. The other members are his brothers and sisters in Christ. More than that, they share his love for the lost and his desire to win them to Christ. For better or worse they are in the work together. Consequently he will find a closer form of fellowship in a mission than perhaps in any other Christian organization. But in order to do this he must be willing to identify himself completely with the mission. A missionary with the Latin America Mission made the following statement:

> *I remember vividly a conversation Ken Strachan [L.A.M. Director] and I had during my first year in Latin America, I had been pretty miserable; nothing had gone the way I expected, my work wasn't particularly stimulating; I felt cut off from friends and activities which had made my life rich and full. My conclusion was that somehow I'd missed the Lord's will, that He certainly had not intended that I be so unproductive and unhappy. Ken's response was kind, but quite different from what I'd expected. He said, "Mary Anne, the trouble is that you've never joined the L.A.M." It is true. I'd given up my job, left my family and friends, but underneath I'd always assumed that if things didn't work out, if the adjustment was too difficult. I could go back. I'd not completely burned my bridges behind me.*[1]

1. Mary Anne Klein, "What Is Maturity?" *Latin America Evangelist,* January–February, 1965.

5

Doing Deputation Work

Deputation work, as it is called, is the first major obstacle encountered by the candidate after he has been accepted by the mission board. This is because almost all missions now require the outgoing missionary to raise his support in full before proceeding to the field. About the only way to do this is to visit various churches in the hope of securing support from each one.

Going into strange churches to appeal for support is not exactly a pleasant prospect for most missionary candidates. It is the last thing they want to do. They do not have the slightest idea where to begin, how to proceed, or when to quit. In fact the very idea scares them to death.

Let it be said at the outset that the experience is not nearly as formidable as the prospect. When a motorist descends into a deep valley the road ahead appears to be much steeper than it really is, but as he begins to climb, the hill seems to level out, and he reaches the top without difficulty. So it is with deputation work. Before one sets out he may be filled with fear, but as he gets into it he finds to his relief that it is not nearly as difficult as he was led to believe.

THE PURPOSE

There is nothing indefinite about deputation work. It has a definite fivefold purpose, and the prospective missionary will find the experience much more exciting and enriching if he understands this.

1. **To secure financial support.** This may not sound like a very "high" purpose, but candor requires that we admit this to be the prime objective of

deputation work. It is not, however, the carnal, mundane exercise that some people think it is, as we shall see.

Full financial support includes three major expenses: outfit, travel, and support. The last mentioned item includes administrative costs in the home office. The missionary candidate is expected to continue his deputation work until all three items are accounted for.

2. To solicit prayer support. Every Christian worker needs the moral support that comes through intercessory prayer, but the foreign missionary has special needs along this line. In a unique way he is engaged in a spiritual battle with the powers of darkness. He does not wrestle against flesh and blood but against demonic powers in heavenly places. As he penetrates farther and farther into enemy-occupied territory (remember, Satan is the god and prince of this world) where the Christian forces are few and feeble and hopelessly outnumbered, he needs to be protected by a constant barrage of prayer.

3. To promote the cause of missions. The missionary is an ambassador for Christ. As such, his interest is much wider than his own work or mission. When he appeals for prayer it is not simply for himself and his work in one small part of the vineyard. He is interested in the cause of Christ in all six continents even though his mission may operate in only one of the six. Like Paul, his concern is for the "regions beyond" where Christ is not known. He will, therefore, bring to his deputation work a global concern, if not a global view. Whenever possible he will put in a good word for missions other than his own. He will realize that the world mission of the Christian church calls for a breadth of understanding and a vision of the lost world not found in many local congregations. As a result of his ministry the churches will be challenged not only to strengthen their stakes but also to lengthen their cords.

4. To edify the church. There is no place for selfishness in Christian service. Deputation ministry is an end in itself as well as a means to an end. If the candidate goes only to get and not to give, he will be a disappointment to himself and to the churches. If he has a proper understanding of his role, however, he will realize that he has something to give to the churches— something that even the pastor cannot provide.

Samuel Rutherford used to say: "What a beautiful yoke is youth and grace, Christ and a young man." One thing more beautiful than Christ and a young man is Christ and a young couple heading for the mission field. It is a thrilling experience to listen to the personal testimonies of a husband and wife who, having turned their backs on the emoluments of the world, are prepared to follow Christ to the ends of the earth. No church member can fail to be impressed by such testimonies if given in humility and in the power of the Holy Spirit. After almost half a century in missionary service I never fail to be blessed when I have the privilege of attending a farewell service for former students leaving for the mission field.

The candidate in deputation work need not feel diffident about his ministry in the local church. He is there to *give* a blessing as well as to *get* one. If he can make a vital contribution to the spiritual life of the church its support will be almost assured. He need have no fears on that score.

5. To recruit other candidates. Young people take their cue these days from their peers, not from their parents or their pastors. It is vitally important, therefore, that they have first-hand acquaintance with young missionaries just starting out. The Student Volunteer Movement is an example of the power of missionary volunteers to attract others to full-time Christian service. Between 1886 and 1920 the SVM was responsible for sending over 20,000 missionaries to the field. The power of example is still a very potent force in human affairs.

THE DISADVANTAGES

It would be nice to say that deputation work is all fun, but that would not be true. There are some drawbacks and these should be acknowledged and discussed.

1. It is time consuming. It usually takes the best part of eighteen months for the average married candidate to gather full support. Some have been known to get it in a matter of weeks. One couple raised their support without taking any meetings at all but simply by writing letters to their friends! Another couple did it in two months. These are the exceptions, however, not the rule. In rare cases the deputation ministry may take so long that the person involved becomes discouraged and decides that the Lord does not want him on the mission field and that this is His way of revealing His will. In the last thirty years, however, I have known only two persons in this category—two out of many hundreds.

But even a year is a long time, especially if the candidate has other responsibilities and cannot give his undivided attention to deputation work. Then again, meetings cannot always be arranged in the desired sequence. One may go for several weeks or months without a speaking engagement, and not all engagements result in financial support. Others provide only a small amount, thus necessitating more meetings involving additional time.

2. It is costly in terms of money. Much depends on mission policy. Some missions assume full responsibility for all deputation expenses, and all offerings received go to the mission. In the case of a single person this works very well, as practically all his expenses on the road will be deputation items. But the married man with a wife and family is in a different situation, unless the mission provides for the family while the father is on deputation. Not many missions do this. They prefer the family to be self-supporting. Either the wife works or the husband has a church which permits him to be away on deputation one weekend in the month.

The candidate with a family has two problems. First, he has to provide for his family while he is away on deputation. Second, with two or three children his support figure will be very high, thus adding to the time it takes to raise the full amount. This past week I received a letter from a former student with four children. It took him almost four years to raise sufficient funds to support such a large family. On more than one occasion he almost gave up, but he persevered and the Lord honored his faith.

3. It is physically enervating. Time and travel combine to make the deputation experience hard on one's physical condition. Long days on the road, late nights, irregular meals, and inadequate sleep are bound to have a debilitating effect on the individual. This is especially true if the travel is extensive and the ministry unduly prolonged.

If the candidate is on the road for six or seven weeks he will find before long that while the spirit is willing, the flesh is weak. The problem is aggravated if he is accompanied by his wife and children. Traveling week after week in a station wagon filled with babies, bundles, bottles, and books, he and his wife can be forgiven if they feel exhausted by the time they return home.

Unfortunately, one trip will probably not be enough. Another and another will be required before all the support is in. Under such circumstances deputation work often turns out to be an endurance test. Our Lord's words, "He that endureth to the end shall be saved," are appropriate here. But this is excellent training for what lies ahead. The mission field is no place for the weak, the weary, or the fainthearted.

THE ADVANTAGES

In spite of the fears entertained by those anticipating deputation ministry, there are several fringe benefits altogether apart from prayer and financial support.

1. It produces self-reliance. John Eliot, missionary to the Indians in Massachusetts, used to say: "Prayer and pains through faith in Jesus Christ will do anything." Prayer and pains—these are the necessary ingredients in all forms of Christian service. Prayer expresses our dependence on God; without Him we can do nothing. Pains involve effort on our part. God does not act alone, nor does man. Paul put it this way: "We are laborers together with God" (I Cor 3:9, KJV). Paul planted and Apollos watered, and God gave the increase, but He did not do it without the active cooperation of Paul and Apollos. It has been said that we should pray as if everything depends on God and work as if everything depends on us.

There is always the temptation, especially on the part of the timid, to sit back and wait for God to assume full responsibility for the entire operation. To this end they pray diligently, asking God to accomplish His purpose in and through them, and in the very act of praying they confirm their own lethargy and fear of failure. This is especially true of those who have a poor self-image, tend to be introverts, and have a natural aversion to anything as demanding as deputation work.

One of the greatest advantages is that the mission requires the candidate to do what otherwise he probably would never do. In this way he is forced to stand on his own feet and help answer his own prayers. In the process he must exercise some initiative, assume some responsibility, and achieve at least a measure of success. He must get down to business, write letters, make phone calls, arrange for meetings, make and change travel plans, confer with pastors, meet with missionary committees, and do many other things incidental to deputation work. At first it may be irksome, but with effort comes experience, with experience comes confidence, and with confidence comes success. When the period of deputation is over the candidate will be a better and stronger character. He will be pleasantly surprised with his own development as a human being. He will have learned lessons and gained victories which will stand him in good stead for the rest of his life. This is no mean achievement.

2. It opens up new vistas. It affords the candidate an opportunity to visit scores of new churches and make hundreds of new friends. On the deputation trail he will visit large churches and small churches, rural churches and urban churches, wealthy churches and poor churches. In this way he will be exposed to a cross section of American church life that only missionaries ever see. In these churches he will meet all kinds of pastors and other Christian workers. Some of them will be very successful; others will be flirting with failure. Some will be in love with the Lord; some will be in love with their work. Others will be in love with their people; and still others will have lost their first love and will be going through the motions without satisfaction to themselves or blessing to others. Through it all his eyes will be opened to the spectrum of the parish ministry, its bright and seamy sides, its victories and defeats, its problems and possibilities. In his fellowship with the pastors of these churches he will learn to rejoice with those who rejoice and weep with those who weep.

He will be entertained in scores of homes where he will be welcomed like a long-lost friend, loved like a son, treated like a prince, and sent on his way rejoicing. In these homes he will encounter some of the most dedicated and wonderful laymen in the country—men and women who will remain his friends for life. While he is on the field they will remember him daily in prayer; when he returns on furlough their homes will be open to him and his family.

3. It provides experience in public speaking. One of the greatest weaknesses of theological education is its failure to provide the student with adequate preaching opportunities. Most seminaries and Bible colleges have one or more courses in homiletics, but the student may have only two or three preaching opportunities in a three-hour course. This is hardly enough to produce proficiency in the art of preaching.

Deputation work affords valuable experience in the preparation and delivery of messages. Granted the candidate will not be expected to preach the kind of exegetical sermon usually delivered on Sunday morning; nevertheless, he will be given speaking opportunities in church services, prayer meetings, youth groups, Sunday school classes, etc. The fact that he will be repeating the same half-dozen messages in various churches will not be a great drawback. This will enable him to correct and improve the talks as he goes along. By the time he has been on the road a month he ought to have some well-developed, well-polished messages. He will have more speaking opportunities in three months of deputation than in three years in seminary. This is an excellent way to begin a preaching career.

HOW TO OBTAIN SPEAKING ENGAGEMENTS

When contemplating deputation work the first problem to be solved is how to secure speaking engagements. It is important that these be lined up well in advance, for pastors are busy and churches usually have their programs arranged months ahead of time. They cannot be expected to alter their own calendar of events to accommodate a missionary candidate whom they have never seen. It helps to know what contacts are available.

1. **Contacts furnished by the mission.** Most missions have a large mailing list of donors, both churches and individuals, who have already shown an interest in supporting world missions. The deputation secretary will usually supply the candidate with a list of churches in a given area. The candidate can then get in touch with the pastors, introduce himself, and ask for an opportunity to share his testimony with the church. Not all pastors will respond positively, for several reasons: (1) The pastor may be inundated with similar requests from other missionaries, (2) The church budget may be fixed for the entire year, in which case no additional items can be added, (3) The church may have a new pastor who is not particularly interested in world missions. In any case it is worth a try. If only one letter in five brings a response, it will be worthwhile.

2. **Contacts obtained through a church directory.** Most denominations publish an annual directory of all their churches and pastors and their addresses. This gives the candidate ready access to the churches most likely to come to his aid. The names and addresses of many independent churches will be found in the annual directory of the Independent Fundamental Churches of America. These are usually listed geographically, state by state, which enables one to see at a glance which churches are within reasonable

traveling distance. It hardly pays a missionary in Connecticut to appeal to a church in California.

3. Contacts acquired through one's alma mater. The prospective missionary should not forget any friends and acquaintances from his college career. This is especially true of the seminary student, whose fellow students will become pastors of churches and will therefore be in a position to help him. Most young pastors are only too willing to help a fellow alumnus heading for the mission field.

4. Contacts in the home town. These include local churches, service clubs, the weekly newspaper, radio and television stations. The editor of the local paper will be happy to run a feature article on a local resident about to undertake a missionary career in some remote region of the world. This kind of human interest article seldom fails to attract attention. Such a newspaper article often leads to speaking engagements in the most unlikely places. The same is true of TV programs, especially in small towns.

5. Contacts through a large missionary conference. A speaking engagement in one church often leads to an invitation to speak in another. This is especially true in a large missionary conference attended by a significant number of outsiders. Some of them will go back to their own churches and report what they have heard.

6. Contacts established by personal correspondence. Nearly everyone has a coterie of Christian friends and relatives who can be counted on to help out when the need arises. A personal letter should be sent to all of these inquiring about the possibilities of speaking in their church.

Deputation work tends to slacken off during the summer months when pastors are on vacation and churches operate on a reduced schedule. On the other hand, the summer provides two special opportunities—vacation Bible schools and summer Bible camps. If the candidate is invited to one of these he should eagerly accept the opportunity.

FOLLOW THROUGH ON CONTACTS

When all possible contacts have been listed, a letter should be prepared and sent to the various churches and groups most likely to respond. The content, style, and tone of the letter is of the utmost importance, especially if the recipient is a total stranger, which is the case most of the time.

The pastor is obviously the key man in the church. The letter should be addressed to him. If his name and title are known, they should by all means be used. Occasionally a pastor may be lukewarm toward missions, or the church may be without a pastor for the time being. In that case it would be better to address the letter to the chairman of the missionary committee.

Great pains should be taken to prepare an attractive, interesting. and informative letter. It should be well constructed and well expressed, and free from all spelling and typing errors. It should contain all pertinent information regarding the candidate, his mission, the country to which he is going, and the kind of work he expects to do. The letter should make some concrete suggestions regarding several possible speaking dates. Included in the letter should be a piece of literature describing the mission, its work, and outreach. When possible, mission stationery should be used. A self-addressed, stamped envelope is always appreciated.

Equally important is the tone of the letter. It is imperative that a good impression be made with the first, perhaps the only, letter. If the recipient is turned off he won't even bother to reply. The tone of the letter should be cordial, courteous, appreciative, accommodating, and sincere.

Not all letters will be answered, and not all answers will include an invitation to speak. If the ratio is one in five the candidate may count himself fortunate. When invitations are given they should be accepted if at all possible. Small churches should not be avoided. Sometimes the best response comes from the smaller churches. Large, wealthy churches are not always the most generous when it comes to missionary support. In addition, the larger churches in the bigger cities are the ones that get the most requests, and they cannot possibly respond affirmatively to even a fraction of them without disrupting their own program. So the candidate should take nothing for granted. He should gladly accept all invitations, hoping that something positive will result.

If after a reasonable length of time there is no response, he may wish to send a second letter or, better still, talk with the pastor on the phone. Great tact is needed not to give offense. If that doesn't produce results, that particular church might as well be written off, at least for the time being.

HOW TO MAKE THE MOST OF THE OPPORTUNITIES

Opportunities are hard to come by. Once secured, they should be used to the best advantage.

1. Visit as many churches as possible. The candidate should not turn down a church because it is small or out of the way. Some of the most fruitful contacts come from such churches. Smaller churches in the rural areas see missionaries less frequently than the big city churches; consequently their members take a more personal interest in the speaker. Rural church members often have more leisure time than their city cousins to devote to personal Bible study, meditation, and prayer. Such Christians make fine prayer partners.

2. Get to the church well ahead of time. This is particularly important when the candidate is visiting a church for the first time and has never met the pastor. He should plan to arrive at least half an hour before the service is scheduled to begin. This will afford ample time to meet the pastor, have a time of prayer, get the "feel" of the church, put out the literature, and set up the projector—if one is to be used. Extra bulbs and an extension cord should always be on hand for emergencies. Projectors have an uncanny way of breaking down at the wrong time!

3. Make as many friends as possible. The candidate should not deliver his message and then go his way. He should stay as long as hospitality is provided without becoming a burden, and take every opportunity to speak personally with the church staff, elders, deacons, missionary committee members, and other leaders. He should make a special effort to cement a lasting friendship with his host and hostess who are usually committed Christians with a heart for world missions. This may entail long hours and late nights, but the effort is worthwhile. It is absolutely essential that he be friendly and manifest a genuine interest in people as people, not simply as donors and prayer partners.

4. Make a list of all interested persons. Most people will be polite, but not all will be interested. The names and addresses of those who show interest should be noted. Included in the notation should be any pertinent details—personal, domestic, and professional—that will enable the candidate to remember them.

5. Leave behind a permanent reminder of the visit. This might be a piece of literature, a prayer card, a colored snapshot, or some other inexpensive memento. In the case of host and hostess, something a little more substantial would be in order. A most acceptable gift would be a paperback on missions or a devotional book, preferably one published by the candidate's own mission.

6. Send a follow-up letter as soon as possible. It is not enough to shake hands and say thank you at the close of the last meeting. Within a week letters of appreciation should be sent to the pastor, the chairman of the missionary committee, and the host and hostess.

HINTS REGARDING SPEAKING ENGAGEMENTS

Not all missionaries are good speakers, but that is no excuse for a poor performance in the pulpit. Most missionaries could improve their speaking ability with a little effort. Fifty years ago the missionary was a hero and his story was exotic if not exciting. Not so today. The problem now is competition. The missionary has to compete with Hollywood and Madison Avenue, to say nothing of the *Today Show* with Jane Pauley and the *Evening News* with Dan Rather. Some suggestions may be in order.

1. Have something to say. Make it something worth hearing, something that nobody else has to offer. Content is important. Every effort should be made to present material that will instruct as well as inspire, so that when the service is over the audience goes home saying, "I heard something tonight I never knew before."

2. Be flexible. The candidate should be prepared for any eventuality. He may expect to speak to the adult class in the Sunday school but discover at the last minute that they want him in the junior department. Or he may have been told that he will have only ten minutes in the opening exercises, only to find to his dismay that he is expected to take the whole period. He should be prepared to speak any time, anywhere, for five minutes or fifty without complaining. He is a guest and should accept whatever opportunity is given to him. His messages should be prepared in such a way that they can be expanded or reduced on the spur of the moment without hesitation, distortion, or confusion. He should have several different messages for children, young people, adults, Sunday service, prayer meeting, etc.

3. Speak forcefully. However timid or shy he may be, the missionary should make every effort to articulate clearly. He has nothing to be shy about. He is an ambassador for Christ. His mandate is clear. His authority is beyond question. His credentials are impeccable. He has indeed a "story to tell to the nations." He also has a word for supporters at home, and he ought to give that word with clarity and authority.

4. Stop on time. There are three basic rules regarding public speaking: Stand up! Speak up! Shut up! Many missionaries spoil a good presentation by continuing to talk beyond their allotted time, to the discomfiture of the audience. Long-winded missionaries can kill a conference the first evening. Few pastors have the courage to stop them when the time is up. The beleaguered hearers have only one way of registering their protest—by staying away the next night.

5. Use slides wisely. Slide presentations can be very effective or they can be downright painful, depending on the way they are used. Slides are seldom effective when the speaker wastes precious time explaining the details of each slide as it appears on the screen. Slides are designed to illustrate, not eliminate, the message. When properly used, the slides become part of an illustrated lecture.

Some missions solve the problem by preparing a tape that is synchronized with the slides. This has several distinct advantages. It guarantees that the missionary will not run overtime. The script of the tape is written out beforehand, revised, and refined, thus assuring that the presentation will be cogent. It also provides the inexperienced candidate with a first-rate talk to go along with his personal testimony.

WHAT A MISSIONARY MESSAGE SHOULD ACCOMPLISH

Missionary talks are a means to an end, not an end in themselves. If properly prepared and forcefully presented, a missionary message should accomplish at least three things.

1. It should impart missionary information. Missionary talks unfortunately tend to be long on inspiration and short on information—good, solid, up-to-date information that will give church members a better understanding of the problems and prospects of the Christian world mission.

2. It should create missionary interest. The information should be conveyed in such a dynamic manner that even nominal church members will have their interest in missions quickened to the point where they will want to hear more.

3. It should result in missionary activity. Interest is good but it is not enough. It should culminate in action. People who have not prayed for missions before will begin to do so. People who have not participated in the "faith promise" will want to share in it. Young people who have been hesitating between two opinions will decide to give serious consideration to the claims of the foreign mission field.

TOPICS FOR MISSIONARY MESSAGES

In most cases the missionary candidate has not been to the field; his knowledge of missionary work, therefore, must of necessity be limited. This, however, need not detract from the effectiveness of the message, especially if he has majored in missions while in Bible college or seminary.

Before he begins his deputation ministry he should decide what he wants to say. If he finds himself in a week-long missionary conference he will need more than one or two talks. Otherwise by Tuesday evening he will have exhausted his repertoire. He should prepare six or eight different talks geared to the various audiences he is likely to encounter.

1. The candidate's life story. Obviously the first, and probably the best, topic is his own testimony. Some people hesitate to give their testimony for fear they will be accused of "always talking about themselves." To add to his uncertainty, the candidate may feel that he is young and inexperienced—both of which are true. This, however, should not deter him from sharing with others what God has done in and through him.

In his testimony he should include his family background, conversion, call to and preparation for the ministry, examples of the leading of the Lord, lessons in the life of faith, and answers to prayer.

Often missionary testimonies are not as effective as they might be because the person has not taken sufficient time and effort to produce a well-conceived and well-constructed talk. The candidate takes for granted that because he knows his own life story so well, there is no need to work over the material. It might not be a bad idea to write it out, paragraph by paragraph, and then go over it several times to make sure that every idea is well expressed and every point is well made. Such a testimony can have a powerful effect on a sympathetic audience.

2. The work of the mission. The candidate should be sufficiently familiar with the history of his mission to enable him to give a good, informative talk on the mission—its origin, history, outreach, methods, principles and practices. To do this successfully will require some reading and research. In a short message of this kind it will not be possible to do more than touch on the highlights of these various areas. Such a talk would be most enlightening to the average church member, many of whom will know the mission only by name.

3. The country of one's choice. By this time the candidate will probably know the country to which he has been assigned. He should then make a thorough study of that country—its geography, history, people, culture, customs, politics, religion, etc. To prepare such a talk will require much study, but it should be done even if only for the candidate's own sake, apart from its possible use in deputation ministry.

Most Americans have only the scantiest knowledge of the world beyond our borders. It will be an education for them to get even a bird's eye view of Indonesia, Nigeria, Venezuela, or the Philippines. I once taught a missions major at Barrington College who was invited to speak to the Women's Missionary Society in a church in Providence, R.I. When she finished she was asked, "When do you return to Indonesia?" She replied, "I'm just a student; I have never been to Indonesia!" The women were flabbergasted. She had been so well prepared and informed in her subject that they thought she was a missionary on furlough. So it can be done.

4. A biblical message on missions. Candidates are not expected to preach. Most manuals warn against it. On the other hand, a seminary graduate who has majored in missions should be able to tackle a message on the Bible basis of missions without too much trouble. This kind of message is best suited to a Sunday morning worship service. Seldom are candidates invited to take the entire morning service. If they participate at all, it is usually to give a short testimony.

Topics for such a biblical presentation might include: Missions in the Plan of God, Missions and the Sovereignty of God, Missions and the Ministry of the Holy Spirit, The Missionary Mandate, The Great Commission, Missions in the Book of Acts, Missions in the Epistles of Paul.

5. Panel discussions. Panel sessions are becoming increasingly popular at the annual missionary conference. They afford an opportunity for the congregation to interact with the missionaries. In this kind of situation the candidate who has majored in missions in Bible college or seminary will have an enormous advantage over others not so fortunate. Such a person will have a fairly adequate grasp of the major problems, trends, and developments in the modern missionary movement and will be able to discuss them intelligently. Those without such an exposure to missions should take a crash course in missions before setting out on deputation work by reading fifteen or twenty short paperbacks on the modern missionary movement. Indeed, the mission under which the candidate plans to serve should require this of all candidates who have not covered this ground in their academic career.

With adequate preparation and prayer, and with the blessing of the Holy Spirit, there is no reason why the deputation ministry of the average candidate should not be rewarding to himself and enriching to the churches.

6

Raising Support

Money was not a big problem in the early church. When Jesus sent out the twelve, He warned them against taking money or extra clothing with them. They were expected to depend on the charity of their converts and the traditional hospitality of the Jewish community. When asked for alms as he was about to enter the temple, Peter replied: "Silver and gold have I none." But it did not seem to hinder his usefulness. He had something money could not buy, and that he shared with the crippled man.

We have come a long way in the intervening years. In 1979 the North American churches gave the handsome sum of $1.15 billion to world missions. This works out at $21,560.00 per missionary, which is a lot of money even by today's inflated standards. Not every missionary receives that amount of money for his own use. There are thousands of institutions overseas and hundreds of offices in the homelands, all of which must get their share, and these are very costly to operate.

THE CURRENT SCENE

The cost of missionary support rises year by year. Between 1971 and 1975 it increased by 80 percent. Today it costs anywhere from $20,000 to $30,000 to support a family of four, depending on the mission and the country involved. Some missions operate more economically than others. Some have a more generous support base for their missionaries. Also, the cost of living varies from country to country. In Japan it is so high that some large Ameri-

63

can firms, IBM among them, are recalling their American personnel and replacing them with nationals.

It now costs more to support a missionary family in some countries than it does to support a pastor and his family in the U.S. The average salary of the American pastor is $16,000 a year. This, however, is misleading, for many pastors have to moonlight to make ends meet. Moreover, many pastors' wives are working outside the home to augment the family income. Missionaries cannot moonlight, so their support figure is high.

Missionaries in the mainline denominations do not have to raise their own support. It is written into the foreign missions budget of the denomination. Those affiliated with the faith missions (IFMA) and the smaller, more conservative denominational missions (EFMA) are expected to raise their support before proceeding to the field. The support figure includes everything required to keep them functioning effectively.

Two devaluations of the American dollar and continuing inflation abroad have played havoc with missionary support during the 1970s. In some countries inflation is running well over 100 percent annually, creating a veritable nightmare for mission treasurers who have to deal with a dozen different currencies. Most missions subscribe to a cost-of-living index provided by the State Department. It gives the cost of living in the major countries of the world on a monthly or a quarterly basis. With this information available to them, the mission boards are able to adjust the support scale up or down as needed. But even with this kind of help it is virtually impossible to keep abreast of galloping inflation in countries like Chile, Argentina, and others.

The evangelical missions have one big advantage over the mainline denominations in their support policy: support is given on a personal basis. To get it the missionary has to appear in person, spend a weekend in the church, share his testimony, and tell about his work. In this way he wins the confidence of the church members who continue to remember him as a personal friend, and not only as a professional missionary. The support he picks up in this way is genuine, personal support; it involves prayer as well as money. The time and effort involved may be considerable, but it pays off in the long run. Without the personal touch this kind of support would be difficult if not impossible to secure.

The mainline denominations have a streamlined operation which saves time and effort but the end result is hardly satisfactory. Their candidates are not required to raise their support, nor are their missionaries on furlough expected to visit the churches. The average local church, therefore, seldom sees a live missionary from one decade to another. The absence of the personal touch is largely responsible for the fact that per capita giving to missions is considerably lower in these denominations than in other churches. As a result, in recent years they have been operating in the red. Unable to generate more interest in missions, they have greatly reduced their missionary force during the last decade.

MYTHS ABOUT MONEY

The average Christian is woefully ignorant of what the Bible has to say about money. As a result, many myths have developed. We have space to mention only a few.

1. There is something unspiritual about money matters. In some Christian circles money is almost a dirty word. Does not the Bible refer to money as "filthy lucre?" Is not the love of money the root of all evil? Does the Bible not roundly condemn such sins as covetousness, selfishness, and greed?

2. There is something unscriptural about financial appeals. Does the Bible not exhort us to make our requests known only to God? Did not Jesus tell us not to allow our right hand to know what our left hand does when giving? Are we not warned against laying up treasures on earth?

3. There is something unseemly about begging for support. It is embarrassing to the churches. It is degrading to the missionary. There is nothing good to be said for it.

4. Full-time Christian workers should live by faith. The laymen in the church "work for a living" and get a paycheck at the end of the week. Christian workers, on the other hand, work for the Lord and should "look to the Lord" for their support.

5. Living by faith is a matter of dollars and cents. It is assumed that a person cannot really live by faith until he has come to the end of all human resources, after which he looks to God alone for the supply of his daily needs.

6. God on His own can supply the needs of His servants. Do not the cattle on a thousand hills belong to Him? Did Jesus not feed five thousand with five loaves and two fishes? Has He not promised to supply all our needs according to His riches in glory by Christ Jesus?

EXPLODING THE MYTHS

It will help the missionary candidate if he can rid his mind of these myths; otherwise they will greatly inhibit him in his deputation ministry. What shall we say about them?

1. Money is not dirty. It is neutral, neither clean nor dirty. It becomes dirty only when sinful man gets his grimy hands on it and uses it for his own selfish ends. Jesus made mention of money in several of His parables, and He Himself resorted to its use. He handled enough money to need a treasurer. That Judas turned out to be a thief does not mean that all treasurers are thieves, however!

Money, far from being a dirty commodity, can be the means of the salvation of souls and the extension of the Kingdom. John Wesley had the right philosophy about money. He said: "Make all you can. Save all you can. Give away all you can." That is precisely what he did. In the first year of his ministry his income was 30 pounds. He kept 28 and gave away two. The next year it increased to 60 pounds. He kept 28 and gave away 32. The third year it was 120 pounds. He lived on 28 and gave the rest away.

General Booth, founder of the Salvation Army, questioned about accepting "tainted" money from non-Christian sources, replied: "I will accept any kind of money—even the Devil's. I'll wash it in the blood of Christ and use it for the glory of God!"

2. There is nothing wrong with financial appeals. Jesus talked freely about money and had some pertinent things to say about its use. He borrowed Peter's boat, the donkey on which He rode into Jerusalem, and the upper room in which He commemorated the Last Supper. It is a safe assumption that He asked for these things; He was too polite to take them without doing so. Paul was not reluctant to ask the Corinthians for money to help the poor saints in Jerusalem.

If the churches were functioning as Christian churches should, there would be no need for candidates to go from church to church asking for support. The churches, with their coffers full, would be looking for candidates to support. And did Jesus not say on one occasion: "It is more blessed to give than to receive"? If the churches really believed this they would be delighted when another missionary came their way, for he would give them the opportunity to get the "bigger" blessing. Kerry Lovering, writing in *Africa Now,* November–December 1976, entitled his lead article, "If one more mission asks me for money, I'll. . . shout 'Praise the Lord!'" It is not the approach of the missionary that is wrong; it is the attitude of the church.

3. The word "begging" is entirely inappropriate. The missionary is *not* a beggar. He is a laborer in the Lord's vineyard, and the laborer is worthy of his hire. Jesus said so. He is also a servant of the church; the church *owes* him a living wage. Every true church is a church for others. The church, like Paul, is a debtor both to the Greeks and to the barbarians. It is under moral obligation to share the gospel with the world, especially that part where Christ has not been named. The church can fulfill this obligation only through the missionary. When the missionary, therefore, comes seeking support he is not a beggar in disgrace; he is a benefactor in disguise.

4. All Christians should live by faith. The Christian life is a life of faith. It commences in faith (Eph 2:8). It continues in faith (Gal 2:20). It culminates in faith (Heb 11:13). This applies to all Christians, not only full-time workers.

Paul said, "Whatsoever is not of faith is sin" (Rom 14:23, KJV). It is a great pity that modern evangelicalism has created such a dichotomy between the layman and the clergy in the Christian church.

5. **Living by faith has nothing to do with money per se.** In some instances it may involve money, but it should never be restricted to money. The great patriarchs listed in Hebrews 11 all lived by faith, yet many of them were men of considerable wealth. This neither helped nor hindered their walk of faith. Modern evangelicals have looked upon George Muller and Hudson Taylor as great men of faith because they lived from day to day not knowing where their next meal would come from. It is a narrow and distorted view of truth to single out these two men as examples of the life of faith. They were chosen vessels to prove to the whole church that it is no vain thing to trust in the living God, but their particular lifestyle was not intended for everyone.

6. **God does supply the needs of His servants.** The question is, "How?" God is prodigal in the exercise of His grace but niggardly in the exercise of His power. He uses extraordinary means only when ordinary means are unavailable or inadequate. The manna fell day by day during the forty years Israel was in the wilderness, but it ceased the day they entered the promised land. They then began to eat corn which they themselves cultivated. Jesus fed the five thousand in the wilderness where there was no food and the people were ready to perish, but on another occasion He *bought* food in Samaria for Himself and His disciples (Jn 4:8).

Missionaries do look to God for the supply of their needs, but everyone knows that these supplies are not sent direct from heaven. They are channeled through the church. In the case of the American church we have money in abundance. There is no need to "pray it down." All we need to do is "pry it out." God is not likely to work miracles for His servants on the mission field when the church at home has the resources to underwrite the entire operation ten times over.

BREAKDOWN OF FUNDS INVOLVED

The total amount of money the candidate is asked to raise includes three major items: outfit, passage, and support.

Most candidates are young people just starting out in life. They have not yet acquired the goods and chattels generally regarded as essential to a comfortable, modest lifestyle. If they are going to a primitive part of the world they must take everything they will need for the first term of service. Naturally, they do not have that kind of money. There is little left over after they have paid their college and seminary debts. Those going to the more advanced countries may find it cheaper to buy these things in the U.S. and transport them halfway around the world than to acquire them at enormously inflated prices after they reach the field. After World War II, laundry soap in Shanghai sold for $2.00 a bar! Today, orange juice in Tokyo costs $1.95 a glass!

Some missionaries now include a car in their outfit. In Europe it is better to buy the car on the spot, but in Latin America a ten-year-old secondhand car may cost twice as much as a new car in the U.S. In any event, cars are expensive to buy and run and adequate provision must be made.

The second item is passage. Almost all missionaries travel by air. Such travel is fast but hardly cheap. A one-way ticket to Nairobi costs $879.00. Four tickets (two adults and two children) would amount to $2,676.00, which is a tidy sum of money. This also must be raised before the candidate and his family proceed to the field. This item, however, will not appear a second time; furlough travel is provided for in the regular support figure.

The third item, support, is the largest of all. It will run anywhere from $20,000 to $30,000 or more a year. That is a lot of money, but one must remember that it includes the *total* amount required to keep a missionary and his family living and functioning as an effective unit on the field.

The support figure is divided into two major categories—personal allowance and other expenses. The personal allowance is that portion which the missionary uses at his own discretion for his own purposes. Most of this goes for food, clothing, education of the children, and other items of a purely personal nature. This usually represents approximately half of the total support figure.

The other half is divided among eight or ten items: work account, car account, social security, health insurance, furlough, pension plan, contingency, administration, etc. These items are kept separate for two reasons. In some countries missionaries are required to pay income tax, and the tax rate is very high. Under this arrangement they are taxed only on their own personal allowance. A second reason is that most of these expenses are incurred at the home base on the missionary's behalf. He never sees the money so it would be confusing to put it into his account. The item for administration is designed to defray the high cost of operating the home office, or offices if there are more than one. The larger faith missions may have four or five regional offices in the U.S. and these costs must also be met. Each missionary is expected to help defray them. The only other way to take care of such expenses would be to have a general or administrative fund, but few donors care to give to such a fund. They much prefer to give directly to what they consider "missionary support."

The amount of money kept at home and posted under administrative expenses varies from mission to mission, depending on the kind of mission involved and the method of accounting used. Interdenominational faith missions have higher overhead costs in the home countries owing to the fact that they require several regional offices in addition to headquarters. Recruiting is also an expensive item for them. Denominational missions, on the other hand, need only one office—headquarters. Again, different missions use different accounting methods. Children in hostels and retired missionaries usually live in the homeland. Should their upkeep be charged against home administration or against missionary support? Some missions do one thing, some another.

There are missions which show only ten percent of income kept at home for administrative purposes. In others, the percentage may run as high as 25 to 30 percent. Ten percent is generally regarded as excellent; 15 percent is good, 20 percent is high. In these days of increasing costs, many churches are taking a second look at mission finance. They naturally want their dollars to go as far as possible.

PERTINENT OBSERVATIONS

There are several things the candidate can do to help achieve his goal. The first is to pray. God works in answer to believing prayer. In his prayers he should make large requests. This is for two reasons. They glorify God and they greatly reduce the time and effort involved. It is to the advantage of both the candidate and the mission if his support comes from 20 churches rather than 40 or 50, as is often the case.

He should pray for the pastors who receive his letter and for the members of the missionary committees as they consider his needs. He should also set dates and goals and pray with these in mind. It is difficult to get specific answers to prayer unless we pray specific prayers. God delights to answer the prayers of great faith.

After visiting a church the candidate will wait patiently, sometimes apprehensively, for some indication of response. Patience will come more easily if certain factors are kept in mind. The decision to take on part of his support will be made by the missionary committee, which may meet only once every month or so. In some churches such a decision has to be passed on to the church board or the finance committee for approval. That will take more time. Also, some churches cannot make any additional commitments until the new mission budget is drawn up and presented to the congregation at the annual business meeting. This process may take six months.

If there is no response within a reasonable time, it is quite proper for the candidate to make a discreet inquiry regarding the matter. This may be done by a letter to the pastor or to the chairman of the missionary committee. Such a letter will have to be very tactful lest a wrong impression be created. Long distance phone calls are very effective in the business world and can be used to good advantage by the missionary candidate. Here again great tact will be required not to give offense. One of my students spent several hundred dollars calling the churches he had visited. The response was amazing. Within a month he had almost all of his support.

When it comes to raising support, evangelical denominational missions have a definite edge over the interdenominational missions. To begin with, they prefer to support their own missionaries. Also, their churches are usually in close and constant touch with headquarters; consequently the pastors and the missionary committee members are well informed regarding their own overseas operations. Independent churches are not always so well informed about the needs and problems of the faith missions. When a denominational church has a surplus in its missions budget it writes to headquarters to ask for a candidate to support. This happens less often among the faith missions, who depend to a large extent on the independent churches. Last year a candidate under the Evangelical Free Church Department of Overseas Missions made a tour of the Evangelical Free churches on the east coast and in six weeks had raised his full support. Some of the churches had written headquarters asking for a candidate to support, so they were ready for him when he arrived. It helps to have that kind of "captive" constituency.

During the fund-raising period, no matter how long it proves to be, the candidate should periodically send out prayer letters to the churches he has visited and the individuals he has contacted. In this way he will keep them posted on his progress and they will be able to pray more intelligently for his needs. Those who have not given might be moved to give, and some who have given might be prompted to increase their support. Of special interest is the departure date. Has it been set? When does he leave? How much support is still needed?

This leads to another question: Will the mission send a candidate out if some support is still lacking? The answer depends on a number of factors. Most boards refuse to allow a missionary to leave for the field until his full support is underwritten. Others will "take a chance" and send him out if only 10 or 15 percent is lacking, hoping that the remainder will come in after his departure. In rare cases, when the personnel needs in an institution are so critical that the entire operation is in jeopardy, the mission will send a person to the field with little or no support. Nurses, and especially doctors, are often desperately needed and are sent out before raising their support in order to keep an institution from closing. In that event the mission board will have to draw on special funds to meet the emergency.

It should be noted that there are a few missions which do not require their candidates to raise their own support. In the IFMA, the Overseas Missionary Fellowship is one such mission. No appeals are made for money and no candidate is expected to raise money for any purpose. All funds go into a general pool and all needs are met from that pool. Among the EFMA missions there is the Christian and Missionary Alliance. Each church sends its missions funds to the Foreign Missions Department at headquarters. In this way sufficient funds are available to meet all needs.

Raising funds may be hard on the flesh but it is good for the spirit. When the young candidate first starts out he is filled with fear and trepidation. How will he ever be able to raise that huge amount of money? It seems like an impossible task. In his dilemma he is cast on the Lord in a new way, and early in his experience, before he ever gets to the field, he learns not to depend on his own understanding or trust in his own ability, but to look to the Lord for the supply of every need.

When the meetings are over he settles down to wait and watch. As the funds come in, sometimes from the most unexpected sources, he rejoices in the goodness of God. Each additional gift not only brings him closer to his desired goal, but it further confirms his call to missionary service. By the time the last dollar is in he is ready to sing the doxology. He is the happiest person in the world. God has provided abundantly above all that he ever dared expect. He will never be the same again. Looking back on the ordeal he decides that he would not be without the experience for the world.

7

Gaining Experience

One problem with many Christian workers is that they have had little or no practical experience before launching their career. This is true of the pastor here at home as well as the missionary going overseas. It is especially important that the latter get some form of practical experience before leaving for the field.

BIBLE COLLEGES

The Bible colleges have made an important contribution to the modern missionary movement; it is doubtful if it could have survived without them. To this day the Bible colleges continue to provide most of the candidates for the evangelical missions. Traditionally the Bible colleges have emphasized Bible, missions, Christian education, church music, and practical work, as it is called. Every student is required to accept some form of Christian service during his time in Bible college. During the four years he may stay with one kind of work, or he may change from one to another. In some instances he engages in six or seven kinds of Christian service during his college career. This has been one of the outstanding features of the Bible school movement and one which has helped to produce so many Christian workers. Moody Bible Institute, located in the heart of Chicago, is in a position to offer its students a smorgasbord of Christian service opportunities. Is there any connection between this and the fact that M.B.I. has produced more missionaries than any other institution in the world? Today, one out of every 18 North American missionaries in the world is an alumnus of that one school.

Not all missionary candidates, however, are products of the Bible college movement. An increasing number are now coming from the secular universities. Many of them come from non-Christian homes. Their first contact with vital Christianity is through Campus Crusade for Christ, Inter-Varsity Christian Fellowship, or the Navigators on the university campuses. From there they go on to seminary.

SEMINARIES

Until recently, all seminaries expected their students to engage in Christian service while in school, but in most cases the arrangements were left to the student. He made the contacts and found the opportunities. He was largely on his own and the program was without structure or supervision. No credit was given for such programs. It was good as far as it went, but it did not go far enough.

Now the seminaries, with a little prodding from the American Theological Association, have taken a second look at their programs and have decided to upgrade, strengthen, and enrich them. Field education, the new term for Christian service, is still required of all students. In addition, the student must enroll in a one-year internship with a local church under the personal supervision of an experienced pastor who has agreed to be part of the seminary program. In this way there is a direct link between the church and the seminary. The pastor is expected to meet weekly with his intern, give guidance, offer counsel, and make suggestions, in this way contributing to his practical training. The program entails anywhere from ten to twenty hours a week and credit is given. This is a big improvement over the former arrangement.

Seminary students who are planning on a missionary career need special training to prepare them for ministry in a cross-cultural situation overseas. This is not easy to provide except in large metropolitan areas such as New York, Philadelphia, Chicago, Los Angeles, Dallas, etc.

In the School of World Mission and Evangelism at Trinity Evangelical Divinity School we offer our missions students a choice of three internship programs, each of which earns six hours of credit. In the first, the student does his internship in a large church with a strong home and foreign missions program. He works under the supervision of the pastor, as do all other interns, but he also works closely with the missionary committee, learning as much as he can about the inner workings of the missions program of a local church. The second option is for the student to do his internship in a non-American church in Chicago—Chinese, Japanese, Korean, Spanish, etc.—of which there are hundreds. His third choice is a summer abroad. Arrangements are made by the School of World Mission and Evangelism in cooperation with the mission of the student's choice. He is required to take some basic missions courses in preparation. While overseas he is under the supervision of a veteran missionary who fills out an evaluation questionnaire at the end of the summer. On his return the student is required to write two reports: one a summary of his summer activities; the other an evaluation of the strengths and weaknesses of church and mission work in the host country. In addition, he has a debriefing session with his professor and the other students in the program.

OVERSEAS EXPERIENCE

There is no doubt that the third option is the best. There is no substitute for personal, practical experience on the mission field. It is one thing to read about missionary work; it is quite another to engage in it, even for a short time.

Not all summer missionary programs carry credit. But with or without credit, the program is abundantly worthwhile. It does several things for the person involved. It affords an opportunity to discover what makes the missionary tick. It gives a first-hand exposure to life and work in a completely different culture. It helps him to understand how Christians, who are often a tiny minority, manage to live and witness in a predominantly non-Christian society. It enables him to clarify his own guidance and ascertain the Lord's will for his life. These are no mean achievements. It is significant that 25 percent of all short-termers eventually sign up as career missionaries. In some missions the percentage runs well over 50 percent.

This kind of in-service training is a developing trend. In the sixties, some missions fought the short-term idea, considering it to be a waste of time, effort, and money, but when the results became known they changed their minds. Today there is hardly a mission that does not encourage potential missionaries to spend a summer abroad.

Inter-Varsity Christian Fellowship used to hold its summer camp in Michigan. Realizing the value of overseas experience, however, they have in recent years transferred the camp to Central America. The mornings are spent in reading, lectures, seminars, and workshops. During the afternoons the campers go out in small groups and engage in evangelistic work. The program is only three or four weeks in length, but the experience gained has lasting value.

Operation Mobilization has probably done more than any other organization to encourage young people to spend a summer in Christian service overseas. Teen Mission, Inc., Youth for Christ International, and other organizations are all making a good contribution in this direction.

STATESIDE EXPERIENCE

Missionary candidates who have had no chance to gain experience should consider the opportunities available at Missionary Internship in Farmington,

Michigan. Four programs are available each year: an eight-month internship program runs from September through May, six concentrated three-week pre-field orientation sessions designed for short-termers and those unable to attend the longer program, two special three-week programs for missionaries on furlough, and a two-week program in language acquisition techniques (PILAT) open to any missionary candidate.

Those who take the eight-month internship program are placed in local churches. They work alongside the pastor in the church for three weeks each month and return to the M.I. campus for one week for training in various aspects of cross-cultural ministry. In this way they get the best of both worlds—practical experience in church work and the opportunity to develop skills and attitudes which will help them to be effective in overseas ministry. Thousands of candidates have been through M.I. and have greatly benefited thereby.

In former years an effort was made to get new missionaries to the field as soon as possible on the assumption that the younger they were, the better and quicker they would learn the language. This is no longer done. The emphasis today is not on youth and language proficiency but on maturity and experience.

Missionaries looking forward to an evangelistic or a church-planting ministry should get some experience in these areas before venturing overseas. Church planting on the mission field often involves starting from scratch and beginning a church on one's own. This is not easy to do even in our own culture where Christianity is the dominant religion. It is much more difficult in a foreign culture where Christians may represent only two or three percent of the population. It is highly desirable, therefore, that all church-planting missionaries get into full-time church work in the U.S. before trying to do the same work overseas. There is much more to church planting than appears on the surface. For this reason many mission boards are now requiring their candidates to take a church for two years before embarking on a missionary career. The experience gained in this way will be invaluable on the mission field.

If the young missionary plans to teach in a Bible school or seminary he should try his hand at teaching here at home. One of my students spent two years at Toccoa Bible College before going to Venezuela to teach in a seminary. During this period he gained considerable experience and acquired some much needed confidence. He was also able to get his lectures into shape. When he began teaching in Venezuela he felt at home from the first day.

Beginning a teaching career in the U.S. has its problems. For the first year or two the young instructor barely manages to keep one jump ahead of his students. It is much more difficult to start in a strange culture, using a foreign language and adapting the material to the needs of the situation in the Third World.

OTHER PERSONNEL

Teachers and preachers are not the only ones who can benefit by practical experience. The same applies to those going into other forms of work: medicine, radio, literature, agriculture, and public health. They too should get some practical experience in this country before undertaking work overseas.

It is especially helpful if the training can be taken in the kind of environment one is likely to encounter on the field. Most of the churches in the Third World are numerically small, financially poor, and located in the rural areas. They do not have much in common with churches in the U.S. Two years in an affluent church in American suburbia is not nearly as valuable as the same time spent in a small, rural church. But in the inner city the budding missionary will find many of the cross-cultural, social, and economic problems peculiar to missionary work overseas. The ghettoes of our inner cities afford an ideal environment for potential missionaries, regardless of the kind of work they hope to do.

Medical personnel will find Cook County Hospital in Chicago an ideal place to do their internship. It is one of the largest hospitals in the country. It is located in the inner city and caters to poor patients, most of whom are on Medicaid. One could hardly ask for a better introduction to a medical career on the mission field.

THIRD WORLD REACTION

It is impossible to overemphasize the importance of practical training in preparation for missionary service. In these days when the business and professional worlds are demanding in-service training of their employees, it is an act of folly for the missionary to embark on his career without a year or two of training in the area of his interest and expertise.

One aspect often overlooked is the reaction of the national churches on the receiving end. Their leaders are very gracious and patient in their treatment of the newly-arrived young missionaries. They expect them to require time to adjust to the country, the climate, the culture, and the new way of doing things. That they are prepared to grant. They are understandably taken aback, however, if they discover that the new missionary has had no practical experience other than what he picked up in college or seminary. Such an imposition is an affront to the selfhood of the churches and leaders in the Third World.

PART TWO

MISSIONARY LIFE

8

Coping with Culture Shock

It is absolutely imperative that the missionary know how to cope with culture shock; otherwise he will swell the ranks of Americans who have gone abroad and made a nuisance of themselves, thus lending credence to the phrase "the ugly American."

> Costly mistakes are being made by diplomats, technicians, military specialists, businessmen, and missionaries because the culturally defined behavior of the people to be assisted is not sufficiently understood and taken into account. In spite of the good will, honest intentions, and, not seldom, dedication, the United States seems to be failing in many of its dealings with other nations... because the overseas Americans only too frequently do not understand the "what" and the "why" of the culture in which they work.[1]

GENERAL OBSERVATIONS

It always helps if a problem can be placed in its proper perspective. Certain observations may be helpful in this regard.

1. Culture shock is real. Ship captains are adamant in their belief that seasickness is a figment of the imagination. Consequently they have no sympathy with passengers who don't show up for dinner the first evening at

1. Louis J. Luzbetak, *The Church and Cultures* (Techny, IL: Divine Word Publications, 1970), p. 14.

sea. Well, both seasickness and culture shock *are* real and no purpose is served by trying to deny or belittle the fact.

Persons suffering from culture shock deserve the understanding and sympathy of those around them. The nationals can't be expected to sympathize because they don't understand it. Missionaries are in the best position to help for they have been through the mill themselves. Unfortunately, some senior missionaries, forgetting how they felt when they first arrived, are not too helpful. They expect too much too soon. They make a difficult situation worse by their lack of sympathy and understanding. Newcomers should not be pampered, but they should be protected until they can develop an immunity to the disease. It is very important that new missionaries be stationed with seasoned, older workers who are aware of the problem and who have a genuine concern to see them succeed. Not all senior missionaries have this gift.

If anyone doubts that culture shock is real he need only read the following quotation:

> Consider the psychological adjustment of a family moved suddenly from Chicago to Calcutta. To the visitor from another land, Chicago has its fantastic aspects, but to the average American woman, in particular, Calcutta is a nightmare of almost sickening intensity. Incredible hordes of people, wrapped, clothed, swathed, scantily covered with flowing robes, white dhotis, billowing pajamas, half-torn shirts, ragged scraps of cloth . . . the heads in turbans, the hoods . . . the saris of green and red and star-studded blue swirling around the frail bare-footed women . . . a red dot on their temples, a red line painted through the part in jet black hair . . . crowds of people on modern streets, more crowds of people teeming in dirty tenement blocks . . . the wooden hovels, the cheap tin and textile shops jammed in motley rows . . . the taxis and the trolleys, packed with dense humanity, men clinging to doors and window frames . . . people huddled in doorways, stretched out like rags on the sidewalks sleeping — or dead? . . . bundles of brown bodies in filthy bedclothes on a shred of mattress here and there, by the dozens, by the hundreds, throughout the city millions without a home. . . . The cattle wandering through the city's streets, cows with dried-up udders, placid beasts resting their huge hulks on sidewalks everywhere, stringy cows trailing their bony haunches betweeen the Fiat and Plymouth and Hillman taxis. . . . But most of all the people, a few rich men in great white garments or smart Western suits, contrasting with the hordes of poor, the upstretched palms of withered beggars. Its all a very far cry from the Loop.[2]

2. Culture shock is not a one-way street. Culture shock is a universal phenomenon. It occurs whenever a person passes from one culture to

2. Harlan Cleveland, et al. *The Overseas Americans* (New York: McGraw-Hill Book Company, 1960), p. 47.

another. It is by no means a one-way street. It happens to Americans going to India. It happens to Africans coming to the U.S. Whenever a person finds himself in an unfamiliar situation surrounded by strange sights and sounds, he is bound to feel a sense of alienation. Nobody thinks his own language is strange, but send him abroad to another language area and he will immediately feel threatened by his inability to communicate.

Those who have not lived or traveled abroad cannot possibly know what culture shock is like; consequently they are in no position to help those afflicted with it. It is a serious problem for the 300,000 foreign students now studying in the U.S. They are bright, affable, industrious, and enthusiastic. They have a fairly good grasp of English, and we take it for granted that they have no problems with our culture. Many of them, however, by their own confession, are desperately lonely and long for understanding and friendship.

3. Culture shock varies in intensity. The farther one is removed from familiar surroundings, the greater will be the sense of shock. Canadians are trying hard to develop a culture of their own. That is right and proper and we wish them well. But frankly, their culture is so much like ours that one can cross from Detroit to Windsor and, except for the red tape with the Customs and Immigration people, hardly be aware that he is in another country.

A visit to England takes one a little farther afield. There, things are slightly different. They have double-decker buses and traffic moves on the left-hand side of the street. Gasoline is called petrol. The hood of a car is the bonnet. Money is divided into pounds, shillings, and pence. Cricket and soccer take the place of football and baseball. But the language is the same, though the accent may be different. The American arriving in England notices these differences, but he would hardly describe the experience as culture shock. It is not until he gets to the Continent that he begins to feel that he is in a different culture, the principal reason being the language.

To experience real culture shock one must go east of Suez. There, *everything* is different. If one wants the ultimate in culture shock he should visit the Baleim Valley of Irian Jaya where the inhabitants are just emerging from the Stone Age.

4. Going up in the social scale is easier than going down. Following the stock market crash in 1929 many millionaires committed suicide when they lost all their money. Being accustomed to affluence they could not live with poverty. Who has ever heard of a poor man winning a million dollars in the Irish sweepstakes and then committing suicide because he couldn't cope with riches? In the same way, a family finds it easier to move from a small house to a larger one than from a large house to a smaller one.

The principle operates in the international arena as well. It is more difficult for an affluent American to adjust to the poverty of India than for an Indian to adjust to the affluence of the U.S. If proof is required one need only consult the immigration statistics to discover how many Indians come to this country to study and remain here for life. It is easier for an Oriental to switch from the ricksha to a Greyhound bus than for a Westerner accustomed to jet travel to use the ricksha.

This is one reason why culture shock is such a problem for missionaries. Over 90 percent of them are Westerners who have left the affluence of the West to live and work in some of the poorest countries of the world. This necessarily causes them a higher degree of culture shock. Eastern missionaries coming to the West—and some have done this—experience culture shock but not to the same extent.

I realize that in referring to one culture as being "higher" or "lower" than another I am leaving myself open to the accusation of cultural chauvinism. I also know that anthropologists prefer not to use such terms as "primitive" or "backward" when speaking of certain tribal groups in the Third World, and I appreciate their sensitivity on this point. The missionaries of the 19th century frequently spoke of the indigenous cultures, even those in India, China, and Japan, in pejorative terms. This was a practice that we do not want to perpetuate in the 20th century.

On the other hand, we may be in danger of going to the other extreme and insisting that all cultures are equally advanced and none is to be referred to as "primitive." I think this also is a mistake. We do not serve the cause of truth by closing our eyes to reality. Even in our own culture there are differences. The farming methods of the Amish in Pennsylvania are certainly primitive compared with the $50,000 combines used in the wheatfields of Kansas. The space capsule that carried Neil Armstrong to the moon was a more sophisticated vehicle than the plane used by the Wright brothers at Kitty Hawk.

For the same reason we would have to confess that the civilization of China during the Ming Dynasty (A.D. 618–906) was superior to European civilization at that time. For hundreds of years China shed the light and luster of its civilization all over eastern Asia, and every year tribute-bearing missions visited China to show respect for its superior culture.

5. Culture shock is usually harder on the wife than on the husband. He has all the diversions afforded by "the work." He goes more places, meets more people, and does more things. The wife, on the other hand, is responsible for the daily chores connected with housekeeping—buying groceries, making meals, washing clothes, handling servants. She more than her husband has to endure the many inconveniences of daily life in a different culture. She is the one who most misses the amenities of Western mechanical civilization.

The wives of businessmen overseas suffer the same fate in spite of a handsome "hardship bonus" designed to ameliorate the inconveniences. In spite of this, many of them cannot cope with culture shock and turn to alcohol.

6. **Culture shock occurs in stages.** The first stage occurs immediately upon arrival in the host country. In the tropics the first thing that strikes one is the hot, enervating climate. Then there is the grinding poverty. Beggars and street urchins follow him with hands outstretched for "baksheesh." The more enterprising grab his luggage and "help" him into a waiting taxi, expecting to receive a tip for the service. His first sally into the marketplace or the bazaar will bring home to him the disturbing fact that *he* is now the foreigner. He can't understand a word that is said, nor can he read the signs on the streets and in the shops. For the first time in his life he cannot communicate. That alone is a traumatic experience.

A Peace Corps volunteer wrote of his early experience in the Philippines:

> *This is the hardest thing I have ever done. Absolutely nothing is familiar and I often feel totally alone . . . . You cannot imagine the gulf between East and West, and it makes me laugh now to think that I expected to bridge it with a smile and a handshake.*[3]

But he soon gets over the initial shock. The very novelty of the situation affords a certain degree of excitement that keeps him going. Besides, he has a lot to write home about. Six months later, when the glamor has worn off and the realities of the situation finally dawn on him, he goes through a second period of culture shock. The language has proved to be more difficult than he expected. He has had several stomach upsets and a nasty bout with dysentery. His three-year-old daughter has prickly heat from top to toe and can't sleep at night. To cap it all, his wife is pregnant. At that point he may well say to himself: "I didn't expect it to be like this!"

This second phase of culture shock is all too common. It has been described by another Peace Corps worker:

> *I live in a picturesque bamboo mat house I built myself. I buy water from a picturesque boy with a burro loaded down with water cans. I read and write under a kerosene lantern, sleep on a cot, and cook on a camp stove. There comes a day when all this suddenly becomes no longer picturesque, no longer quaint, but furiously frustrating; and you want like crazy to get out of there, to go home.*[4]

Just when he is beginning to feel at home he will receive notice that furlough has been granted. He is then in for a third dose of culture shock. After finally adjusting to and beginning to appreciate the culture of his adopted country, the missionary must face the ordeal of readjusting to the affluence of the American way of life. Each succeeding furlough is more difficult than the last, for two reasons: he has been away longer and is now

3. Quoted by Roy Hoopes, *The Complete Peace Corps Guide* (New York: Dell Publications, 1966), p. 179.
4. Ibid., p. 187.

more at home in the alien culture than in his own; and lifestyles in America are changing more rapidly and more drastically with each passing decade.

If he was shocked by the poverty when he first went to the field, he is now shocked by the affluence of the U.S. He can hardly believe his eyes when he sees dogs and cats eating "pure meat products" enriched with vitamins and minerals. He is entertained in fabulous homes with wall-to-wall carpets, costly draperies, colored TV, modern electric kitchens, and elegantly appointed bathrooms. But worse than the wealth is the waste that goes with it. Coming from a world of unrelieved hunger he finds it unimaginable that anyone should leave food on his plate. He is glad to be home again, but he feels out of place. He has lived with poverty, hunger, and disease and can never quite forget it. Let no one underestimate the trauma of reentry.

This is one reason why veteran missionaries often prefer to remain in the country where they have served when they reach retirement. By that time they have become so immersed in the life and culture of their adopted country that only an ultimatum from headquarters will bring them home. Given their own way they would prefer to live out their days and be buried in the land of their adoption. The prospect of returning to the U.S. has little appeal for them.

7. Missionaries react differently to culture shock. No two missionaries are exactly alike; consequently they react differently to their environment. For one it is the climate; he loses every ounce of energy when the thermometer goes above one hundred. Another loves the heat. For one it is the flies by day and the mosquitoes by night; he can't get to sleep if one mosquito is buzzing around his head. Another falls asleep the moment his head hits the pillow so he is oblivious to the mosquitoes. For one it is bedbugs; he doesn't mind mosquitoes but he hates bedbugs. One missionary despises the constant noise of native "music" far into the night. Another finds the music soothing and thus conducive to sleep. For some it is the lack of variety in the diet; they long for a cold, crisp salad, a glass of orange juice, a dish of ice cream, or a piece of lemon meringue pie. Some missionaries are scared to death of snakes, others of rats, to say nothing of elephants and crocodiles! Some miss the four seasons of the northern hemisphere. It has been said: "One man's peach is another man's poison." This is certainly true on the mission field. No two missionaries react to their total environment in exactly the same way.

CONTRIBUTING FACTORS

Culture shock doesn't take place in a vacuum. It is the result of a combination of physical, social, economic, and other factors that form the warp and woof of life in the Third World. We can cover only the major factors.

1. **Climate.** The American missionary is particularly vulnerable at this point. Central heating in the winter and air conditioning in the summer have accustomed him to a 70-degree temperature twelve months in the year. Climate is one of the most frequent causes of culture shock.

Much depends on where one is located. The highlands of Kenya are very different from the rain forests of Zaire, though both are close to the equator. The difference is due to altitude. Many mission lands lie on or close to the equator, and that means *heat*. Along with heat is humidity, and the combination can be overpowering. In Taiwan it is necessary to change clothes two or three times a day just to keep dry. In many countries there are two seasons, wet and dry. During the dry season they go without rain for three or four months, resulting in dust storms that cover everything with a thick layer of dust. In the rainy season it rains for weeks on end, during which time it is just about impossible to dry clothes. Mildew appears almost overnight on books, leather goods, and food. In the meantime children break out in prickly heat. Adults go to bed with a fan in one hand and a towel in the other. Under such conditions both work and sleep become a problem. Without electricity it is impossible to get relief until the weather breaks. By that time the missionary and his family are physically, if not mentally, exhausted. Little wonder that missionaries need a long vacation during the hot season.

2. **Poverty.** Beverly Nichols, in his book, *Verdict on India*, says that the Indians are so poor that they can live on the smell of an oil rag. Obviously this is an exaggeration, but it conveys the idea of extreme poverty he intended. Here in the U.S. we have pockets of poverty with many thousands of people on relief, but at least they have a roof over their heads and utilities in their homes, and some even own cars. But in many parts of the world the poverty is so extreme as to defy description. The slum areas surrounding the larger cities are places of incredible hardship, with hundreds of thousands of poverty-stricken families living at subsistence level. Beggars abound. Thievery and pilferage, necessary for survival, are a way of life. Such poverty the missionary has never seen, not even on television. The fact that he cannot possibly solve the problem by himself exacerbates the situation and adds to his sense of frustration. It leaves him with a sick feeling in the pit of his stomach.

3. **Hunger.** Poverty is never alone; it is always accompanied by other calamities, one of which is hunger. At the World Food Conference held in Rome in 1974, they referred to some countries, such as Bangladesh, as "basket cases." No matter how much help they are given, it will not be enough to stave off starvation in the long run. The suggestion was made that maybe we should abandon these countries to their certain doom and concentrate on the more hopeful cases. Such a suggestion is unthinkable, yet the fact that it was made is some indication of the extent of the problem in some of the poorer, more populous countries.

To those of us who live in the U.S. these are cold, lifeless statistics, and "statistics don't bleed." But the missionary has to face this kind of situation, not through the medium of the press or television, which is bad enough, but in person. To us, "famine" is a word in the dictionary. We have never seen it for ourselves, and we have probably never gone to bed hungry except when we were sick or on a diet. How different it is with the missionary. In times of famine he has to give all his time and attention to feeding the hungry in a desperate attempt to save lives, all the while knowing that the lives he saves will be doomed to live with hunger even when the famine is over. No man can live in that kind of environment and not be affected by it.

4. Disease. The socialist governments in the Third World are devoting huge sums of money to the advancement of medical science and health care, but they still have much to do. Some diseases, such as smallpox, have been completely wiped out with the help of the World Health Organization. Malaria has been eliminated in Sri Lanka and other countries, but medical and dental care is still inadequate and confined largely to the bigger cities. In the towns and rural areas, disease continues unchecked. Only in China has the government solved the problem of health care delivery in the rural areas.

It is not uncommon to see children with eyes full of pus, heads covered with sores, distended bellies, and disfigured bodies. As for malnutrition with its permanent damage to brain and body, it is chronic. The usual childhood diseases take their annual toll. Infant mortality is high; half of the children die before reaching school age, if indeed they go to school at all. Personal hygiene and public sanitation are unknown, with the result that millions of people die needlessly every year. To make matters worse, the brain drain from East to West has robbed these countries of the medical expertise they so badly need.[5]

It is difficult for the missionary to see all the sickness, disease, and malnutrition around him and not be able to do anything to alleviate the situation.

5. Language. The factors mentioned above are all physical, but culture shock has other causes as well. One of them is language. This factor can be overcome with time and effort, but in the beginning it is a powerful cause of culture shock.

One does not realize the contribution communication makes to one's sense of well being until he finds himself in a foreign country completely unable to communicate. There is such a thing as "silent language," and music, so we are told, is a "universal language." Neither of these, however, is a substitute for verbal communication. One of the most traumatic experiences occurs when the missionary on his arrival is reduced to sign language.

5. According to the American Medical Association there are 64,000 foreign doctors in the U.S. at the present time.

He is overcome by a feeling of helplessness. He can't locate the restroom in the airport. He can't make a phone call. He can't even ask the way into town. Fortunately, in the international airports he will probably find somebody who understands English, and a senior missionary will almost certainly be on hand to help him through Customs and Immigration. But that does not solve his problem. He still can't say a word in his own behalf.

He will lose no time in beginning to learn the language, but it will be several years before he can communicate freely, fluently, and accurately in the vernacular. Until then he will suffer his full share of frustration.

6. Strange customs. Culture shock is precipitated by the anxiety that results from losing all the familiar signs and symbols of social intercourse. These signs include the thousand-and-one ways in which we orient ourselves to the situations encountered in the daily routine of life: when to shake hands and what to say when we meet people, when and how to give tips, how to handle servants, how to make purchases, when to accept and when to refuse invitations, how to entertain friends, when to take statements seriously and when not to. Cues to these situations may be words, gestures, facial expressions, or customs acquired by all of us in the course of growing up and which are a part of our culture. We all depend on hundreds of such cues, most of which have long since become part of our subconscious, and we use or interpret them without any conscious effort.

When the missionary enters a strange culture all or most of these familiar cues are gone. Consequently he feels like a fish out of water. This inevitably gives rise to a feeling of uncertainty and anxiety. If people, friends or strangers, laugh when he does or says the wrong thing, his problem is compounded. Not everyone can laugh at himself, especially when everyone else is laughing at him. This kind of anxiety is a very real part of culture shock.

7. Minor inconveniences. In addition to these major factors there are a host of lesser problems which may be grouped together as "minor inconveniences."

Nothing seems to work as well in a foreign culture as in the U.S. The house or apartment may have indoor plumbing, but the water may be turned off from 6 p.m. to 6 a.m. every night. That means no bath after a hot, sticky day. It also means that the toilet can be flushed only once after 6 p.m. When morning comes the missionary rushes to take his bath, only to discover that everyone else in the block is doing the same and the water pressure is reduced to a trickle.

The same is true of electricity. It is now quite common in the larger cities, but the power may be on only during certain hours in the evening. At 10 p.m. all the lights go out. Moreover, each room may have only one bulb in the middle of the ceiling and no outlets for floor or table lamps. Reading then becomes a problem.

In the larger cities the missionary will be happy that there is a telephone in the house. This he regards as a great convenience until he discovers that it takes half an hour to make a call. The operator is asleep at the switchboard, or she is out to lunch, or the lines are down, or the equipment is out of order. A long distance call may take several hours to complete.

These are illustrations of the many minor inconveniences which occur in the course of the average day. Each one is too insignificant to fuss over, but taken together they become a formidable challenge to the missionary's peace of mind. Patience is not usually his outstanding virtue, but he will need a great deal of it.

HOW TO OVERCOME CULTURE SHOCK

Culture shock is a real and troublesome problem, but it can be conquered. It will help immensely if the missionary does not give way to self-pity or despair. There are certain things he can do to ameliorate the situation.

1. Remember Jesus and the Incarnation. Jesus was the first and greatest missionary (Heb 3:1) and His ministry was the prototype for ours. "As my Father hath sent me, even so send I you" is what He said to His disciples after the Resurrection (John 20:21, KJV). In the days of His flesh He was known as a Man of sorrows, and He actually learned obedience by the things which He suffered (Heb 5:8). In this way He became the author and finisher of our faith (Heb 12:1).

If the missionary thinks his experience with culture shock is bad, he should remember Jesus and His experience. Paul had this in mind when he wrote: "Ye know the grace of our Lord Jesus Christ, that, though he was rich, yet for your sakes he became poor, that ye through his poverty might be rich" (2 Cor 8:9, KJV). How infinitely rich He was in heaven! How desperately poor He became on earth! The contrast between the two is quite beyond our powers of imagination. His culture shock when He left the "ivory palaces" and came into this "world of woe" is something we shall never understand.

Moreover, He not only became a man, but He humbled Himself and became a servant (Phil 2:7). He was the only person who had the right to choose the family into which He would be born, and He deliberately bypassed the homes of the rich, the mighty, and the noble in choosing the humble home of Joseph and Mary. The apostle Peter reminds us that He left us an example that we should follow in His steps (1 Pet 2:21). Jesus Himself taught us that the disciple is not above his master, nor the servant above his lord (Matt 10:24).

2. Recognize that culture shock is a normal reaction. Culture shock is not some strange behavioral trait exhibited by only a small number of weak people. It is a universal phenomenon and should be accepted as such. The missionary is a human being with human feelings and he will have a perfectly human reaction to his environment. He should not, therefore, be unduly discouraged. Above all, he should not blame his feelings on a lack of dedication. His is a normal reaction to a cultural change; it has nothing to do with spirituality.

It is at this point that the devil often attacks the new missionary and sows the seeds of doubt in his mind. Before long, he builds up a guilt complex which can rob him of his joy in the Lord's service.

3. Recall that others have survived. In the depth of depression it is easy for the missionary to imagine the worst. But the depression will pass if he hangs in there for another month or two. The language *will* come. The work *will* prosper. The rainy season *will* end. The sun *will* shine again. Others have been through the same experience and they survived; there is no reason for him to think that he will not. It may be hard to believe, but not only will he survive, he will go on to succeed.

4. Learn the language as quickly as possible. Without a doubt one of the hardest things to endure in a foreign country is the inability to communicate. It is imperative, therefore, that this impediment be removed as soon as possible. Life will take on an altogether different complexion when one is able to converse with friends and neighbors; and when the new missionary has acquired enough fluency to permit him to start teaching and preaching he will be well on his way to overcoming culture shock.

5. Participate in the social life of the people. Until one has learned the language there is always the temptation to confine one's social life to the American community. Business and professional people seldom get beyond the circle of their own compatriots. It is known as the "cocktail circuit." Such people never overcome their culture shock. Even after being in the country for years they still feel like strangers. The missionary doesn't have the cocktail circuit to worry about, but he may, through timidity, shyness, or an inability to make friends easily, confine his social contacts to other missionaries in the city or community. This is a serious mistake.

The missionaries most likely to succeed are those who are able to mix and mingle with people and make friends easily. Every effort should be made to make friends among the nationals, to play as well as to work with them, to meet them in their homes as well as in the church, to sit and chat and enjoy social fellowship. Such social intercourse not only helps greatly with the learning of the language, it also helps take one's mind off the petty annoyances which are a regular part of culture shock.

6. Look for the good things in the culture. Norman Vincent Peale wasn't the first to discover the power of positive thinking. Paul preached it long ago when he wrote to the Christians at Philippi: "Whatsoever things are true, whatsoever things are honest, whatsoever things are just, whatsoever things are pure, whatsoever things are lovely, whatsoever things are of good report; if there be any virtue, and if there be any praise, think on these things" (Phil 4:8, KJV).

There are pleasant and unpleasant aspects to every culture. There is always a tendency to become preoccupied with the unpleasant aspects. They have a way of standing out, of attracting attention, and of grating on one's nerves. By an act of the will the new missionary can concentrate on the pleasant things. He can appreciate them and thank God for them. If he does this he will soon discover that the pleasant aspects outnumber and overshadow the unpleasant ones.

7. **Forget about life back in the U.S.** It is natural, almost inevitable, for the newcomer to compare the manners and mores of the host country with those of "the good old U.S.A." This should be avoided at all costs, especially by the career missionary who expects to spend the rest of his life in the country of his adoption. The sooner he forgets about the "wonders" and "beauties" of the American way of life, the more quickly he will adjust to the culture of the host country and the more effective a missionary he will become.

Holiday Inns, McDonald's hamburgers, Baskin-Robbins' 31 flavors of ice cream, Poppin' Fresh pies, the World Series, the Super Bowl, the Tournament of Roses—all are things of the past and should be forgotten. When furlough time comes around he will be able to enjoy them again.

8. **Trust God for grace.** Paul said: "I have learned in whatsoever state I am therewith to be content. I know both how to be abased and I know how to abound" (Phil 4:11–12, KJV). Lest anyone think that he achieved this in his own strength he was careful to say: "By the grace of God I am what I am" (1 Cor 15:10, KJV). And when God refused to remove the thorn in his flesh His word to Paul was: "My grace is sufficient for thee; for my strength is made perfect in weakness" (2 Cor 12:9, KJV).

The missionary can hope for nothing more and he can get along with nothing less. If he is a missionary by the will of God and is serving God in the place of His appointment, God is able to make all grace abound toward him, that he, always having all sufficiency in all things, may abound unto every good work (2 Cor 9:8).

> *Finding, following, keeping, struggling,*
> *Is He sure to bless?*
> *Saints, apostles, prophets, martyrs*
> *Answer, "Yes!"*

9

Adjusting to Missionary Life

The two most valuable assets a missionary can possess are versatility and adaptability. Most Americans are not particularly good at adapting. We expect others to speak English; we make little or no attempt to speak their languages. American tourists have been known to get angry when they couldn't buy hot dogs in Spain or Coca-Cola in Timbuktu. We expect others to adjust to our ways; we do not readily adjust to theirs. This kind of chauvinism is bad enough in the tourist; it is unpardonable in the missionary.

It is only reasonable that the missionary should be the one to adjust. He is a guest and is not, therefore, expected to rearrange the furniture. He will be in the country for a comparatively short time and will be outnumbered by the nationals, who have no intention of changing their ways. If changes are to be made, the missionary must make them.

ADJUSTING TO THE PHYSICAL ENVIRONMENT

At the heart of the Christian gospel is the Incarnation. "The Word became flesh and dwelt among us" (Jn 1:14, KJV). The missionary must lead an incarnational life. He must recognize that the people among whom he labors are not merely souls to be saved but people—whole people—with physical, mental, and material needs. To minister to these people effectively he must pitch his tent among them, travel their roads, visit their homes, and sleep in their beds. In short, he must do his best to adjust to their physical environment.

1. Housing. Nowhere in the world is housing more elaborate, commodious, or luxurious, than in the United States. Visitors to the U.S., including Europeans, are amazed at the large, beautifully appointed suburban homes with all kinds of labor-saving appliances, lush green lawns front and back, and two or three cars in the driveway.

In contrast, houses in many other parts of the world tend to be small, dingy, poorly constructed, dimly lighted, and plainly furnished. This is one area where the American missionary has to make a major adjustment. He must be content with a much smaller house with modest furnishings and few, if any, of the electrical gadgets so common at home.

Some missionaries have taken chrome kitchen sets and elaborate bedroom and living-room furniture with them to the field. Perhaps a case can be made for some of the smaller time-saving appliances, but one wonders if American missionaries are, by their well-appointed homes, erecting an unnecessary barrier between them and the nationals. The standard of living maintained by American missionaries is usually higher than that of most other missionaries.

The missionary naturally wants to make his home as comfortable as possible. It is the one place where he can relax, kick off his shoes, and be himself. This is understandable and not altogether wrong. One room in the house, however, preferably the room in which guests are received, should be sufficiently indigenous in decor to make nationals feel welcome. The missionary is not likely to make converts unless he first makes friends. He will do this more easily if he keeps open house.

2. Food. Americans consume 3200 calories a day and have an unbelievable variety of foods from which to choose. America is the only country in the world where calories are removed from human food and added to dog food! The missionary coming from such a background will have problems when it comes to eating.

It is difficult for the missionary, accustomed as he is to the bewildering variety of foods in the supermarket, to realize that baby food, fresh meats, and fresh fruits and vegetables year round, are either unknown or exceedingly difficult to obtain in many parts of the world. A large proportion of the world's population still eats what it can get in season. Millions seek their bread one day at a time with no assurance that it can be found.

More and more Americans are eating out. It is estimated that one meal out of three is now taken outside the home. This is the result of two factors: more women are working now than ever before, and making a meal at the end of the day is something of a burden. With at least two checks coming into the home each payday, more money is available for such extras as eating out.

Such delectable items as milk shakes, Big Macs, and hot dogs, the delight of American youngsters, are unknown in most parts of the Third World. Coca-Cola, the most ubiquitous soft drink in the world, may be available but only in the larger cities and at a price beyond the missionary's reach.

Among my most vivid memories of China are the few visits we made to Shanghai. A group of us would get together and make a beeline for the Chocolate Shop on Bubbling Well Road, where we shamelessly indulged in the luxury of honest-to-goodness ice cream sundaes, cokes, and confectionery of various kinds. Such visits occurred with distressing infrequency—once every year or two until the war broke out, and then they stopped altogether.

The missionary will find that he must change many of his eating habits. He must learn to get along without Kellogg's corn flakes, Kraft cheese, Betty Crocker cake mixes, Campbell's soups, and a hundred other foods taken for granted in the U.S. There is rice, but not minute rice; wheat, but not wheat thins. In a word, the vast majority of the thousands of items in the American supermarket will not be available. That may require some major adjustments and the burden will fall more heavily on the wife than on the husband.

3. Clothing. Clothing in any society serves many purposes. It may meet the demands of protection, modesty, and comfort. It may also function as a symbol of sex, age, occupation, or status. It may simply serve some decorative purpose. At first the national dress may appear strange, but the missionary will not be long in the country before he discovers that there are good physical and material reasons as well as esthetic considerations for most attire. He may find it both convenient and comfortable to adopt the national dress, especially in climates of extreme heat or cold. The nationals have been there for a long time and they usually know what is best.

While there is no essential connection between clothing and modesty, every society has its own definition of modest attire. It is in the missionary's interest to discover early in his career what is and what is not acceptable attire for all occasions. In some societies green is worn only by prostitutes. In some it is immodest for a woman to expose her elbow. Until recently women in the Far East wore long sleeves and high necklines. To wear anything else was considered suggestive if not seductive. For women missionaries to ignore such customs would be disastrous.

In some parts of Europe the American missionary can be identified by the shoes he wears. It is a small matter, but apparently not too small to attract the attention of the Europeans, whose own standard of living is not exactly low. Japanese men have adopted Western dress, but the cut and color of their clothes are very conservative. Colored shirts and loud ties are definitely not the "in" thing in Japan. Missionaries should bear this in mind when they buy their wardrobe. It is exceedingly difficult to win the Japanese to Christ. Why make it more so by wearing clothes which are offensive to their taste?

4. Lifestyle. The free and easy lifestyle which in recent years has become the hallmark of American culture is by no means acceptable in all parts of the world. Miniskirts, popular in the 1960s, were banned by some governments in Africa. Long hair for men is forbidden in Singapore, where barbers are on hand at the international airport to cut the locks of those wishing to enter the city! The Peace Corps has been expelled from more than 20 countries around the world. In some instances the reason given for this was that they presented a slovenly lifestyle that corrupted the youth of the country. American tourists are notoriously insensitive to the feelings of others; and by their casual, often careless, appearance they offend their hosts. The missionary must avoid such conduct.

The standard of living is about as high in the U.S. as anywhere in the world, the per capita income being about $9500 a year. The average for most Third World countries is from $300 to $400 a year. In India it is $140, but 40% of the people live below the poverty level which is $90. Obviously the American missionary in these countries will have to do something about the enormous disparity between his lifestyle and that of the nationals.

No one is suggesting that the missionary try to live at the level of the nationals. In some countries this would be impossible. It would injure his health and incapacitate him for service. But in many countries he could do with less than he has in the past. Does he need to take with him all his household goods and appliances? The fact that he has enjoyed them in the U.S. is not sufficient reason for taking them abroad. Does he really need a car? Could he get along with a bicycle? What about public transportation which is what everyone else uses?

Today's missionary needs to be reminded of the words of Jesus: "A man's life does not consist in the abundance of his possessions" (Lk 12:15, RSV). Stanley Jones used to say that there are two ways in which a person can be rich. One is in the multiplicity of his possessions; the other is in the simplicity of his wants. It is to be feared that many Christian missionaries belong in the first category, not the second.

ADJUSTING TO THE SOCIAL ENVIRONMENT

Man is a gregarious creature. It is not good for him to dwell alone. He finds happiness in fellowship with others. Interpersonal relations are very important to him.

1. The law of hospitality. In the frontier days Americans practiced hospitality, but as a society becomes more affluent and the individual becomes more self-reliant, hospitality tends to diminish. This is what has happened in American culture, and the hospitality that remains is carried on to a large extent in the restaurant and not the home.

This is not so in other cultures. In the Middle East and the Orient, hospitality is a way of life. Homes are always open to friends, and especially to relatives. Guests are always welcome no matter at what hour of the day or night they arrive. They are free to stay as long as they like. As for relatives, they are regarded as part of the extended family. When tragedy strikes or when needs arise they always look to their relatives for help, and they seldom look in vain. No inconvenience is too great to endure for the sake of relatives. When a married man comes to the U.S. to study, his wife and children return to the ancestral home or move in with a married brother or sister. Sharing is a part of life. The rich share their wealth and the poor share their poverty. It is a beautiful way to live.

It often poses a problem for the missionary, however. In no time at all he finds himself on the receiving end of this hospitality and he doesn't know how to react. He has been taught that it is more blessed to give than to receive, but he has never seen it operate on such a grand scale. The temptation is for him to accept more hospitality than he is prepared to reciprocate. Unless he goes out of his way to *show* hospitality, it will soon become one-way traffic to the detriment of all concerned.

Missionaries in the Orient are usually embarrassed by the hospitality heaped on them by their friends. It is quite impossible to outdo the Orientals in generosity, but that is no reason for not trying! Missionaries, particularly wives, should try to develop the habit of hospitality even though it may be costly in time and money. The New Testament has much to say about hospitality, and it was a qualification for holding office in the early church.

2. Segregation of the sexes. In the West, especially in the U.S., the segregation of the sexes is a thing of the past. Today we have unisex clothing, hairdos, and lifestyles. The women smoke, drink, gamble, and curse along with the men. In the business world secretaries accompany their bosses on business trips. On the university campuses men and women students live in the same dorms, use the same washrooms, and even share the same beds. Such promiscuity is scandalous in most parts of the Third World, where men and women still go their separate ways. Throughout much of Asia, women are still regarded as second-class citizens and treated accordingly. In the Muslim world the women have their own quarters in the family compound. Those who live in Pakistan and Bangladesh still observe *purdah* when they venture out on the streets. Husband and wife are seldom seen together in public. They certainly don't walk down the street arm in arm. Any show of affection in public is frowned on even in Christian circles. In church services the men usually occupy one side of the sanctuary and the women the other.

These customs are being slowly but surely undermined, especially among the young in the larger cities; but in the towns and the rural areas the separation of the sexes is still rigidly maintained, and anyone who fails to comply is immediately suspect.

In all such situations the missionary must be prepared to change his lifestyle in order not to give offense. During our early years in China my wife and I never went to church together. I walked ahead and she followed a discreet three hundred feet behind me! Only after our two sons were old enough to go to church with us did we decide to come and go as a family. The presence of the children made sufficient difference to render such an innovation permissible, if not desirable.

Even in the most progressive countries the missionary must be careful not to show too much attention to members of the opposite sex, especially if a third party is not present. Such conduct is totally unacceptable. That is one of the reasons why certain governments asked Peace Corps volunteers in their countries to leave.

Some missionaries consider it their duty to teach their converts what Christian love is all about, especially as it relates to the Christian family. If they want to show affection in public they do so, hoping thereby to be an example to the believers, but there is grave danger of giving offense to believers and unbelievers alike. It is not necessary for Christian converts to adopt Western ways of expressing love. In cultures where holding hands, kissing, and embracing in public are taboo, the missionary is well advised to refrain from any expression of romantic love. It may cramp his style but it will save him from offending the nationals.

3. Stratification of society. Not only are women and girls regarded as inferior to men and boys, but the society itself is divided into higher and lower strata. The outstanding example is the caste system in India. But even in other parts of the world there is a great gap between the literate and the illiterate, the rich and the poor, the white-collar worker and the blue-collar worker, the teacher and the student, the master and the servant.

In Confucian culture the scholar has always been at the top of the social totem pole. To this day there is a clear line of demarcation between the teacher and the pupil, except in present-day China where the Communists have deliberately destroyed all such distinctions. In the Orient students stand when the teacher enters the room and remain standing until he gives them the sign to be seated. The American missionary with his free and easy outlook on life doesn't always accept the more formal aspects of Oriental culture. He insists on absolute equality between him and his students, to the great discomfort of the students.

In some countries the social classes are so well defined that each has its own mode of address. There is one way to address a servant or an employee, another way to address a friend or a neighbor, and still another to address a parent or a teacher. Such distinctions are a sign of culture, and woe betide the missionary who deliberately ignores them.

In other countries there is no middle class such as we have here in the U.S. There is a small, wealthy ruling class at the top and all others belong to the lower class. It is virtually impossible to minister to both classes at once. A missionary called to minister to the professional class—doctors, lawyers, government and military personnel—will have to live and move in those circles if he wants to be effective. If on the other hand he is called to minister to the lower class he will automatically be cut off from the higher group. He may wish to be all things to all men, as Paul was, but he will find it an impossible task. He will have to confine his efforts to one group or the other. This does not mean that he sanctions class distinctions. It simply means that he recognizes the realities of the social situation and is willing to identify with one group in order to win its members to Christ.

4. Practice of propriety. In many non-Western societies there is an elaborate system of social etiquette. Nowhere is this more clearly seen than in the Orient, where it receives its highest expression. The Chinese word for this is *li,* variously translated as good manners, politeness, respect, and etiquette.

Confucius was the great practitioner of *li.* On one occasion the sage said: "If the mat is not arranged correctly I will not sit down." He went so far as to say that he would not eat fruit out of season! In Confucian culture *li* governs all relations. Without it one is barely civilized. That is one reason why Westerners in China were known as "barbarians." Orientals are extremely polite, and their politeness is often elaborately expressed. It may take ten minutes to arrange the seating at a banquet, but no one will occupy the place of honor, including the guest in whose honor the banquet was held in the first place! Each person wants to outdo the other in his expression of self-depreciation. Paul's words, "Let each esteem other better than themselves," make good sense to the Orientals.

Confucius once said, *"Li to ren puh kwai"*—nobody blames one for being too polite—but to the foreigner this may appear to be too much of a good thing. The average Westerner is in no danger of being thought too polite. He is more likely to err in the other direction. His problem is to appear polite enough in a culture where etiquette is the most essential element of social intercourse, and it is understood, appreciated, and observed by all.

5. Practice of talking price. This can be most exasperating to the Westerner. In the West every commodity bears a price tag, and except for second-hand cars the price advertised is the price paid. Not so in other parts of the world. Prices are not marked and in most cases are not even fixed. The buyer has to ask the price, and the seller begins by naming an inflated figure which may be twice what he really expects to get. The buyer counters with an offer that is much lower than he is prepared to pay. Then the bargaining begins. The seller comes down in price and the buyer goes up until after a while they come together somewhere between the two original figures, and both parties are happy.

This system usually works quite well and everyone takes it for granted. One feels a certain satisfaction in being able to drive a hard bargain. Occasionally one party will take advantage of the other if the circumstances are favorable. In hiring a ricksha, for example, much will depend on the weather, the time of day, the amount of luggage one has, and how far he wants to travel. If it is raining hard late at night and there is only one ricksha at the railroad station, the customer is at the mercy of the ricksha puller.

The rub comes when foreigners are charged two or three times what the nationals pay. The reason for this is twofold. First, by local standards the foreigner is a rich person and can afford to pay more. Second, he probably doesn't know the right price anyway so he won't know he's being cheated. This works a hardship on the missionary who usually ends up paying more than a national would for the same article or service. This should not unduly distress him, however. He *is* rich compared with the local populace and is therefore expected to pay more. If, however, he has lived in the city or town for a while, he will have an easier time. The merchants will recognize him and realize that he is acquainted with the local situation, including prevailing prices. In some cases the missionary, *because* he is a foreigner, will be given preferential treatment. The proprietor of the shop might insist on giving the article to him. So it works both ways. More often than not he will pay more, but on some occasions he will be treated as an "honored guest" and presented with a gift. The missionary must learn to play the game with patience and good will, knowing that such conduct is a good advertisement for the gospel.

6. **Role of the middleman.** Americans prefer to do business directly, man to man, without beating around the bush or wasting time waiting for others to help. If we don't get an immediate response we get on the telephone, call the person involved, and close the deal as quickly and expeditiously as possible.

This is not the way business is conducted in other parts of the world where the services of a middleman are indispensable in conducting all important transactions, be they business, financial, or social. Buying and selling property, hiring and firing servants, marrying the young, and burying the dead—all call for the services of a middleman, who will take great pains to conclude the business at hand in a manner that will be in the best interests of all concerned. In some cases he may be paid for his services; in others he will not. The middleman is usually a friend of one of the parties, and he is glad to do the favor. It is regarded as an honor to be asked to act in this capacity.

Missionaries as a group tend to be active and aggressive. They prefer to manage their own affairs. This has worked well for them at home so why not on the mission field? Many a missionary has come to grief because he was unwilling to take advantage of the services of a middleman. The missionary who has a faithful friend, Christian or non-Christian, who understands the local situation, who has the confidence of the community, and who is willing to act on his behalf when important business has to be transacted, should be very thankful.

This is also true in church affairs, especially when discipline becomes a problem. It is usually a mistake for the missionary to take matters into his own hands and try to solve the problem by himself. The nationals understand the nuances of their own culture much better than the missionary does and are therefore in a better position to offer advice and make decisions. Some missionaries have done irreparable damage to their usefulness in the national church by forgetting or neglecting this important principle.

7. Loss of face. Nobody likes to be humiliated in the eyes of his friends, but in the Orient, "loss of face" is the greatest of all misfortunes. Sin is not so much a matter of wrong doing as of being found out. In some societies a man's word is his bond. To ask for a written receipt is to impugn his integrity and cause loss of face. To transfer a person from one position to another, even on the same level, may be interpreted by him as a vote of non-confidence and therefore a loss of face. To probe into the financial report submitted by the church treasurer, or even to ask for a clarification of certain items, would most certainly offend him. This is one reason why the churches in the Third World have so much trouble with money matters. To ask questions is to excite suspicion. To excite suspicion is to cause the person to lose face.

Church discipline is an extremely delicate area, especially if the offender is an officer or a leader. The crucial question is not how to discipline him but how to accomplish this without causing him to lose face to the point where he will never again be able to raise his head in public. In all such situations loss of face seems to be more important than either the reputation of the church or the rehabilitation of the culprit. This is one reason why church discipline, always a problem, is so exceedingly difficult in some societies.

The missionary is vulnerable at this point. If he insists on the church's dealing with the matter in an open, aboveboard, Western way he may do more harm than good. He will become the life-long enemy of the offender, and the church itself may not recover from the trauma of the unhappy episode.

8. No sense of time. The Western world operates by the clock. We punch in at 8:30 in the morning and we punch out again at 4:30 in the evening. Coffee breaks occur twice a day and last 15 minutes. Trains, buses, and planes all run on time—most of the time. But in the Third World, people take life at a much more leisurely pace and enjoy themselves in the process. Meetings *never* start on time; they are not supposed to. The deacons meeting may be announced for three o'clock. The first deacon arrives about 3:45; the second at four o'clock; the third 15 minutes later. By 4:30 the last one has arrived and the meeting gets under way. The missionary takes a dim view of this procedure. He was there at 3:00 and expected the meeting to be over by 4:30. While he was fretting and fuming the others were having a good time of fellowship—drinking tea, eating watermelon seeds, chatting, laughing, and greeting each latecomer as he arrived.

Buses may or may not leave on time. They may not even leave until the next day, depending on the weather, the supply of gas, the condition of the tires, the availability of a driver, and the number of passengers. And when the bus—often an open truck—starts out in the morning there is no guarantee that it will reach its destination that night. If it breaks down or gets stuck in a mudhole or if there is no ferry at the river, the passengers may have to sit on the side of the road for a day or two until help arrives. This does not greatly disturb the nationals. They have learned to take this kind of thing in their stride. They may even settle down to enjoy their stay. The missionary usually has a different reaction. He is not happy with the unexpected turn of events. He is in a hurry. He has important things to do. He wants to be on his way. He needs to follow their lead and learn to endure with patience, if not actually to enjoy, the difficulties and delays which are a part of life in his area of the world.

ADJUSTING TO THE RELIGIOUS ENVIRONMENT

In some respects this is the most important adjustment of all. The missionary is a purveyor of religion; at least that is the way he appears to the people. His main business is to make converts to the Christian faith. This naturally brings him into contact with other religious movements, institutions and customs.

1. **Confronting the non-Christian religions.** One of the first things to strike the new missionary is the size and strength of the non-Christian religions. He knew they were there, but he didn't expect them to be so powerful and so pervasive. The Christian presence resembles a small island surrounded by a sea of Hinduism, Buddhism, or Islam, depending on where he is. For the first time in his life he knows what it is to be part of a religious minority—weak, poor, despised, and sometimes persecuted. Mosques, temples, shrines, and pagodas outnumber churches a hundred to one. They are big and beautiful while the churches are small and plain, and the congregations are numerically insignificant.

The power of the non-Christian religions must be seen and felt to be appreciated. The reaction to the Christian message will run the gamut from ready acceptance in Africa to polite complacency in Thailand, broad toleration in India, active opposition in Malaysia, and outright persecution in the Middle East. The great ethnic religions are undergoing a resurgence at home and are reaching out in missionary work around the world.

In his approach to these people the missionary will have to find new ways of expressing the Christian gospel. He will have to use terms that are intelligible to the listeners. This will require a good deal of adaptation on his part and is one reason why a study of the non-Christian religions should be part of every missionary's training.

2. **Religion in everyday life.** Here in the U.S. there is complete separation of church and state. Religion is a private affair, mostly confined to Sunday morning. This is not true in other parts of the world, where religion is an integral part of everyday life. Morning prayers, daily ablutions, lighting candles, burning incense, arranging flowers, preparing food—all have religious significance. Setting out on a long journey, building a house, launching a boat, starting a business—all are the occasion for some kind of religious ceremony. Hindus and Muslims in particular take their religion seriously

and practice their religious rites in public and in private. It is a moving sight to see thousands of Muslims, all dressed in long, flowing robes, kneeling in the city plaza praying with their faces toward Mecca.

The missionary will not be long in one of these countries before he realizes what a strong hold the native religion has on the people and how difficult it will be to win them to Christ. He will need a double portion of the Spirit of God if he is to have an impact on the religious power structures of the world.

3. Cooperation with the national church. The presence of the indigenous church in all parts of the world is the great new fact of our day. The missionary must recognize that fact and act accordingly. The day is past when he could go his own way and do his own thing without consulting the church. He will not only have to work with and under the church leaders, who may have less education than himself, but he will also have to work with facilities that are vastly inferior to those of the large, well organized, wealthy churches in the U.S. Church furniture, Sunday school supplies, Christian literature, and other facilities and services taken for granted in the U.S. are largely missing on the mission field. Illiteracy adds to the problems of Christian education. To fit into this kind of church situation will require a good deal of adjustment on the part of the missionary.

4. Adjusting to institutional life. This problem is especially acute for medical and educational workers. They too will have to work without many of the facilities and services available in the U.S. The hospitals will be old, the equipment will be obsolete, sanitary conditions will be unsatisfactory, wards will be overcrowded, supplies will be difficult to secure, bills will be hard to collect, and patients won't do what they are told. These and other problems will be the daily lot of the medical missionary. He will survive only if he knows how to adjust.

The educational missionary may be better off, but not by much. He too will have to get along without many of the facilities available at home. If he teaches in a seminary he will find the level of instruction much lower than in the U.S. Most seminaries operate on two levels, some on three. Only a handful offer post-college programs. Housing and dining facilities will be primitive. The library, the heart of any school, will probably have less than 10,000 volumes, and fewer than half of these will be in the vernacular. Up-to-date textbooks will be scarce, and those that are available will probably be in English. As for mechanical equipment, the teacher should consider himself lucky if there is one overhead projector for the entire school. Photocopiers will be non-existent. Imagine a seminary professor getting along without a duplicating machine!

Regardless of the kind of work he will be doing, the new missionary will have a good deal of adjusting to do before he can effectively carry out his ministry for Christ, and the adjustments will involve both his life and his work. The major adjustments will come during the first term of service. After that it will be comparatively smooth sailing, although certain minor adjustments will have to be made from time to time. This business of assimilating another culture requires a lifetime of effort. Prospective missionaries will be interested in a very helpful article by Ronald A. Iwasko entitled "Making the First-Term Missionary," which appeared in *Emissary*, Vol. IX, No. 3, April 1978 published by the Evangelical Missions Information Service, Box 794, Wheaton, Illinois, 60187.

10

Maintaining One's Health

According to a study made by the Missionary Research Library in New York, ill health is the greatest single cause of missionary dropouts. Physical health problems account for 20.3 percent and mental health problems for 5.6 percent, making a total of 25.9 percent.

Health and happiness belong together. Both are essential to a successful missionary career. No one can be truly effective over a long period of time unless he is basically happy in his work, and happiness depends to a large degree on health. It has been said that the greatest saints are the greatest sufferers. That has been true in rare cases. Fanny Crosby was blind for most of her life and she wrote some of the finest hymns in the book. Others like her, fortified by a double portion of God's grace, have been able to rise above their infirmities and lead useful, productive lives. But they were the exception, not the rule. Most of us would have to confess that sickness is a serious handicap. A throbbing toothache is not particularly conducive to a spirit of prayer. We pray and work better when we are well. It is important then that the missionary take steps to maintain his health.

HEALTH HAZARDS

It is common knowledge that health hazards are greater in the Third World countries than here in the U.S. Contagious diseases such as polio and tuberculosis, which have been eliminated in the West, are still a problem in other parts of the world. The mortality rate among children is especially high.

Public sanitation is inadequate at best; consequently, drinking water must be boiled even in some "modern" cities. In the rural areas there are very few safe wells; rivers, ponds, and stagnant pools constitute the water supply. The women do the family laundry at one end of the pond and draw the family drinking water from the other. There is no indoor plumbing. Toilets, both private and public, are little more than holes in the ground. Human waste is used to fertilize the vegetable gardens. This results in luxuriant growth but is a great danger to health. There is no garbage pickup; refuse is thrown into the streets. If sewers exist they are often open and the children splash and swim in them.

Personal hygiene is practically unknown in many places. Toothpaste and soap are luxuries which only the rich can afford. There are no detergents or deodorants. Most of the peasants are unschooled so they have no knowledge of germs. Once a contagious disease gets started it runs rampant through a community, resulting in many deaths. The only bathing facility is the public bathhouse, usually reserved for men only.

FOOD SUPPLY

The food situation varies from country to country. In some parts of the world there are all kinds of fruits and vegetables most of the year, but in other countries food is always a problem.

1. The problem of variety. Living in the U.S. has spoiled us. In our supermarkets there can be found a bewildering assortment of food for every member of the family, including the canary and the cat. Fresh fruits and vegetables are available in season and out. Somewhere on the rows and rows of shelves one can find whatever his palate craves. The only limitation is the amount of money in the pocketbook, and even that is no longer a problem if one has a credit card.

This is not true on the mission field. Take breakfast cereal as an example. To the delight of our children and the dismay of their mothers, we have 35 or 40 kinds of dry cereal to choose from. On the field the only kind of cereal available may be ground wheat or corn, which must be cooked and eaten hot.

What about meat? That too is in short supply. In Muslim countries pork will be unobtainable. In India, where the cow is a sacred animal, beef is taboo. Fish may be had only if there is a river nearby. Fowl is acceptable to most people though not always available. It has one big advantage; it is sold alive so the buyer knows that the meat is fresh.

2. The problem of nutrition. Hunger and malnutrition are two of the greatest health problems in the Third World. It is estimated that half of the world's children go to bed hungry every night. Many of them suffer irreparable brain damage in their early years because of a lack of protein and vitamins in their diet. Others are chronically thin, weak, and ill, unable to function at peak capacity as normal human beings. Obesity, one of the great health problems in the West, is rarely a problem in the Third World. As for "decalorizing" food, it is unknown in most countries. In Asia and many parts of Latin America the need is for more, not fewer, calories. In countries such as India, Pakistan, Bangladesh, and Haiti the daily per capita consumption of calories is less than half of what it is in the U.S.

Reduced to simple terms, the problem is too many people and not enough land. Every square foot of arable land is under extensive cultivation. The soil becomes "tired" from overuse with no rotation of crops and no chance to lie fallow. Even in countries where the food supply is fairly plentiful the nutritional value is low. It takes much more food to provide the same amount of nutrition.

Not many missionaries are forced to live on a reduced diet, even in time of famine. They usually get enough to eat. Food is available but it is not nutritious. The missionary often ends up doing what the nationals do; he eats more to get the nutrition he needs. Protein and vitamins are always a serious problem, for two reasons. First, the regular diet tends to be starchy. Second, meat, fish, and fowl—good sources of protein—usually are not plentiful and therefore expensive.

3. The problem of contamination. In countries where the climate is hot nine months of the year, where the people know little or nothing about germs, and where human waste is used as fertilizer, contamination is a continual problem. Dysentery, the biggest killer of children, is caused by contaminated food or water. So are hepatitis and typhoid fever.

Though milk is a nutritious food it may be dangerous. If it comes from cows infected with tuberculosis it can pass on the disease. Even when it comes from healthy cows it is not always safe, for the vendors have a way of making their supply go farther by adding water. One rule should *never* be broken: *Do not drink unboiled water.* A missionary friend of mine succumbed to temptation on a hot summer day and drank a glass of unboiled water. For weeks he lay at death's door with typhoid fever. He survived the attack but had paid dearly for his lesson.

4. The problem of supply. In the U.S., supply is seldom a problem except when a nationwide strike occurs and transportation breaks down. But it is often a problem on the mission field, depending on several factors: location, climate, transportation, etc.

In the tropics, where two and sometimes three crops a year are possible, there is usually a fairly steady supply of food. In colder regions fruits and vegetables are available only in season, which may be only a month or so. But while it lasts, fruit is plentiful and cheap. Missionaries usually take advantage of this by buying large quantities to preserve.

In the larger cities such as Tokyo, Manila, Nairobi, and Caracas, all kinds of foodstuffs, including canned goods, are available most of the year. If the canned goods are imported the price is likely to be out of reach for the missionary. In the smaller towns and the rural areas the supply will naturally be less plentiful. Missionaries who live in the jungle have to learn to live on local produce, supplemented by what can be flown in by Mission Aviation Fellowship. In some parts of Africa the missionaries depend on hunting for most of their meat.

Missionaries in the rural areas often have gardens in which they grow such Western fruits and vegetables as strawberries, melons, cucumbers, tomatoes, green beans, peas, etc., some of which can be preserved. These and other plants were introduced to Asia and Africa by the missionaries of the nineteenth century.

5. The problem of preservation. The Third World is rapidly catching up with the technology of the West, but refrigeration is still a long way off. It is a luxury that most people cannot afford; therefore the facilities are not available. Some missionaries solve the problem by bringing a kerosene refrigerator. Without refrigeration the preservation of food is a major problem. Meat must be eaten the day it is killed, milk turns sour overnight, and eggs remain fresh only a day or two. In very hot weather many missionaries do not bother with meat and eggs. They substitute peanuts and soybeans.

6. The problem of palatability. When all other food problems have been solved—and that may take a long time—there still remains the problem of palatability. In China the food is delicious and Chinese food is enjoyed the world over, but missionaries in other countries may not be so fortunate. Raw fish, a staple in Japan, takes some getting used to. In some countries the food is greasy and spicy; in others it is sour; and in still others it is sticky-sweet.

Much depends on what one has been accustomed to. In the West we eat pork but would gag on dog meat. We eat snails but not snakes, rabbits but not rats, dandelions but not daisies. The only explanation for this is habit. We are accustomed to eating certain things and therefore we like them. In other cultures they have different likes and dislikes, and the missionary is expected to like what they like. While still at home he sang: "Where He Leads Me I Will Follow." On the mission field he learns to sing: "What They Feed Me I Will Swallow." It takes time and effort, and more than once he will gag or regurgitate; but with determination and the help of the Lord it can be done.

Before leaving the matter of food it might not be out of place to remark that in many ways the missionary's diet, with all of its limitations, is often more wholesome than the food consumed here in the West. The American diet, for all of its variety, is anything but well balanced. Some nutritionists are now talking about "junk food" and advising us to avoid it. American food tends to be too rich, too sweet, too high in calories, and therefore too fattening. Sugar is one of the villains; let me tell you how I know this from personal experience.

Because of the Sino-Japanese War our first term in China lasted ten years. During most of that time we had very little sugar, and towards the end none at all. Immediately upon our return to the U.S. for furlough I went to the dentist for a checkup, fully expecting him to find a mouthful of cavities. To my great surprise—and his—there were none. He asked what we had used to clean our teeth in China and I told him: bicarbonate of soda. He expressed approval, remarking that the toothpaste used in this country is mostly junk. But that is not the end of the story. When I visited him after a year on furlough he found two cavities. The culprit? Sugar!

My wife and I both enjoyed good health throughout our years in China. To be sure, the Lord was good to us, but on the human level I am persuaded that the simple, wholesome food had much to do with it.

HEALTH PROBLEMS WITH CHILDREN

Missionary children, familiarly known as MKs, are a great joy to their parents and are often a definite asset in their work, but from a physical point of view they are particularly vulnerable. There are several reasons for this. First, like all children they have a tendency to put everything into their mouths. Second, they do not understand the laws of health and do not realize when they are running a risk. Third, they are often left in the care of an amah who may or may not do as she is told. Fourth, they play with children from local homes where sanitation is unknown and where disease is rife. Tuberculosis and dysentery are common. Infections of all kinds abound.

Two families, colleagues of ours in China, lost children to dysentery. Our own two boys came down with it and the younger one almost died. At one point the doctor did not expect him to live through the night. After suffering for a whole summer he looked for all the world like a famine baby.

PREGNANCY AND CHILDBIRTH

It is not uncommon for missionary families to have four or five children, most of them born on the mission field where both pregnancy and childbirth can be hazardous.

The nine months of pregnancy may be an anxious time even here at home where medical facilities are immediately available and monthly checkups are routine. On the mission field the difficulties and dangers are multiplied many times. Some missionaries are several days away from the nearest hospital, which makes regular checkups impossible. Without professional advice and care, complications may become critical. It can be a time of testing for both husband and wife.

Will the mother travel, perhaps hundreds of miles, to a mission hospital for the birth of the child, or will she remain at home in the hope that a doctor will be able to reach her in time? There are few doctors and they are usually assigned to a hospital. Some hospitals have only one doctor on the staff, in which case he could hardly leave for a maternity case two or three days journey away, especially when no one can be sure whether the baby's arrival will be early or late. It is more feasible for the mother to go to the hospital, but this may involve an arduous journey by overcrowded bus or a hike over high mountains. In recent years Mission Aviation Fellowship has performed an outstanding service by transporting missionaries back and forth between hospital and home, reducing travel time by as much as 90 percent, relieving anxiety, and in some instances saving lives. Unfortunately MAF is operating in only twenty countries, which leaves many missionaries without this kind of transportation.

MEDICAL FACILITIES ON THE INCREASE

Modern scientific medicine and surgery were introduced to the Third World by missionaries during the nineteenth century, and for many years they were the only practitioners of modern medicine. But in this latter half of the twentieth century conditions are rapidly changing. Most of the newly independent countries, of which there are almost a hundred, have opted for socialism rather than capitalism. Socialized medicine is the order of the day, and with tax money the governments have greatly expanded various health care facilities. Many mission hospitals in these countries have been taken over by the department of health and welfare.

Most of the government hospitals are located in the larger cities, which leaves the towns and rural areas still without medical facilities. In the less developed countries there may be no medical facilities outside the capital city. The missionary therefore has to be his own doctor. It is only fair to say that in many countries, through no fault of their own, the governments have had to sacrifice quality for quantity, multiplying hospitals and clinics in order to meet the colossal needs of a burgeoning population.

PRACTICAL SUGGESTIONS

In the absence of medical facilities the missionary can do many things to take care of himself and his family. Some of these will be prompted by experience; others are dictated by common sense. In either case he should do all he can to insure a full measure of health and strength. He owes it to himself, his family, and to the Lord. His body is the temple of the Holy Spirit, which is a potent reason for taking good care of it.

1. **Be fit before you leave.** Take care of all physical deficiencies and abnormalities before leaving for the field. Every candidate must have a thorough medical checkup as part of the application process. Most existing problems will be revealed at that time. If the problem is of a serious nature and cannot be corrected he will not be accepted by the mission. In all other cases it should be taken care of, if necessary by surgery. When the problem is chronic rather than acute there is always the temptation to postpone

action. It is an act of folly to take a chance and proceed to the mission field hoping that it will go away. It is much more likely to recur at a later time when medical attention will not be so readily available.

2. Take every reasonable precaution. Do not take unnecessary risks. Better be safe than sorry. In areas where malaria is prevalent use a mosquito net, or better still, install screens on all doors and windows. Again, be sure to boil all drinking water unless you are in a modern city where water pollution is not a problem.

3. Get sufficient exercise. Years ago this advice would have been unnecessary, for the missionaries either walked or rode a bicycle, which gave them all the exercise they needed. But more and more missionaries are using cars, which cuts down on their activity. Others are engaged in sedentary work—Bible translation, for instance—and get no exercise at all. All missionaries should make a special effort to get some exercise each day to keep themselves in shape.

4. Get adequate rest. The average person requires at least seven hours of sleep a night. In the tropics, where the climate tends to be enervating, more may be needed. If the nationals feel the need for an afternoon siesta, it is safe to assume that the missionary will also benefit from one. American missionaries have been known to take the American rat race with them to the field, only to discover that the body has a way of kicking back when it is abused.

5. Take an annual vacation. This may appear to be a luxury in the eyes of the nationals who are accustomed to working seven days a week fifty-two weeks a year. They might be able to stand such a routine, but not the missionary. It is essential that at least once a year he have a change of pace and an opportunity to rest and relax away from the demands and responsibilities of his work. This is a must in the tropics. Fortunately in most tropical countries there are cool mountain resorts to which the missionaries can go when they need to get away.

6. Have an annual checkup. This can coincide with the annual vacation without involving any additional time or travel. It should be made a regular part of the vacation schedule. "An ounce of prevention is worth a pound of cure" is no cliche on the mission field.

7. Keep books and medicines handy. It has been said that a little knowledge is a dangerous thing. No knowledge at all can be even more dangerous. A few books on first aid, health care, and even minor surgery should be a part of every missionary's library. Every home should have a medicine cabinet in which are stored some of the more common medicines, simple medical instruments, and such basic supplies as gauze, cotton swabs, bandages, etc.

8. Take out health insurance. Most mission boards see that all their missionaries are covered by Blue Cross and Blue Shield or some comparable health insurance plan. If for any reason the mission does not do it, the missionary should make his own plans for adequate coverage.

9. Do not give way to fear. The missionary should take all reasonable precautions. Having done so, he should not allow fear of illness or accident to incapacitate him for his work. One Swedish missionary, when asked how he managed to cope with life on the mission field, replied: "I trust God and drink strong coffee." With or without coffee, the missionary always has the Lord, and ultimately his trust is in God. If he does his part by maintaining a well-balanced diet, getting sufficient rest, and taking some exercise each day, he can trust the Lord for the rest.

He will have to take *some* risks. That is implicit in his vocation. It was involved in his initial decision to follow Christ to the ends of the earth. In spite of all the precautions they take, some missionaries do have physical problems. One friend of ours contracted polio in the Philippines and spent the remainder of his life in an iron lung. Some pick up germs and parasites which render them unable to continue their missionary work. All these risks are present, but it should not discourage or deter them. Paul had his thorn in the flesh and learned to live with it. He even used it as an occasion to display the power of Christ.

10. One final word. It is easy to exaggerate the difficulties and dangers of the mission field. Life is hard, but the human organism has remarkable powers of adaptation and survival. It is not nearly as easy to die as some people think! I remember my early experiences in China. My first trip to a rural church involved a 25-mile bicycle ride in the summer heat. When I arrived about three o'clock in the afternoon I was good for nothing. Instead of preaching I lay on a camp cot nursing a throbbing headache. Next day I was glad to go home again. A year later I was able to cycle a hundred miles over rough roads in all kinds of weather and arrive in good shape for a two-hour service.

It was the same with the food. In my early visits to the country churches I thought I would not survive without my usual intake of sugar. Not only did I survive, but I soon came to the point where I didn't even miss it. When it comes to our metabolism we certainly are "fearfully and wonderfully made."

11

Cultivating the Mind

The vast majority of today's missionaries are college graduates. Many have seminary training. In addition, they are well screened by their respective candidate committees. It is a safe assumption that they have good minds. That is a great asset.

But the mind, like the body, has a way of deteriorating. It too must be cultivated or atrophy will set in, and the older we get, the faster we deteriorate. Medical experts tell us that beginning at about forty years of age, the brain loses 100,000 cells a day that are not replaced.

All persons as they grow older are in danger of slowing down and losing interest in their work, their family, their community, and even their hobbies. The missionary is no different.

To begin with, he worked so hard during his academic career that he feels entitled to a "vacation" from study. Once on vacation he finds it difficult to get off. Never again does he hit the books with the same degree of interest and intensity. He has "graduated." He can now afford to coast along on the momentum of his past learning.

Second, on most mission fields he will have few intellectual peers with whom he can talk shop. If he is located in one of the more primitive parts of the world most of his converts will be illiterate. In other areas some church members may be high school graduates; few will have had college training. In places like Japan, Korea, and Taiwan, of course, he will have plenty of intellectual competition. Indeed, he may have a hard time keeping up. But in many places his immediate friends will have attended grade school only, or high school at best. It will be difficult for them to offer him much of an intellectual challenge.

In the area of his expertise—theology—he will be head and shoulders above the congregations to which he ministers. There is little incentive for him to go deeper in his own study of Bible and theology. It will be years before anyone overtakes him in that area. Even if he is teaching in a Bible college, his seminary notes will stand him in good stead for a long time to come. Or so he may think!

The missionary is in grave danger at this point. Without realizing it he may allow his mind to stagnate. Only when he returns on furlough does he become aware of the ground he has lost.

HOW THE MISSIONARY CAN HELP HIMSELF

The missionary is by no means helpless. There are certain things he can do to prevent mental atrophy.

1. Good reading habits. Not all college students have a passion for learning. Once out of college they sell their textbooks and buy other things. Seminary graduates are a different breed. Realizing that books are the tools of their trade, they acquire as many as they can during their seminary days and seldom do they sell them afterwards.

Regardless of whether he is a college or a seminary graduate, however, the missionary should take with him every good book that he possesses. Here at home the pastor can always borrow from a fellow pastor or from a seminary library or even from the community library, but the only books to which the missionary has access are his own. In his library he should have light reading for relaxation, heavy reading to stretch and stimulate his mind, and theological and technical books to be used as tools in his teaching and preaching ministry.

Having the books will do no good unless he reads them. He should set aside some time each day for reading and jealously guard it against all intruders. This will not be easy, but the attempt should be made.

2. Keep abreast of world events. The missionary, if he is true to his high calling, is an internationalist. He believes with John Wesley that the world is his parish. His church is a universal institution. His Bible is a universal book. His gospel is a universal message. His Master is the Lord of history and the King of the world. This being so, he *must* be interested in world events.

There are various ways in which he can achieve this goal. He should listen each day to the international news broadcasts over the Voice of America or the British Broadcasting Corporation. He should subscribe to *Time, Newsweek,* or *US News and World Report.* One of these is a must.

Then there are national and regional journals such as *Africa Report, Middle East Journal,* and *Far Eastern Review,* which he should read.

Every missionary should keep in touch with church and mission work around the world. The following journals will help: *International Review of Mission, Evangelical Missions Quarterly, Pulse* (six regional editions), *Missionary News Service, World Vision, IFMA News Bulletin, Information Bulletin* (Lausanne Committee), and *Global Report* (WEF).

Those interested in missiological studies will have a choice of *Missiology: An International Review, Bulletin of Scottish Institute of Missionary Studies, Missionalia, Occasional Bulletin of Missionary Research,* and *IAMS News Letter.*

To keep informed about theological developments in the Third World he may read *Indian Journal of Theology, Journal of Theology of Southern Africa, Northeast Asia Journal of Theology, Southeast Asia Journal of Theology, Ghana Bulletin of Theology, Theological Fraternity Bulletin* (Latin America), *Asia Theological News, Theological Education Today, Theological News, Evangelical Review of Theology,* and *Gospel in Context.*

Now that one-third of the world's population lives under Communism, the fate of the church in those countries is of vital interest to every Christian. Several journals are available: *Religion in Communist Lands, China Notes, Sparks, Religion and Communism,* and *LWF Marxism and China Study: Information Letter.*

Missionaries in the larger countries will have access to several national periodicals. In Japan, for instance, there are three: *Japan Christian Quarterly, Japan Harvest,* and *Japan Missionary Bulletin.* The same is true of India.

Those wishing to follow events in the ecumenical movement may subscribe to the *Ecumenical Review, Ecumenical Press Service, One World, WCC Exchange*—all published by the World Council of Churches. Africa missionaries can hardly afford to be without the *AACC Bulletin;* those in Asia should read the *CCA News.*

Other periodicals of value include *Church Growth Bulletin, Lutheran World, Christianity Today, Eternity,* and *Moody Monthly.*

3. Subscribe to daily newspapers. All the large countries and some of the smaller ones have at least one good English language newspaper. In addition, it is wise to subscribe to a good vernacular newspaper, either daily or weekly. Not many missionaries bother with a vernacular newspaper. This is a mistake. If one wants to get the feel of the country it is necessary to have access to news presented from an indigenous point of view.

4. Engage in creative writing. There is no finer mental discipline than writing. Creative writing might begin with short stories, magazine articles, news reports, tracts, pamphlets, or brochures. Practice leads to fluency.

Who knows? The missionary may eventually become a writer. Those with aesthetic tastes could try poetry or music. Every mission publishes its own house organ and editors welcome well-written articles. All of this will require time, thought, and effort, but it will be a good investment.

5. Enroll in a local university. If the missionary cannot find intellectual peers in the Christian community, he should try elsewhere. If there is a university in his city, he may wish to enroll in a course or two. This will not only help him to keep up to date in his particular discipline, it will also afford opportunities for wider friendship and witness. It may even open the door to a part-time teaching position on the faculty. Qualified English teachers are in great demand in some parts of the Third World. If such an opening occurs he may wish to accept it. Daily contact with the students will help to keep him on his toes intellectually.

6. Take up a hobby. Not many missionaries have a hobby, partly from lack of time and partly because facilities may not be available. One China missionary made a hobby of writing the complicated Chinese characters with the Chinese writing brush. Each evening after everyone else had gone to bed he sat up for an hour or two practising his characters. In time he became so adept that he was asked by his Chinese friends to write scrolls for decorative purposes. That was indeed a high honor. The Chinese who saw the scrolls couldn't believe they were written by a foreigner.

A missionary in Japan took up railroading as a hobby and became something of an expert. This gave him an entrée to the railroad officials, some of whom became his good friends.

There is no end to the number of hobbies open to missionaries. Having a hobby has therapeutic as well as intrinsic value. By all means give it some thought.

HOW TO OBTAIN READING MATERIAL

Books are the life blood of a person's intellectual well being. He should endeavor to acquire as many as he can. This is a costly undertaking, however, and the average missionary may not have the funds to purchase the books and journals listed in this chapter. They should not be regarded as a luxury, however; they are as necessary for his mind as food is for his body.

There are several ways for a missionary to acquire the books he desires.

1. Encourage friends to give books. Birthdays and Christmas are the two occasions in the year when missionaries receive special gifts from supporting churches, friends, and relatives. They should be encouraged to send books instead of money. Book postage is comparatively cheap and books enter most countries duty free, which makes them doubly welcome.

2. Join a book club. In the U.S. there are various kinds of book clubs—religious, classical, professional, and popular. By joining such a club the missionary can be sure of a steady supply of good books automatically month after month. One drawback is unwanted books. It is more cumbersome to return them from overseas than from the U.S. Another problem is pilferage. Popular books in English are very attractive and hard to get in the Third World. The temptation for post office personnel to help themselves to books is sometimes irresistible.

3. Organize a circulating library. Twelve families in a given mission or country can get together, pool their resources, and arrange among themselves to buy a book a month. Each family will buy one book a year. The books will be passed around on a monthly basis from one family to another until they have been read by all twelve members of the group. In this way each family buys a book of its own choice and reads eleven other books free of charge. For the plan to be successful, however, someone must see that the books are kept circulating. No family should keep a book longer than a month; otherwise the plan will break down.

4. Order books from home. If the missionary keeps a checking account in the U.S. (which most do) he can order books as they come off the press and pay for them by check. He can find book ads and book reviews in Christian periodicals, the best source of information on new books.

HOW THE MISSIONS CAN HELP

Mission administrators at home and overseas are doing a superb job in caring for the physical and material needs of their members, but for some strange reason they have not done so well for the intellectual needs. It may be they assume that the missionary has already received all the intellectual training he needs, or perhaps they think he will buy books without their prompting. For whatever reason, no specific plans are made to meet his intellectual needs. There are, however, several ways in which the missions can help.

1. Make funds for books available. Some churches in the U.S. are now including in the annual budget an item of several hundred dollars to be given to the pastor for the purchase of books. This is a specially designated amount, over and above his salary, on which he does not have to pay income tax. He must spend the money on books, but that is no hardship to the average pastor. This is an excellent idea. It enables him to buy at least one good book a month and to subscribe to half-a-dozen periodicals each year, all of which will greatly enrich his ministry.

The missions could do for their missionaries what these churches are doing for their pastors by including in their support figure an item designated for books. The money would have to be used for that purpose. This would provide the missionary with the means to acquire whatever books he wants in the course of the year.

2. Buy books in quantity. The missions could include in their administrative budget an item to cover the cost of one or two books to be ordered each year for all missionaries. From time to time books appear that every missionary should read, but for one reason or another he never gets around to it. He doesn't have the money, or he doesn't know of its existence, or he is just too busy to order it. The mission could order enough copies to send one to each missionary unit on the field.

Books ordered in large numbers to be given away free can be bought at a 50 or 60 percent discount. This would bring a $7.95 book down to $3.18. Two hundred copies at $3.18 would amount to $636.00. With $80.00 added for postage the total would come to $716.00. The annual budget of a mission with 200 missionaries runs between two and three million dollars. If two books a year were ordered, the amount would be $1,432.00, less than .05 percent of the total budget. What mission could not afford so small an expense for so crucial an item? It would be one of the best investments it could possibly make.

3. Make provision for study programs on furlough. There is another way in which the missions can help. They can encourage missionaries on furlough to take advantage of study programs. Continuing education is becoming increasingly popular; many professional and business men are utilizing it to help in their careers. Missionaries are beginning to recognize its value but there are several serious problems.

Many missions have a one-sided view of the purpose of furlough. It is supposed to provide physical rest and relaxation in a climate conducive to the rehabilitation of the human organism. Every missionary is expected to take one month of complete rest before beginning deputation work. But what about the mind? Are its needs less important than those of the body? If the body needs rest and relaxation, the mind needs exercise and stimulation.

Furlough study poses two problems, one of time and the other of money. It should not be too difficult to solve the time problem. The supporting churches and the mission board should get together and come to an understanding regarding the amount of time to be spent in deputation work. The churches should not demand that all their missionaries visit them on every furlough.

The second problem is money. Every missionary receives a furlough allowance, but it barely covers food, rent, and other basic needs. There is nothing left over for such a "luxury" as tuition. This problem could be solved by unilateral mission action. Nearly every mission has written into the missionary's support figure a large item for furlough, of which the largest part is for travel. During the four years he is overseas, funds are set aside each month for furlough, retirement, administrative expenses, etc. A small monthly item could be added to provide for tuition as part of the overall furlough expense. Such an item, it seems to me, would not only be legitimate, but it would prove to be extremely beneficial to both the missionary and the mission.

However it is accomplished, the missionary's intellectual life should be cultivated. The missionary, his mission, and even the home church should consider the matter seriously and make a determined effort to solve the problem.

"The people who measure up most consistently overseas are those who not only have resources within themselves for creative living, but do what is needful to keep their minds nourished and their spirits renewed."[1]

---

1. John Rosengrant et al, *Assignment: Overseas* (New York: Thomas Y. Crowell, 1966), p. 109.

12

Nourishing the Soul

Whatever else the missionary may be, he must be a man of God. To be a man of God he must love the Lord with all his heart and with all his mind. To do this he must learn to cultivate both his spiritual life and his intellectual life.

This is not easy to do. The average Christian does not realize the extent to which we at home depend on others for the stimulation of our spiritual and intellectual life. We have church services, Bible classes, prayer meetings, weekend retreats, choir practice, seminars, workshops, Christian radio and TV programs, Christian journals, missionary periodicals, devotional books, sermons and sacred music on tapes in our homes and cars, and an unlimited supply of Christian literature of all kinds for all ages. One wonders what American Christians would do if all these spiritual props on which they have come to lean were suddenly removed.

As every missionary knows to his sorrow, most of these things are either missing or exceedingly scarce on the mission field. If he is to survive spiritually he must do so on his own initiative. If he allows either heart or mind to atrophy he will be in deep trouble.

THE SPIRITUAL LIFE

This is most important. If his spiritual life dries up, the missionary might as well come home and sell insurance. There are few sights more pathetic than a spiritually defeated missionary trying to keep up his ministry. It is of the utmost importance that he devise ways of maintaining his spiritual life.

He must continue to grow in grace and in the knowledge of the Lord Jesus Christ long after he goes to the mission field. Otherwise his life will be barren and his ministry ineffective.

All Christian workers have the same problem, but with the missionary there are graver consequences. He has all the problems of the pastor at home, but he also has some which are peculiar to life on the field. There are several reasons why his spiritual life is likely to suffer.

1. The wear and tear of life. The Christian worker at home has the many amenities of Western technology, including labor-saving devices which render housework less demanding and time-consuming. Life on the mission field is quite different. Heat, dirt, delays, disappointments, language problems, cultural barriers, children to be taught, visitors to be seen, and innumerable other irritations and interruptions all crowd into every 16-hour day. All of this continues week after week, month after month, year after year. Little wonder that the missionary finds, as Jesus did, that virtue has gone out of him.

2. The fierce spiritual warfare. This is not confined to the mission field, but certainly the battle is fiercest in that arena. Satan will not suffer his kingdom to be invaded or his authority challenged by the Christian missionary. Sooner or later the missionary will feel the full fury of his wrath. Satan may attack his mind, body, or soul, but attack he will, and the missionary will need the protection of the whole armor of God.

3. Lack of privacy and leisure. Non-Western societies tend to be open and easy-going. People get up and go to bed with the chickens. Without clocks to cramp their style they arrange the affairs of the day by the location of the sun in the sky, and when the sun is obscured by clouds they simply "play it by ear." They come and go as they please, stay as long as they like, converse for hours on end, and ask the most personal questions. Even when the missionary is at home he finds it difficult to maintain anything resembling a schedule. On safari he might as well forget it; privacy will be impossible. This too is a constant drain on his spiritual and psychological resources.

4. Lack of Christian fellowship. Missionaries in pioneer church-planting work often find themselves with little or no Christian fellowship. In the early stages the Christians are few in number, often illiterate or semi-literate, and unable to make much of a contribution to the missionary's need for mature Christian fellowship. Church services are not noted for either dignity or decorum. Congregational singing leaves much to be desired. Sermons are hardly a model of homiletical expertise. Under such conditions the missionary craves fellowship on a higher level.

I shall never forget the first English church service we attended after ten years in rural China. It took place in Bowen Memorial Church in Bombay. The pastor was an Anglo-Indian, a graduate of Drew University, handsome, intellectual, and eloquent. My parched spirit drank in the entire service. From the invocation to the benediction it was a blessing to my soul. I had forgotten how quiet, beautiful, and dignified a worship service could be. The 30-minute sermon was a feast for my mind as well as my heart. The special number by the choir was "music to my ears." Perhaps the most moving part of the service was the pastoral prayer. To my unaccustomed ears it sounded more like poetry than prose. It had depth as well as breadth, inspiration as well as aspiration, and praise as well as petition. As I sat through the service I felt like Jacob at Bethel when he said, "This is none other than the house of God, and this is the gate of heaven" (Gen 28:17, RSV).

5. Lack of social contacts. Man is a gregarious creature with varied social needs. The Christian missionary is no exception. Very few of these needs, however, are met in most situations on the mission field. Unless he is located in Tokyo, Singapore, Salisbury, Buenos Aires, Paris, or some other metropolitan center he will have few social contacts other than those provided by the small group of believers.

There are no community concerts, no symphony orchestras, no university lectures. He does not have television, and even if he did there would be no World Series or Stanley Cup playoffs. Most high days and holidays come and go unnoticed. The only American holiday he celebrates is Labor Day and he does that by working all day! He has no telephone; consequently neither he nor his wife can chat on the phone with friends and loved ones. To top it off, his children are away at school nine or ten months of the year. Only those who have lived in such isolation can possibly appreciate what it is like to be without an adequate social life. In time, this lack of social contacts affects his spiritual life as well.

PRACTICAL SUGGESTIONS

There is nothing mystical about the Christian life. Like all other forms of life it is governed by laws, the first of which is the law of cultivation. The life of Christ that is imparted to the believer at the time of his conversion is not an automatically on-going, self-sustaining kind of life. It has no built-in momentum that will carry it along indefinitely. It must be nourished by the means of grace that God has made available to all believers.

Another law of the spiritual life is the law of gradualism. Lasting growth is slow and steady. The slower the development, the stronger the growth. Mushrooms spring up overnight but perish in a day or two. The redwoods of California took hundreds of years to achieve their full height, but they have been with us for 2000 years. Jesus expressed it this way: "For the earth bringeth forth fruit of herself; first the blade, then the ear, after that the full corn in the ear" (Mk 4:28, KJV). This law is universal and inexorable. We ignore it at our peril. All kinds of problems arise when we demand instant growth. A. W. Tozer said it as well as anyone:

> *It is hardly a matter of wonder that the country that gave the world instant tea and instant coffee should be the one to give it instant Christianity . . . . By instant Christianity I mean the kind found almost everywhere in gospel circles and which is born of the notion that we may discharge our total obligation to our own souls by one act of faith, or at the most by two, and be relieved thereafter of all anxiety about our own spiritual condition . . . . By trying to pack all of salvation into one experience, or two, the advocates of instant Christianity flaunt the law of development which runs through all nature.* [1]

1. Maintain the quiet time. It is not in society, however Christian it may be, that the soul grows the most but in communion with God. Meetings are good, body-life sessions are helpful, fellowship is enriching; but in the final analysis, real and lasting spiritual growth ultimately depends on communion with God, not on fellowship with others.

Americans do not take kindly to this idea. The last thing they want is to be alone. When they get fed up with the rat race in the city they head for the hills or the beaches, but they take along their transistor radios to drown out the unbearable silence. Truckers have their CB radios to provide endless chatter with perfect strangers. It seems that Americans can endure anything but solitude.

Christians have the same tendency. We have come to depend too much on others. The present emphasis on body life is good and has New Testament sanction, but it can be carried too far. No one knows this better than the missionary who has no Christian fellowship. If he is to survive spiritually he must cultivate the habit of communion with God. It is imperative that he establish and maintain a daily quiet time when he can be alone with God.

Maintaining a quiet time is more difficult than establishing it. Somehow life on the mission field is different—more hectic and disorganized. Events are less predictable; interruptions are more numerous. Plans are more difficult to make, engagements more difficult to keep, and schedules more difficult to control. The missionary's routine is likely to be interrupted a dozen times a day. He will not find it easy to maintain his quiet time, but it must be done if he is to be a power for God.

2. Devotional use of the Bible. The Bible is the missionary's most valuable tool. His mandate, his message, his methods, and his motivation are all derived from the Bible. He uses it constantly in the preparation of his messages. Yet it is possible for him to do all this and not get any spiritual food for his own soul. For that he must use the Bible as a devotional book.

---

1. A. W. Tozer, *That Incredible Christian* (Harrisburg, PA: Christian Publications, 1964), p. 24.

There are basically two approaches to Bible study. One is for the preparation of sermons, the other for the cultivation of the soul. In the former the Bible is often reduced to a textbook. In the latter it is God's love letter to His children. In these two approaches the purpose, the procedure, and the results are all different. The missionary needs to read the Bible each day for his own edification—to inform his mind, strengthen his faith, warm his heart, deepen his love, quicken his zeal, and energize his will—so that as a person, not as a preacher, he may grow in grace and in the knowledge of the Lord Jesus Christ.

One problem with daily Bible reading is that familiarity with the words tends to reduce the impact of the message. By and by, the effort becomes mechanical and the reader complains that he gets nothing out of it. This can best be overcome by using several versions, such as the Revised Standard Version, the American Standard Version, the International Bible, the New International Bible, and the Good News Bible. Some readers prefer freer translations such as Weymouth, Moffat, Goodspeed, or, more recently, J. B. Phillips. Ken Taylor's Living Bible, a paraphrase, not a translation, is the most popular of all and is very stimulating.

3. The habit of prayer. If, as Montgomery says, prayer is the Christian's "vital breath" and his "native air," the missionary had better cultivate the habit. Here again he will encounter problems. Prayer can become a joy or a drudgery depending on the circumstances. If he confines his prayers to his own work or even to the wider work of his own mission, he may soon find that prayer begins to pall. Paul exhorted his converts to pray for all saints (Eph 6:18), all men (1 Tim 2:1), and all things (Phil 4:6). The missionary will do well to follow Paul's exhortation and broaden his prayers to include the worldwide interests of the kingdom.

There are two basic problems that militate against the missionary maintaining a daily prayer schedule. One is the fact that when work piles up and he is pressed for time, prayer is the first thing to be neglected. Second, once neglect sets in, it is difficult to overcome it. The reason for this is that prayer is a habit. An instinct works in reverse. The longer one denies an instinct the stronger it becomes until, like hunger, it gets the better of us and we have to satisfy the craving. Not so with prayer. Prayer is a habit, not an instinct. The less we pray, the less we want to pray; the less we want to pray, the less we do pray. The missionary must not allow himself to fall into that vicious cycle. He must remember that prayer is a habit to be cultivated. It will help if he has a set time and place for daily prayer. When the time arrives he will pray whether or not he feels like it. There is no other way to live a life of prayer.

4. Reading devotional books. Bible commentaries, dictionaries, etc., the stock-in-trade of every missionary, come in handy in preparing messages, but frankly they are of little value in feeding the soul. For that purpose he needs devotional books. Some authors have specialized in this kind of literature: Andrew Murray, Stephen Olford, Oswald Sanders, Alan Redpath, A. W. Tozer, Oswald Chambers, Stuart Briscoe, to name only a few. Books of poetry should not be overlooked.

An often neglected source of devotional reading is the hymnal. Some hymnals are especially rich in devotional hymns. *Consecration and Faith* and the *Keswick Hymnal*, both published in England, are among the best. These devotional hymns can be used with great effect to express not only one's aspirations to holiness but also one's ascriptions of praise. Their use will greatly enrich the daily devotional period.

In recent years cassettes dealing with various aspects of the Christian life have become available. Thousands of titles are carried by Encounter Ministries (Stephen Olford), Campus Crusade for Christ, Navigators, and others. There is no longer any reason for the missionary to be spiritually isolated from the home constituency even though he is physically isolated.

5. Good sacred music. One thing the missionary has always missed on the field is good music. In former days he had to provide his own music, and all he had was a small portable organ. Today the situation is much improved. Cassette tapes with classical and sacred music are available and are fairly cheap. Every missionary should have on hand a good supply of sacred music. Home churches could send this sort of thing to their missionaries as Christmas or birthday gifts. What is Christmas without Christmas carols?

6. Family devotions. In addition to his own quiet time the missionary should conduct family prayers each day. This is especially important when the children are young, before they leave for boarding school. Even after the children have gone, it is a good idea for husband and wife, and any other members of the household, to gather each day for prayer and the reading of the Word of God.

During our time in China we had family prayers each morning. This gave us an opportunity to teach our two boys to memorize Scripture. They learned the Ten Commandments, the Lord's Prayer, the Beatitudes, and the Twenty-third Psalm, as well as the Apostles' Creed and other expressions of Christian faith. We also sang hymns together, in this way introducing the children to the great hymns of the church. Probably nothing brings the family together more effectively than daily family devotions.

7. Get away for a change. Sooner or later the daily routine, coupled with cramped quarters and close colleagues, will get the better of the missionary. It is not only rest that he needs but a complete change of scenery as well as a change of pace. He needs to get away—away from the environment, the climate, the work, the institution, even his fellow workers. Otherwise his physical condition is bound to deteriorate and that will definitely have a deleterious effect on his spiritual condition. It is absolutely essential that he enjoy a period of complete rest and relaxation once a year.

8. Take advantage of the annual field conference. I personally can vouch for the value of the field conference. I still remember the one which was held in our part of China in 1943. Owing to the Sino-Japanese War it was the only conference held in North Anhwei in five years. All the missionaries except one family were first termers, young and green. To make matters worse we were left without a provincial superintendent. Finally one of the regional superintendents managed to get through the Japanese lines to visit us. We had five glorious days together, three meetings a day. For my wife and me it was not a change of environment, for the conference met on our compound, but it was a complete change of pace. And the deeper life ministry of R. Ernest Thompson was like a blood transfusion to a dying man. It was the most thrilling conference I ever had the privilege to attend.

13

Learning the Language

Very few Americans are bilingual, in contrast to Europeans, most of whom speak two or three languages. Practically every German can speak French and most Frenchmen can speak German. In Switzerland they speak four languages. Since English is the *lingua franca* of the world, most Europeans speak it fairly well.

Here in the U.S. the situation is different. Most ethnic groups learn to speak English after they are here for a generation, and they soon forget their mother tongue. Consequently few are really bilingual. We have always taught foreign languages in college and university, and more recently we have introduced them at the elementary level.

There is still much to be accomplished, however. Even our foreign diplomats are not required to know the language of the country to which they are sent. Edwin O. Reischauer, Kennedy's ambassador to Japan in the early 1960s, was the first American ambassador who could speak Japanese. He was an MK and his wife was a native of Japan. The Japanese loved it!

The British government sends its young men who are going into the diplomatic corps to the School of Oriental and African Languages. The Russians go one step farther. They train their diplomats from youth by selecting the sharp youngsters with linguistic gifts and sending them to a special school where they are immersed in the language and culture of the countries to which they hope to go.

If the men of the world attach that much importance to learning the language, it is incumbent on every missionary to see to it that he masters the language as soon as possible after reaching the field.

OBSERVATIONS

1. A knowledge of the vernacular is essential to missionary work. The effectiveness of a missionary depends to a large extent on his ability to communicate in the local language in a culturally relevant manner. English is readily understood by educated people in all former British colonies, and it is possible to get along with English, but that is not good enough. Also, it is always possible to use an interpreter, but this is rarely desirable unless the speaker is a person of world renown whom people will want to hear just to be able to say they have done so. It is conceivable that some short-term missionaries might have an effective ministry without learning the language, but this would be a rare exception. Other things being equal, missionary work cannot be effective over a long period of time without at least a working knowledge of the language.

2. Some missionaries have to learn two or three languages. Missionaries going to former Francophone Africa must learn French, the official language in many countries of Africa. For that reason it is necessary for them to spend at least a year in France, Belgium, or Switzerland studying French.

From France they may go to Zaire. There they will discover four trade languages, one of which they will have to learn. In addition they may have to learn a tribal language if they want to communicate effectively with the local people who know only the tribal dialect. The educated people will speak French. The businessmen and traders will speak the trade language. The rest of the people will speak one of the 250 tribal languages.

A similar situation arises in Angola, Mozambique, and Brazil, where Portuguese is the official language and all educated people speak it fluently. In addition there are trade languages and tribal dialects. Most missionaries in such situations must eventually learn three languages, which is no easy matter.

It is best to learn only one language at a time. A child can "pick up" two or three languages simultaneously. This he will do naturally as he plays with friends who speak the languages. The situation is different, however, with an adult. He must learn the language; he can't just pick it up. He will save himself endless trouble if he tackles them one at a time. It is important, therefore, that the missionary not be transferred to another language area until he has mastered the first language.

3. Not all languages are equally difficult. The easiest of all are those languages which use the English alphabet as the base such as French, German, Italian, Spanish, and other European languages. In many cases the pronunciation is similar if not identical. But the farther removed from English, the more difficult the language becomes for the American missionary to learn. It is obviously more difficult to master Chinese, Japanese, and Arabic than the languages of Europe. The written form of these languages has nothing in common with English or any language based on the English alphabet.

The Chinese ideographs, known as "characters," are the most difficult of all. There is no alphabet as we know it. Most Chinese words are made up of two parts, the radical and the phonetic. There are 214 radicals and 888 phonetics. The radical usually gives a clue to the meaning and the phonetic to the pronunciation. Possible combinations of the two are almost endless. To use the Chinese-English dictionary one must first master all the radicals in their proper order and be able to distinguish them from the phonetics. Each word is listed according to the radical and the number of strokes in the phonetic. To make matters worse, Chinese is a tonal language. In Mandarin there are four tones; in Cantonese there are nine! The same word spoken in nine different tones will have nine different meanings. Obviously, Chinese cannot be learned in "thirteen easy lessons." On the other hand, the grammar is simple—no tenses or conjugations of verbs and no gender of nouns. The Communists, in an effort to simplify the written language, have produced the Mao Script, in which the ten or more strokes of the more complicated characters have been reduced to three or four.

4. The need for proficiency differs according to the nature of the work.

From a linguistic point of view missionaries may be divided into four groups. The first group includes teachers in schools for missionaries' children, office secretaries, radio technicians, hostesses in mission homes, etc. They have little need for a knowledge of the language. Their work does not require that they speak the vernacular, though it does help if they want to travel, attend church, go visiting, or make purchases.

The second group includes physicians, surgeons, and other medical and technical personnel who are in daily contact with the people but are not required to do much teaching or preaching. They spend most of their time treating patients and this can be done with a small but selective vocabulary, with some help now and then from an interpreter. This is one reason why mission boards will accept doctors who are older than the other candidates.

The third group includes most general missionaries, especially evangelistic and church-planting missionaries whose main task is teaching and preaching. For them it is necessary to get a thorough grasp of the language, its vocabulary, grammar, idiom, pronunciation, etc. It is essential that the truth of the gospel be communicated fluently and accurately so that there will be no misunderstanding on the part of the listeners.

The fourth group comprises those who are engaged in full-time literature work as translators, writers, or editors. Bible translators must have a working knowledge of Greek and Hebrew as well as a complete mastery of the vernacular. The British and Foreign Bible Society will not accept a manuscript from any missionary who has not been in the culture for at least ten years. They believe that it takes that long for a person to learn the intricacies and nuances of a foreign language. It is easier to preach a sermon in a foreign language than it is to write an article or edit a magazine. That requires immense skill and finesse.

5. Success depends on several factors—aptitude, motivation, and opportunity. It is difficult to say which is the most important. There are those who favor motivation, saying that if a person is sufficiently motivated he can achieve his goal regardless of other factors. Barney and Larson take this view. "People with low aptitude can learn if they are motivated. At the same time people with very high aptitude test scores may fail miserably, because they lack motivation."[1]

Personally I am not persuaded that this is always the case. Most missionaries are highly motivated but not all do well at learning the language. Some have impaired their health in an effort to do so and have not succeeded. On the other hand, missionaries with linguistic skills usually breeze through the course with very little trouble. Those who are born mimics have no difficulty with the spoken language.

No less important is the matter of opportunity. Most languages require two or three years of arduous study. It is essential that conditions conducive to study be provided. If the new missionaries are expected to shoulder responsibility too soon they may never become fluent in the language and that will affect their entire future ministry. Mothers with small children are at a great disadvantage. They almost always fall behind their husbands, for the simple reason that their domestic duties occupy so much of their time and energy that they have little opportunity for study. Field superintendents should make sure that all new missionaries are given ample opportunity for the study of the language. It is not enough to set deadlines and impose penalties. Free time must be provided or the deadlines will come and go with no significant progress.

6. Language study is a long process. This may be a blessing in disguise, at least in the Orient.

> Simultaneous with the laborious process of mastering the subtleties of the language, is the harder task of exploring the involutions of an oriental mind, and it is providentially appointed that language is acquired but slowly. Were the gift of tongues so freely imparted that the newcomer could express himself easily from the beginning, his loss would far exceed his gain. Exuberances, enthusiasms and effusiveness are things to hold in check until he so handle the language that he knows exactly what its idiom conveys.[2]

We found that in China it took us about three years before we could readily understand everything that was said, but when it came to speaking

---

1. *Evangelical Missions Quarterly*, Fall, 1967, p. 36.
2. Mildred Cable and Francesca French, *Ambassadors for Christ* (London: Hodder & Stoughton, 1935), pp. 56, 57.

we were thinking in English and speaking in Chinese. That meant that somewhere between the brain and the lips it was necessary to shift gears. This made for halting speech. After another two years something in the brain clicked. We then began to *think* in Chinese and that made all the difference in the world.

As we have already said, some languages are more difficult to acquire than others, but even in the so-called "primitive" areas the languages are not as simple as one might expect. Dan Crawford discovered a language in Central Africa that has nouns in twelve genders and verbs with thirty-two tenses. In the Tetzell language there are twenty-five words for "carry."

Let it be said for the comfort of the timid that most missionaries, in spite of many discouragements and drawbacks, finally succeed in learning the language. According to a Missionary Research Library survey, failure to learn the language accounted for fewer than two percent of the dropouts. On the other hand, it must be admitted that only a small number of missionaries ever learn to speak like the nationals. Vocabulary is usually limited and pronunciation is seldom perfect. People who speak English with a German accent are likely to speak Quechua with a German accent also. The very best speakers are usually the MKs, who never had to learn the language; they picked it up as children and speak it with no trace of an accent.

One problem with missionaries is that they tend to be content with a limited vocabulary. After five or six years of formal language study they cease to be concerned about further progress. They have enough language to permit them to do their work with a fair degree of success. They forget that language assimilation is a lifelong process for most persons and they end up with what might be called a theological vocabulary, excellent for teaching and preaching but wholly inadequate for general use with students and other intellectuals.

To be really proficient the missionary should be able to read, write, and speak the language. Not many China missionaries ever learned to write the Chinese characters. They are too difficult and involved. They wrote their exams in the Romanized form; i.e., they used the English alphabet to spell out the sounds of the Chinese characters. When it was necessary to write a Chinese letter they got their teachers to do it for them. The few missionaries who made the effort to master the intricate Chinese characters were greatly appreciated by their Chinese colleagues.

7. Not all communication is at the same level. In Japan there are two levels of speech. One is used in ordinary conversation; the other, a more formal style, is used in preaching. In the Middle East there are three levels of Arabic: classical, newspaper, and spoken.

> *Classical Arabic is the language of the Bible and the Qur'an. It is extremely complex in comparison with spoken Arabic. The missionary must know this form of Arabic if he is ever to read the Bible, the Qur'an, or*

classical literature or if he ever hopes to write any tracts. Since Classical Arabic is thought by many Arabs to be the very language of God in Heaven, sermons are better received if they are preached in this form. With every insertion of a word of spoken Arabic, the sermon is considered to be that much more cheapened. Sermons in spoken Arabic are understood but not appreciated. On the other hand, sermons in Classical are admired but not understood, because only a very few Arabs receive a thorough education in Classical Arabic.[3]

All of this adds to the difficulties faced by the missionary when he starts to learn the language. It is always easier to engage in casual conversation than to deliver a formal sermon. In countries such as Japan, where form is as important as substance, it is essential that the missionary be able to communicate on both levels.

9. Missionaries should be placed according to language proficiency. So far as proficiency in the language is concerned, missionaries can be categorized as strong, normal, and weak. This fact should be borne in mind when assignments are made. Those with real language problems should not be sent where they will have to learn two or three languages. One new language will be all they can handle. Let others with more linguistic skill take on the more difficult assignments.

OBSTACLES TO LANGUAGE LEARNING

Some obstacles are subjective, others are objective. Some can be removed and others are a fact of life with which the missionary will have to live. In any case they prove to be a serious problem, especially if several are found in a given situation.

1. Lack of self-discipline. In the study of the language, self-discipline may make all the difference between success and failure. Unfortunately not all missionaries have mastered the art of self-discipline. In a structured program in language school they fare pretty well, doing the required work and keeping up with their peers. On their own, however, they find it exceedingly difficult to keep their nose to the grindstone hour after hour, day after day. They discover along with Solomon that much study is a weariness of the flesh (Ecc 12:12). And the farther they fall behind, the more apathetic they become.

2. Lack of adequate opportunities for study. Most missionaries spend the first year or two in a structured program of a language school or university. During this time they give ten to twelve hours each day to uninter-

3. Ray Marchand, "Square Pegs in Round Holes," *Baptist Mid-Missions Harvest Report*, Summer 1970.

rupted study. It is much different, however, when they leave the school and get out into the work. How much time will they have to devote to language study? Sometimes, through no fault of their own, they are suddenly burdened with responsibilities which take them away from their studies. The senior missionary falls sick or returns home on furlough, leaving the new missionary not only to fend for himself but also to assume responsibility for the work. In this case language study is bound to suffer, with results that may hinder his usefulness for the rest of his life. It is very important that the new missionary be spared this problem.

3. Lack of basic tools. This was a universal problem for the pioneers of the 19th century. Many of them had to begin from scratch and forge their own tools as they went along. This problem is not common today except in pioneer areas where the language has not yet been reduced to writing. In that case the missionary will have to prepare his own tools. This is not as difficult as it once was, for Wycliffe Bible Translators have developed scientific techniques that make language learning much easier than it used to be. A very helpful tool is *Language Acquisition Made Practical,* by Tom and Betty Brewster.

4. Lack of qualified teachers. Grammar and language analysis can be learned from senior missionaries, but reading and speaking must be learned from the nationals, preferably nationals with a good education and teaching experience. Such teachers are available in the language schools and the universities. The problem arises when the missionary is on his own. Such teachers may not be available, and if they are, he may not have the money to hire them. Each missionary's support figure should include an amount, however small, to help cover this expense.

5. Too many interruptions. Interruptions are bound to occur, but every effort should be made to keep them to a minimum. One missionary in Africa was transferred seven times during her first term of service. She found the experience so unsettling that she did not return for a second term.

Some interruptions cannot be avoided. The missionary may contract typhoid fever or infectious hepatitis and be out of service for several months. He may have to substitute for a missionary suddenly sent home on sick leave. Regardless of the occasion, any interruption will play havoc with his language study. If there are too many interruptions, he may never become a good speaker.

6. A tendency to discouragement. Rare is the missionary who can spend two or three years in language study without giving way to discouragement. After six months of concentrated study with little progress in the spoken language, he reaches saturation point. One day he says to himself: "This language is just too difficult. I'll never be able to master it." His mind may go back home to his pal in seminary who now has a flourishing church in California and is preaching eloquent sermons to a packed congregation every Sunday morning. His spirits may be so low that he wonders: "Why slug it out here when I could be preaching at home?"

At this point he should remember two things. First, he is not the only one who has felt that way. Second, God has promised wisdom to those who ask (James 1:5). One China missionary, a good friend of mine, was so utterly discouraged at his lack of progress in language school that he took time out to spend three days in prayer and fasting, asking God for special help. On the third day his attention was directed to Joshua 1:3, KJV: "Every place that the sole of your foot shall tread upon, that have I given unto you." He accepted this as God's message to him, and taking the textbook, *The Sacred Edict*, he put it on the floor and stood on it, thanking God for His promise of help. From that day he had no further trouble. He went on to learn the spoken language so fluently that he became the best speaker in the China Inland Mission. Later on he was asked to become the director of the mission's language school in Anking! God *does* answer prayer. He *does* give the ability to learn a difficult language. When discouragement comes the missionary, instead of giving up in despair, should seek help from God, who delights to give wisdom to those who ask.

ADVANTAGES OF LEARNING THE LANGUAGE

Learning a foreign language is always a difficult task, but it definitely pays off. There are several advantages.

1. It promotes rapport with the people. If the missionary is to be successful he must devise some way of ingratiating himself with the people among whom he has come to live and serve. There is no better way than to learn their language. This is the greatest compliment one can pay to any people. They will deeply appreciate the effort even if his language lacks finesse.

The most conspicuous thing about the missionary is his foreignness. It sticks out all over him—his white skin, his blue eyes, his fair hair, his big nose, sometimes even his loud mouth! People keep their distance, not knowing quite how to approach him, what to say, or how to behave—until he opens his mouth and speaks their language. Immediately they break into a broad smile. They know he must be their friend if he has learned their language.

2. It affords an insight into culture. In recent years a good deal of attention has been given to the gospel and culture. The two most important ingredients in any culture are language and religion. If the missionary is ever to understand and appreciate the culture he must have a working knowledge of both. Without this he will not get very far in his understanding of the people or their culture.

In these days of jet travel it is possible for the missionary to transport himself physically to any part of the globe in a matter of hours. It may take him months, even years, however, to arrive psychologically. This will not occur until he has come to understand the culture, and this can best be accomplished by learning the language.

3. It makes possible an effective communication of the gospel. In the Christian gospel the missionary believes he possesses the truth concerning God, man, sin, and salvation. This is a life-or-death message, depending on the reception given to it by the hearer, as Paul indicates in 2 Corinthians 2: 14–17. This being so, it is imperative that the gospel be preached in terms that can be readily understood. This is why missionaries in Africa take the pains to learn two, sometimes three, languages. To be really effective they must preach in the "heart" language of the people, the language to which they were born, the one they know best. They may know the trade language and have a smattering of French or English or Portuguese, but in order to comprehend the full import of the gospel they must hear it in their native tongue. Harold Cook tells of an educated Filipino who said to him one day: "English speaks to our heads; but our own language speaks to our hearts."[4]

One European missionary, fluent in seven languages, was asked in which language she prayed. She replied: "I pray in German; that's the language in which I was saved." To her, German was her heart language.

Charles Brent, Episcopal missionary to the Philippines in the early part of the century, deplored his inability to communicate effectively with the people:

> I get both impatient and sad because I am unable to speak the tongue of the people. It is the only way to reach and win them—to become one with them in language and life. The approaching Feast of the Nativity reminds one that God reached man by settling, so to speak, among the sons of men and reaching them through their own life, appealing to them in their own language. Who would venture to improve on God's way?[5]

4. It gives the missionary a sense of confidence. Part of culture shock is the missionary's sense of insecurity because of his inability to communicate. This should not last long enough to be a factor in his ministry. It is essential that the missionary have a sufficient command of the language, written and spoken, to enable him to cope with any situation as it develops. If he is dependent for information on friends and neighbors he will always be at a serious disadvantage. He should have such a grasp of the tribal dialect as well as the national language that he will be in command of the situation. This is especially true when the political situation deteriorates and decisions have to be made—decisions affecting the missionary, his family, and his work. At

4. Harold Cook, *An Introduction to the Study of Christian Missions* (Chicago: Moody Press, 1954), p. 130.
5. *Missiology*, July 1973, p. 385

home he will have to deal with contractors, repairmen, shopkeepers, public officials, and church leaders. On the road he will meet airline personnel, immigration officials, policemen, soldiers, even taxi drivers, all of whom could give him a hard time unless he can converse freely on a variety of subjects, not only the gospel. This was a problem during the Sino-Japanese War. The missionaries in occupied China didn't know Japanese so they were unable to hold their own with the Japanese officers who interrogated and harrassed them.

HOW BEST TO LEARN A LANGUAGE

There are tricks in every trade, and each missionary when he gets to the field will have to work out his own arrangements and methods for language study. There are, however, certain general principles which apply to every situation. The following suggestions should prove helpful.

1. **Learn the fundamentals at home.** With the exception of French and Spanish, it is not advisable to learn a foreign language in this country unless there are special circumstances that require it. During World War II Harvard, Yale, and a few other universities held crash courses in Chinese for the GIs going into the China theater of the war. The fundamentals of learning a language can be acquired before leaving for the field. Summer courses are available at the Toronto Institute of Linguistics and the Summer Institute of Linguistics (Wycliffe) in Norman, Oklahoma. The Toronto program is better for the general missionary. The Wycliffe program is much longer and more thorough, having been designed especially for Bible translators. Phonetics is an excellent introductory course which will be of immense value to any prospective missionary, regardless of where he goes or which language he has to learn.

2. **Take formal training on the field.** This should be done at a language school or university. In some countries there are special language schools which provide an excellent program for all expatriates wishing to learn the language. One of the best known schools is in Costa Rica, where thousands of missionaries have learned Spanish. In Europe there are universities which offer accelerated language courses for foreign students.

All missionaries should begin their language study in such a school or university if possible. The advantages include a structured program, fully qualified instructors, the latest audio facilities and equipment, an academic atmosphere conducive to serious study, peer students learning the same language, and living in the homes of nationals where the only language spoken is the one to be learned. Under these conditions the student makes rapid and solid progress. Under no circumstances should the new missionary try to go it alone when such services are available, regardless of the cost of the program.

3. Continue to study after language school. Language school usually lasts about a year. After it is over the missionary is on his own but he still has a good deal of hard study before him. It is imperative that the mission make provision for this second stage of the study program, which will probably continue through the remainder of the first term. Otherwise, the missionary is not likely ever to become an effective speaker.

The problem during this stage is one of time. It is essential that the missionary be free to pursue his study of the language unencumbered by other responsibilities. During the second year he will still spend most of his time in study. Only in his third year should he be expected to get into the work, and even then it should be a gradual process. He will find it helpful to read vernacular newspapers and listen to local radio broadcasts. One missionary in Zaire wrote:

> I find it helpful to subscribe to La Selection Hebdomadaire (weekly edition) of Le Monde, the leading Parisian newspaper; I listen to the Paris radio once or twice a day and read books in French. If I did not do this my French would rapidly slip, and I would be throwing away all the time that I had spent and all that the mission board invested in me.[6]

4. Take advantage of social contacts. The very best way to learn a language is to immerse oneself completely in the culture. A missionary to Japan wrote: "In my limited experience the language was mastered not by those whose scholarly abilities kept up a grueling study every day, but by those who got out among the people and found uses for what they had studied."[7]

Social contacts should not be restricted to church circles. Speaking of the situation in Africa a missionary wrote: "Social contacts have been woefully lacking. Most contacts between missionaries and Zairians have been in church, in meetings, in the context of their work, and on the level of employer to househelp—hardly the optimal contact for language learning."[8]

It is simply a matter of record that the missionary with the most fruitful contacts is the one who learns the language the best. The most rapid progress is made by a single missionary who lives with a national family. A couple in the same situation do not learn quite so fast, for they often succumb to the temptation to speak to each other in English. Unfortunately, when missionaries get together they invariably use English, thus impeding their progress in the language. They do the same in the home. This is a natural thing to do, especially if there are small children in the family and this is their only contact with English.

A China missionary who became very proficient in the language, attributed his prowess to the fact that as a single worker he spent two full years

6. Donald S. Deer, "The Missionary Language-learning Program," *Missiology: An International Review,* January 1975, p. 97.
7. Joseph L. Cannon, *For Missionaries Only* (Grand Rapids: Baker Book House, 1969), p. 64.
8. Deer, "Language-learning Program," p. 96.

with a team of Chinese evangelists, and for all that time he heard and spoke nothing but Chinese. That's the way to learn a language.

5. Begin speaking as soon as possible. The only way to learn a language is to *speak* it. In the early stages mistakes will be made and that scares many people. Two kinds of persons are reluctant to speak: introverts and perfectionists. Both refuse to speak the language until they can speak it well, but their motives are different. The introvert is shy, self-conscious, and retiring; he fears what others will think of his feeble efforts. The extrovert, on the other hand, couldn't care less what people think about him. He has a good time doing what he wants to do, and in doing it he makes progress.

The perfectionist has a different problem. He must measure up to his own high standards of performance, and if he doesn't, he clams up. Cannon says:

> Scholars are sometimes perfectionists and they are unwilling to go through the childish mistakes and embarrassment necessary to learning a foreign language. One must become a baby, a little child, with lisps and stutters, willing to be laughed at when a humorous error is made, willing to go through the monotony and humility of numerous repetitions and corrections.[9]

The nationals will laugh when an error is made, but their laughter ought to be a cue to the speaker that he has made a mistake. Imagine how difficult progress would be if the people didn't laugh! The new missionary should not fear the laughter of his friends or resent the criticisms of his teachers; he should welcome it. Stanley Jones used to say: "My critics are the unpaid guardians of my soul." The young missionary should be thankful for them.

6. Keep a notebook on hand. A very few missionaries are blessed with a photographic memory. Once introduced to a new word or phrase they have it in their mental computer forever. Such a person will have no need for a notebook. Most of us, however, will be wise to use one extensively, jotting down every new word, sound, saying, and proverb, with the appropriate English translation.

Keeping these items in a notebook enables one to review his vocabulary periodically, and there is no substitute for review. During my years in China I used small two-by-three cards on which I wrote thousands of new words, two-character combinations, and four-character expressions which I culled from the newspaper and picked up in conversation. On the back I wrote the English translation. I arranged the cards in bundles of a hundred and eventually had dozens of bundles. These I kept in a cloth bag which I took with me whenever I visited the rural churches. Between meetings I would go over the cards one by one. The difficult ones I kept at the top of the bundle;

9. Cannon, *Missionaries*, p. 65.

the others were allowed to drop to the bottom. In this way I was constantly reviewing. I continued this practice during all my fifteen years in China.

Language learning is a lifetime process. There is always more to learn, new words to be added to the vocabulary, new expressions to be mastered. I heard of one China missionary who, when he had finished his sixth and last examination, offered his Chinese-English dictionary to a young missionary, saying he had no further use for it! It goes without saying that he was not widely known for his knowledge of the language.

14

Enjoying Single Blessedness

Women on the mission field outnumber the men by a ratio of approximately six to four, which means that there are about 11,000 single ladies in the missionary force today whose chances of getting married are very slim. It doesn't seem to bother them, however; they took it into account when they decided on a missionary career.

In recent years, women volunteers have greatly outnumbered the men. Too many of the men are saying: "Here am I, Lord, send my sister." In some missions the ratio is higher than six to four. Interestingly enough, they are the missions working in the hard areas of the world. The more difficult and dangerous the work, the higher the ratio of women to men. The Red Sea Mission Team, working in what is doubtless the most difficult and barren of all mission fields, at one time had 13 couples, two single men, and 30 single ladies in its membership! This may be all right in these days when the women are demanding access to all jobs open to men, but it does seem incongruous that single women should so greatly outnumber the men in those places where the going is so hard.

HISTORICAL DEVELOPMENTS

The ratio was not always so high, however. In the early years of the modern missionary movement there were no single lady missionaries. The work was considered too difficult and dangerous for "unprotected" single ladies. Besides, women were not supposed to take a prominent part in church life. Their role was to be 'keeper of the home." A few single ladies

143

did go to the field, but they were already engaged and went out to make a home for a missionary already out there.

The prejudice against single lady missionaries was deepseated and long-standing. Some of this grew out of the biblical teaching concerning the place of women in public worship. Some of it was purely cultural and reflected the status of women in American society at that time. Women were expected to do no more than stand behind their menfolk, supporting missionary endeavors with their gifts and prayers.

The time came, however, when they were no longer content with such secondary roles. The first major breakthrough came in 1800 when Miss Mary Webb formed the Boston Female Society for Missionary Purposes. For several decades the main work of this society was to support home missions on the frontier and among the Indians. Cent Societies sprang up in various parts of New England. Membership requirements were simple: a cent a week, or 52 cents a year! During the first two years the Boston Female Society gave all its collections to the Massachusetts Missionary Society. Later on the funds were divided between the Congregationalists and the Baptists. First from Boston and then from a wider area, pennies flowed into the coffers of the Cent Society. In 1811 the Massachusetts Missionary Society received more than $1,200 from this source, most of which went for the purchase of Bibles, Testaments, hymnbooks, catechisms, spelling books, primers, etc., for home missionary work.

Following the formation of the American Board of Commissioners for Foreign Missions in 1810, women began to show an interest in service overseas. In 1812 they formed six Female Foreign Missionary Societies in Massachusetts and Connecticut. Single lady missionaries, however, got their start in home missions among the American Indians. Apparently the "reverend fathers" on the mission boards considered life among the Indians safer than life in "heathen" lands. In 1820 three young ladies were employed in Rhode Island and Massachusetts as schoolteachers by the Society for the Propagation of the Gospel among the Indians and Others in North America. Six other women, members of the United Foreign Mission Society, worked for a time among the Osages, west of the Mississippi River.

Little by little, prejudice against single lady missionaries in foreign service gave way to practical consideration. The missionary wives found it impossible to make a home for their husbands, raise a family, and meet the appalling needs of the women and girls on the field all at the same time. Once again necessity proved to be the mother of invention and single lady missionaries were accepted for foreign service, but not without opposition and misgiving on the part of many who considered such action unnecessary and irresponsible.

Cynthia Farrar made history when, as the first single lady to become a career missionary overseas, she was sent to India by the American Board of Commissioners in 1827. For thirty-five years she engaged in educational work among the girls, some of them high class caste Hindus. Single ladies were also sent to the Sandwich Islands during the 1830s. Other boards became involved and began sending out single women during that decade. In its first fifty years the American Board sent out 124 single women, thirty overseas and the remainder to Indian missions at home. In 1860 eleven were serving overseas and only four in Indian missions.

Then as now, the women considered the concessions made in their favor "too little and too late," so they took it upon themselves to establish their own missionary societies. The first was the Zenana and Bible Medical Mission founded in Great Britain in 1852. This was followed by the Woman's Union Missionary Society in Boston in 1860. Both of these societies retained their exclusively female membership until the 1960s, when recruitment and other problems prompted them to open their membership to men, married and single. The two missions merged in 1976. It is now known as the BMMF International. Other Female Societies included the Hancock Female Tract Society, the New Haven Female Education Society, and the Female Bible Societies of New York and Philadelphia. During the nineteenth century many of the mainline denominations formed their own Woman's Foreign Missionary Boards. These were fully autonomous sending and supporting agencies. They have long since been incorporated into the foreign boards of these denominations.

When single ladies first began going to the mission field it was with the understanding that they would go as members of a household. Apparently they still needed the "protection" that came from living with a married couple. When Charlotte White, a widow, made application to the American Board she stated: "My wishes are to reside in their family in the character of a sister to Mrs. Hough and a sister in the Lord." The mission took affirmative action: "Resolved, that the Board hear with pleasure the desire of sister White to attach herself to the family of brother Hough, to accompany them to India, and to render service to the mission."[1]

The single ladies were limited in their missionary activities. They could not minister to men so they turned their attention to the women and girls. In this area they served with distinction, in two directions: education and medicine. In those long ago days female education was unknown in mission lands; consequently the missionaries had to go from door to door imploring the parents to allow their girls to attend school. The notion was so novel that most of the parents were flabbergasted and refused to have anything to do with the missionaries. Others, however, realizing the advantages of education, permitted their girls to attend.

Some of these lady missionaries became outstanding educators and the schools they established developed into institutions of international reputation. They usually began in a single room in a missionary bungalow with a handful of shy, giggling girls. Before long they had a well organized school.

1. R. Pierce Beaver, *All Loves Excelling* (Grand Rapids: William B. Eerdmans Publishing Company, 1968), p. 65.

Elementary schools developed into high schools, and high schools into colleges and universities. Isabella Thoburn began in Lucknow (India) in 1870 with six little girls in a rented room and a man with a club outside the door to protect them. During thirty-one years of ministry, Miss Thoburn, a dynamic teacher and an able administrator, established a number of schools, trained Biblewomen, and engaged in other forms of missionary work. One development led to another until finally she founded a college for girls which was named the Isabella Thoburn College.

Lydia Mary Fay was the first single American woman missionary in China. In 1890 she opened a boarding school in Shanghai which became St. John's University. Some famous women's colleges were Ginling College in Nanking, the Woman's Christian College of Japan in Tokyo, the Woman's Christian College in Madras, and the American College for Girls in Istanbul. From a purely sociological point of view, female education was the greatest single contribution made by Christian missions to the elevation of women in the Third World.

Dame Edith Brown, honored by the British Crown, established a medical institution in Ludhiana in north India. Other famous women missionaries included Amy Carmichael and Mary Slessor. It is quite impossible to exaggerate the contribution made to Christian missions by the single ladies who helped to lead the way in the nineteenth century. The institutions they founded are still viable operations after more than a hundred years.

One of these famous women, Eleanor Macomber, had many great achievements in Burma in the first half of the nineteenth century:

> *The spectacle of a weak, friendless, lone woman removing from Maulmain to Dong Yhan, and there, with no husband, no father, no brother, establishing public worship, opening her house for prayer and praise, and gathering schools in the midst of wild and unlettered natives, is one of full moral grandeur. The idea of performing such work alone, the idea of a defenseless woman going into a besotted nation, among a drunken, sensual people, and lifting them up to the privileges of a refined faith, a pure religion, is an idea worthy of an angel.*[2]

OBSERVATIONS

In this discussion we are concerned with single *women*. Little or nothing will be said about single men until the end of the chapter, where a short treatment will be given. The reason for this is the fact that the overwhelming majority of single career missionaries are women. Few single men go out into the field. Those who do so usually manage to find a wife and establish a home within a year or two. In my day in China (1935–1950) there were only two men in the China Inland Mission that were not married, but there were

---

2. Daniel C. Eddy, *Ministering Women: Heroines of the Missionary Enterprise* (London: Arthur Hall, Virtue, n.d.), p. 124.

several hundred single ladies. Obviously any discussion of celibacy in missions should concentrate on the women.

1. The ratio of women to men. This is not nearly so high as is sometimes reported. It has been said that women outnumber the men two to one, three to one, even four or five to one. That may be true of one or two small missions, but it is not true across the board. Women *do* outnumber men, but the ratio is much more modest, approximately six to four. This may not be all bad. In fact, some consider it to be a good thing.

Mabel Williamson, herself a single missionary, said: "Before I came to the mission field I thought that the reason that there were more women than men on the field was that more women were wholly consecrated to the cause of Christ; but after I had been out for some time I changed my mind. Now I believe that God calls more women than men because *more women are needed.*"[3]

2. The ability to cope. Someone has said that if a person is not happy in his own home he won't be happy anywhere. This is true in the long run. Everyone needs a happy home if he is to derive any satisfaction from life. When it comes to making a home on the mission field, married couples, for obvious reasons, fare the best, and single women do a much better job than single men. Even married men, left on their own for any length of time, soon come to the end of their resources, and the house is reduced to a shambles. This past week I heard of a missionary friend on furlough who was keeping house for his children while his wife was away. Just before she returned, his oldest son said to him: "Gee, Dad, as a housekeeper you're a disaster!"

If this is true of married men, it is much more so of single men on the field. There are few sights more pathetic than two single men trying to fend for themselves. They call it "batching." It might be better termed "botching!" Mabel Williamson remarks: "Even where two single men are together, 'batching it' is usually a sorry business; but when the call of the Lord comes He will give grace. In that respect it is much easier for women. Two unmarried women can live together and make a home that seems like a home; most men do not seem to have that gift!"[4] That may be the understatement of the year!

With a little effort and ingenuity, single ladies can make a home that in all respects is as happy and wholesome as one established by a married couple. They usually have the artistic taste to make their home attractive, and their culinary ability guarantees wholesome, nutritious, well-balanced meals.

3. Marriage prospects are dim. The young lady who doesn't marry before going to the field has almost no chance of doing so after she gets there. The single man, on the other hand, has no such problem. At the annual field

3. Mabel Williamson, *Have We No Rights?* (Chicago: Moody Press, 1973), p. 62.
4. Ibid., pp. 64–65.

conference he will probably be the only eligible bachelor, surrounded by ten or twelve single ladies whose eyes are all turned in his direction. This is their one opportunity in the year to have personal contact with a prospective husband, and any observable response on his part is likely to set tongues wagging and hearts fluttering!

When a single lady volunteers for missionary service she knows that she probably faces single blessedness for the rest of her life. This is no mean consideration. It takes a strong personality as well as a dedicated heart to make that kind of decision.

Celibacy is not for everyone. Some try it and find that they don't have what it takes. Helen Roseveare was one of these. She writes: "I returned to England from my first missionary term with one determination: I would get married. . . . I wanted a fellow surgeon who would serve with me in the Congo. And I was willing to chuck everything to get what I wanted." Fortunately the Lord in His grace met her and satisfied the deepest longings of her heart and she returned to Zaire for another term of service. "Not only did the Lord bring satisfaction and release, but He also brought a new lightness of heart and a new joy. Then I saw other things. From that moment I realized the privilege of single service to God."[5]

Not all single missionaries achieve the victory that Dr. Roseveare did. Some refuse to return to the field after the first furlough unless they find a husband to go with them. Others become so desperate for love that they marry the first man, usually not a missionary, who proposes to them. In some cases it turns out well. Both husband and wife find ways of serving the Lord at home, some of them in the pastorate, others in business. It is unwise to pass judgment in such cases. Only the Lord and the person concerned know all that is involved. It is comforting to know that our heavenly Father knows our frame and remembers that we are dust (Psalm 103:14). No one who has not been through such an experience should criticize.

On the other hand there are many single missionaries who have no great desire to get married, and even if they do, they soon get over it. One of them wrote: "When I was in my twenties I sometimes vaguely hoped that I would get married some time; but with me it was never a strong desire. For most of my time on the mission field, I think I was really thankful that I wasn't married." She gave almost forty years to missionary service, first in China and later in a primitive part of the Philippines, and only mission policy persuaded her to retire at sixty-five.

Let no one imagine that remaining single holds no problems for Christians completely dedicated to the will of God. Dedicated persons, including missionaries, are human beings with God-given human instincts and desires, and when these basic desires are unmet there is bound to be some tension. Referring to this problem Evelyn Mumaw poses the question: "Can Christ really satisfy these longings?" Her reply is:

5. *Moody Monthy,* December 1976.

The answer depends on what the question means. If it means "Does having Christ in your life take away your desire to be married, or keep you from missing the companionship of a husband, or erase your biological hungers for sex fulfillment?" the answer is no. [6]

While the married state is to be regarded as normal in human society, one is not justified in assuming that somehow single persons are only "half" persons. Jesus was the only perfectly integrated person who ever lived and He enjoyed a life of celibacy. Miss Mumaw has a pertinent observation at this point:

The fact that Jesus Himself found it preferable to live and do His work as a single person is significant. Marriage was not a requirement for perfection of personhood or fulfillment of the highest purposes of His life. It is the privilege of the single adult to identify with Him in His singleness. [7]

4. Single missionaries are not wallflowers. Many single missionaries are among the most attractive women in the world. They are not single because they never had a chance to get married. Some of them had more than one offer of marriage before going to the field, but they rejected them because they didn't want anything, including marriage, to come between them and the Lord they had promised to serve on the mission field. This I consider to be the ultimate in personal dedication.

One missionary lady turned down a very attractive marriage proposal and went to Zambia. After five years on the field she returned home to find the young man still waiting for her. Again he proposed, but again she rejected him. She was called to missionary work and he was not; how could they become man and wife? She bravely returned to Zambia where she is still serving. That kind of dedication is not at all rare in mission circles.

With few exceptions the single lady missionaries are well integrated personalities—intelligent, competent, and articulate. They are every bit as attractive as their married colleagues.

5. Single missionaries do well. In spite of the handicaps under which they function, the single missionaries do exceedingly well. They are able to surmount their difficulties, solve their problems, sublimate their sexual desires, and harness all the powers of mind, heart, and will to the service of Christ. They are neither misfits nor problems. They did not choose the mission field because they could not "make it" at home; nor was the missionary career an escape from the more competitive vocations available in the homeland. They are usually socially well-adjusted persons, strong characters, self-reliant, self-effacing, and self-denying. They don't go around bemoaning their lot in life. Most of them are hard workers who have learned to

6. *The Gospel Message,* Spring 1978, p. 6.
7. Ibid.

endure hardness for Jesus' sake. They are found in all the difficult and dangerous places of the world, including pioneer work in primitive areas where only men should be expected to go. The churches at home and overseas owe a tremendous debt to the thousands of single ladies who have given themselves unreservedly to the work of missions.

They have done it all with no thought of recognition or reward. Seldom have they been elected or appointed to high office. Few have been given executive or administrative responsibility, though they have the ability to assume both. They haven't been in on the decision-making process even when their work and welfare were involved. Humbly, quietly, and cheerfully, they have done the work assigned to them without question or complaint. When it comes right down to missionary work they carry the lion's share. They do more than the missionary wives and often more than the missionary husbands. If they were to be suddenly withdrawn it is doubtful if the missionary enterprise could continue. It would certainly suffer a massive setback. Hats off to these gallant gals who have voluntarily foregone husband, home, and children in order to build the kingdom of God on earth. Great will be their reward in heaven!

ADVANTAGES

In spite of the many drawbacks to celibacy on the mission field there are several solid advantages, and these should be discussed.

1. Freedom from family responsibilities. From a purely personal and selfish point of view this is perhaps the greatest of all the advantages. It is the one mentioned most often when the single ladies are asked for an opinion.

The apostle Paul, himself either single or widowed, warned that married people have a price to pay. He called it "trouble in the flesh" (1 Cor 7:28). He went on to acknowledge that the married man cares for the things of the world, how he may please his wife, and the wife how she may please her husband; the single person, however, is concerned for the things of the Lord and how he may please Him (1 Cor 7:32–34). Other things being equal, this is a fair statement regarding the essential difference between matrimony and celibacy for the Christian. If this is true of life in general, and it is, it is much more so for those engaged in missionary work, which demands a different and more rigorous lifestyle.

Most missionary marriages result in children, usually three or four. This alone imposes a heavy burden on the parents, especially the mother. It almost removes her from missionary work while the children are young. With four children growing up, there will be young ones in the home for at least fifteen consecutive years. During that time the mother will be almost completely immobilized. The single missionaries are completely free of this great burden; consequently they can give all their time to language study, missionary work, and the cultivation of their own spiritual life. This is a great advantage.

Freedom from family responsibilities is especially desirable when war, drought, earthquake, famine, flood, or some other major disaster makes evacuation necessary. During the Sino-Japanese War and later during the civil war between the Nationalists and the Communists, I was separated from my wife and two boys on three occasions for a total of twenty-seven months. On each occasion they were on one side of the battle line and I on the other. During two of those separations letters did not get through for three months. My last thought at night and my first thought in the morning were: "I wonder how Winnie and the boys are." When our city of Fowyang was surrounded, first by the Japanese and later by the Communist armies, and everything on wheels had been commandeered by the military, evacuation with a wife and family was a nightmare. I couldn't help but think enviously of the Roman Catholic missionaries in the Jesuit mission in the same city. When the enemy was banging on the north gate of the city they could hop on their bicycles and escape through the south gate. Things weren't that simple for us.

The single missionaries have only their own safety to consider and half the time they don't bother about that. The older ones especially insist on remaining at their posts regardless of danger. They are prepared to face death rather than leave their Christian friends without the help and protection they can give. They say with Paul: "For to me to live is Christ; and to die is gain" (Phil 1:21, KJV). If worse comes to the worst and they get caught in the crossfire of the contending forces, or they are killed by an exploding bomb, or shot, accidentally or otherwise, by a drunken soldier, so what? They go home to heaven in a blaze of glory!

2. Closer contact with the nationals. "Nationals" in this context refers to women and girls, among whom most of their work is done. Single ladies can keep open house much more readily than a married couple can, especially if there are children around to care for. Women and girls visit in their homes at all times of the day or night, stay as long as they wish, and have the time of their lives. When mealtime comes it is a simple matter to add a cup of rice and a handful of vegetables to the pot. The single ladies feel free to visit the women in their homes, where again they may have a meal together.

Women and girls will think twice before barging in on a married couple for fear the husband may be present, or the children may need attention, or the mother may be busy. With the single ladies there are no such inhibitions. Their door is always open, and they always seem to have time to sit, to chat, to read the Scriptures, to sing, to pray. So it comes about that real rapport develops between the women and girls and the single missionary ladies.

Sadie Custer of the Overseas Missionary Fellowship spent over forty years in missionary service. Her ministry was Bible teaching in the rural churches. She stayed out for four to six weeks at a time, usually living in the homes of the nationals. In her testimony she said:

> God has promised a hundredfold to those who leave houses, or brothers, or sisters, or father or mother for the Lord's sake. He shall receive a hundredfold now in this time. The Lord has given me a thousandfold. Every time I went into a mud house in China, a board house in Malaysia, or a slate house in the mountains of Taiwan I accepted it as part of God's promise for now. And what shall I say of the brothers and sisters, fathers and mothers? One dear pastor's wife asked if she might call me "Mother" whereupon all the children of that congregation promptly gave me the title of "Grandma!"

Because of her close contacts with the nationals, the single missionary is in a much better position to appreciate and accept the national culture. Married couples with children almost have to retain a more Western lifestyle, whereas the single missionary, with only herself to think of, finds it easier to wear native dress, eat native food, and generally to adopt a native lifestyle.

3. **More time for the work.** Missionary wives make no bones about it; their first responsibility is to the family, not the work. As long as the children are young and need a mother's attention the mission agrees with them. Without family responsibilities the single ladies can give their entire time to the work.

The ladies who worked with us in North Anhwei were "on the road" most of the time. One of them conducted reading classes for the country women. Each session lasted three weeks; she then moved on to the next place and repeated the performance. Two other ladies were engaged in a short-term Bible school ministry for the outstation leaders in eight districts. Each school lasted six weeks; they then moved on to another place for another six weeks. In the slack seasons when the country people had more free time, the ladies were on the road for months on end, teaching six or eight hours a day, six days a week, with two or three meetings on Sunday. They did more work in a year than the married women were able to accomplish in a whole term.

4. **Greater proficiency in the language.** The men in our mission were obliged to complete six sections of formal language study, each culminating in a ten-hour written and oral exam. Each section required the best part of a year of hard work. The women had to do only four sections, but many of the single ladies did all six sections required of the men. All missionaries were expected to *read* and *speak* Chinese. No one, not even the men, was required to learn to write more than 1,000 characters. The single ladies in our part of North Anhwei, however, went the second mile and learned to write the beautiful but complicated Chinese characters with such proficiency that they were able to write their own Chinese letters instead of asking their teachers to write for them.

Because they had more time for individual study they did well with the book work, and because of their close and constant contact with the nationals they learned the spoken language much more quickly and accurately than the married women were able to. As a matter of fact, many of the married women had difficulty getting through the four required language sections before furlough. The only way to learn to swim is to *swim*. The only way to learn to speak a foreign language is to *speak* it; and because the single ladies had more opportunities to speak they usually surpassed the married women in language proficiency.

5. Greater freedom of movement. One of the bugbears of missions is the shortage of workers. When a missionary falls sick or goes home on furlough or for any other reason must leave his place of service, someone must be sent to fill the vacancy. In a large mission with many stations and much coming and going, the procedure sometimes resembles musical chairs. In such a situation it is helpful to have people who are mobile, who can be transferred from one place to another with a minimum of disruption to all concerned. The single worker can make a real contribution in these circumstances. She can pack all her worldly goods and chattels on a wheelbarrow, or a sampan, or a small motor launch and proceed without further difficulty or delay to the new assignment; and when she gets there she can settle in in a matter of hours.

Moving a family is something else. Besides personal effects for two parents and three or four children, there are books, bedding, furniture, pictures, kitchen utensils, toys, and many other things essential to family life.

6. Personal support less expensive. The very best investment of the missionary dollar is in the personal support of an unmarried missionary. It has become exceedingly costly to support a missionary family with three or four children when only one person is engaged in full-time missionary work. Not only do the children have to be supported while they are at home, their support must continue when they go to school. To this must be added the expense of operating a school for them. With 300 students, 20 missionary teachers, dozens of helpers and servants, utilities, food, books, supplies, and other items, it is an expensive undertaking.

This is an area where Roman Catholic missionaries have an advantage over the Protestant missionaries. They all take a vow of celibacy; consequently, there are no children to worry about. If celibacy prevailed among Protestant missionaries the individual support figure would be cut in half.

DISADVANTAGES

It would be nice to be able to say that there are no disadvantages, but that would not be true. In this, as in most other things, there are liabilities as well as assets. We now examine briefly some of the disadvantages, though it is apparent that they are far outweighed by the advantages.

1. The stigma of celibacy. Someone has said that a man is only half a man until he is married; the same has probably been said of a woman. Even in Western society, until very recent times an unmarried person has been regarded as an anomaly. This attitude is much more pronounced in the Third World, where celibacy is practically unknown.

Throughout the non-Western world, people have always married young, established large families, idolized children and grandchildren, and generally supported and strengthened family ties. In many societies the social unit is the extended family, which may include forty or fifty persons spread over three or even four generations. Celibacy is unknown in situations like this.

This means that the single missionary is something of an oddity to the nationals. All kinds of questions are asked: How old are you? Why aren't you married? Why didn't your parents arrange for a marriage? Can't you have children? Who will support you when you are old? The questions go on and on, and the missionary is expected to give a full and frank reply to all of them. This idea must not be overdone, however. They come to accept the fact that she is single and completely overlook it in time. Several things contribute to this change of attitude. They know she is a foreigner and they expect foreigners to be different. They recognize her superior education and they respect her for that. Most of all, they experience her Christian love and compassion, and people the world over respond to love.

2. No choice of companions. Missionaries are usually assigned to certain cities and institutions by the field council. Seldom do they consult the wishes of the persons involved. It is assumed that missionaries can get along together without too much trouble. As a result, incompatibility may become a problem.

When a new worker is expected, all kinds of questions run through the mind: What will the other girl be like? How will I relate to her? What about her background, upbringing, education, hobbies? Does she have any idiosyncrasies? Is she an introvert or an extrovert? Will she be loquacious and bore me with her everlasting chatter? Will she object to my playing the violin in the evening? Will she share my interest in art, my love of music, my passion for neatness? Will she insist on going to bed early when I like to burn the midnight oil? Is she fussy about her food or will she eat anything I put before her? Will she carry her full share of the household chores or will I have to do it all? Similar questions plague the thinking of the new missionary. She is apprehensive about her senior missionary.

The problem of incompatibility should not be underestimated. It is the greatest single problem in interpersonal relationships. Here in the U.S. it is reckoned that 35 percent of all persons who change their jobs do so because they can't get along either with the boss or with their fellow employees. But on the mission field such an option is not open. Missionaries have no voice in the choice of their fellow workers, nor are they allowed, except in extreme cases, to change jobs. They are expected to stay where they are and "work things out." The Holy Spirit does give grace, but the human factors are always present and they don't yield easily even to the influence of the Holy Spirit. If incompatibility reaches the point where both individuals are virtually incapacitated for spiritual work, to say nothing of spiritual warfare, the mission should step in and separate the two. There is biblical precedent for such action. Paul and Barnabas had the problem of incompatibility to contend with and they could not solve it, so they went their separate ways (Acts 15:36–41).

3. A sense of loneliness. Even though single workers do not usually live alone, there is still a gnawing sense of loneliness.

> *If single workers could share the most difficult part of their work, they would probably agree that it is loneliness. Married folks have each other and their families. Single folks have their work and a busy life among the multitudes of people, but they can face loneliness at the end of a busy day and be far away from any with whom they can share their joys and burdens.*[8]

In the last few decades Western lifestyles have changed remarkably. Children are no longer wanted; it costs too much to rear them. Besides, they interfere with one's freedom. Increasingly, young people are settling for the single life, or they are putting off marriage until some future time. This has made it necessary for the churches to introduce a new program to meet the needs of a new group, the single adults. Apparently these persons are not troubled by loneliness or they wouldn't have chosen the single lifestyle.

It should be remembered, however, that single blessedness in the U.S. is different from the same thing on the mission field. Here the single ladies have an almost unlimited variety of options before them. They may live in beautifully appointed apartments with all the modern conveniences. With the "equal pay for equal work" syndrome in full operation, their salaries are high enough to enable them to do whatever they please. For relaxation they can chat on the phone, watch color television, or read the daily paper or the weekly newsmagazines. When they want to get away from the apartment they can go to church, attend a movie, go to a concert, or attend cultural or sporting events. When they get fed up with their own cooking they have a choice of a dozen nearby restaurants. With a car at their disposal they can head for the hills or the shore any weekend they wish. With indoor swimming pools, tennis courts, sauna baths, and skating rinks, they can enjoy their favorite sports twelve months of the year. They may spend their summer vacation in Europe, the Christmas holidays in Florida, or Easter in California. It would be surprising if, with all these diversions, our single gals were afflicted with loneliness!

8. Marjorie A. Collins, *Manual for Accepted Missionary Candidates* (South Pasadena, CA: William Carey Library, 1972), p. 87.

But the single missionary finds herself in an entirely different world where most of these social, recreational, and cultural amenities are not available, and if they are, she has neither the time nor the money to take advantage of them.

The single missionary's only diversion is her work. After a stint among the rural churches she returns to the city, but it is hardly "coming home." She doesn't have a home in the real sense of the word, and returning to a fellow worker is hardly the same as coming home to a wife and family. When she gets home she may find that her fellow worker has just left for a short-term Bible school in the west district, so she returns to an empty house. Is that really coming home?

4. Limitations of effectiveness. The fact that society in most of the Third World is dominated by men means that the single lady missionary has a number of strikes against her. She can have a marvelous ministry among the women and girls, and this should never be minimized, but that very fact tends to diminish her opportunities for ministry among the men.

The Third World is rapidly being influenced by Western culture (not always by its best features) and little by little the women are being liberated, but they are still usually regarded as second-class citizens and are expected to know and keep their proper place in society. It is difficult, therefore, for the men to regard the single lady missionary as an equal in their work.

The situation is further complicated by the rigid segregation of the sexes. Men and women sit in different parts of the church. Husbands and wives are seldom seen on the street together. For a man to be caught in private conversation with a member of the opposite sex would be sure to excite suspicion if not to invite censure.

This being so, the single lady missionary is limited in what she can do with and for the men. She will have to exercise great caution and discretion in all her contacts so that everything is open and aboveboard and there is no occasion whatever for gossip or scandal.

Wherever the work is initiated by single ladies the church is likely to be made up largely of women and girls. It will be difficult to attract men. The church, therefore, will lack leadership and may take years to get on its feet. Once firmly established, however, the few men members will more readily accept leadership posts offered to them. So there are compensating factors, though it is correct to say that on the whole it is difficult for single ladies to establish and bring to maturity a strong, well-balanced, indigenous church.

LIVING ARRANGEMENTS

In the beginning God said, "It is not good for man to dwell alone." The word "man" in that instance is used in the generic sense; it includes the woman also. When Jesus sent out the twelve and the seventy He sent them two by two. On each of his three missionary journeys Paul had at least one companion, sometimes more. When he broke with Barnabas, he chose Silas to take his place rather than go on alone.

It is an act of folly for a single lady missionary to live and labor all by herself. It may be necessary in rare instances for a short time, but it should never become the rule. That was the problem with Margaret Sparhawk in Elisabeth Elliot's novel, *No Graven Image*. She was entirely on her own and as a result had some traumatic experiences. For reasons of safety, companionship, and propriety a single lady should always have a fellow worker. This can be arranged in a number of ways.

1. Living with a married couple. This was the common practice in the nineteenth century. In those days most of the single ladies went out with the understanding and purpose of becoming part of an existing missionary household. They were expected, among other things, to help the missionary wife with the care and education of the children and, when needed, with the household chores. This is no longer the practice. Some single ladies may live with a married couple, but that is the exception. It is much better than living alone, but it has problems both for the single person and for the couple. If there are children, that becomes an additional complication.

The great benefit for the single lady is that she doesn't have to set up house for herself nor does she have to worry about making meals and handling servants. She will, however, forever feel that she is an outsider and therefore doesn't really "belong." She may feel that her presence in the dining-room twenty-one times a week is hard on the privacy of the couple— and it is.

One advantage accruing to the couple is that when the man of the house is away for weeks on end, as some of them are, the wife has a companion. Young children may become a problem for the single worker, however. They may impose on her good nature and make demands on her time and strength to the point of frustration. On the whole the arrangement is not a good one.

2. Living with other single workers. This is a big improvement on living with a family. Two single ladies on a station are better than three. Where there are three there is always a tendency for two to form a close relationship at the expense of the third. If this continues for any length of time it is bound to affect the morale of the station.

If two ladies live together, compatibility is of the utmost importance. Without a certain degree of basic compatibility life can be very trying, making it impossible for the partnership to continue.

In the larger centers, where there may be thirty or forty missionaries, the single ladies may decide to set up house together. With six or seven in the group they have a viable operation with all kinds of fellowship and fun. Here compatibility is not so important, for the larger group offers a variety of personality traits.

When all things are considered, the single lady missionaries manage to hit it off pretty well. Some remain together on the same station for years, some for decades.

3. **Living with nationals.** Some missions arrange for their new missionaries, married and single, to live with a national family for a year or two while they are learning the language. This is an excellent way to master a language, but is hard on the patience, both of the missionaries and of the national family.

Some single ladies strike up a close friendship with a Biblewoman or a school teacher or a medical technician, and they decide to live together. This too is an excellent arrangment, but it has its drawbacks. At what level will they live? The level of the missionary or the level of the national worker? Will they eat food cooked in Western style or national style? Will such a close friendship between a missionary and a national excite jealousy on the part of other national workers who would like the "prestige" of living in the home of a missionary? On the other hand, would the other missionaries resent the fact that one of their own has shattered missionary solidarity by forging such close links with a national worker? Does the national possess enough "sophistication" to enable the two persons to live together over a long period of time in genuine harmony?

ROLES THEY CAN FILL

In spite of the handicaps discussed in the foregoing pages, the fact remains that single women missionaries are still needed and still wanted by both church and mission leaders in all parts of the world. They are today filling every conceivable role in missionary ranks, from management positions to photography and radio announcing. According to a study prepared for the Evangelical Foreign Missions Association Executives' Retreat in 1965 by D. L. Cornell, General Secretary of Worldwide Evangelization Crusade, 5,867 single lady missionaries were engaged in forty different kinds of work divided into six categories: Business and Administration (426); General Missionary Work (1763); Educational Work (1628); Medical Work (1274); Literature (734); and Radio and Recording (42).

Nurses, with a total of 1117, were at the top of the list, followed by general evangelism (898), secondary school teachers (470), linguists/translators (444), elementary school teachers (361), Bible school teachers (322), teachers in schools for MKs (284), and general office/stenographic workers (281). Thirty-eight are listed under office management. Only three or four could be considered executives and they belonged at that time to two missions made up of women only.

Evangelical missions have been slow to open executive posts to women, single or married. A minor breakthrough came in September 1978 when Dr.

Lois McKinney of Conservative Baptists was appointed Director of CAMEO (Committee to Assist Ministry Education Overseas). It is to be hoped that in the near future women missionaries will be appointed or elected to the decision-making bodies of the various boards and committees. A beginning has been made in field committees, where women missionaries are serving in various capacities, but very few boards on the home front have women members. If women outnumber the men six to four it would seem only right that they should have more than token representation in administrative posts.

That women are capable of holding executive positions has been demonstrated on more than one occasion. For over forty years Amy Carmichael was the director of the Dohnavur Fellowship in India. Miss Joy Ridderhoff was the founder and for almost forty years the director of Gospel Recordings. For many years Mrs. Wallace Paddon was president of the Woman's Union Missionary Society. She was followed by her husband, who remained in office until it merged with the BMMF International in 1976.

As more and more young women in the Third World go on for higher education and from there into the professions, often as single persons, the role of the single woman missionary will become increasingly easy and accepted. Her success will depend on a number of factors: age, academic background, professional competence, ability to articulate, and, above all, spiritual insight and influence. Humility and sincerity continue to be definite assets. In other words, sex is becoming less and less important. If the missionary can deliver the goods, she will be accepted by almost everyone.

In certain cultures she will still have to exhibit a "meek and quiet spirit" if she wants to have an effective ministry. She must not be so aggressive that she will be accused of lording it over the national pastors. In Africa, where the Christians have come from a tribal background, the pastors have taken the place, at least in the minds of their parishioners, of the tribal chiefs. They therefore tend to be dictatorial, and the people wish to have it that way; they are comfortable with this arrangement. A similar situation exists in Japan, where the pastors, all of them highly educated, call the shots and expect the churches to follow their leadership. In all cultures of this kind the single woman missionary, regardless of her gifts and achievements, will have to walk softly and accept gladly the leadership of strong-minded pastors. If she can do that there should be no trouble.

A final word about the single woman missionary:

> *Clearly, the most important thing about a woman in the mind of God is not whether she is single or married, but whether she is rightly related to the Lord and His church. Whether she is single or married is important only as it relates to the will of God for her life.* [9]

9. *The Gospel Message*, Spring 1978, p. 6.

A WORD ABOUT SINGLE MEN

The time has come to give serious consideration to the advisability of calling for an elite corps of single men who will forego marriage for at least one term of service. They are needed to maintain and strengthen the Christian presence in certain parts of the world where the political situation is so explosive as to make it unwise to send families or single women. Missionaries of the Roman Catholic Church, because they are single, have been able to remain at their posts when Protestant missionaries were obliged to withdraw.

Conditions since World War II have been the most turbulent in the history of modern missions. Never in the last three centuries has there been such widespread social unrest, economic chaos, and political instability. In country after country, church and mission work has been disrupted: Nigeria, Zaire, Chad, Burundi, Ethiopia, Rhodesia, China, Vietnam, Laos, Cambodia, Sudan, Egypt, Burma, Chile, Cuba, Iraq, Malaysia, Thailand, Pakistan, India, and the list goes on. In some countries the missionaries were expelled. In others they left of their own accord when the situation became untenable. In nearly every instance casualties were sustained. In Rhodesia and Zaire whole families were wiped out.

The question arises: Is it right to send women and children into these danger zones when the risk to life and limb is so great? Has the time not come to call for a corps of Christian commandos—the spiritual counterpart of the U.S. Marines—who, because they are young, strong, brave, and free, will be able to man the Christian outposts in the various danger spots around the world.

Non-Christians all over the world—Communists, nationalists, revolutionaries, terrorists, guerrillas—are on the march, giving themselves without reserve and without regret to social and political crusades in all six continents. They have one consuming passion: to change the world and make it over in their image. To achieve their purpose they are willing to forego home, family, friends, fortune, and if necessary, life itself. Is the Christian church in our day unable to match this kind of dedication? If so, the future is dark indeed.

15

Being a Wife

Being a wife, at home or abroad, is both a high privilege and a sacred responsibility. After creating Adam, God said that it was not good for man to dwell alone, so He proceeded to make a mate for him. Woman, therefore, is the completion of man. Solomon said: "Whoso findeth a wife findeth a good thing, and obtaineth favor of the Lord" (Prov 18:22, KJV).

If this is true of men in general it is even more true of missionaries who live and labor in a foreign culture. Perhaps that is one reason why there are so few unmarried men on the mission field. They may go out single, but they don't remain single very long. Almost without exception they soon marry, and if later on they become widowers they marry again. William Carey had three wives; so did Adoniram Judson. Hudson Taylor had two.

MISSIONARY WIVES DIFFER FROM THEIR STATESIDE COUNTERPARTS

This they do in a number of ways.

1. They are more directly involved in the work. Pastors' wives help out in various capacities, such as singing in the choir and teaching a Sunday School class; but very few of them are directly involved in church work, certainly not to the same extent as missionary wives on the field. They are full members of the mission and are expected to make their full contribution. When they have small children to care for, they must of necessity give some time to them, but that is not their prime occupation. Later on when the children go to school they give their full time to the work.

161

2. They work more closely with their husbands. Both are full-time missionaries and engaged in the same work. He may be a doctor, she a nurse. He may be a school principal, she a teacher. He may be a radio technician, she a script writer. In all instances they work in the same institution under the same auspices.

3. They are more directly involved in the life of their children. In America the children spend a good part of the day in school. After school they play with their friends and come home only when darkness puts an end to their activities. Even when they are at home in the evening hours, they probably spend most of the time in their room doing homework or watching TV.

It is not so with the missionary family. During the early years the mother is totally responsible for her children's welfare and hardly lets them out of her sight. If they don't go to a boarding school she becomes their teacher. In sickness she is their nurse. She is always there when they need her. It is no wonder that a very strong bond of affection develops between the missionary mother and her children.

MISSIONARY WIVES DIFFER FROM OTHER EXPATRIATE WIVES

Missionaries are not the only ones who live abroad. Businessmen, professionals and military and diplomatic personnel outnumber the missionaries, and most of them have wives. Missionary wives, however, differ from the others in several respects.

1. They have to meet stiff qualifications. The other wives go out as homemakers for their husbands and no qualifications are required of them. The sponsoring agency, be it private or public, is interested only in the husband, who is an employee of the agency. This is not true of missionary wives. They have to meet the same high standards—physical, intellectual, psychological, and spiritual—as their husbands. If they don't measure up, both they and their husbands are disqualified.

2. They are regarded as full-time members of the sponsoring agency. In their case it is the mission board. They have the same rights and privileges as their husbands, including the same remuneration. The other wives are not employees of the sponsoring agency, nor do they receive any remuneration. The husband is given a fixed salary regardless of whether he is single or married.

3. They enjoy a more satisfying lifestyle. They can't afford the luxuries available to the business and professional people, nor do they have access to the PX like the military and diplomatic personnel, but in spite of that they live a fuller, richer, more productive life than the other wives. They are living examples of the fact that a man's life does not consist in the abundance of things that he possesses (Luke 12:15). They derive their satisfaction not from their environment but from their work, their husbands, their children, and their Christian friends, many of whom are their own converts. They know the language and thus can enjoy a quiet social life, converse freely with friends, neighbors, students, merchants, peasants, soldiers, workmen, local officials, school teachers, and a host of other interesting people, all of whom add greatly to the enrichment of life. The other wives, unable to speak the language, are confined to the American "ghetto" where they are caught up in a highly organized social whirl which includes bridge parties in the morning, cocktails in the afternoon, and dinners in the evening, always with the same people. It doesn't take long for that kind of lifestyle to pall.

4. They stand up better under pressure. The casualty rate among other wives is distressingly high. Many business firms have found that the high turnover among overseas employees is due in considerable measure to the wives' failure to adjust.

> *The women, perhaps more than the men, have been unable to cope with the shocks of differences and the pressures of change and uncertainty. While their husbands have usually had some experience in dealing with representatives from overseas, the wives have been thrown into a new environment with little or no knowledge of their role. . . . In a few cases, promising young men in foreign service have transferred or terminated because of the frustrations or behavioral errors of their wives.* [1]

This happens even though such families are given fabulous salaries to induce them to go abroad and furnished with special bonuses to compensate for accepting a "hardship post."

Missionary wives, on the other hand, have a "sense of call" which enables them to endure greater hardships with fewer amenities and do it cheerfully for Christ's sake. That makes all the difference in the world.

GETTING A HUSBAND

Forty years ago most new missionaries went out single, which meant that they had to find a mate after they reached the field. Today the situation has changed. The majority of men go out married. This has obvious advantages. Almost half of the women go out single. Most of them remain single for the rest of their lives, the reason being that there are not enough men to go around.

1. Courtship. This is rendered difficult by two factors. First, the choice is very limited, opportunities to meet eligible bachelors being few and far

1. John Rosengrant, *Assignment Overseas* (New York: Thomas Y. Crowell, 1966), pp. 101–102.

between. Second, once engaged it is exceedingly difficult to carry on a normal kind of courtship.

Other things being equal, missionaries would rather marry other missionaries, preferably in their own mission. This causes the fewest problems. But in any country the bachelors in one's own mission are few indeed—one or two at the most. It is possible to marry outside the mission, in which case the wife usually joins the husband's mission. She might marry a non-missionary, but then she would have to give up her missionary career.

Missionaries usually meet once a year at the annual field conference. This is the time when romances are likely to blossom. The conference lasts only one week, however; that doesn't give either party much time for reflection. Whatever is done has to be done in a hurry! It is not unusual for an engagement to be announced at the close of the conference. How can the couple be assured that there is sufficient compatibility to make a happy marriage? Of necessity some risks must be taken.

The period of courtship is short and not always sweet. When the conference is over, the couple go their separate ways, not to meet again, perhaps, until the wedding day. Courtship can be carried on by correspondence, but it is a poor substitute for the physical presence, especially when the mails are uncertain at best. In some countries, China for instance, the couple could not be seen together in public anyway, since this would offend the sensibilities of the people. According to Chinese custom the bride and groom never exchanged a word or a glance until their wedding day! Apparently missionaries found a way around some of these extreme social customs, but it was not easy.

The following paragraphs, taken from a prayer letter from Thailand, give a good picture of how it works on the mission field.

> On the eve of my ascent up into Miaoland I must share with you the wonderful thing God has done for me. He has joined my heart in love and betrothal to Don Rulison. I can't tell you all the details, but I will try to show a little of how your prayers for His will have been answered.
>
> I went through five days of conference blissfully busy taking notes as one of the secretaries and absolutely oblivious of what was about to occur. Then when the conference had closed, within twenty-four short hours Don had opened his heart to me and God gave me perfect peace to decide to be his wife and help-meet.
>
> Don left almost immediately for his station. The Carlsons asked him to come back so that we could have time together and so he returned on Thanksgiving Day. . . . We had a golden week together in Chiengmai before we boarded the train to a common parting place from which Don went west and I went east with my two fellow-workers. Mail deliveries will be comparatively infrequent, so we are cast on the Lord for everything.

2. Marriage. Weddings on the mission field, especially in the less-developed countries, are much less elaborate than here at home. It's just as well since both the finances and the facilities are often lacking. A China missionary on his way to his wedding was accosted by bandits who robbed him of his possessions. At the wedding, when they came to the part of the ceremony where the groom says to his bride, "With all my earthly goods I thee endow," a fellow missionary in the second row nudged the colleague sitting beside him and whispered: "There go his Bible and toothbrush!" During the Sino-Japanese War one missionary bride made her wedding dress from a nylon parachute used by an American airman who bailed out over China.

In many instances it is necessary to have two ceremonies—a civil one to make it legal and a religious one to make it meaningful. One couple wrote: "After two weddings in two churches, by two pastors in two countries, on two continents on the same day, we now feel well married." That took some hustling!

The wedding, though it may be simple, is usually a well planned, well executed, and meaningful service. Many of the expensive frills that are a necessary part of a homeside wedding are missing, but with substitution and improvisation it is usually surprisingly beautiful. The biggest drawback is the absence of relatives, especially parents, but with jet travel and more money and time, some parents do fly out for the wedding. Occasionally the couple will wait until furlough when they can have the wedding at home.

The absence of friends and relatives from home is compensated for by the presence of local Christians and nationals from other countries. One account read: "Our wedding day began at 10:00 a.m. with our religious ceremony and garden reception at the North Africa Mission Chapel in Tangier. About 100 people attended, representing eleven nationalities, American, English, Spanish, French, Arabic, German, Dutch, Jewish, Cuban, Canadian and Swiss." What missionary wouldn't feel happy in an international gathering like that?

RELATING TO HER HUSBAND

This is not always easy under the best of conditions. It is sometimes very difficult on the mission field. While both husband and wife are missionaries of equal standing, where they will live and what they will do are generally determined by the gifts and vocation of the husband. The wife goes with him to be his helpmeet, to make a home for him and the children, and to do the hundred-and-one other things that fall to the lot of the wife in traditional society.

The wife's role on the mission field is basically the same as that of the wife at home. In both instances she is responsible for establishing and maintaining the home and caring for the physical and emotional needs of the family.

Let no one be deceived, however, into making the facile assumption that there exists a high positive correlation between the two roles, for they are performed within a specific social structure, cultural setting, and physical environment. All three are radically different for the missionary than they are for her sisters here in the U.S. In male dominated societies, such as Latin America, the Orient, and the Muslim world, the missionary wife is expected to be subservient to her husband, at least in public.

The amount of time that a husband and wife spend together can place a strain on their relationship. In some cases they see too much of each other. They not only live together but they work together. That means that they are together seven days a week with little or no diversion or company. After a while that can become a problem. In America, some senior citizens fear the coming of retirement. The wife says: "I don't know how I'm going to adjust to having Harry at home all the time." Well, on the mission field some couples don't have to wait until retirement to experience that problem. Harry is always at home!

Then there is the other extreme: the husband who is seldom at home. Some husbands are out on preaching tours for weeks on end, and the wife is left to fend for herself with three or four children to care for. Worse still, there may be long periods of separation occasioned by some upheaval such as famine, civil war, plague, revolution, etc. During such times it is customary for the women and children to be evacuated while the husbands remain at the station. It may be months before they see each other again, and in the meantime mails may be disrupted.

DIVISION OF LABOR

We have already remarked on the fact that missionary wives are closely involved in the mission work. This may be a problem. The husband may make unreasonable demands of his wife to the point where she will actually become ill, either physically or emotionally. Some husbands are so devoted to the work that they neglect their duty to their wives and children. The husband has all the excitement of traveling, teaching, preaching, ministering, etc., while the wife remains at home burdened with household responsibilities and the care of the children, and with no one of her intellectual caliber with whom she can have fellowship. Pearl Buck's father was one of these hard-working, dedicated missionaries who left his wife and children for long periods of time. The story, a rather sad one, is told in her book, *The Fighting Angel*. Not a few missionary couples have come to grief over this kind of problem.

On the other hand, the wife can be too demanding and expect her husband to help her with the chores and the children, to the neglect of the work. This tendency is more prevalent in American women than those of other nationalities. American husbands as a rule give their wives more help than any other men in the world. It is part of our way of life. When the wife gets to the field and finds herself without many of the amenities of American civilization her tendency is to fall back on her ever loving, ever willing husband. Before long he may be giving an abnormal amount of time and energy to domestic affairs which are rightfully the responsibility of the wife. This does not go unnoticed by the nationals. Juan Isais in his intriguing book, *The Other Side of the Coin,* conjures up an imaginary situation where nationals and missionaries are engaging in an "Hour of Confession," each telling what he doesn't like about the other. One national, Ignacio by name, said:

> *Please forgive me if I am wrong. What bothers me is that some of you . . . well, almost the majority of missionaries seem to spend more time going to market, putting children to bed, talking among themselves, and running to the post office than serving directly in the work. And another thing I can't stand is that every time I invite a missionary to eat with me, or I am invited to eat with him, his wife always has to be consulted first. I wish you could be like us, putting your wives in the proper place where they belong, according to the Bible.*[2]

On the other hand, culture shock is harder on the wife than on the husband.

> *Culture shock affects both man and wife when they venture abroad for the first time. But the husband's shock is cushioned by the comfortable continuity of his profession—he spends most of his time soldiering, engineering, teaching, or whatever he has been doing at home. The wife is the one who must adjust to dirt and heat in the home, worry about health and schools, get used to the invasion of her privacy by omnipresent servants, and try to learn a strange tongue in two or three distracted hours a week.*[3]

PARTICIPATING IN THE WORK

The Women's Liberation Movement in the U.S. is demanding more rights for women, especially in the area of employment. In this connection it is interesting to note that women on the mission field have always enjoyed greater vocational freedom than women at home. Missions pioneered in two areas: medicine and education; and in both fields, women missionaries were in the vanguard. Dr. Ida Scudder established the first medical school for women in India in 1918. Isabella Thoburn opened the first college for girls in 1870.

Assuming that the wife has time for the work, what opportunities are available to her? Much depends on her training and skills. If she has all the qualifications of her husband, the field is wide open. She can do anything her

2. Juan H. Isais, *The Other Side of the Coin* (Grand Rapids: Eerdmans, 1966), p. 43.
3. Harlan Cleveland et al, *The Overseas Americans* (New York: McGraw-Hill, 1960), p. 46.

husband does. Most wives have at least a college education and not a few of them have advanced degrees. Men with a seminary education have an edge over their wives, but this gap will disappear as more and more women attend seminary. Many of them are fully qualified to teach the more technical subjects such as music, Christian education, art, history, hygiene, science, and English at the college level. Some of them became outstanding authors, among them Pearl Buck, Elisabeth Elliot, Isabel Kuhn, Geraldine Taylor, Rosalind Goforth, Mildred Cable, and Francesca French.

Mrs. Tuggy, in her book, *The Missionary Wife and Her work,* lists fifty-four kinds of work in which the missionary wife can make a significant contribution. These cover the gamut of missionary endeavor. Many wives are very gifted and can turn their hand to almost anything that needs to be done. Almost all wives are required, sometime in their career, to engage in work for which they have had no previous training. They usually do a good job.

As might be expected, women missionaries not working in an institution or engaged in technical work such as writing, editing, translation, etc., end up working with women and children. One reason for this is that these two classes have special needs. Another reason is that segregation makes it impossible for men to work with women, so they are likely to be neglected. So segregated were the sexes in the nineteenth century that some early missions were made up entirely of women, the idea being that this was the only way to reach the national womenfolk in their own quarters.

Working with women and children can be difficult and discouraging. For the most part the women in these countries are poor, ignorant, illiterate, undernourished, overworked, often despised and neglected, sometimes threatened and abused. In some countries they are little better than beasts of burden, doing all the heavy work while their husbands visit in the bazaars, haggle in the marketplaces, drink in the bars, bask in the sun, and generally enjoy life with their friends. They are expected to slave for their husbands, bearing them ten or twelve children, cooking their meals, making and mending their clothes, and ministering to their personal welfare. They get little in return.

This is where the missionary wife comes in. With the proper combination of courage, wisdom, compassion, love, and tact she can have a marvelous ministry to these downtrodden women who have never known anything but hardship. They respond with alacrity to anyone who shows a personal interest in their welfare. The Christian gospel, with its emphasis on love, its offer of peace and pardon, its promise of power, and its message of hope, makes a strong appeal to them, and many of them accept Christ and develop into beautiful Christian characters. Naturally a bond of affection grows between them and the missionary wives, something rarely seen in the Western world. In times of persecution not only have they refused to deny the Lord but they have risked their lives to save their missionary friends.

ADJUSTING TO A DUAL ROLE

In addition to her many problems is the greatest dilemma of all. How can she be a missionary and a wife at the same time and do justice to both? Where does her responsibility to the family end and her responsibility to the Lord begin, or should it be the other way round? In any case, she has a problem of the first magnitude.

Her feelings of frustration will be all the greater if she was single when she first went to the field, for then she will have had several years of complete freedom to engage in missionary work. Then she had only one problem—how to please the Lord. Now she has two—how to please the Lord and how to serve her family at the same time. And the fact that she is a missionary by calling only accentuates the feeling of guilt that may arise in her heart. She fears that she has fallen short in both roles, which again adds to her misery. She may even come to the point where she actually becomes jealous of her husband because of the freedom he enjoys. She may secretly resent the fact that he has learned the language faster and is a better speaker than she is, that he is free to come and go, meet people, attend conferences, fraternize with the national leaders, entertain public officials, etc.

The only way to solve this problem is for the wife to come to terms with reality and recognize that as long as the children are young her first responsibility is to them, and that in caring for them she is actually doing God service. The day will come when the children will go to school. Then she will be free to give most of her time to the work. In the meantime she will have to possess her soul in patience and remember that even a cup of cold water given to a stranger will not go unrewarded.

Husband and wife are a team. They must learn to work as well as live together. There will be times when the work must take precedence over the family; there are other times when the family must take precedence over the work. The Lord understands this. He knows our frame; He remembers that we are dust (Ps 103:14), and He does not expect of us more than we can give. There are times when the husband will have to "neglect" his wife in order to fulfill his calling as a missionary. It is to be hoped that these times will not come too often nor last too long. There are other times when family considerations will take precedence over missionary obligations. Those who have an understanding and sympathetic spouse are spared much pain. If their love for each other is deep and strong and surpassed only by their love for the Lord, there will be few if any problems that cannot be solved.

Anyone interested in reading about the trials and tribulations of family life on the mission field should consult Mabel Williamson's book, *Have We No Rights?*, Chapter 8, "The Right to a Normal Home Life." It is a vivid but realistic account of the joys and sorrows, the expectations and frustrations of a young couple starting out in a missionary career.

16

Making a Home

Most women at some time in their lives want to marry, and every married woman wants a home to call her own. This is only natural and it has the sanction of Holy Scripture. Every other institution—school, club, government, hospital, bank, office, factory, association—has been made by man. The home was established by God; it is therefore unique. God has ordained that the human race should live in families, and that each family should establish its own home. The home is the cement that holds society together. When it disintegrates, society comes apart at the seams. That is what is taking place in the U.S. at the present time and it doesn't augur well for the future. It may yet turn out to be the greatest single problem that we face— worse than inflation, the energy crisis, unemployment, or anything else. It is at the bottom of many of the ills that plague our society—crime, violence, pornography, child abuse, vandalism, and juvenile delinquency.

Homemaking is not the prime purpose of the missionary enterprise, but it is a very important ingredient. A well ordered home is essential to the well-being of each member of the family. This is just as true for the missionary on the field as it is for the pastor or Christian layman at home. Homemaking on the field is much the same as it is in the U.S. There are some differences, however, and it is with these that we want to deal.

SETTING UP HOUSE

Studies show that American mothers overseas are concerned about four things: housing, health, education, and servants. Missionary mothers are not different from others. They share these concerns, though in a different way and to a lesser extent. Housing is not nearly so great a problem for missionaries as for others, for two reasons. First, missionaries are prepared to accept a lower standard of living, so if they have to settle for substandard housing they are not unduly disturbed. Second, housing in one form or another is usually provided by the mission.

1. A bygone era. In the "good old days" missionary housing was quite adequate. In many instances it was elaborate. Houses were large and ceilings were high, porches were wide and windows were many, allowing the air to circulate freely. Often the house was set in a large compound surrounded by high walls and decorated with lawns, trees, shrubs, and flowers. Some even had tennis courts. This was made possible by the fact that land was extremely cheap. Labor was unbelievably low, a carpenter costing about ten cents a day in American currency. Local materials were equally cheap. Little wonder that missions invested in land and buildings.

2. Changing times. Following World War II, things changed. Instead of buying land and erecting buildings, many mission boards decided to rent. This permitted more mobility, did away with the ugly colonial image, placed missionaries where they belong—among the people, and greatly reduced property losses occasioned by civil war, riots, and other social and political upheavals.

This worked well during the fifties and sixties; but in the seventies, rents have soared so drastically that missionaries are now finding even modest housing almost beyond their means. For the first time in history it costs more to live abroad than in the U.S. An apartment that would rent for $300.00 a month here costs two or three times that amount in Tokyo or Sao Paulo. Some missions, especially in Japan, now regret that they didn't buy property after the war when it was much cheaper than it is today.

3. In primitive areas. In less developed countries missionaries often have to build their own houses. They are usually very simple with mud floors, adobe walls, and thatched roofs. The windows may be little more than openings in the walls. In such situations most of the amenities of modern civilization—running water, indoor plumbing, electricity—are missing. Cooking is done on an improvised stove or simply on a cluster of heated stones. Food lacks nutrition and must be supplemented with minerals and vitamins to insure a balanced diet. In the tropics, where the temperature may be in the nineties six months of the year, heat and humidity can be very enervating. That is why the missionaries usually take a month's vacation each year and head for the hill stations to get relief from the unrelenting heat.

4. In modern cities. In some overcrowded cities such as Caracas, Singapore, and Hong Kong, high-rise apartments are the only housing available.

Missionaries in a church-planting ministry use their apartment as house and meeting place until the congregation is able to buy or rent a meeting place of its own.

Utilities are also a problem. A missionary in Brazil paid $3,000 to have his telephone installed. In Tehran the installation charge is $950.00 and the waiting period may be two years.

The average American home has an endless array of household appliances. Once regarded as a luxury, they are now considered a necessity, and an increasing number of missionaries are taking them to the field. Small appliances are cheap to buy and easy to transport, so they constitute no great problem. The large appliances include, in order of importance, refrigerator, washer, and dryer. These are not only exceedingly convenient but they save endless time for the busy missionary. They can be used only where electricity is available, however, and even then there are many problems. One Foreign Service wife wrote:

> My refrigerator works fine in the winter, but not in the summer. I asked for a new one. I got a new one. Now I've got two and neither one works. You go to iron, the electricity goes off and you can't iron, and the pump stops and you have no water. The food spoils because the refrigerator is on the blink. You can't drink the local water. You ask them to do something. You go away for a week and they don't do it. I find my gorge rising.[1]

RAISING CHILDREN

We used to think that raising children on the mission field was more difficult than it is at home, but in recent years we have had second thoughts on the matter. With drugs in the schools, violence in the streets, crime everywhere, and sex and violence on TV, we are by no means sure that present-day conditions are conducive to the rearing of children in the Christian faith. Most missionary parents now agree that, taking everything into consideration including the fact that they must go to boarding school, rearing children on the field is preferable to rearing them in the U.S. This is not to suggest that there are no problems. Some of the major ones are discussed below.

1. The advantages of having children on the mission field. In spite of all the problems involved, children are a definite asset on the field. Very few parents would want to be without them. There are several advantages to having children.

Children round out and complete the family circle. A family without children isn't really a family at all—just a married couple. This is very important in the Third World, where celibacy is practically unknown and

1. Harlan Cleveland et al, *The Overseas Americans* (New York: McGraw-Hill, 1960), p. 49.

where small families are rare. Catholic missionaries are at a serious disadvantage in this respect; it is all but impossible for them to get close to the national people because their lifestyle seems unnatural and strange. It is also important to the nationals to carry on the family name; that is one reason why boys are preferred to girls. The birth of a child, especially a boy, is a supremely happy occasion in the Orient. When a woman is expecting a child we say she is pregnant. The Chinese say, "She has happiness!"—a much more beautiful expression. It is a glad day for the missionary couple when the first child comes to bless and brighten their home. One missionary wrote:

> *The Japanese love children. My husband says, "When I got married I felt myself heightened in the estimation of the Japanese; and when our first child was born, I went up another notch." Likewise the same could be said when our first boy arrived.* [2]

Children bring a second blessing. They win their way into the hearts and homes of the people, disarming prejudice and dispelling fear, and opening up opportunities which their parents can turn to good account. Children are universally loved. They are pure, innocent, unaffected, and outgoing. They have a natural way of ingratiating themselves with friends and neighbors without waiting for a formal introduction. Their friendship is immediate, their curiosity is boundless, their laughter is spontaneous. They make friends wherever they go. They are especially helpful when their parents move into a new neighborhood. They help to break the ice. In the first week they come to know everyone in the block. This is good public relations for missionary parents.

There is a third way in which MKs make a contribution. They provide an example of what a wholesome Christian home is really like. The Chinese have an expression: "One picture is worth a hundred words." The missionary can expound the biblical teaching on family life, but it isn't until the converts see an example that they get the full meaning. "It may be stated categorically that the presence of a loving, well-behaved missionary child is of the greatest possible blessing in missionary work." [3]

2. The problems. In many mission fields MKs lack recreational facilities, educational materials, and suitable playmates. Toys and games, so plentiful at home, are unknown in many countries of the Third World, but they can be taken out from home or sent out later. As for parks and playgrounds, nobody has ever heard of them, so missionary children have to be content with the games they can play in their own backyard, assuming they have a backyard.

Educational materials in English are unobtainable except in a few places

---

2. Quoted in *The Missionary Wife and Her Work* by Joy Turner Tuggy (Chicago: Moody Press, 1966), p. 52.
3. Ibid., p. 53.

like Nigeria, India, and Rhodesia. Bright, multicolored storybooks, comic books, records, drawing paper, poster board, pictures, puzzles, crayons, etc., which are a regular part of the American child's preschool experience, are not available at any price.

Playmates are also a problem. Most of the local children come from poor families who have little understanding of personal hygiene. Eye, ear, and throat infections are common. Tuberculosis is everywhere. No attempt is made to isolate persons with whooping cough, scarlet fever, or any of the more infectious diseases. Lack of public sanitation accentuates the spread of disease. Dysentery can be picked up by eating one piece of contaminated food. Missionary mothers can be forgiven if they worry about the health of their children, especially when they know that 50 percent of the local children die before reaching the age of seven.

Lack of suitable food for young children is also a problem. Baby food, a godsend to American mothers, is not to be had. Cow's milk is seldom available. Unboiled water is forbidden in the home, but the mother can never be sure that the children won't forget and drink it outside.

3. The children and the work. To what extent should the children participate in the work of their parents? Should they go with them on their evangelistic tours? Or should they remain at home? If they go, then mother can go along with them and the family remains together. Dr. and Mrs. Jonathan Goforth did this in China, but they lost six of their twelve children. Some missionaries make a practice of taking the children with them when they go on tour, but if the children are young they will occupy so much of the mother's time that both she and they might as well remain at home. Others prefer to play it safe, so the mother stays at home with the children. Much will depend on the kind of exposure the children will get, how long they will be away, and under what conditions they will live while on the road.

If the father goes alone, he will be free to give his entire time and thought to the work, but without his wife he will be unable to minister to the women. Each family must decide on its own course of action in the light of local circumstances, the demands of the work, the opportunities for service, and the potential for success.

Some parents are overprotective, keeping their children from all contacts which might contaminate them. The nationals may be offended by this, for they would fail to understand the rationale for the action. Other parents go to the other extreme and drag their children with them wherever they go, allowing them full freedom to fraternize with the other children, trusting the Lord to protect them from infection, danger, and disease. The wise course probably lies somewhere between these two extremes. If one has a pathological fear of dirt and disease he should not go to the mission field in the first place; but it is not necessarily an act of faith to needlessly expose oneself or one's children to known danger or disease. God expects us to use our common sense. He also expects us to obey His commands and do His work, and sometimes this involves a certain degree of risk which we must be prepared to take. We can always have the assurance that if we are in God's will and doing God's work we shall have His protection.

HANDLING SERVANTS

Americans who hear that missionaries have three or four servants sometimes raise their eyebrows in surprise and ask, "How come?" The answer is simple. There are two kinds of servants, human and mechanical. Here at home we have all kinds of mechanical gadgets that reduce labor, save time, and increase efficiency, and we accept and use them without giving them a thought. The servants employed by the missionaries do for them what the electrical appliances do for us.

1. **Reasons for having servants.** According to Joy Tuggy two-thirds of the missionary mothers employ servants most of the time.[4] They include cooks, housemaids, amahs, handymen, watercarriers, gardeners, goatherds, and others. The number of servants depends on the country they are in, the size of the family, the ages of the children, the demands of the work, and the income of the missionary. In the more advanced parts of the world servants are not needed any more than they are in the U.S. But in the less developed countries, and especially in the primitive areas, they are indispensable to the total operation of the mission station. Without them the efficiency quotient of the missionaries would be drastically reduced. Take water as an example. In many places water is a big problem, particularly during the dry season. Every drop of water—for drinking, cooking, laundry, and bathing—must be carried from a stream two miles away. Obviously a water boy is no luxury in that situation.

Another reason why missionaries employ servants is that the cost in many instances is unbelievably low. In our day in China we hired a cook, a housemaid, and a goatherd for a monthly cost of less than ten dollars. It would be foolish for missionaries to do their own menial tasks when help is available at such reasonable rates. True, the scene has changed greatly in the intervening years, but there are still areas of the world where the living standards and the pay scales are low.

2. **The proper number.** A family may have anywhere from one to three or four servants depending on their needs. A couple without children can get along without servants much better than a family with children. The most helpful servant is the cook, especially if he or she is willing to do other chores as well. He is usually the "head" servant. He is the best trained and the highest paid, and he takes responsibility for the other servants. Where there are several young children an amah (child's nurse) is a great asset to the

4. Ibid., p. 107.

family. If milk is not available the missionary may have to keep a cow or a couple of goats. In that case a goatherd will be necessary. Children of the nationals seem to get along without milk, but it is an essential part of the diet of all children.

3. The importance of training. Servants are not an unmixed blessing. They present two problems: training and supervision. Christians usually make the best servants. They are more likely to be honest and industrious. In a pioneering situation there may be no converts to draw from. Servants should be chosen with great care and on a trial basis. This should be made clear at the beginning. It is often easier to hire a servant than to fire one.

Training the servants is the responsibility of the mother, and she will need a great deal of wisdom and patience for the job. It will help immensely if she can communicate with them in their own language. She should bear in mind that when they first come they will be scared to death, so she should do her best to set them at ease. Most of the things she tries to teach them will seem utterly strange, if not foolish, to them. Such simple items as sweeping floors and making beds may be a new experience. Setting a table with cloth and napkins, cups and saucers, and knives and forks will be extremely complicated until it is learned. In short, living with and working for the missionary will introduce these simple, rustic people to a brand new world for which nothing has prepared them. It will take time and effort to train them and the instructions will have to be repeated time and time again.

Patience pays off, however. It is amazing how quickly servants will catch on and take over. Some are quicker and brighter than others, but on the whole they work out very well.

4. The need for supervision. Most servants need constant supervision. Some are slow, some are dull, some are lazy, some are dishonest, some are prone to illness, and some are given to lying. When the missionary appears to be so affluent and the servant and his family are so poor, the temptation to pilfer is almost irresistible. They sometimes help themselves to food, not things, unless they can pawn or sell them. One way to help alleviate the problem is to give them a living wage—enough to support their entire family—and thus reduce the need to pilfer. Keep temptation to a minimum by storing foodstuffs and other items in places where pilfering will not be easy.

In China the cooks did all the buying and reckoned accounts with the mistress each evening. This was both good and bad. It was good in that the cook could always drive a better bargain than the missionary could and thus save money. It was bad in that some cooks took advantage of the situation and pocketed all or part of the savings made possible by their ability to "talk price." This was an old Chinese custom and they thought nothing of it. It greatly distressed some missionaries and often led to ugly altercations. Other missionaries, wiser in their ways, regarded the practice as a form of commission that, according to Chinese tradition, belonged to the cook. In any event the amount was not large, though over a long period of time it could add up to a tidy sum.

Amahs in charge of the children require careful watching. They don't always do what they are told, for the simple reason that what they are told runs counter to what they have done all their lives. Their way of raising children is fundamentally different from ours. Ours makes sense to us, but not to them, so there is the temptation to accept orders but not always to obey them, especially when the mistress is not there to scold. The amahs come to love their charges and they show their love in the only way they know how— by being permissive and indulgent. The children naturally take kindly to this treatment and in no time at all become "spoiled brats," much to the consternation of the parents. To be successful in dealing with her servants the missionary mother will need intuition, patience, firmness, and kindness in just the right proportions.

5. **Handle with care.** In handling servants care must be exercised not to interfere unnecessarily with their social status. Americans, with their flair for egalitarianism, are the worst offenders. They insist on treating their servants as members of the family. This upsets the servants. They don't know how to respond. They know that as servants there are certain well defined proprieties they are supposed to observe, and this they are quite willing to do. But along comes the missionary and throws them into a dither by patting them on the back, laughing, joking, fraternizing with them, and generally treating them as equals. This is not only frowned upon by the community, but it is very unnerving to the servants themselves. They don't want to break their own code of social etiquette. It is better for all concerned if the missionary maintains a certain dignity and distance.

In some societies even servants have their own social hierarchy and values. This is particularly true in India where caste, a socio-economic system, determines the occupation of the individual. Every Indian knows the subcaste to which he belongs and the occupations related thereto. Cooks, waiters, sweepers, barbers, butchers, scavengers—all have their own particular niche to fill. To expect a waiter to clean the bathroom is to expect the impossible. To force him to do so would precipitate a row in which all the servants would take sides against the missionary. The only way to obviate this kind of situation is to hire the right kind of servant for the right kind of job.

6. **Fringe benefits.** Many missionaries, in addition to training the servants in household chores, train them to do other useful things such as knitting, sewing, crocheting, dressmaking, etc. The male servants may be trained to become carpenters, masons, tinsmiths, mechanics, etc. The more aggressive ones catch on quickly and make phenomenal progress. They begin at the bottom of the ladder as illiterate, unskilled servants. From

goatherd they become house boy; from house boy they move up to cook. Along the way they learn to read and write, and later they may go to school. After graduation they become evangelists or teachers; many of them become pastors. A Trinity graduate from Africa, now working on his Ph. D. in Education at Michigan State, began twenty years ago as a house boy in the home of a single lady missionary in Nigeria. When he returns to Nigeria he will be the pastor of a large church and president of a theological seminary. This points up one of the essential differences between missionaries and anthropologists. The anthropologists, after spending six months or a year studying a primitive tribe in some remote region of the world, come home and write a book about their findings; but they leave the people as they found them—ignorant, illiterate, fearful, emaciated, diseased, superstitious, and with no hope of ever becoming anything else. The missionary, on the other hand, stays with them, identifies with them, takes them into his heart and home, shares with them the transforming gospel of Jesus Christ, teaches them to read and write, and helps them to learn a trade, thereby emancipating them from social and economic bondage. In a word, the anthropologist treats them as objects to be studied, whereas the missionary loves them as persons for whom Christ died.

EXTENDING HOSPITALITY

Hospitality was so important in the early church that it was one of the qualifications for leadership as outlined by Paul in his letters to Timothy. Hospitality was widely practiced on the American frontier when survival often depended on the concerted effort of the community. In more recent times American Christians have overlooked the importance of hospitality. It is becoming increasingly difficult to get housing for missionaries on furlough and other groups engaged in a traveling ministry.

There are several reasons for this. Houses tend to be smaller, which puts spare room at a premium. More than half of the married women are working, many of them full time. This means that leisure time is also at a premium. Instead of entertaining in the home, therefore, the practice of eating out is becoming more popular. On the mission field, hospitality is still widely practiced. Among the Orientals and the Arabs it is the law of life.

1. **To outsiders.** Some mission stations are located in strategic centers at the crossroads of the world where there is a constant stream of travelers—anthropologists, archeologists, and historians as well as a motley crew of globetrotters. More often than not these Westerners make their way to the mission compound, introduce themselves, request hospitality, and proceed to stay as long as they like.

When entertaining such visitors, the hostess usually does herself proud by preparing the best Western meal her meager pantry will permit. Sometimes this means bringing out the last package of Jello, or the last can of salmon, or the last jar of strawberry preserves. Globetrotters sometimes partake of these delicacies and then report to the home constituency that "missionaries live like kings." One church threatened to drop my support when a GI visited our headquarters in Shanghai, enjoyed the food and fellowship, and then told his home church that the CIM compound in Shanghai was "as luxurious as Buckingham Palace." The church demanded an explanation. In reply I confessed that I was at a disadvantage. Never having been to Buckingham Palace I was not in a position to compare the two. I did, however, describe the compound as accurately and honestly as I could, explaining the rationale for all the "luxury." I got no reply. I assume my explanation was satisfactory. At least my support was not cut off.

2. **To fellow missionaries.** Missionaries on trek almost always stay with other missionaries. In smaller places there are no suitable hotels. In the larger cities, where hotels are available, the prices are beyond the reach of the average missionary. On a 27-day journey across central China in the fall of 1944, not once was I obliged to sleep in an inn. I always managed to find a church or an outstation or a missionary home where I was welcomed with open arms by Chinese and missionaries alike, and most of them were not affiliated with my mission.

In practically all of the capital cities of the world there are mission homes and hostels open to missionaries of all denominations. These homes usually have a full-time host and hostess and a number of servants to help with the work. The guests are expected to pay a nominal amount for room and board. In the smaller towns and cities where travelers are less numerous and hospitality is on a personal basis the missionaries may or may not pay, depending on the affiliation of the mission, the length of stay, and the degree of friendship involved. If no charge is made, a substantial tip is always left for the servants involved in extra work.

3. **To national Christians.** Of more immediate concern to the missionary mother is hospitality involving the nationals. In earlier days it was not customary to extend hospitality to national Christians. In Africa even church leaders were entertained outside on the verandah. Seldom if ever were they invited into the home even for a cup of tea. In China, when missionaries and nationals traveled together on evangelistic teams the missionaries were entertained in the mission home (if there was one) and the Chinese were entertained in the church (again, if there was one). If there was neither church nor mission they all went to an inn. When it came to giving feasts it was almost always the Chinese who invited the missionaries; seldom did the missionaries return the compliment. This was a serious social faux pas.

One reason for the segregation was the fact that the missionaries followed a Western lifestyle, living in Western-style houses and eating Western meals with knife and fork. Sophisticated Chinese living in Shanghai or Nanking would feel at home in such an atmosphere, but the church leaders upcountry were a different breed. They definitely did not appreciate Western food. I remember inviting an outstation leader, Ma Ping-kuang, for dinner on one occasion. He was so flustered by the foreignness of the food, the dishes, the cutlery, and the surroundings that he only nibbled at the food. I was told afterwards by the city pastor that he was so embarrassed that he lost his appetite. He found the food unpalatable, the atmosphere strange, and the sharp knife and pronged fork positively dangerous. Under such handicaps he didn't even enjoy the fellowship. I learned a lesson from that episode. We should have served Chinese food with chopsticks. Then he would have appreciated both the food and the fellowship.

Another problem that we had was that the missionaries ate three meals a day whereas the Chinese ate only two. This meant that when we were eating they were working, and when they were eating we were working. That left only a few hours each day when both were free. I have vowed a thousand times that if we ever return to China we will take with us only a toothbrush and a Bible. We will have two meals a day. We will eat Chinese food. We will use chopsticks. Then I will be able to invite the outstation leaders to a meal when they come to town. This would not work any great hardship on me or my wife; Chinese food is not hard to take!

If the missionary hostess is to extend hospitality to church leaders, to say nothing of rank-and-file Christians, she will have to accommodate herself to their way of cooking and eating. Otherwise they may eat the food but they will not enjoy it.

17

Educating the Children

The greatest problem facing missionary parents is the education of their children. More time, thought, and money are spent on this than on any other problem. The fact that the overwhelming majority of missionaries are college graduates means that it takes on added significance in their thinking. They naturally want their children to have as good an education as they had, if not better. This concern is shared by mission executives, most of whom have children of their own, which gives them double reason to be interested in this important matter.

Roman Catholic missionaries do not face this problem. They have done an excellent job in providing education for their converts and other nationals, but not a single Roman Catholic school for MKs exists. They are fortunate in a way to be free of this cause for concern and expense.

OPTIONS OPEN TO PARENTS

In the nineteenth century there were few if any options. Today, with greater facilities on the field and jet travel around the world, parents have a number of options not available in the early days of the missionary enterprise. Most missions today give the parents the right to choose how they will handle the education of their children.

1. **The children may be taught by the parents.** In this case the mother becomes the teacher and a good deal of her day will be spent in the "classroom." Most mothers, being college graduates, have the necessary

qualifications, short, perhaps, of teacher certification, but the mother will not be obliged to make up her own curriculum. She may elect to use the Calvert Correspondence Course, which takes the student right through high school. Some parents keep their children at home through elementary school and send them to the mission school for their high school training.

2. **The children may be educated in the U.S.** This was a common practice in the early days before schools for MKs were available. Some missions, like the Sudan Interior Mission, operated a school for their own children in the U.S. and Canada. This practice has been discontinued. If the children come to the homeland for their education, they usually live in a mission-sponsored hostel and attend a nearby public school. This cuts down on effort and expense. Some parents prefer to send their children to independent Christian schools such as Wheaton Academy, Ben Lippen, Hampton-Dubois, or Stony Brook. Others arrange for the children to live with relatives and attend a public school.

3. **The children may be educated in a mission school.** This is the most common practice and on the whole it works out well for all concerned, parents as well as children. These schools are to be found in all parts of the mission field. In India and some other large countries there are several. The Overseas Missionary Fellowship, Africa Inland Mission, Sudan Interior Mission, CAM International, the Christian and Missionary Alliance, and other missions are large enough to warrant operating their own schools in different parts of the world. If there is room they accept children from other missions, but the fees for them are considerably higher. In some places several missions pool their resources of men and money and support a union school which the children of all cooperating missions attend. Morrison Academy in Taiwan and Faith Academy in the Philippines are in this category.

These are all boarding schools, though there are always some commuters, especially if the school is located in a large city. Enrollment generally runs in the neighborhood of three hundred, large enough to permit a good athletic program, but the physical facilities are nothing like the two- and three-million-dollar edifices here at home. Faculty members and administrators are all missionaries, most of them career missionaries, though there are some short-termers. Some of these schools have an excellent record and reputation, so much so that business and professional people and the diplomatic corps prefer to have their children attend them if possible. Henry Luce, founder and one-time editor of *Time* magazine, was a student at the Chefoo School operated by the China Inland Mission. Graduating seniors took the Oxford matriculation exams before leaving Chefoo.

4. **The children may attend an American school overseas.** With an increasing number of American families living abroad these schools are fairly common. Some of them are independently endowed, while some are spon-

sored by the U.S. government, especially where there is a large concentration of GIs. Some schools are maintained by the large oil companies. With 40,000 American technicians in Saudi Arabia, American schools are a must. In all these schools first choice goes to the children of the GIs and the oil company employees, but where there is room, MKs are welcome.

5. The children may attend local schools with the nationals. Up to the present this has not been practicable except in a very few countries where the educational standards are comparable to those in the West. The situation, however, is changing, and more and more MKs are attending local schools, especially in Europe where the standards are high and the curriculum similar to that in Canadian and American schools. As a matter of fact, the high schools in France and Germany are ahead of American schools when it comes to academic load and student performance. Besides being perfectly bilingual, MKs from Europe usually skip a grade when they transfer to American schools. MKs in the Third World are not quite so fortunate. Standards are low, facilities are poor, and performance is weak. In addition, to be fluent in a European language is much more advantageous to the MK than to be fluent in Telugu, Tagalog, or Thai, unless he returns to that part of the world later on.

THE PROS AND CONS OF THE VARIOUS OPTIONS

1. If the children are taught at home. Here the disadvantages greatly outweigh the advantages. The one big advantage is that the children remain with their parents, and to some parents this is of paramount importance. They are persuaded that children should not be separated from their parents under any circumstances. They therefore refuse even to contemplate sending little Johnny or Mary off to school at the tender age of six. From a purely emotional point of view the very suggestion is repugnant. Moreover, they would consider such conduct a betrayal of their God-given responsibility to rear their own children in the fear of God according to biblical principles.

The disadvantages are rather formidable. To begin with, a major portion of the mother's time must be devoted to teaching the children. Little time is left for missionary work. Most missions regard the wife/mother as a full-time missionary, although they are reasonable enough to know that children demand a certain amount of a mother's time during their early years. But, if the children are educated at home, she may be tied down for fifteen or twenty years, depending on the number of children involved.

Interruptions are bound to take her out of the "classroom." No matter how hard she tries to maintain a consistent teaching schedule, there will be demands on her time. If she is a nurse there will be outpatients who can't be turned away. Visitors from far and near will arrive unannounced and expect to see the wife as well as the husband. Other emergencies will crop up from time to time, and such interruptions are apt to disrupt the teaching schedule.

The children on their part will suffer certain disabilities. The "school" will be too small to afford competition. If there are three children, each will be in a different grade. Under these conditions they may lose interest in their studies. School then becomes all work and no fun. Discipline becomes a problem when the mother is also the teacher. One mother insisted that her daughter call her "Mrs. Jones" during class hours. "It's pretty hard to keep up *that* pretense," she confessed. "What do you do when your pupil suddenly hugs you and says, 'Oh Mummy, I love you. Let's stop now?'"

Textbooks will be available, but there will be no library facilities. Extracurricular activities, especially athletics, are almost impossible. Children need their parents, to be sure, but they also need peers with whom they can identify. If half a dozen families living in the same area cooperated in providing schooling for their youngsters, it would be a big improvement on the isolated family with few if any social contacts.

2. If the children are sent to the U.S. The pros and cons of this situation depend to some extent on the arrangements—whether the children will live in a school or hostel or in the home of a relative. The advantages include an American education with all the fun and frills. They will be in a comparatively safe country where revolution and civil war are not likely to occur. By getting their elementary education in the States they will be spared the trauma of "reentry" during high school or college years.

Several disadvantages should be noted. The children will see their parents only every three or four years when they come home on furlough, though nowadays some missions do send the children to the field for a summer halfway through their parents' term of service. They may not be happy living with friends or relatives. They may come to feel that their presence in the family is an imposition, especially if the guardians grow weary of the responsibility of having MKs in the home. If problems arise, the child may not feel free to share them with relatives. The Christian influence of the home may not be strong enough to offset the secular and worldly influence of the school.

These disadvantages are somewhat mitigated if they live in a Christian boarding school or a hostel with other MKs.

3. If the children attend a school for MKs overseas. From many points of view this seems to be the best of the five options. Certainly it has more advantages than disadvantages. First of all, this arrangement sets both parents free for full-time missionary service, and that is the purpose for which they became missionaries in the first place. In a mission school the children will have plenty of companions of their own age and culture with whom to live, study, and play. They will receive a well-rounded education in a structured program in an academic atmosphere conducive to study. In addition, they will have a variety of extracurricular activities not available if they had remained at home with their parents. There will be adequate medical care with a doctor and nurse on call 24 hours a day, which is more than school-children have in the U.S. In a mission school they enjoy a communal lifestyle which is good preparation for later life and they learn to take responsibility for making their own beds and keeping their rooms and belongings in order. They operate on bells thus acquiring the habit of promptness. Such a regimen may sound harsh to homeside Americans with their permissive lifestyle, but when everyone else is doing the same thing it doesn't occur to the individual to complain, much less rebel. He comes to like the system because he finds that it makes possible a well-ordered, happy communal life.

One of the truly great advantages of this kind of school is the dedication of the staff—administration, teachers, and houseparents. I daresay that the average MK gets more tender loving care than his American counterpart does from either his parents or his teachers. Only those who have seen these schools in action can possibly appreciate the extent to which the staff members give themselves to the students. It is a beautiful arrangement and quite unique.

The physical facilities are no match for those available here in the States, but the academic program is often superior. Our sons began the study of Roman history in the third grade and Latin in the fifth, and that was back in the 1940s. Both boys skipped a grade when they transferred to the American school system, and the older one graduated from high school when he had just turned sixteen.

There are, however, some drawbacks. It can be a very traumatic experience for a child of six to leave home for boarding school. Most children adjust very well, but there are always the few who find the ordeal painful. It is equally hard, in some ways harder, for the parents. The children soon make many new friends at school and there are houseparents and teachers to care for them; but the parents have no one to take the place of the absent children. This is the greatest sacrifice that missionaries are called upon to make.

With staff members who devote all of their time to the welfare of the children, it is not surprising that they live contented and happy lives. They eagerly look for mail from home and are elated when it comes, but there is no time for homesickness, and the wise parent will rejoice that it is so. There are some failures; some children do grow up to resent their parents for sending them away to school. The vast majority, however, take it in their stride and benefit from the experience.

One serious disadvantage is that the mission school, because of its cloistered atmosphere, does not adequately prepare the teenager for his return to American society. This has always been a problem, but with the deteriorating situation in American high schools—drugs, alcohol, sex, and vandalism—it has assumed gargantuan proportions. Because of this, some parents are now remaining at home after their fourth or fifth furlough to make a home for their teenage children. The high schooler is the one who suffers most. Those who enter college, especially a Christian college, fare much better, but even they have their problems.

4. If the children attend an American school overseas. Here the disadvantages seriously outweigh the advantages. The prevailing atmosphere in these schools is thoroughly secular and worldly with no religious emphasis, much less religious training. The teachers, while they may be professionally competent, may not be as dedicated as those in a mission school. The moral standards are often lax in the extreme. All of these conditions exist in the school systems here in the U.S., but with this difference: overseas they are boarding schools where the MK will be exposed to this kind of hostile climate without the offsetting influence of a Christian home. Tuition and other costs are much higher than in mission schools—so high, in fact, that very few missionaries can afford to send their children to them.

5. If the children attend local schools overseas. With educational facilities and standards improving rapidly in all parts of the world, this is becoming an attractive possibility. In Europe the common practice is to send missionary children to the local schools. Such an arrangement enables the MK to live at home. It also enhances his opportunity to become bilingual and bicultural. These schools are usually part of the tax-supported system so the fees, if any, are low.

On the minus side there are other factors. The curriculum might be so foreign that he will find himself ill prepared to enter college when he returns to the U.S. If he goes to school in one of the less developed countries the academic standards may be so low that he will become frustrated. In countries where nationalism runs high, an anti-foreign bias may be strong enough to make life miserable for him. One family in Latin America had to remove their two boys from the local school when they could no longer endure the anti-gringo sentiment in the student body. Their parents wrote in an August 1974 prayer letter:

> You have probably heard us say that we would never send our kids away to school! Well, with somewhat red, but very happy faces, we have to admit that we have changed our tune. Our two boys returned to the same secular English-speaking school in Cartagena last year where all our children had studied previously. However, in the four years that we were gone, the school has changed. There are practically no North American children now, and the peer pressure and anti-gringo feelings are much stronger than we anticipated.
>
> After much prayer and wrestling with the problem, in the middle of the year we sent the boys to a missionary kids' school in Quito, Ecuador, run by the Christian and Missionary Alliance. The benefits in spiritual life, academic standing, sports, and other activities, far offset our dislike of having them away from home.

In a predominantly Catholic country a Protestant child might be the victim of discrimination. Since Vatican II this is less likely to occur, however. In a Muslim country the MK is sure to stick out like a sore thumb. He might even be obliged to participate in religious practices.

GENERAL OBSERVATIONS

1. **Separation from children is part of missionary life.** The majority of missionary recruits are married and some of them already have one or two children. They know when they sign up for missionary duty that this is part of the deal; it comes as no surprise. Most of them have already faced up to the ordeal. Missionary life, more than any other form of Christian service, involves a great deal of sacrifice, and part of that sacrifice is separation from children. This is not something altogether new. Our Lord doubtless had this in mind when He gave His marching orders to His disciples: "He that loveth father or mother more than me is not worthy of me; and he that loveth son or daughter more than me is not worthy of me" (Matt 10:37, KJV). There are some couples who simply cannot face the prospect of parting with their children under any circumstances. They usually drop out of the race before or during candidate school.

2. **Sending children away to school is not as difficult as some people imagine.** At first sight it appears cold, callous, cruel, even inhumane, but on further reflection and understanding it is not cruel, either for the parents or for the children. Spurgeon used to say: "You don't get dying grace for living moments." But when dying grace is needed, it is available. God gives grace and strength day by day *as we need them.* Nobody pretends that it is easy, but most missionary parents will testify to the fact that, when the time came, God gave the necessary grace. His grace is sufficient for our every need, and His strength is made perfect in our weakness. Paul found it so, and so has every missionary since his day. In addition, it affords a sense of satisfaction to know that what they are doing is not for their own profit but for the glory of God. In the final analysis it is an act of obedience, and they know that if they obey God He will make Himself responsible for all the consequences that flow from their action. They know, too, that if they disobey God they will be responsible for the consequences of their disobedience. That knowledge makes all the difference in the world. His commandments are not grievous (1 Jn 5:3). His yoke is easy and His burden is light (Matt 11:30). His ways are ways of pleasantness and all His paths are peace (Prov 3:17).

3. **Missionaries are not the only ones with this problem.** Several million Americans now live overseas, including business and professional people and the diplomatic corps. Most of them are married and some have children of school age, some of whom have to go away to boarding school. Tens of thousands of seamen are even worse off. They see their wives and children

only once or twice a year when the ship calls at the home port. In England many people send their children to private boarding schools. These children see their parents only during vacation periods. If these people can endure the trauma of separation, surely missionaries should be able to do the same.

4. Life in a mission school is usually happy and wholesome. This does not mean that every MK sails through school without difficulty. The first few days are the hardest. Most children settle in with little or no problem, others take days, and a few take even longer to make the adjustment. Much depends on the extent to which the parents prepared the child for the break. Some parents do a better job than others. With our sons, we always spoke of going to school as a great adventure, telling them about the many things they would have at school which were not available on the mission station, and describing life at school as rewarding and exciting. As a result, they went to school without any tears or regrets and made the adjustment with a minimum of trouble.

A great deal depends on the temperament of the child. Those who are shy and timid have much more difficulty than those who are friendly and outgoing. Neither teachers nor parents have much control in this kind of situation.

Teachers and houseparents are always on hand to welcome newcomers to the school. If they spot a child with special problems, they go out of their way to help him. They see to it that such a child gets a double share of tender loving care. Once he becomes accustomed to the community lifestyle of the school he settles down, makes friends, and has a good time.

5. The vast majority of MKs turn out well. In some schools, as high as 90 percent of the graduates go on to college, where they usually get scholarships, make good grades, and acquire lifelong friends. They may be less sophisticated than American youngsters, but they are usually more mature. They have read more books, visited more places, talked to more people, and made more friends. They are usually bicultural and can speak at least two languages fluently. They are accustomed to world travel, which in itself is an education. They have experienced in real life many of the exciting and exotic things available to us only on television. The percentage of MKs who go to college and do well when they get there is considerably higher than for the population as a whole. Most of them go into the professions— law, medicine, the pastorate, the diplomatic corps, and teaching. Not a few return to the field as missionaries. Not many have the desire to go into business simply to make money and live well.

Invariably they are cosmopolitan in outlook. The State Department and the multinational corporations like to get MKs because of their understanding of world affairs, their empathy for other peoples and cultures, and their general ability to feel at home in any society.

It is a mistake to pity them. Actually, they are to be congratulated. They have enjoyed privileges and experiences unknown to American youngsters. Far from being misfits and oddballs with warped personalities, they are, on the whole, beautiful people, intelligent, responsible, resourceful, industrious, and successful.

On the other side of the ledger, it should be acknowledged that some MKs do become casualties. For a variety of reasons they resent their upbringing, turn against their parents, rebel against authority, and carry a grudge for the rest of their lives. Some become drug addicts or alcoholics. Others lose their faith and blame God for their plight. Exact figures relating to such casualties are not available, but they constitute only a very small minority of the total number of MKs.

HOW TO INSURE SUCCESS

Like any human enterprise, missionary schools will not succeed without concerted effort on the part of all concerned.

1. The ultimate responsibility lies with the mission board. The problem is too big and too complicated to be solved by the parents, even acting in concert. Only the mission board has the ability, the authority, and the funds necessary to support and conduct a well organized school of any size. If the mission wants to keep its missionaries happy, it must provide adequate educational facilities for their children. These include suitable property, adequate buildings, competent teachers, capable houseparents, a strong curriculum, high academic standards, extracurricular activities, and the necessary funds. All of this is quite beyond the ability of the parents.

Most mission boards take this responsibility very seriously, and on the whole they do a good job with the resources they have. The larger missions, with greater resources in men and money, can maintain better schools.

2. Staff members play a significant role. The mission should provide all the facilities mentioned above, but success is not assured by facilities alone. The teachers and houseparents are crucial to the entire operation, for in a real sense they are surrogate parents.

One of the greatest problems is attracting qualified teachers. Competent, dedicated Christian teachers are difficult to come by. Most missionaries want to be on the cutting edge of a church-planting ministry; they don't want to be "sidetracked" into teaching in a school for MKs. Very few people volunteer for this kind of work. Usually they have to be taken out of other work and assigned to the school, some of them on an interim basis to meet a pressing need. Furlough every four years further complicates the problem. Not many candidates apply to the missions for the specific purpose of teaching in a school for MKs, though the number is increasing. In recent years more and more teachers have been short-termers. Furlough for them means the termination of their contract and they do not return.

If not enough candidates apply to teach in the schools, it becomes necessary for the school administration to recruit directly. This is not easy. Personal interviews are not possible. All business must be transacted by correspondence. When a teacher is hired he (or she) must then raise his support and travel expenses, and that will run into well over $10,000 a year and may take a long time.

Teachers in a mission school must have more than academic qualifications. They must have spiritual qualifications as well. Among these is a special sense of call to this particular form of Christian service. This is their contribution to missionary work. In that sense they are real missionaries. They are just as much a part of the missionary enterprise as the evangelist in the bazaar or the professor in the Bible school or the Bible translator in the jungle. That is true of houseparents as well. They too must have a definite sense of call.

3. Parents have their role to play. They begin by providing the right combination of discipline and love that makes for a strong family life and will continue to undergird the child long after he has gone away to school. A missionary in Japan expressed it well when he said:

> As far as raising children abroad is concerned, whether it is an advantage or not depends on how happy the home is, because the home is so much more important abroad. In most circumstances, the child doesn't have as much to do outside the home, and therefore falls heavily back on the home. The parents really therefore have more responsibility than in the States.[1]

It is the parents' responsibility to prepare the child for boarding school. If they do a good job he should have no problem leaving home or adjusting to life in school. This assignment requires both wisdom and tact. If it is possible, a previous visit to the school should be arranged. This will do much to allay any fears the child may have and pave the way for a smooth matriculation.

Parting is hard, but not as hard as might be imagined. It is usually worse for the parents than for the child. Most parents take their children to school the first time they go; after that they usually travel in groups with one missionary escorting a dozen or more youngsters. It is best for the parents not to prolong their stay at the school. Overnight or a weekend is plenty. The child settles in more quickly and easily if the break is clean. Some parents are surprised when their child has to be summoned from the playground to say good-bye and receive a quick farewell kiss. Ian Hay, General Director of the Sudan Interior Mission, has this reassuring word:

1. Harlan Cleveland, et al. *The Overseas Americans* (New York: McGraw-Hill, 1960), p. 57.

> *As one who has been Principal of a school where hundreds of children of*
> *missionaries have received their education, starting from an age as low as*
> *five or six years, I can declare fervently that 99% of the children rapidly*
> *overcome their homesickness in the busy activities of school, and respond*
> *to happy, healthy companionship. They do not forget, or lose their love*
> *for their parents. . . . God can, through these experiences, tie these*
> *families in closer bonds, not separate them.*[2]

Parents can help keep family ties intact by communicating with their children on a regular basis. Most schools set aside an hour each week when all the children write home. It is imperative that the parents reciprocate by writing a weekly letter also. Birthdays should always be remembered with cards, gifts, money, etc. Vacation periods should be used to the greatest possible advantage. Most schools have fairly long vacations staggered throughout the year when the children can spend time at home. Wise parents will take advantage of these times, giving themselves as far as possible to the children, arranging for games, parties, picnics, camping and hunting trips, and other activities. It is not the amount of time they spend together but the quality of time that really counts. Better a month of close and precious fellowship than half a year of casual communication.

In the tropics the schools are usually located in the highlands where the climate is cool and invigorating. In that case the parents usually spend their summer vacation with the children at school. It would be an act of folly to expose the children to the heat and dust of the plains.

Two of the difficult times for an MK are furlough and coming home for the last time to enter college. The father is expected to spend most of his furlough time doing deputation work. If he goes by himself the family is alone. If he takes the family with him the experience can be a nightmare— long trips during the day, meetings every evening, being entertained in a different home every night, snatching a meal here and there, always on the go and seldom able to enjoy a quiet family time together.

Both housing and schooling are problems during furlough. The majority of missionary families have to find their own housing. Most of them receive a rental allowance but it is seldom sufficient to meet the minimum costs in an urban situation where vacant apartments are few and rents are high.

Most MKs come home for their college education. That separation is, in some respects, more difficult than the separation when he went to boarding school. Now for the first time he is entirely on his own, with no place to call home. Most of them spend the vacations with grandparents or other relatives. Sometimes a roommate issues an invitation to spend the holiday at his home. If he has to stay on campus, with the cafeteria closed and the dorm empty, he begins to realize what it costs to be an MK.

Money is also a problem. Coming from the mission field, he has not been

2. James Romaine Beck, *Parental Preparation of Missionary Children for Boarding School* (Taipei, Taiwan: Mei Ya Publications, 1968), p. 31.

able to save for college. Part-time jobs and babysitting—lucrative sources of income for American young people—are not available to them. Nor are their parents able to do more than give token financial help. Some missions now continue partial support through college. It doesn't pay all the bills, but it helps. Most MKs qualify for scholarships based on need. In one way or another their financial needs are met, but it is a life of faith and he has no guarantee that he will be able to meet next semester's bills.

During the summer vacation he may have to move off campus and find his own lodgings. It might be difficult for him to find employment without the usual leads that come through family connections. All told, the lot of the MK is an uncertain one until he finishes college, marries, and settles down in his own home.

Having discussed the problem from all angles, I can do no better than sum it up in the words of another:

> Most missionaries do not neglect their children and are trying their best under various circumstances. But the failure to find a satisfactory solution to children's education probably causes more missionaries to leave the field than anything else. Even so, educating children should not be our primary goal in life as missionaries. If that were the case, we should not have left home in the first place. Children must learn to share in the mission of their parents. If we teach them that their education is more important than preaching the gospel in the field that Christ has led us to, then will they not consider the work of Christ a hindrance to their progress, and a resented competitor of secondary importance? We are never going to educate our children properly for Christ unless we are fully dedicated ourselves. Children must learn in a happy way that they are not the center of the universe, and that the central purpose of the lives of the missionary parents is not the satisfying of their every whim.[3]

3. Joseph L. Cannon, *For Missionaries Only* (Grand Rapids: Baker Book House, 1969), pp. 81–82.

18

Getting Along with Others

Harold Cook wrote: "It is not the opposition from outside that causes most breakdowns in the missionary ranks; it is dissensions within."[1] It may come as a surprise to the supporters at home, but it is common knowledge on the field that the missionary's greatest problem is how to get along with his fellow missionaries. The question may well be asked: Why does anyone as spiritual as the missionary is reputed to be have trouble along this line? Having forsaken all for the sake of the gospel, and having adjusted to life in a different culture, surely they should be able to live together in peace and harmony. Before we condemn them out of hand we should take a look at the bigger picture.

WITH FELLOW MISSIONARIES

We may find it difficult to account for such behavior, but there are some contributing factors which go a long way toward explaining it.

1. They are human beings. Missionaries are men with the same passions as ourselves. They are fashioned from the same clay, and they have the treasure of the gospel in earthen vessels. They may have hearts of gold, but they have feet of clay. They have their headaches and their hangups, their blind spots and their pet peeves, their prejudices and their passions. They

---

1. Harold R. Cook, *Missionary Life and Work* (Chicago: Moody Press, 1959), p. 117.

even have their doubts and fears. They are not angels; they are not even saints, except in the making; there is still room for improvement.

2. They are strong personalities. There are a few meek and mild missionaries, but they are definitely in the minority. Most of them are strong-minded persons with wills and ideas of their own. That's what made them missionaries in the first place. The weaker characters fell by the wayside or were rejected by the mission. The mission wanted leaders—people with purpose, passion, and push—and they got them. Now they have to live with them! What was an asset as a candidate may be a liability as a missionary.

3. Personality clashes. Personality is a subtle thing. It is made up of a number of complex entities—mind, heart, will—and is influenced by heredity, environment, training, and other potent factors. Some personalities click and others clash, and often there is no rational explanation. Certain people when thrown together "hit it off" while others don't. It happens at home and it happens on the mission field, but there it is more difficult to cope with.

4. Behavioral traits. These may be either good or bad. The good ones cause no trouble. The bad ones do—laziness, selfishness, tardiness, loquaciousness, censoriousness, and so on. Some missionaries are just plain lazy; thus they end up not carrying their weight. Others never come to meals or meetings on time. Others monopolize the conversation, talking interminably about themselves and their children.

A large number of faith missions are international in membership, a fact which often makes it easy to indulge in criticism if one is so inclined. English missionaries drink tea; Americans prefer coffee. The English like hot breakfast cereal served with hot milk; Americans eat cold cereal with cold milk. The English have a daily ritual known as afternoon tea while Americans take a morning coffee break. British missionaries tend to be more formal, more polished, more reserved. They handle the English language better than we Americans do. Americans, with their free-and-easy, happy-go-lucky, back-slapping behavior, can be a constant irritant to the more sophisticated English. It is easy to see how two families in the same station could have problems relating to each other.

5. Close quarters. The fact that many missionaries are thrown together in close quarters greatly exacerbates an already difficult situation.

> *Petty annoyances and irritations may come to be magnified far out of measure. Under other circumstances these things usually would be overlooked. But the mannerism that wouldn't bother you at all if you saw a person only occasionally, becomes unbearable when you have to be with him morning, afternoon, and evening, every day of the week.*[2]

2. Ibid, pp. 118–119.

Christian workers in an institution in the U.S. do not usually live in the same institution. At five o'clock they take off for home. That affords them a great measure of relief, a relief not available to the missionaries who have to live with their problems around the clock seven days a week. That is hard on the flesh. Anyone who has lived in a concentration camp during wartime has a good idea how difficult human relationships become in cramped quarters.

6. Inability to choose fellow workers. Living together in close quarters is not too bad if one has the opportunity to choose his companions. Students live together in college dorms, but they are usually able to choose their roommates. If a student doesn't like his roommate, he can always ask to have his room changed. Missionaries cannot do so. They do not choose the individuals with whom they must live and work, nor can they be changed except in rare cases.

7. Lack of diversion. Christian workers at home have all kinds of extracurricular activities to break the monotony of the weekly grind. They have access to parks, concerts, races, museums, art galleries, tennis, golf, movies, amateur and professional sports, parades, special events on Memorial Day, Independence Day, and Labor Day. Easter, Thanksgiving, and Christmas usually bring families together for feasting and fellowship.

Missionaries in the larger cities do have some of these activities for diversion, but those in the small towns and the primitive areas are completely without any kind of recreation. After a while the cultural isolation gets them down and they become irritable, almost without knowing why.

8. The presence of children. Married couples with young children have the hardest time. If the adults don't have anything to worry about, the children often provide it. They don't always play together harmoniously. Parents may have to step in to restore peace. An aggressive or selfish child can upset a whole neighborhood. When this happens at home the mother can say to her child: "Leave so-and-so alone! Go play with someone else." But on the mission field there may not be anyone else. Unfortunately, the naughty child may be the son or daughter of your coworkers. To make matters worse, some parents don't discipline their children or even correct them when they squabble with others. Missionary mothers who believe in discipline find this kind of behavior hard to take.

It is true that missionaries have their share of interpersonal problems, but there are extenuating circumstances which we should take into account before we pass judgment on them. "Let him that is without sin cast the first stone" (John 8:7). Those who have not lived under the conditions described above are in no position to criticize them for failure in this regard. Instead we should be praying that God will give them a double portion of His grace and cause His strength to be made perfect on their weakness.

SOME OF THE PROBLEMS

What is it specifically that causes friction among missionaries?

1. A critical spirit. This seems to be Enemy Number 1 in mission circles. "By far the most serious overt threat to missionary relationships, the greatest danger of all, is criticism of one another."[3]

To criticize others is a universal practice. He is a rare individual who never indulges in negative criticism. Criticism, it would seem, is the favorite indoor pastime of most people. This is especially true of those engaged in institutional work where personal contact on a daily basis is very close. It is for this reason that the problem looms so large among missionaries. They too form an intimate circle with close contacts. Much of the daily conversation revolves around the work and the workers, and it is always easy to drift into criticism. If one is looking for imperfection it isn't hard to find, and it is always easier to spot the mote in the other fellow's eye than to detect the beam in one's own. Under these conditions one can very easily and unconsciously develop a critical spirit.

Sometimes criticism takes the form of gossip with no particular malice involved. At other times it is a convenient way of exalting oneself and denigrating others. In either case it is detrimental to the spirit of unity so essential for a Christian community. Criticism has a way of feeding on itself. It grows, like a cancer in the body, until it destroys the harmony of the entire group.

2. Jealousy. Jealousy is not nearly so common as criticism, but when it strikes it is deadly. It can do an enormous amount of injury to the individual himself as well as to others who may be involved. It was jealousy that prompted Aaron and Miriam to murmur against Moses because he had married an Ethiopian woman. They said: "Hath the Lord indeed spoken only by Moses? Hath he not spoken also by us?" (Num 12:2 KJV). The seriousness of the sin can be seen from the kind of judgment that fell on Miriam. The Lord's anger was kindled and He cursed her with leprosy.

We find the same sin in the twelve apostles on their last journey to Jerusalem. They fell to bickering among themselves as to which of them was the greatest. That they should have succumbed to this sort of thing after spending three years in fellowship with the humblest Man who ever lived is an indication of how deepseated this tendency is.

Missionaries have this problem; the very fact that they are a small, close-knit group makes jealousy all the more likely. Missionary wives vie with one another when it comes to entertaining. Each wants to put on a better spread. Missionary mothers want their children to outperform the others. The missionary who has difficulty with the language will envy the one with obvious linguistic ability, and if the good speaker is younger than the other, the jealousy may run deep indeed. An older missionary may resent

3. Ibid., p. 124.

the fact that a younger man has been given a position of leadership ahead of him. Some missionaries are preferred above others by the nationals and singled out for preferential treatment. This is hard on the less popular, less gifted missionaries who may come to resent their more "successful" colleagues.

Money sometimes becomes an occasion for jealousy. The great majority of missionaries receive the same remuneration; but in some missions the workers get only what is pledged toward their support. If the support drops they take the loss. In some international missions the home councils insist that their missionaries live at the level provided by the home office. Under this system Americans often have a much higher income than Britishers, even though they belong to the same mission, live in the same city, and engage in the same work. Disparity of this sort can lead to jealousy. Fortunately this kind of situation is not common, but it does exist. Let no one assume that missionaries are too spiritual to be moved by such carnal considerations. It has been said that to touch a man's pocketbook is to touch the apple of his eye. Missionaries are just as vulnerable at this point.

A very serious form of jealousy may arise where one or two single women live on the same station with a married couple. With or without provocation the wife may become jealous of one or the other of these ladies, especially if the husband shows them any attention. Usually the husband, the only man on the station, will do many things for the single ladies. Some wives resent this and complain that their husbands do more for the gals than they do for them. If the single ladies happen to be young, pretty, and vivacious, the wife has added reason for jealousy.

HOW TO COPE WITH THE SITUATION

As long as missionaries live under abnormal conditions, there are bound to be interpersonal problems. They will never be completely solved, but with effort they can be reduced to manageable proportions. There are some things that can be done, and if everyone does his part, missionary life will be more pleasant.

1. Be sensitive. Study your fellow missionary. Everyone has his pet peeve. Find out what his is *and avoid it*. If he lacks a sense of humor, don't expect him to laugh at your jokes, and never crack a joke at his expense. If he doesn't like to lend out his tools, don't ask to borrow them. If he has a quick temper, don't unnecessarily provoke him to anger. In a word, get to know his idiosyncrasies and hope that he will get to know yours.

2. Be considerate. If you are a host, be considerate of your guests. If you are a guest, be considerate of your host. Paul expressed it beautifully when he said: "Look not every man on his own things, but every man also on the things of others" (Phil 2:4, KJV). The missionary's first concern is to please the Lord. His second is to keep his fellow missionaries happy. This he cannot do if he rides roughshod over their sensibilities.

When strife threatened to destroy the relationship between Abraham and Lot, Abraham said to Lot: "Let there be no strife, I pray thee, between me and thee. Is not the whole land before thee? . . . if thou wilt take the left hand, then I will go to the right; or if thou depart to the right hand, then I will go to the left" (Gen 13:8–9, KJV). Missionaries don't have land to divide among themselves, but there are dozens of practical ways in which they can show consideration, thus reducing the potential for strife.

If your colleagues take a siesta every afternoon and you don't, be sure that your children don't raise a rumpus while they are resting. If you are invited to dinner and the meal is late, wait graciously and patiently until it is served. There is probably good reason for the delay. If your junior missionaries are not able to keep up with your pace, don't scold and find fault. Remember that you were once a new missionary. If hot water is available only twice a week, don't insist on taking a bath every day.

3. Be courteous. The dictionary defines courtesy as having and showing good manners. In ancient China Confucius extolled the virtues of the "princely man." In medieval times they had their knights who practiced chivalry. In more recent times the English have had their "gentlemen," who formed the backbone of the aristocracy. Here in the U.S. we have paid scant attention to the finer things of life. We have been more interested in the acquisition of wealth, the pursuit of happiness, and the achievement of fame than in the development of the social graces. We tend to be more careless and more casual in our dealings with others, and, with the advent of the Women's Liberation Movement, we have all but thrown courtesy to the winds.

There is something to be said for the old way of life with its compassion for the weak, its deference to women, and its veneration of the elderly. Courtesy is the oil that lubricates the intricate machinery of interpersonal relationships and reduces friction to a minimum. When people live in close quarters as missionaries do, courtesy goes a long way towards maintaining harmony in the group.

4. Be generous. Nobody likes a stingy person. Selfishness has no place in Christian service, least of all on the mission field. It will sour a relationship more quickly than anything else.

Generosity is at the heart of the Christian gospel. God loved the world and gave His Son (John 3:16). Jesus said that it is more blessed to give than to receive (Acts 20:35). The early Christians got the point. They had all things in common, sharing their goods and services (Acts 4:32). Stanley Jones said on one occasion: "If I have something that my brother needs more than I do, I am duty bound, as a Christian, to let him have it."

When generosity is mentioned, the mind turns almost instinctively to money, but generosity is much more than money. It includes an expansive mood, a liberal mind, a charitable spirit, and a magnanimous character. It includes going the second mile, sharing the extra garment, lending a helping hand, doing more than is required. It involves entertaining strangers, helping one's friends, loving one's enemies, doing good to all, and not hoping for anything in return.

This kind of generosity never fails to reap benefits. Jesus said so. "Give and it shall be given unto you; good measure, pressed down and shaken together, and running over, shall men give into your bosom" (Luke 6:38, KJV).

5. Be patient. This is harder for some people than for others. Missionaries by nature are not usually known for their patience. They tend to be activists, always on the go—working, traveling, teaching, preaching, healing, helping, building. Patience is not their outstanding virtue. This is a serious handicap because in many non-Western cultures impatience is regarded as a grievous sin, more serious than lying, cheating, or stealing. One veteran said to a group of missionaries about to leave for China: "When you get to China either you'll learn patience or you won't, and if you don't, you'll have a hard time." He was right. Missionaries must learn to be patient—patient with themselves as well as with their fellow workers and their national brethren. All of them are but Christians in the making; God is not finished with them yet.

6. Be humble. Unregenerate human nature is basically proud. Pride was the occasion of Satan's fall. The same was true of Adam. Even the regenerate person is not beyond the reach of pride. It dogs his steps wherever he goes, even to the mission field. There are various forms of pride: pride of face, place, race, and grace, and the last is the most arrogant of all.

My first junior missionary wasn't on the station one week before he berated me for my lack of spirituality. He claimed that as a result of his spiritual experience that took place in the language school, his Adamic nature had been eradicated, root and branch. His "old man," he said, was dead and buried with Christ. Henceforth no temptation could reach him from within, only from without. He then proceeded to criticize me for not having had a similar experience, and he concluded by saying that if he were not a better missionary than I, he would at least have the courage to go home!

Within a year he had left the mission; within another year he had left China; and before long he had completely left the Lord. I was reminded of Paul's admonition: "Let him that thinketh he standeth, take heed lest he fall" (1 Cor 10:12, KJV).

Missionaries need to walk humbly with their God, recognizing the deceitfulness of their hearts, the innate weakness of the flesh, and the ever-present propensity to pride. At the same time they must seek to love the Lord with all their hearts and to esteem others better than themselves.

WITH THE ADMINISTRATION

The overwhelming majority of present-day missionaries are members of some mission, denominational or interdenominational. As such, they are expected to cooperate with the administration.

1. **The responsibilities of the mission.** On the home front there are various secretaries, committees, councils, etc., that are responsible for recruitment of new workers, selection and appointment of candidates, raising and disbursing of funds, publication and distribution of literature, preparation of slides and cassettes, lining up speaking engagements, securing passports and visas, and, finally, making arrangements for travel to the field. Without these vital services, rendered cheerfully and without cost, the candidates would be at a serious disadvantage.

Then there is the field council with the usual committees and subcommittees. Above that there may be a regional or even an international council. The decisions made at these various levels will, sooner or later, affect the life, work, and welfare of every member of the mission. It is important that the new missionary understand the organizational structure under which he will be working and fit into it as best he can. While overseas he is responsible to the field administration. When he returns home on furlough he reverts to the home administration. In either case he is a man under authority and is expected to act accordingly.

Every reputable mission has clearly defined guidelines designed to regulate the life and the work of the missionary. These are usually spelled out in some detail in the *Mission Handbook*. They are sometimes referred to simply as the P & P—Principles and Practices. Every missionary must be thoroughly acquainted with them.

Included in the responsibilities of the administration are oversight, evaluation, and discipline. The young missionary is not left to his own resources. He is placed with a senior missionary until he can function on his own. As a junior missionary he is expected to operate according to the policies established by the field council. At the end of each term of service there is an opportunity for evaluation. This is conducted by the field council in cooperation with fellow missionaries. Sometimes national leaders are asked for their input. If the overall evaluation is favorable, the missionary will be permitted to return for another term of service. If not, he will be asked to remain at home.

Now and again—not very often—it is necessary to exercise discipline. When this happens the offender is asked to resign from the mission. This occurs only when there has been a serious lapse in faith or conduct.

2. **The responsibilities of the missionary.** Nowadays people are more concerned with rights than with responsibilities. Some young people are reluctant to join a mission lest their freedom of action be curtailed. They prefer to make their own plans and do their own thing.

Joining a mission is not the only way to lose one's freedom. When a person gets married his freedom is cut in half. When the first child comes along his freedom is reduced again. Anyone who isn't prepared for that kind of arrangement shouldn't get married. The same applies to membership in a mission. It carries both privilege and responsibility. It is impossible to have one without the other.

When all is said and done, there is little to fear. Many mission agencies have been in existence for almost a hundred years. The rules and regulations they have adopted have been tried and tested by several generations of missionaries and have proved to be both beneficent and benign. They are designed to help, not hinder, the missionary in the conduct of his work. He is better off with them than without them.

Guidance can be a problem. It should be noted that there are two kinds of guidance, personal guidance and group guidance. If the missionary is working entirely on his own, he has only his personal guidance to worry about, but if he is a member of a team he has to reckon with group guidance as well.

What happens when group guidance and personal guidance clash? In that event some kind of compromise must be worked out. This should not prove to be difficult. The majority of mission leaders are fair-minded, warm-hearted men with a good share of wisdom, sympathy, and experience. They have no desire to force the missionary to violate his sense of guidance and end up like a square peg in a round hole. That would be disastrous.

It should be borne in mind that neither form of guidance is infallible. Both sides, therefore, must be prepared for further light on a given problem. Under ordinary conditions the mission will do its best to satisfy the gut feelings of the missionary. In an emergency involving the continuity of a school or hospital program, however, the individual will be asked to fill the post for six months until a suitable substitute can be found. At the end of that time the missionary will be free to pursue the work that is closest to his heart. This seems like an equitable settlement.

If the missionary insists, however, on starting a new work—a hospital, college, radio station, or some other big project—for which the mission has neither the mandate nor the money, the field council will refuse his request. The missionary then has two choices; he can accept the ruling of the council or he can resign. He should be very sure of his guidance before resigning.

In my day in China there was a new missionary who felt strongly that the Lord wanted him in the province of Shansi in North China. The mission was equally certain that he should go to Chekiang in South China. The mission yielded and allowed him to proceed to Shansi. He was there only a year when he wrote to headquarters in Shanghai asking for a transfer to Chekiang! The request was granted. Given good will and common sense on both sides and the helping, healing influence of the Holy Spirit, no problem should prove insoluble.

The missionary should be prepared to shoulder his responsibility vis-à-

vis the administration. The mission should be able to count on his understanding, appreciation, loyalty, cooperation, and, on occasion, his submis-
sion.

WITH NATIONAL WORKERS

Since the collapse of the colonial system following the war, church-
mission relations have suddenly taken on vast importance. The great new
fact of our era is the emergence of a large number of independent churches
in the Third World.

One might have imagined that the advent of independence would bring a
decrease in church-mission tensions. Instead, in many instances they have
increased, so much so that the IFMA/EFMA member missions held a conference in Green Lake, Wisconsin, in the fall of 1971 to discuss the whole
problem of church-mission tensions. For the best part of a week 400 mission
leaders grappled with the question. If both sides show good will the problem
can be solved. In the meantime the missionaries are faced with the problem
of how to get along with thousands of national workers—pastors, evangelists,
Biblewomen, teachers, administrators, technicians, and others.

The role of the missionary is a changing one. First he was the master;
then he became the partner; today he is the servant. Even here at home it is
not easy to play the role of the servant. It is much more difficult on the
mission field. As a servant the missionary must learn to relate to a fully
independent church that has neither the funds nor the expertise available to
the Western missions.

The tensions are heightened by the fact that the national leaders want
change and want it in a hurry, while the missions many times are satisfied
with the status quo and consequently have a tendency to drag their feet.

The moral responsibility rests heavily with the missions. They, more
than the churches, are to blame for the present impasse. It is therefore up to
them to take the initiative to bring about peaceful change. Some missions
have a better record than others, among them the Christian and Missionary
Alliance, Sudan Interior Mission, Overseas Missionary Fellowship, Latin
America Mission, to mention only a few. These missions, by anticipating the
needs and demands of the national churches, have always been one jump
ahead of them. There has, therefore, been little or no tension. Other missions, unfortunately, have not done as well.

The call for moratorium stems largely from this fact. Rightly or wrongly
the national church leaders feel that as long as the missionaries are present
they will not be able to achieve authentic selfhood. It is in this kind of milieu
that today's missionary must function. It will help immensely if he has the
proper understanding and attitude.

1. **Understand them as a people.** It is not enough to understand them as
individuals. He must know them as a people: their history, heritage,

sociopolitical systems, culture and customs, racial characteristics, and national aspirations. To achieve this it is necessary to engage in special studies designed to acquaint him with the people and the country of his adoption. Only as he knows something of the people as a whole will he be able to relate to the individuals with whom he has to work.

2. Trust them as leaders. The missionaries have been leaders so long that it is difficult for them to step aside and watch the nationals take over. They will make mistakes. We made our share of mistakes and the world didn't come to an end. They should be allowed to make their mistakes without losing our confidence. The missionaries should stand with them and behind them in prayer, giving them all the support and sympathy they need. This will not be easy but it must be done if the churches are to survive.

3. Love them as brothers. Bishop Azariah of India made a most stirring address at the Edinburgh Missionary Conference of 1910. He said:

> *My personal observation has revealed to me the fact that the relationship between the European missionaries and the Indian workers is far from what it ought to be, and that a certain aloofness, a lack of mutual understanding and openness, a great lack of frank intercourse and friendliness exists throughout the country.*

He closed with a moving appeal:

> *Through all the ages to come the Indian church will rise up in gratitude to attest the heroism and self-denying labours of the missionary body. You have given your goods to feed the poor. You have given your bodies to be burned. We also ask for love. Give us FRIENDS.* [4]

In spite of the many differences between the nationals and the missionaries, they are our brothers, bought with the same blood, infused with the same Spirit, members of the same family, heirs of the same kingdom, servants of the same Lord, preachers of the same gospel. The things we have in common far outweigh the differences between us. If we love them—really love them—they will overlook many of our faults and failings. If we lack love, everything else is an exercise in futility, and they have an uncanny way of knowing whether or not we love them.

4. Treat them as equals. There is a great outward disparity between the missionary and the national worker. The missionary usually has more education to his credit, more ideas in his head, more books in his library, more equipment in his office, and more money in his pocket; but that doesn't make him any better than the nationals. They are not one bit inferior to him

4. *World Missionary Conference*, 1910, Vol. 9, p. 315.

in areas where it really counts: human worth, personal dignity, self-respect, social awareness, mental acumen, common sense, ability to communicate, and potential for success.

Now that the churches in the Third World are waking up to their responsibility for world evangelization, it is more necessary than ever that the missionary learn to work with nationals on a basis of equality and mutuality. Chinese church leaders in a conference in the Philippines in March 1978 made this statement:

> Dear missionary brothers and sisters: In the past one and a half centuries, you have brought the Gospel to us. We thank you, we respect you, and we love you. From this day, we are partners of the Gospel. We will work hand in hand; we will help each other; and we will be faithful to the end. Together, and by His grace, we will bring the Gospel to the end of the earth.

At the same meeting the missionaries acknowledged the failures of the past, and added:

> We pledge our unreserved support in all areas of your missionary thrust. We desire that you will feel free to call on us for counsel, for encouragement, for training, and even for work where we can be of assistance.

One delegate expressed what was believed to be the sentiment of the entire group:

> Cooperation between Chinese and Westerners should be well planned on an equal basis, with an attitude of openness, love, and patience. This cooperation should be on all levels and in all areas. The task is too great. We cannot afford the time and effort involved if we think only of "We Chinese" and "We Westerners." We all belong to Christ, and all need to join together to fulfill the great commission that Jesus has given to us.[5]

There is still room, plenty of room, on the mission field for the right kind of missionary with the right understanding, the right attitude, and the right motives. The indigenous churches still need—and still want—missionaries of the right stripe. When Leslie Newbigin visited Africa in the 1960s, the African leaders with one voice said to him: "Send us missionaries who will be one with us, live with us, work with us, die with us, and lay their bones with ours here in Africa."[6]

5. Chinese World Pulse, Vol. 2, No. 1, May 1978.
6. World Mission Newsletter, Vol. VIII, No. 1, January 1961.

19

Keeping in Touch

When my wife and I left for China on August 30, 1935, over a hundred friends gathered at Windsor Station in Montreal to see us off. After singing "God will take care of you" and other appropriate hymns, they pumped our hands, said their fond farewells, and promised to pray for us.

The first Christmas in China we received about 130 Christmas cards. Obviously the friends back home were keeping their promise. The second Christmas, however, we received only 60 cards. By the time the third Christmas rolled around, the number dropped to about 30. It was clearly a case of "out of sight, out of mind."

It is essential that missionaries in the thick of the battle for the souls of men have the moral and spiritual support of the home constituency. To retain that support it is necessary to keep the lines of communication open year after year. The responsibility for this rests not with the friends at home but with the missionary on the field; hence the importance of keeping in touch.

PRAYER LETTERS

By far the most effective way to keep in touch is by means of prayer letters. Two things should be borne in mind. First, if prayer letters are to achieve their purpose they must be *read*. Second, to be read they must be attractive and interesting. Both ideas are important.

The missionary must not assume that his letters will be read. To begin with, the folks back home are busy. In many cases both husband and wife hold full-time jobs. The children, with their school and other activities, require an inordinate amount of time and attention. In addition there are the demands of the church, the P.T.A., and other civic associations to be met. When they come home at the end of the day they are weary in body and mind. An uninteresting prayer letter from a missionary halfway around the world hardly merits a second glance.

In addition, most prayer letters are mailed second class and are, therefore, part of a growing pile of what has come to be called "junk mail." Much of the junk mail is never opened, much less read; it goes directly into the wastepaper basket. What will save the prayer letter from the same fate? The prayer letter, unlike the junk mail, will probably be opened, but it will be read only if it is attractive and interesting. Otherwise the recipient will read the first paragraph and put it aside, saying to himself: "I'll read it when I have more time," and promptly forget all about it. Appearance and content largely determine whether or not a prayer letter is read.

1. Attractive in appearance. So important are image and appearance that large commercial and industrial firms hire industrial psychologists to help them sell their products. Nothing is taken for granted. Everything possible is done to make the article appealing to the customer. The shape of the bottle, the size of the carton, the picture on the cover, the color of the wrapper—all are important in the art of selling in the free enterprise system. Advertising in the U.S. is a 70-billion-dollar-a-year industry. The missionary should remember all of this when he sits down to write his prayer letter.

Most prayer letters are produced on a typewriter and run off on some kind of duplicating machine. The missionary sends the original to the home office, or to the home church, or to one of several agencies that specialize in printing and mailing out letters. Sometimes they are sent by air mail directly from the field to the prayer supporters at home. This greatly increases the cost, but it has one advantage—people like receiving letters with beautiful, exotic foreign stamps!

It is essential that the letter be free from errors in typing, spelling, punctuation, and grammar. There should be two or three spaces between paragraphs and a wide margin on all four sides. A crowded letter gives a messy appearance.

Every typewriter has a number of keys that can be used for decorative purposes, such as #, %, &, *, +, !, =. These can be used to make boxes, dividers, and other devices designed to attract attention or provide variety.

Drawings, sketches, decals, pictures, or photos can be used to great effect, especially if they tie in with the contents. These should reflect as far as possible the indigenous culture. Photos should show people rather than places and individuals rather than large groups. When a letter deals with the erection of a building, snapshots of the various stages of construction are suitable. Action pictures and natural poses are preferable to posed pictures.

A picture of the family every three or four years is always welcome and a snap of the new baby is a must.

In the first letter it is a good idea to include a small map indicating the relation of the country to the continent and the relation of your city to the country. In a large country like Zaire, India, or Brazil it is helpful if the reader knows where the writer is located. This is especially true when trouble breaks out. It enables the prayer supporters to determine whether or not the missionary and his family are in the danger zone.

The writer may wish to develop a "trademark" or a special format of his own. I have in my file scores of such letters and they are very attractive. One family in Nigeria came up with a unique approach. The letters purported to be written not by themselves but by their suitcase and they were signed "Sammy Suitcase"! This was good only as long as they were on the go. When they settled down, "Sammy" had to sign off for good.

With a little imagination there is no end to the possibilities. Some missionaries use the mission name and logo at the top of each letter as a regular practice. Others weave their own name into the caption. Some examples are: Hahn Herald, Pretol's Progress, News from Head's Quarters, Petersen's Page, Embossed Notes. Others use the name of the country: Porthole on Portugal, Calapan Chronicle, Taiwan Topics. One family in Venezuela settled for TELL-A-LETTER, using the initials of the six names in the Loy family.

Some prayer letters are written from the point of view of the children and are signed by one of them. One family in their first letter from the field asked nine questions and had each member of the family give his or her answer. Some of the questions were: What do you like best about Kenya? What do you miss most? What has been the hardest to adjust to? Are you glad you came? What surprised you most? What would you like most from America? It was a very interesting and revealing letter.

One letter from Kuala Lumpur carried this heading: *The R's in our life!* Six paragraphs, all beginning with "R," discussed Riots, Rain, Redirection, Reflection, Responsibilities, and Requests. The "R" in each case was printed large and black to make it stand out, and each paragraph was illustrated with an appropriate drawing. The overall effect was striking.

For a while, TEAM missionaries in Japan used a beautiful 10 x 16 inch printed form which folded into three parts. On the cover were the words, "A Peep into Japan." Opening two screen "doors" revealed a sketch of a Japanese family in the dining room. On the large inside sheet was a fact-filled description of Japanese life and culture, each paragraph appropriately illustrated with a colored drawing. On the remaining half of the back side was a personal letter from the missionary. This served a double purpose. It afforded a glimpse into Japanese life in general and included news of the missionary family as well. A form of this kind can be used by all the members of the mission.

Most missionaries continue to use white stock, though colored stock is almost as cheap and certainly more attractive. In some parts of the world, however, colored stock may not be available. When using colored stock, care should be taken to use a different colored ink. Dark green ink on light green stock is very difficult to read. The same is true of other colors.

For their year-end letters some missionaries are now using paper with a Christmas motif. This kind of stock is available in an increasing number of countries. It can also be ordered from home, but that would probably add to the cost.

Speaking of cost brings up the point that postage is becoming a problem for some, depending on the number of letters in each mailing. International airmail is 40 cents for the first half ounce for first-class mail. To send letters by sea would hardly be worth the effort; the news would be two or three months old by the time it was received.

To help with mailing costs some missions are now undertaking to reproduce and mail out all prayer letters. The cost for this service is written into the missionary's support figure, so his account is automatically charged with the expense.

If neither the mission nor the home church can assume responsibility for sending out prayer letters, the missionary could get help from one of the following agencies:

Christian Services Fellowship
5716 Benton Avenue South
Minneapolis, MN 55437.

Missionary Letter Service
RD 4
Gettysburg, PA 17325

Missionary Mailings
Route 4, Box 120-A
Thief River Falls, MN 56701.

Missionary Letters, Inc.
334 East Wesley Street
Wheaton, IL 60187.

King's Missionary Letter Service
19303 Freemont Avenue N.
Seattle, WA 98133

2. Interesting in content. Appearance, important as it is, is no substitute for content. A beautifully prepared letter will attract the attention of the recipient to the point where he will *begin* to read, but by itself it is not enough to insure that he will read it through. If the content is poor it is certain that later letters, however attractive, will not be read, which leads to the conclusion that appearance alone is not enough. If letters are to be effective over a long period of time they must be interesting and informative.

The most important part of any letter is the first paragraph. If that fails to get attention the letter may well remain unread. In some letters the first paragraph is the weakest. It begins with a vague general statement or, worse still, an apology for not having written sooner. Some missionaries feel that they must appear spiritual so they quote Scripture. Most readers have learned to skip the first paragraph and move down to the second where, presumably, the news begins. If it doesn't, they discard the letter. There is nothing wrong with quoting Scripture provided it is appropriate to the occasion.

One letter in my file contains three quotations from Scripture: "The eternal God is thy refuge and underneath are the everlasting arms" (Deut 33:27, KJV); "The rain descended, and the floods came" (Matt 7:27, KJV); and "Neither shall any plague come nigh thy dwelling" (Psalm 91:10, KJV). The first verse introduces a paragraph which describes the goodness of God through another year. The second is related to a paragraph telling about recent floods that inundated the roads and made travel impossible, but also brought fertility to the soil. The third one concerns an outbreak of amebic dysentery that decimated the population. That use of Scripture is not only permissible, it is highly desirable.

Here are several examples of sharp, eye-catching introductions. "Give a man a fish and he will eat for a day. Teach him to fish and he will eat forever. Here in Kenya we are involved in teaching, so that in the years to come, should the Lord tarry, the church of Africa will be able to carry on its own program." Another letter begins: "Death is a reality one is never far from. Yesterday morning Nathan's teacher and her husband were stabbed to death in the school courtyard." Still another begins: "There is a young girl just outside the compound lying in the ditch. She is sick and needs food. She is going to die soon. What shall we do?"

Christmas letters usually start off with the greetings so common to that season of the year. Not this one. "Last Christmas in Singapore, our jovial Santa Claus was much frustrated by not being able to find a single chimney in our big mission home. He sadly shook his head, lamenting, 'No chimney! No chimney!' This year if he called on us he could toast his toes with us around our fireplace—one of those welcome experiences we are having after three years of solid summer in the tropics."

Another Christmas letter begins: "A WHITE CHRISTMAS and a JOYOUS CHRISTMAS from your missionary friends, Gordon and Vera in Lion City—Singapore. We shall wake up Christmas morning with the temperature 72°F. Seventy miles south will sleep the equator. . . . Expansive Singapore harbor will quiver with boats from every nation under heaven. Three quarters of a million Chinese will kowtow, not to the Savior, but to big business. Malays, Indians, Indonesians, and Europeans will play a minor refrain; but few of them will bow in worship to the Savior of the world."

Even a letter about candidate school can begin with a paragraph packed with action and suspense. "SCENE: Eight frightened, tense-looking individuals. One in the corner nervously biting her fingernails; another on a chair trying to relax by playing with a baby; three others huddled together on a couch discussing their plight in subdued tones; one in the kitchen downing a glass of water; the other two just standing by the door . . . concentrating on disguising their anxiety. P.O.W.s? No. Just ordinary missionary candidates waiting for the S.I.M. Council to accept or reject them for service in Africa."

What about the length and frequency of prayer letters? Madison Avenue has gone back to the long, four-page advertising letter and some Christian organizations have followed suit. I doubt the wisdom of this move, perhaps because I usually throw such letters away without reading them. The length of the letter will depend to some extent on the circumstances at the time. A two-page, or even a three-page, letter may be warranted if there is some momentous event to describe. Anyone who attempts a three-page letter should be an exceptionally good writer. Otherwise a one-page job seems best.

To keep it down to one page the writer will have to do some pruning, but that is a necessary part of good writing. Very few professional writers are satisfied with the first, or even the second, draft of an article. They write and rewrite it several times until the finished product is as close to perfection as they can make it. The missionary should do no less.

How often should the missionary send out a prayer letter? Once a quarter is too often, unless a special event calls for a special letter. Once every six months is better, but even that may be too often. Once a year seems to be an ideal schedule. If the schedule calls for two letters a year, one, written preferably in December, should give the highlights for the entire year. Whether the letters go out once a quarter or once or twice a year doesn't matter nearly as much as sending them out on time. Once the missionary has decided on his timetable he should stick to it religiously, avoiding procrastination like the plague; otherwise, his prayer support at home will be sure to suffer. He is busy, but not too busy to write prayer letters. These are the lifeline between the missionary and his supporting constituency at home. He should write his letter on time even if he has to neglect something else.

In one letter he should tell something about his family. The other one could deal with one major topic, too long and involved to be included in the year-end letter. Appropriate items for such a letter may be earthquakes, famines, floods, civil wars, evangelistic crusades, church conferences, special workshops, problems and progress in medical work, community development, agricultural missions, theological education by extension, etc. The finest prayer letters I have ever received are written by Drs. Tom and Cynthia Hale of Nepal. Their letters are usually several pages long, but they are so well written that one is compelled to read to the end. Each letter deals with a different aspect of medical work in Nepal, and they are all very interesting and most enlightening. I wish more missionaries would write that kind of letter. The supporters at home would have a much better understanding of the problems and developments of the modern missionary movement.

Many prayer letters are unsatisfactory from the point of view of content. It is apparent that the writer either was in a hurry and lacked the time to do a good job, or he ran out of good material and had to make his bricks without straw. Either way, the end result is a disappointment to the reader.

Two things are essential to producing a good letter—interesting material and hard work. Let's face it, to write an interesting, informative letter takes time, thought, patience, prayer, and hard work. It is fatal for the missionary to depend on the inspiration of the moment. Every missionary should have some plan for collecting pertinent material as he goes along. The 19th century missionaries, aware that they were making history, kept voluminous diaries in which they recorded all important events. Today's missionaries have neither the knack nor the need to keep a diary; consequently they sometimes have difficulty in putting a letter together.

In the absence of a diary the missionary should have some kind of record book in which the year's events are set down. In addition he should keep a manila folder marked "Prayer Letter" in which he keeps odds and ends: magazine articles, newspaper clippings, quotations, illustrations, letters, stories, anecdotes, etc. Then when he comes to write his prayer letter, he will not have to spend half a day racking his brain to find something to say. He will have sufficient material for several letters and need only select the items he wishes to use in the one at hand.

Style is important. Each missionary should develop his own style rather than copy another person's. It is a good idea to take a writer's manual to the field, or to study the articles in a popular periodical like the *Reader's Digest*. He may never become a first-class writer, but with a little study and effort he can improve his style to the point where his letters will be a pleasure to read. Above all, he should aim at brevity, clarity, and cogency.

One thing the writer should never do is preach! Missionaries are among the most spiritually-minded people in the world, pious as well as practical, devout as well as dedicated. There is therefore always the temptation to "preach" when writing a prayer letter. This should be strenuously resisted. Readers at home look for information, not inspiration. They want news to fuel their prayers, not blessed thoughts to warm their hearts. These they can get from their pastor or from devotional books or Christian periodicals.

There should be some continuity from one letter to the next. If the March letter requested prayer for a specific problem, the next letter should indicate whether or not the prayer was answered. People pray better if they know their prayers are being answered.

It is helpful for prayer purposes if at the end of the letter there is a short line of items for prayer and praise. This enables the recipient to pray about these matters without having to reread the entire letter each time.

Prayer letters should always be signed in full. All letters should also carry the writer's full address. Only this week I received two letters with no indication of the whereabouts of the writers. When there is a change of address this fact should be drawn to the attention of the reader; otherwise it may pass unnoticed. From time to time the recipients should be asked to notify the writer of any change of address.

CASSETTES

In recent years cassettes have become available and nearly everyone has a small recorder. This makes it possible for the churches at home to hear their missionaries speak. This method of communication is more personal than a letter can ever be.

Some missions are now making extensive use of cassettes. The Evangelical Free Church Department of Overseas Missions makes a monthly tape which they send to some 400 churches in the U.S. and Canada. They are used in the midweek prayer services and missionary and other meetings. They are general in content and give a broad picture of the work. This is an excellent way for the churches to keep in touch with events and developments in ten different fields. Special prayer requests are always included.

It would be difficult and costly for the individual missionary to send tapes to all the people on his mailing list, but he may wish to make a small number of tapes and send them to the churches to which he and his wife belong and to other supporting churches with which they are closely associated. Tapes can be used to great advantage during the annual missionary conference. Missionaries should do their best to make them as interesting and informative as possible. They should plan ahead exactly what they want to say, as briefly and clearly as they can. The tapes should be mailed well in advance of the conference to be sure they arrive in time.

Some of the larger churches which can afford it arrange for a long-distance telephone conversation with their missionaries during the annual conference. While writing this chapter I received the following in a prayer letter from Taiwan: "May 6 brought a lovely surprise. Our home church (Christ Church, Oakbrook) had let us know that they would be putting through a phone call from the service to us during their missionary festival so we were ready when the phone rang. After Pastor DeKruyter talked with us he put Margie, Robby, and Jill on the phone. We were so overcome we couldn't think what to say! There were about 900 in the audience listening to it all."[1]

The tape ministry is a two-way street. Some churches tape the Sunday morning service and send it to all their missionaries, regardless of the number. Others make a tape once a month. Some send the Sunday bulletin to their missionaries. In this and other ways the home churches can minister to their missionaries overseas. This type of ministry is exceedingly valuable, especially to missionaries in primitive areas where they lack fellowship and seldom if ever hear a "meaty" sermon or good music.

1. Letter from George and Ruth Steed, June 1978.

20

Furlough

The dictionary defines furlough as "a leave of absence from duty, granted especially to a soldier." In military life the enlisted person gets a month's leave for every year of service. This is "furlough." The word has been taken over by the missions and is in common use in church circles.

Furloughs used to come every seven years, but in this jet age they now occur much more often, usually once every four years. In some missions there is a choice, depending on the length of service, of four, six, eight, ten, or twelve months of furlough.

Some missions arrange for their workers to have a mini furlough—two or three months—every two years. The Sudan Interior Mission uses charter flights every June and September to transport the missionaries back and forth. This enables them to return home every two years for a short time rather than every four years for a longer period. By using charter flights the cost is cut in half, making the operation quite economical. It has some added advantages: it does not interfere with the schooling of the children, it makes it possible for parents to keep in touch with their teenagers at home, and it is less disruptive of the work on the field.

If missionaries return on furlough once every four years, it means that in any given year 25 percent of the total missionary force is at home on furlough. This inevitably leads to problems for mission executives, both on the field and here at home. Actually, furloughs are a headache for most missions. This is one problem that the Roman Catholics do not have. Their missionaries seldom come home on furlough. They are moved about from place to place and are sometimes called home for service, but they do not have a regular furlough as Protestant missionaries do.

THE PURPOSE

Furlough is an integral part of missionary life and it has definite purposes.

1. **Rejuvenation.** Most missionaries live under conditions that are not conducive to physical or mental health. After four years of isolation in a steaming jungle with a diet that lacks nutrition and variety and a climate that is always hot and humid even during the night, they are physically and psychologically exhausted. During World War II it was discovered that the American GI lost 50 percent of his combat efficiency after one year in the jungles of New Guinea.

There have been a few missionaries who have stayed on the field for thirty or forty years without a furlough. Amy Carmichael of Dohnavur was one of these, but even she might have profited from a furlough now and then, for in her later years she became completely incapacitated. Most missionaries, men as well as women, find that their "combat efficiency" is greatly reduced after four years of arduous service. It is imperative that they return to the familiar surroundings of the U.S. with its moderate climate, its abundant and nutritious food, and its complete change of scenery.

The first order of business upon return is a medical checkup. If surgery is required it is undertaken immediately so that restoration to health may be achieved at the earliest possible moment. If a special diet or medication is recommended it likewise is begun immediately. Missionaries usually come home looking pale and thin, but by the time they have been in the U.S. three months they are beginning to look like themselves again.

Rejuvenation includes more than the physical. It involves the psychological, the social, the cultural, and the spiritual as well. Children born on the mission field need to be exposed to the American way of life, to say nothing of brushing up on their English.

Part of the rejuvenation process is the joy of family reunion. The grandparents have never seen their grandchildren and can hardly wait for them to come home. The parents are anxious to show off their new children. Fellowship with family and loved ones is very precious, especially when they are Christians and can enter wholeheartedly into the joys and sorrows, the delights and disappointments, of missionary life.

Spiritual rejuvenation is by no means the least in importance. It is always a joy to return to the supporting churches, especially the home church, and to bask in the warmth of Christian fellowship. The Sunday morning worship service in a beautiful sanctuary with carpets on the floor, cushions in the pew, and draperies at the windows has a soothing effect on the spirit of the weary missionary who for years has been worshiping in a primitive bamboo structure with a thatched roof and mud floor, backless benches for pews, people coming and going, dogs and chickens wandering in and out, and crying babies demanding to be fed.

2. Preparation. It is generally assumed that the missionary will return to the field. The purpose of furlough is not simply to restore him to health and strength but to prepare him for another term of service. An important part of the preparation is personal development. The missionary on furlough wants to do everything he can to make up for lost time, to catch up on the many things he missed, and to read the books that have been published while he was away, books that he has seen advertised in Christian journals but never had the opportunity to read.

As part of his personal development he may want to get back into academic life, to stretch his mind as well as to warm his heart. The best way to do this is to attend university or, better still, to enroll in seminary, where he will enjoy a form of mental stimulation not available on the mission field.

Mission boards should encourage their missionaries to take advantage of some kind of continuing education and should provide financial help to make it possible for them to do so. Single missionaries (mostly women) are the best situated when it comes to continuing education. They have no family responsibilities and are free to spend a semester or two in an educational institution. Their personal allowance together with their work account will permit them to live and eat in the school and probably have something left over for tuition. Married men with families have a harder time. They will have to leave the family at home and go to school by themselves or find off-campus housing to accommodate the family. In either case they will need financial help, for when tuition charges are added to everything else, the bill can climb pretty high. If the family men are to get further schooling the mission boards will have to make adequate provision for them.

Many evangelical seminaries now offer a Master of Arts in missiology. Others, among them Trinity and Fuller, have a Doctor of Missiology program. Special arrangements are made for missionaries to do their residence work during furlough and write their thesis or dissertation after they return to the field. Some schools allow five years for the completion of the thesis. Others offer extension courses which can be taken on the field and applied towards a degree program when they come home on furlough.

Missionaries must be released from deputation work in order to profit by these opportunities; otherwise they will be burning the candle at both ends and by the time they are ready to return to the field they will be physical and nervous wrecks. If necessary, furlough should be extended for six months or a year to permit the completion of the course of study. It is exceedingly important that missionaries get the most out of their furlough, intellectually and spiritually as well as physically and socially. On the field they have been on the giving end until they have just about run dry. Furlough is the time for them to recharge their batteries. There is no better way to do this than to spend some time in an academic institution where they will be stimulated by fellowship with other students and challenged by the instruction of the classroom. In recent years hundreds of missionaries have testified to the inestimable value of this kind of continuing education.

In many cases missionaries must increase their financial support to the level required by the mission before returning to the field. In some faith missions the members receive only what is actually sent in for their support. During their four years overseas there is bound to be some attrition in the amount of support pledged. This is due to many factors at the local level: failure of churches and individuals to follow through on their commitments, change of pastors, death of supporters, church splits, and other disruptive factors.

Missions are loath to send their members back to the field until their full support has been underwritten by interested churches and individuals. This usually means that they must visit the supporting churches or advise them by letter of their specific needs. This is not nearly as difficult as raising support as candidates, but it does require time and patience.

3. Deputation. Faith missions with few exceptions expect their missionaries to visit the supporting churches while they are on furlough. The purpose is fourfold: to report on their work; to recruit new missionaries; to solicit prayer support; and, as mentioned above, to regain lost financial support.

It is definitely not a good idea to take the family on deputation tours. The rugged pace is too hard on the mother and the children. Besides, it is difficult for the churches to provide hospitality for a family that needs three bedrooms. It is better all around for the father to go on deputation by himself, even though it means separation from the family.

Not all missionaries are good speakers, but that doesn't mean that they are not good missionaries. This should be borne in mind when the mission sets up the deputation schedule. Church members should also remember this when they evaluate the missionary's message. He is there to report on his work, not to preach a sermon. Churches that have supported the missionary and his family through the years with their prayers and their money should welcome his report whether or not he is an eloquent speaker.

Care should be taken, however, when the mission sets up the speaking tour. As a rule only good speakers should be sent to colleges and seminaries where they are completely unknown and are likely to be judged solely on their platform performance. A poor speaker is almost sure to leave a bad impression with the students, most of whom are accustomed to professors who are good communicators, and who are apt to be critical of poor speakers. Inevitably the missionary will be compared with the professor and the comparison will not always be in his favor. If the missionary speaker does not measure up to their standards the students will be turned off.

The missionary on furlough has one definite advantage over the missionary candidate when it comes to deputation work. He has been on the field, has had personal experience in the work, and therefore can speak with authority. He must not assume, however, that either he or his message will be well received simply because he has been a missionary. Every message should be carefully thought out, well prepared, and well delivered. There is no excuse for a poor performance.

The greatest temptation facing the missionary speaker is to run overtime. Time and again missionaries have been guilty of speaking too long and thereby ruining the entire effect of the message. There are several reasons for this strange behavior: first, he is full of his message; second, he naturally has a lot to tell; and third, he is accustomed on the field to speaking from 60 to 90 minutes. To be suddenly cut down to 20 or 30 minutes is a real hardship. If he is wise he will stay within the time limits set for him. Nothing destroys the interest of a congregation more quickly than a longwinded speaker—even a good one.

4. Recruitment. If the missionary enterprise of our day is to continue its momentum, it must get its full quota of new workers each year. Some of the larger missions need eighty or ninety new missionaries annually just to maintain their existing commitments. Few are getting that many. Recruitment is a major concern of candidate secretaries.

A study done by the Missionary Research Library of New York shows that more missionary recruits are influenced by missionaries than by pastors, parents, Sunday school teachers, or anybody else. This being so, the missionary on furlough occupies a strategic place in the missionary movement. Without his influence the number of recruits would be considerably lower than it is.

The best place for recruiting new missionaries is the college campus. That's where the young people are, not in the churches. Not many of them attend the annual missionary conference in the local church.

To have an effective recruiting ministry on campus the missionary should try to arrange for an extended stay; one chapel service is seldom enough. There are several ways in which he can do this. He can enroll in the school and spend a whole semester there. He can become the missionary-in-residence, in which capacity he may be able to remain for a month or more. He can accept an invitation to join the faculty for a year. In any of these capacities he will have ample opportunity to contact students. As a student he will live in the dorm and eat in the dining room as well as attend classes. As the missionary-in-residence he need neither study nor teach. He will simply be there to make himself available to anyone who wishes to speak with him. As a professor he may teach such courses as missionary anthropology, cross-cultural communications, non-Christian religions, health care delivery in developing countries, etc. If he has a Ph. D. in biblical studies he might be invited to teach New Testament, Old Testament, or Systematic

Theology. More and more, qualified missionaries are being invited to teach for a semester in colleges and seminaries. They bring a freshness to the academic climate of the school which is very invigorating.

One missionary on furlough enrolled in the School of World Mission at Trinity Evangelical Divinity School in the early 1970s. When he came home he asked the Lord to give him five recruits to take back to Bangladesh. At the end of his year at Trinity three men and two women were preparing to go to Bangladesh. Today that team is doing an unusually fine piece of church planting work in one of the most difficult fields in the world.

THE BENEFITS

The benefits of furlough are many. Only a few can be discussed here.

1. **Change of scenery.** It begins with the climate. In many areas of the world there are only two seasons, wet and dry, and neither of them provides much variety. One of the refreshing features of furlough is the change of seasons in the Northern Hemisphere. Snow is fascinating to those who have been living in the steaming tropics. Then spring comes when nature comes out of hibernation and decks herself in her prettiest attire. Summer is vacation time when people head for the mountains and the beaches. If the temperature climbs beyond eighty there is air conditioning to relieve the heat. Autumn brings sunny days, cool nights, and foliage that defies description.

Who but the missionary can appreciate the privilege of eating fresh vegetables and drinking unboiled water? Or visiting McDonald's or the Pizza Hut or Baskin Robbins? Paved roads, even in the rural areas without goats, cows, or camels to compete with, are a joy. Traveling the super highways with their well-stocked restaurants and clean service stations every twenty miles or so is sheer delight. As for the supermarkets, they appear to be the last stop just before heaven! And what a relief not to have flies, fleas, bedbugs, cockroaches, snakes, and scorpions to worry about.

2. **Change of pace.** Furlough is a time for rest and relaxation with friends and loved ones. It includes picnics, outings, ball games, ice capades, Memorial Day, Fourth of July, Labor Day, and the most American holiday of all, Thanksgiving Day. No one bangs on the door at five o'clock in the morning. Visitors give advance notice of their intended visit. Meals are seldom interrupted by people calling for help. Law and order prevail. Peace and quiet are maintained. Privacy, the sweetest of the social amenities, is assured both day and night. When he gets the urge to travel there is the family car waiting to take him and his wife and children, swiftly and safely, wherever they want to go. The endless and rapid pace of missionary life is for the time forgotten and he thoroughly enjoys the change.

3. Reunion with family and friends. Four years is a long time to be away from those you love best. The years have brought many changes. The ten-year-old niece is now a young lady in her teens. The seventeen-year-old nephew is married. Grandma is a little greyer and grandad is a little balder—and maybe stouter. It is a thrill to witness their joy as they meet, sometimes for the first time, their grandchildren, who have never seen a football game, a high school band, a supermarket, a golf course, a television set, or a fire engine; and how they enjoy taking them on a shopping spree or to the swimming pool or a baseball game.

4. Contact with the home church. Here the missionary finds the people who have stood behind him with their gifts and their prayers. He will have a lot to tell and also much to learn. Here too, changes have taken place. The church has grown almost beyond recognition. Perhaps the sanctuary has been enlarged and a Christian Education building has been erected. The membership of the missionary committee has changed and a new pastor has recently been installed. The church members probably will have a shower for the returning missionaries. Their first Sunday at home the family will be invited to come to the platform to be introduced to the congregation. That will be the beginning of a year of rich Christian fellowship.

Contact with the home church involves a good deal more than making a report to the congregation or speaking at the annual missionary conference. There is no reason why both husband and wife should not become actively involved in the life and ministry of the church for the entire year. They could teach a Sunday school class, or serve on the missionary committee, or act as sponsor of the youth group, attending their meetings, outings, and other special activities. In this way the people of the church, including the young people, could get to know them more intimately. The husband might be asked to help out with some of the pastoral duties such as home visitation, hospital calls, and leading some of the services.

5. Visit to headquarters. It is important that missionaries on furlough renew personal contact with the home office, not only to conduct business but also to spend time in prayer, fellowship, and evaluation. Some mission boards have all missionaries on furlough gather at a central place for a retreat. In some cases it coincides with the annual candidate school. This gives the new workers the opportunity to meet the missionaries with whom they will be working when they get to the field. The interaction between these two groups is very helpful. It also gives the board an opportunity to meet personally with each missionary unit to discuss all the ramifications of life and work overseas. If the missionaries have any grievances, this is the time and place to air them. If the board has any misgivings about the missionary's work, this provides an excellent opportunity to talk about the matters of concern without making him feel that he is "called on the carpet."

Such a retreat will be costly in terms of money. The mission will have to provide travel expenses there and back, but the funds will be well invested. An outstanding Bible teacher may be invited to bring a series of devotional messages for their enrichment and encouragement. Fellowship among the missionaries is very important, especially in a large mission that has work in ten or twenty countries. Without such a retreat the missionaries in Zaire will know only the other missionaries in Zaire; they will never become acquainted with those in other countries. A retreat of this kind would go a long way toward promoting a strong family spirit among the members of the mission.

6. **Restocking equipment and supplies.** Equipment has a way of breaking down and supplies have a way of running out. Both need to be replenished and furlough is the time to do it. The missionary has already been on the field and knows exactly what is needed for effective service. Some things were never used or turned out to be more trouble than they were worth. These he will discard. Some articles are obtainable only in this country. Others may be obtained overseas, but the price is two or three times what it is here in the U.S. It is to his advantage to purchase them here even if he has to pay duty on them when he returns to the field.

Supporting churches, especially the home church, are always interested in getting a list of the items needed. The missionary should not hesitate to make the list available to individuals and churches who inquire. In this way he may get some things he would not have the funds to buy. It is marvelous to see the way in which the Lord supplies the needs when they become known.

THE PROBLEMS

Each furlough has its own peculiar features. The first is always the most exciting, both to the missionary and to his family at home. It is a happy day when he gets word that furlough has been granted and he is instructed to get ready to go home. He can hardly wait for the time to arrive. He assumes, and probably rightly so, that his friends and relatives at home are just as excited as he is. Later furloughs are never quite the same, and by the time number seven rolls around he would just as soon skip it. His adopted country is now his "native" land and furlough is something of an intrusion.

1. **Leaving the field.** It begins with a certain amount of red tape. The town mayor, the chief of police, the director of taxes, and other officials must be satisfied that he is leaving legally. Something must be done with his household goods and personal effects. They will have to be stored in some out-of-the-way place where they won't clutter things up for those who come to replace him. If the station remains vacant while he is away there is no guarantee that his possessions will be there when he returns. Friends, Christian and otherwise, may "borrow" them in his absence and it might be

difficult to retrieve them when he returns. This is especially true in time of riot, civil war, and other upheavals. Before leaving China to come home on furlough in 1945 towards the end of the Sino-Japanese War, we sold every stick of furniture and thus saved ourselves much trouble when we returned in 1946.

When contemplating furlough it is a good idea to plan ahead. In the case of an international marriage the couple must decide whether to spend their furlough in Australia (her country) or in the States(his country), or whether to split it between the two. The time of year is also important. I would not advise a person from the tropics to arrive in the windy, snowbound city of Chicago in January! June is much better. Also, what about the children's schooling? To arrive home in the middle of a semester imposes a serious hardship on them. It helps immensely if they can enter school at the beginning of the academic year.

Furlough often provides a convenient and economical way to visit certain parts of the world that hold a particular attraction—Europe, London, the Holy Land, Greece. This too requires some advance planning. It is better to visit these places when the children are old enough to appreciate them, in which case it might be wise to wait until the second or third furlough. Traveling extensively with young children is not convenient in any case.

2. Housing for the family. This is the most vexing problem of furlough, especially in recent years when the cost of housing has gone sky high. Most missions give the family a rental allowance, but it seldom pays the full cost of decent housing these days. The missionary is in no position to buy so he has to rent, but rents are also high and houses for rent are very scarce. Apartments are cheaper but they seldom have more than two bedrooms, which is not enough for a family with children of both sexes.

It is definitely not wise to share a house with relatives unless it is a very large house belonging to grandparents who live alone. Even then there may be problems when the initial welcome has worn off. Grandparents love their grandchildren, but having them around *all* the time can be wearing.

Some missionaries who have access to special funds are now buying a house at home and renting it out while they are on the field. In this way they can keep up the monthly payments and have a place of their own on furlough. This is the only way a missionary family can ever hope to build up equity for their later years.

Some churches are now making provision for their missionaries on furlough by buying or building furnished apartments. Everything is provided, including kitchen utensils, towels in the bathroom, linen on the beds, and food in the freezer. The Southern Baptist churches have over 200 of these homes and apartments in 19 states. A complete list of housing is mailed to all missionaries twice a year. Missionaries write directly to the church to request the use of the home they prefer. Additional information is supplied regarding schools, transportation, recreational facilities, cultural features, community events, opportunities for continuing education, etc. Given this kind of information the family looking forward to furlough is able to make their plans well in advance. It would solve one of furlough's greatest problems if every missionary-minded church would invest in a second parsonage and reserve it for missionaries on furlough.

3. Schooling for the children. This is the second major problem of furlough and one that is uppermost in the minds of parents when making their plans. The sudden change from a school for MKs to one of our schools in the U.S. can be a traumatic experience. It is hard on teenagers, especially girls. Some of the local school systems in the larger cities are wracked with problems—discipline, drugs, vandalism, violence—which make the learning process almost impossible. Even in the suburbs the situation isn't much better. In this kind of milieu the MK is very self-conscious and often feels threatened.

Younger children adjust more readily and fit into the American scene with less difficulty. Older teenagers find the teen subculture strange at best. The far-out dress fads, the loud music, the foul language, the preoccupation with sex, the frivolity and immaturity of many of the students, the lack of discipline in the classroom—all make life difficult for an MK. Equally difficult to understand is the total lack of interest in international news. For these and other reasons an MK would find himself more at home in a Christian high school; but they are not available in every community, and where they are, the fees are high.

There are academic problems as well. Some MKs are ahead of their American peers and skip a year when they enter school in the U.S. Others may be somewhat behind in science and U.S. history. If they enter in the middle of the year their problems are just that much greater.

4. Relating to the home church. If the church is missionary-minded, problems in this area probably will not exist, but not all churches are missionary-minded. Much will depend on the attitude and interest of the pastor. He may be new to the church and not personally acquainted with the missionaries. Besides, his interest in missions may be superficial and his participation without enthusiasm. Apart from acknowledging their presence at the first Sunday morning service, he might never again mention their name. He may be concerned only for the growth of *his* church and *his* work. Missions is something "out there" where only missionaries are supposed to function.

The missionary may have problems relating to the church members. The American scene is changing so rapidly that he could be a trifle bewildered when he first gets back into the swing of things. The American church is not far behind the world; it too is changing. It is becoming more secular, more worldly, more affluent, and more self-centered. The worship service on Sunday morning is still well attended; there may even be two services. The

Sunday evening attendance may be one-third as many; and as for the mid-week prayer meeting, only a handful of the faithful few ever bother to turn out. He could get the impression that the church is no longer a spiritual power house, that individual members are content to enjoy their religion rather than to practice it. They give much of their time and energy to the pursuit of happiness and spend a disproportionate amount of their income on themselves. Each time he comes home the people have new and more luxurious cars and larger and more expensive homes with more elaborate furnishings. The affluence of the church members is in sharp contrast to the poverty he has been accustomed to on the field where most of his converts have two suits of clothes, one for the warm weather and the other for the cold.

He also finds that discipline and dedication are virtues that are rapidly disappearing from the American churches, including some evangelical ones. Divorce, which used to be a problem for the world, is now a problem for the churches. Thirty years ago it was becoming common in the world. Twenty years ago it became a problem in the liberal churches. Today it is becoming a problem in the evangelical churches. Elders and deacons are often divorced. Even pastors have been known to run off with a woman in the congregation. I heard of one pastor who has been divorced twice and now has his third wife, whom he married while still the pastor of an evangelical church. Pre-marital sex is by no means unknown in evangelical circles and young people engaging in this kind of behavior are given a church wedding when they decide to get married, no questions asked. All of this seems very strange to the missionary. He wonders how far the home church can go in the direction of the world without losing completely its role as the salt of the earth and the light of the world.

On each recurring furlough he and his wife find the home church just a little closer to the world, and this disturbs them.

5. Returning to the field. Furlough is predicated on the assumption that the missionary will return to the field, but this should not be taken for granted. He or a member of his family may have a health problem that prevents his return. His record on the field may be such that it would be a waste of time and money to send him back. There may be a vacancy on the home staff which he will be asked to fill, or he may remain at home for several years to see his children through high school and into college. Some missionaries, particularly single ladies, remain at home to care for their aged parents who have no one else to look after them.

Most missionaries after they have been at home for six months are ready to return. Their furlough has served it purpose. They have seen all their friends and relatives and have visited all the supporting churches. At this point they become homesick for the mission field. As for the MKs, they can hardly wait to "go home." Home for them is not the U.S. but the country in which they were born, whose language they learned before they spoke

English, and whose way of life has become an integral part of their cultural heritage. They feel more at home there than here.

Before returning to the field for another term it is necessary to get clearance from the mission board. If his record has been good this should pose no problem, but it is a formality to be reckoned with. If for any reason he is not needed or not wanted on the field his service should be terminated. Furlough is a time for evaluation. It is an opportunity for both the missionary and the board to assess the effectiveness of his ministry. If a change is called for, this is an ideal time to make it with a minimum amount of embarrassment. Missionary work is not for everyone and the sooner this is discovered the better. If perchance he decides to terminate his service, the board and the supporting home church should do their best to make the transition as smooth as possible. All too often a stigma attaches to the missionary who fails to return to the field. He is referred to as a "casualty." This is unfortunate.

If the missionary does return to the field, the church should arrange for a commissioning service just before he leaves. He and his family should once again be commended to the Lord and to the ministry of the Word. The service should take place during the morning worship service when the entire congregation is present. It will not only strengthen the hands of the missionary but also remind the church members of their duty to support him with their prayers while he is gone. This might be a good time to take up a "prayer pledge." Just as the congregation pledges their financial support during the annual missionary conference, so now they should pledge their prayer support. It would also be a nice gesture if the church were to give him and his family a going-away gift. Missionaries always have special needs and can always use more money, especially when they have to travel.

The commissioning service should not be a perfunctory affair. The entire service that morning should be devoted to world missions. Either the missionary should be asked to speak or the pastor should bring a missionary message from the Bible. It is an excellent opportunity to remind the church of its responsibility for the evangelization of the world.

When the missionary returns to the field, where is he to locate? Does he return to his former place of work or does he break new ground? Much will depend upon mission policy and the local circumstances prevailing on the field at the time. Some missions prefer to move their workers around. They are expected to plant a new church during each term, in which case they do not return to their former location.

On the other hand, continuity is a good thing, especially in a country like Japan. It takes the Japanese a long time to establish rapport with strangers and they don't appreciate having to deal with too many different missionaries in a short span of time. Language is an important factor. No missionary should be expected to learn a new language or even a new dialect unless circumstances over which the mission has no control make it necessary, as when a country closes to missionary work and he must either remain at home or be sent to another field. It is exceedingly difficult and very time consuming for a person over forty to learn a new language.

Finally the day arrives when he must board the plane and be on his way. This means parting from friends and loved ones, and this is never easy. There is a certain excitement about going out the first time, but on the second and third occasions much of the glamour is gone. He now *knows* what missionary work is like. He may feel that he is leaving his parents for the last time. They may be getting on in years, or their health may be impaired, and they may not be expected to live much longer. Under such conditions it is particularly difficult to leave. It is even harder for the parents left behind. They know that the chances of their seeing their children and grandchildren again may be slim.

Worse still, the returning missionaries may have to leave one or two of their teenage children at home. That is the greatest sacrifice of all. It is bad enough to be separated from them while they are in school on the field; it is much harder to leave them at home for a period of three or four years, not knowing how they will fare in the meantime. A million questions pass through their minds: How will they adjust to the American culture? Where will they go to college? How will they pay their bills? Where will they spend the Christmas holidays? Will they be able to get work during the summer vacation? Will they have any health problems? Will they find the right husband or wife?

At our station in Fowyang, Anhwei, China, we and our senior missionaries used to have a prayer meeting every Saturday evening. We always closed with the singing of Amy Carmichael's hymn which so beautifully expresses the longings of every missionary parent's heart:

> *Father, hear us, we are praying,*
> *Hear the words our hearts are saying,*
> *We are praying for our children.*
>
> *Keep them from the powers of evil,*
> *From the secret, hidden peril,*
> *Father, hear us for our children.*
>
> *From the whirlpool that would suck them,*
> *From the treacherous quicksand pluck them,*
> *Father, hear us for our children.*
>
> *From the worldling's hollow gladness,*
> *From the sting of faithless sadness,*
> *Father, Father, keep our children.*
>
> *Through life's troubled waters steer them,*
> *Through life's bitter battle cheer them,*
> *Father, Father, be Thou near them.*
>
> *Read the language of our longing,*
> *Read the wordless pleadings thronging,*
> *Holy Father, for our children.*
>
> *And wherever they may bide,*
> *Lead them Home at eventide.*

PART THREE

MISSIONARY WORK

21

Getting into the Work

Starting a new career is both exciting and frightening at the same time. The seminary graduate delivers his first sermon with some degree of trepidation. It may take him two or three months to get into the swing of things, even in an established church in familiar surroundings. How much more difficult it is for the missionary. For him, *everything* is new. The society is overwhelmingly non-Christian. The people are mostly indifferent, some of them hostile. The Christians, predominantly women and children, are few in number and of little standing in the community. Less than half of them can read. There may be some "rice" Christians, more interested in what they can get than in the milk and meat of the Word. The church building is nothing more than a three-room dwelling made of adobe and thatch. In this strange milieu the new missionary may be quite bewildered, wondering what to do and how to begin.

Before he even gets started dozens of questions will come to mind. In preaching to the "heathen," should he begin with the creation, the Ten Commandments, the holiness of God, the love of Christ, or the sinfulness of man? In teaching the Christians should he concentrate on the Old Testament or the New? When dealing with the life of Christ should he emphasize the parables or the miracles or both? When using illustrations should he follow Jesus, whose illustrations were taken from an agricultural setting, or Paul, whose illustrations came from a cosmopolitan background?

In his evangelistic work should he go to the people in the bazaar, the teashop, and the village plaza, or should he invite them into the street chapel? Should he try to win the children through the parents or the parents

through the children? What about the women? Should he make any attempt
to contact them, or should he leave them to the Biblewoman? Should he sell
Scripture Portions or give them away? What about beggars? Should he give
them money? What about hecklers? Should they be answered or ignored?
How should he deal with opposition, harrassment, and persecution? Turn
the other cheek? Go the second mile? Or call the police?

ASSET OR LIABILITY?

Is the new missionary an asset or a liability? Actually, he is both. In the
beginning he must be regarded as a liability. For the first year or so he
cannot speak the language so he is not able to make much of a contribution.
He requires a good deal of counsel and supervision from the church and
mission leaders, who must take the time and trouble to introduce him to
missionary life and work. During this period he will of necessity be a con-
sumer, not a producer. In that sense he is a liability.

But he will not remain a liability for long. After a year or two, when he
has become proficient in the language and can take an active part in the
work, he will definitely be an asset. The time required for this transition
differs from person to person. Much will depend on his understanding of his
own role, the state of his health, his progress in the language, his opportunities for service, and the help he gets from others. But sooner or later, if
he sticks with it, he will become a missionary in the full sense of the term.

THE NEW MISSIONARY'S ATTITUDE

Someone has said: "A good start is right smart." In beginning a new
career, with all of its uncertainties and imponderables, there are few things
as important as attitude. If the new worker starts off with a positive attitude
he will probably succeed. A negative attitude, on the other hand, often leads
to failure. It is impossible to overemphasize the importance of attitude.

1. **Gratitude for the privilege of Christian service.** Paul said: "I thank
Christ Jesus our Lord, who hath enabled me, for that he counted me faithful,
putting me into the ministry" (1 Tim 1:12, KJV). Full-time service is not for
everyone. It is reserved for those who have been specially called by God
(Heb 5:4). Paul was extremely grateful that he had been appointed a
preacher, an apostle, and a teacher (2 Tim 1:11). The new missionary will
feel the same way. He will be forever grateful for the grace that called him
into the service of Jesus Christ.

2. **Wonder and excitement at being a missionary.** Not all servants of
God are missionaries. Paul never ceased to wonder at the grace that called
him to preach among the Gentiles the unsearchable riches of Christ (Eph
3:8). It was his joy to preach the gospel "not where Christ was named" (Rom

15:20, KJV). He delighted in the fact that he was sent "far hence to the Gentiles" (Acts 22:21, KJV). He was convinced that to be Christ's ambassador to a lost world, to be guided by His Spirit, entrusted with His Word, and endued with His power, is the highest honor that can be conferred on any man.

3. Willingness to learn. The new missionary has been through college and seminary and probably has several advanced degrees. This does not mean that he has nothing left to learn. He should not equate education with maturity or confuse learning with experience. In spite of all his years of training he still has much to learn. He does not have all the answers. He doesn't even know all the questions. He will be wise to listen and learn, realizing that there are a host of new ideas, new methods, new problems, and new patterns of work. Some day he will be a leader; for the present he is a follower. And he will be a better leader if he is a good follower. He will be able to learn from his missionary colleagues, even the veterans who appear to be slightly behind the times, and he can learn much from the national church leaders. There is no room on the mission field for the cocksure recruit who knows it all and is unwilling to learn.

4. Desire to please. His first responsibility is to please God (Gal 1:10). This does not necessarily preclude the desirability of pleasing one's fellow workers. Speaking of our conduct towards a weaker brother, Paul admonishes us to act charitably in the spirit of Christ, giving the other person the benefit of the doubt. He goes on to say: "He that in these things serveth Christ is acceptable to God and approved of men" (Rom 14:18, KJV). It is important that the new missionary have the approbation of his colleagues, foreign and national, especially those who are older and have had more experience than he. Some missionaries judge their fidelity to God by the number of fellow workers they can alienate. When working with a group of spiritual people—which the missionary usually does—he will best please God by pleasing his colleagues. Their wishes should have a direct bearing on his conduct. He will not go far wrong by trying to measure up to their expectations of him. They are his friends. They wish him well. They want him to succeed. The least he can do is respond by doing his best to please.

5. Confidence to succeed. His confidence, of course, is in the Lord, not in himself. The new missionary is confronted with a formidable array of hostile forces sufficient to strike fear into the stoutest heart, but he is licked before he starts if he looks only at the circumstances and forgets the treasure he has in his earthen vessel—the power that is of God and not of himself (2 Cor 4:7). No man was more conscious of his own spiritual bankruptcy than Paul, yet time and again he expresses complete confidence in the power of God in his life and ministry. He said: "I am sure that when I come unto you I shall come in the fulness of the blessing of the gospel of Christ" (Rom 15:29,

KJV). His gospel, he said, came not in word only, but also in power, and in the Holy Ghost, and in much assurance, or conviction (1 Thess 1:5). He expected results and he got them.

The new missionary starting out will feel like the ten spies on their scouting mission in Canaan. When they saw the size and strength of the enemy they felt like grasshoppers. As a result of their report the children of Israel wandered forty years in the wilderness. Their problem was lack of faith in the power of God to operate on their behalf. Their enemies were formidable, but they forgot that God was greater than all their enemies. So it is with the new missionary. He sees the obvious—the powers of darkness arrayed against him—and if he is not careful he will succumb to unbelief and lose the battle. He needs confidence, not in himself but in the Lord and in the power of His might. He must remember the words of John: "Greater is he that is in you than he that is in the world" (1 John 4:4, KJV).

QUALITIES OF A GOOD SENIOR MISSIONARY

New workers are sent to a station where they will be under the guidance of senior missionaries. This is one of the fringe benefits of belonging to a mission. Unfortunately not all veteran missionaries make good "senior" missionaries. It requires a special kind of missionary to take a raw recruit under his wing, introduce him to the various groups in the community, initiate him into the culture, help him with the intricacies of the language, introduce him to new methods of work, and in general provide him with comfort, counsel, friendship, encouragement, and anything else he might need in the early months of his career.

1. Genuine interest in helping new workers. Not all missionaries are happy to receive new workers right out of language school. There are various reasons for this. In some cases they are too busy and don't have the time, and the job is a time-consuming one. Some may have the time but not the inclination; they are already carrying heavy responsibilities and don't want to add to them. Some missionaries feel that they don't have the necessary gifts for this kind of work and prefer that the newcomers be sent elsewhere. In a few cases, local circumstances may make it inadvisable to accept new missionaries.

Whatever the reason, their wishes should be respected. If they don't want new missionaries they should not be forced to accept them except under dire circumstances. To do so will lead to frustration for both parties.

2. A good grasp of the language. The new missionary's first responsibility is to learn the language in the shortest possible time. He will be helped immensely if his senior missionary is a good speaker; otherwise it will be a case of the blind leading the blind. Moreover, if he is not a good speaker he probably will not be a very effective worker. He will not, therefore, be a good example for the younger missionary to follow. It is important that the younger person get a good impression of missionary proficiency, with the hope that one day he too will achieve the same degree of proficiency. If the senior missionary is still unable to speak fluently after ten years in the country, the younger one is likely to become discouraged, and this will affect his entire outlook.

3. Good rapport with the nationals. Not all missionaries are on friendly terms with their national brethren. Sometimes it is the fault of the missionaries, while other times it is the fault of the nationals. Regardless of where the fault lies, it is not wise to send a young missionary into that kind of awkward situation. He is almost sure to be influenced by the bad feelings of the missionary-in-charge, and once such feelings have been acquired it is very difficult to get rid of them.

4. Some degree of success. Some missionaries are more successful than others. If at all possible, the mission board should assign the new worker to a senior missionary with a good track record. Good teachers produce good students. Good coaches produce good athletes. Good senior missionaries produce good junior missionaries. The new missionary should be favorably impressed with what he sees of missionary life and work. This cannot occur unless he is teamed with an older missionary whose ministry has been blessed by the Lord to the salvation of souls and the building up of the church. The standards set by the senior partner—his linguistic ability, his intellectual prowess, his love and his concern for the people, his teaching and preaching ministry—will continue to beckon the young missionary throughout his entire career. Having seen success in his senior missionary, he will not settle for less himself.

5. Patience and understanding. In June of 1978 two young men died in a U.S. Army camp at Fort Jackson, South Carolina, on their first day of training. The exercises they were forced to perform were too much for them and they succumbed to the heat and fatigue. This is an extreme case and should not be taken as an example of army life, but it demonstrates a potential danger to all recruits.

Missionaries face similar problems. They too are in danger of exhaustion, physically and psychologically. Senior missionaries can do much to alleviate the pressure and thus insure a smooth, successful period of adjustment to missionary life and work. Many veterans forget what it is like to be a rookie. They have twenty or thirty years of experience behind them. By this time they have become completely inured to the difficulties and trials of missionary service. They can take anything in their stride. Nothing seems to faze them. It is difficult for such missionaries to appreciate the problems of the newcomer. They have long since forgotten their own problems at that stage, and there is a tendency to overdrive the younger missionary, to expect more than he can produce.

It is important that the older, more seasoned worker be aware of this fact and act accordingly. He will have to put forth a determined effort to slow down to the point where the young man can keep up. If the newcomer knows that he has the wholehearted sympathy and support of his senior partner, his chances of success will be much greater.

QUALITIES OF A GOOD NATIONAL LEADER

As the new missionary gets into the work he will find that he has to relate to the church and its leaders. In this, too, he will need all the moral support he can get. Some church leaders are better than others when it comes to handling the foreign missionary. The new missionary is fortunate if he has a wise senior missionary and a helpful national leader during the early years of his career.

1. **Sympathy with the whole missionary idea.** In recent years we have heard much about the demand for moratorium. It calls for the withdrawal of all foreign men and money for a period of five years, after which the situation will be reviewed. Some of the advocates of moratorium have made some rather abrasive statements which, if taken seriously, would spell the doom of the missionary enterprise as we know it. Some have said that the best thing the missionary can do for the cause of Christ is to go home!

These men are probably sincere. At any rate, they are entitled to their own views. It would be an act of consummate folly, however, to send a new missionary to work with a church whose leaders are opposed to all missionaries, good and bad. When the mission assigns the new worker it should make sure that the church in that area is willing to receive him. A hostile national leader can make life pretty miserable for a young missionary.

2. **Understanding of the missionary lifestyle.** Very few missionaries have been able to get down to the economic level of the people and survive. This often causes misunderstanding on the part of the national church leaders. They are jealous of the higher standard of living maintained by the missionaries and resent the fact that they don't enjoy the same privileges. Such leaders are not likely to look with favor on the arrival of a new missionary; consequently they could not be expected to help introduce him to the work. Other leaders take a more sympathetic view, especially those who have been in the U.S. and have firsthand knowledge of the missionary's former standard of living and the "sacrifice" he has already made in order to become a missionary. It helps immensely if the new recruit can count on the sympathy and support of the national church leaders.

3. **Ability to work with foreigners.** We knew two pastors in China, Pastor Hsing and Pastor Tsui. Both were good and godly men who have now

gone to their reward. Pastor Hsing was very fond of the missionaries. As far as he was concerned they could do no wrong. In any controversy between church and mission he could always be counted on to take the part of the mission. Pastor Tsui was of an entirely different stripe. He seemed to have a basic antiforeign streak in his makeup. On the surface he was always polite, but he was ill at ease when dealing with missionaries. He could love them but he could not like them. Such xenophobia is by no means confined to the Chinese. There are Americans who dislike foreigners. It seems to be a congenital weakness found in certain people. To get off to a good start the new missionary should be sent to work with a national leader who likes foreigners and can cooperate wholeheartedly with them.

4. Courage to correct the missionary. The new missionary is bound to make mistakes, especially in the use of the language. He will learn by his mistakes only if they are pointed out to him. Otherwise he will continue to repeat them. It is important, therefore, that the national leader have the courage to correct the missionary when he is wrong. This will not be an easy thing for him to do. Oriental people are painfully polite and find it difficult to point out the faults of others. Moreover, they hate to lose face and they assume the same is true of the missionary. To correct a missionary, especially in public, would cause him to lose face. This they are loath to do. So the missionary goes uncorrected.

5. Success in church work. The national leader may be a pastor, an evangelist, a Biblewoman, or even a layman, but he should have experienced the blessing of the Lord in his ministry. If he is a pastor his church should be a growing one. If he is an evangelist he should be an effective soul winner. If she is a Biblewoman she should have the gift of teaching and a fruitful ministry among the women of the church. It is essential that the missionary's first contact with church life be encouraging and challenging. Not all churches on the mission field are growing; not all pastors are successful leaders. Some have lost the vision and are carrying on in a mechanical fashion. Others have become weary and are ready to quit. Some are at loggerheads with their deacons and elders; as a result church life is at a standstill. To send the new missionary to work with such a church would be disastrous.

THE MISSIONARY'S FIRST ASSIGNMENT

After spending his first year in language school, the missionary is assigned to a field of service. This first assignment is crucial and should be made a matter of prayer by both the mission and the missionary. I shall never forget the thrill that we experienced when my wife and I received our assignment during an interview with the general director of the mission. We might have been sent to any one of 300 stations in the fifteen provinces of China. During the seven months that we had been in language school we had set aside time each day to ask for God's special guidance in the matter of our assignment. For years we had anticipated work among the tribal peoples of Southwest China, but as we prayed that vision receded and the province of Anhwei moved into the center of our thinking. It was to Fowyang in North Anhwei that we were sent in April 1936! During thirteen years of war and civil war never once did we doubt that we were in Fowyang by the will of God.

What factors should be borne in mind when he is given his first assignment?

1. Where he can use his training and skill. Today's recruit is vocation conscious. During his educational career he has received special training and developed certain skills. Naturally he wants to use them as fully as possible. Few experiences are more frustrating than to be trained to do one thing and then be expected to do something entirely different. It happens frequently in military service, always to the bitter disappointment of the recruit. Field councils and superintendents should see that the young worker has some assurance that he will be able to use his special training to good advantage.

Surgeons should be attached to a hospital, not expected to function in a jungle clinic. The same goes for nurses. Seminary graduates with a Ph. D. in Old Testament should not be asked to correct Bible correspondence courses. Their place is in a high level seminary. A man from a business background with a C.P.A. or an M.B.A. should not be asked to teach in a school for MKs. He should be given an administrative post, either overseas or in the home office.

There are exceptions. Persons with a degree in science, engineering, archaeology, or electronics will have little opportunity to use their particular skills in the service of their own mission. They may, however, be seconded to a university, Christian or secular, where the demand for this kind of talent is still high. Several missions encourage this practice. Such missionaries can have a vital ministry to the intellectuals, who are generally neglected by most missions.

2. Where he can gain valuable experience. His first assignment will probably not be his permanent one. He may be asked to do church planting for two years before teaching in a seminary. This is an excellent procedure and one that is being used increasingly. Whether the appointment is permanent or not, it should offer the kind of experience that will stand him in good stead in the years to come.

3. Where he can achieve a measure of success. The parable of the sower in Matthew 13 warns us that not all soil is productive. The first three kinds of soil in the parable produced nothing of lasting value. Even in the case of the good soil the results were not uniformly good—anywhere from thirty to a hundredfold. It is important that the new missionary be sent to a part of the vineyard where the soil will be at least partially productive, where he can get sufficient results to encourage him to believe that he will have an effective ministry in the future.

4. Where he can make a contribution. The church or station to which he is assigned may be ideal from many points of view, but the question always arises: Can the new missionary make a real contribution in that particular location? He may be wanted but not needed. Every new missionary likes to feel that he is appreciated not only for what he is but also for what he can do. In the early years his contribution will of necessity be modest, but even a minor contribution will afford him a sense of satisfaction.

The first two years on the field actually put the capstone on his preparation and training for the ministry to which God has called him. Having weathered that experience he will face the future with faith, optimism and hope, having already learned that he can count on God for wisdom, guidance, and help in meeting the demands that are made upon him.

22

Evangelistic Work

Evangelism is at the heart of the missionary movement. Missionary work that doesn't include evangelism isn't missionary work at all. This applies to the auxiliary enterprises of the Christian mission—hospitals, schools, and other institutions—as well as to the primary avenues of outreach. A school or hospital is a missionary institution only if it has a strong Christian witness.

At home and abroad there is a growing interest in evangelism. Billy Graham more than any other person is responsible for this phenomenon. It is largely through his influence that evangelism has become respectable in ecumenical circles. The Berlin Congress on Evangelism in 1966 spawned dozens of national and regional congresses on the same theme. In recent years the National Council of Churches, the World Council of Churches, and even the Roman Catholic Church have all devoted considerable time and attention to various aspects of evangelism. George W. Peters, returning from a trip overseas, said: "The peoples of the Third World are more eager to hear the gospel than we are to preach it. This is indeed the day of salvation."

Never before in history have the non-Christian peoples of the world been so open to the claims of Christ. Millions in all walks of life are showing an unprecedented interest in the Christian faith. Animists in Africa, Buddhists in East Asia, Hindus in India, and even Muslims in the Middle East are reading Christian literature, listening to Christian broadcasts, and enrolling in Bible correspondence courses in record numbers. Everywhere the Holy Spirit is at work, creating a genuine hunger for the Bread of Life. This quest for spiritual reality is not confined to the poverty-stricken masses. It includes

teachers, students, government officials, and successful business and professional people whose hearts God has touched.

DEFINITION OF EVANGELISM

While we thank God for the worldwide interest in evangelism, we are
appalled at the widespread confusion about evangelism. In this period of
modern missions there has never been so much discussion and debate about
it as there is at the present time. At a recent joint meeting of the Interdenominational Foreign Mission Association and the Evangelical Foreign
Missions Association Dr. Peters had this to say:

> *Theological issues are confronting us and they are coming upon us in full
> force. The first issue that meets us again and again is the concept of
> evangelism. . . . I have had more questions in India, Japan, and the
> Philippines about evangelism than I have ever had before. What really is
> evangelism? In every one of the seminars in India one of the very first
> requests was: Define for us evangelism. What do you really mean by
> evangelism?*[1]

The definitions are legion. The Madras Conference of the International
Missionary Council came up with 31 definitions, some by Western missionaries and others by Third World leaders. Michael Green defines evangelism as "proclaiming the good news of salvation to men and women with a
view to their conversion to Christ and incorporation in his Church."[2] J. I.
Packer suggests the simplest definition of all: "Evangelism is just preaching
the gospel, the evangel."[3]

John Stott agrees with Packer and says that "the essence of evangelism
lies in the faithful proclamation of the gospel."[4] He refuses to define evangelism in terms of recipients, results, or methods; evangelism must be defined
only in terms of the message.

In any discussion of evangelism we must make sure that we adhere
faithfully to the biblical meaning of the term. The words "evangelism" and
"mission" are often used interchangeably. This is a mistake which has led to
much fruitless discussion. Evangelism is a much narrower concept than
mission. John Stott has defined mission as embracing "everything which God
sends His people into the world to do."[5] Evangelism, on the other hand,

1. George W. Peters, "Issues Confronting Evangelical Missions," in *Evangelical Missions
Tomorrow*, Wade T. Coggins and E. L. Frizen, Jr., eds. (South Pasadena, CA: William Carey
Library, 1977), p. 162.
2. Michael Green, *Evangelism in the Early Church* (Grand Rapids: Wm. B. Eerdmans Publishing Company, 1970), p. 71.
3. J. I. Packer, *Evangelism and the Sovereignty of God* (London: Inter-Varsity Fellowship,
1961), p. 41.
4. John R. W. Stott, *Christian Mission in the Modern World* (Downers Grove, IL: InterVarsity
Press, 1975), p. 40.
5. Ibid., p. 35.

involves only the proclamation of the gospel. All evangelism is mission; not all mission is evangelism.

Two words in the New Testament are pertinent to this discussion. One is a noun, *euangelion*; it means "good news" and occurs seventy-five times. The other is a verb, *euangelizomai*; it means "to publish good news" and occurs twenty-four times. The gospel is the evangel, the good news. Evangelism is the act of proclaiming the good news.

THE MESSAGE OF EVANGELISM

The gospel has many facets but only one theme. This comes out clearly in the Acts of the Apostles. Immediately following his conversion, Paul "preached Christ" in Damascus (Acts 9:20, KJV). In Corinth, his preaching was confined to "Jesus Christ and him crucified" (1 Cor 2:2, KJV). The other apostles did the same. Everywhere they went they preached "Jesus and the Resurrection" (Acts 2:24; 4:2; 4:33, KJV).

On one occasion Stanley Jones was asked: "What does Christianity have that Hinduism does not?" His reply was: "Jesus Christ." The Christian religion centers around a unique person, Jesus Christ. Remove Him from Christianity and there is nothing left but ethical teachings which can be found in other religions. The central fact of Christianity is the person of Christ. The crucial question is not, "What do you think of Gautama, or Mohammed, or Karl Marx?" but "What think ye of Christ? Whose Son is He?" Man's eternal destiny depends on his answer to that question.

The gospel is Christocentric in two ways: it pertains to His person and His work.

The New Testament teaches, and the early church believed, that Jesus Christ is a unique person. He is the Son of God, who, in the Incarnation, became the Son of Man that through His death and resurrection He might become the one and only Savior and Sovereign of the universe.

Along with the person of Christ goes the work of Christ. The work of Christ that forms the heart of the gospel is reduced by Paul to three propositions: He died for our sins, He was buried, He rose again from the dead—all in accordance with the Scripture (1 Cor 15:1–3).

His work, like His person, was unique. He didn't die as a prophet, or as a reformer, or even as a martyr. He died as a Savior, the *only* Savior of the world (1 Pet 3:18). He gave His life and shed His blood for the remission of sins (Mt 26:28). His death was part of God's eternal plan and purpose (Acts 4:27–28) and could be brought about only in God's way, in God's time, and with God's consent (John 19:11). In death as well as in life He occupied a solitary throne.

The word *gospel* means "good news"—not any kind of good news but the Good News that "God was in Christ reconciling the world unto himself" (2 Cor 5:19, KJV). This is the message that the church has to share with a lost and dying world. When Count Zinzendorf sent his Moravian missionaries out on their task of world evangelization he gave them strict instructions to preach the gospel and forget theology. "The heathen," he insisted, "already know of the existence of God. What they need to hear about is the love of Christ." The gospel message can be summed up in three statements: God loved the world; Christ died for all; whosoever shall call on the name of the Lord shall be saved.

THE PRIORITY OF EVANGELISM

In view of the fact that evangelism is not social action, or community development, or nation building, or humanitarian service, what is its place in the broad spectrum of mission? There is today a heavy emphasis on the holistic approach of the gospel: ministering to the total needs of the whole man in the total context of his physical, social, economic, and political environment. Those who espouse this approach are reluctant to single out evangelism as being any more important than any other aspect of the Christian mission. Hence we have various viewpoints. There are those who believe that evangelism is the sole task of the church. Others conceive it to be the primary task. Still others regard it simply as one of many activities of the church.[6] Orlando Costas in his book, *The Church and Its Mission*, rejects the term "primary" and prefers to speak of the "total" task of the church. For him, social action and evangelism are both integral parts of the church's mission.

Much depends on one's understanding of the word salvation. If the resurrection of Christ has inaugurated a new age in which all men are already part of the new creation of which Christ is the Head, then the only thing left is the realization of *shalom*—God's beneficent reign over creation, involving peace, prosperity, security, human rights, and social justice as outlined in Psalm 85. In such a context personal salvation is not only irrelevant, it is unnecessary. Evangelism, then, can be "nothing but the realization of hope, a function of expectancy."[7]

Evangelicals have always maintained that evangelism is the primary mission of the church. Billy Graham is the best-known representative of this point of view. This is reflected in Article IV of the Lausanne Covenant: "To evangelize is to spread the good news that Jesus Christ died for our sins and was raised from the dead according to the Scriptures, and that as reigning Lord he now offers the forgiveness of sins and the liberating gift of the Spirit to all who repent and believe."

A study of the New Testament makes it difficult to escape the conclusion

6. A discussion of these and other viewpoints will be found in an article by Ronald J. Sider, "Evangelism, Salvation and Social Justice," in *International Review of Mission*, July 1975, pp. 251–255.
7. J. C. Hoekendijk, "The Call to Evangelism," in *Eye of the Storm*, Donald McGavran, ed. (Waco, TX: Word Books, 1972), p. 47.

that both Jesus and the apostles gave highest priority to the preaching of the gospel with a view to the salvation of individuals. The reason for this is not hard to find. It is found in the biblical doctrine of man.

Man was made in the beginning *by* God and *for* God; God intended him to find his highest happiness in fellowship with Himself. But sin entered man's life and God went out. As a result, man is not only a sinner, he is a lost sinner. That means that he is alienated from the life of God (Eph 4:18), ignorant of the truth of God (Rom 1:25), hostile to the law of God (Rom 8:7), disobedient to the will of God (Tit 3:3), and exposed to the wrath of God (John 3:36). The Bible clearly teaches that there are two destinies open to man. One involves everlasting happiness in the presence of God and the holy angels (Luke 15:10; Rev 22:3–5; 1 Thess 4:17); the other involves everlasting misery in the company of the devil and his angels (Matt 25:41). The New Testament speaks of two gates, one wide and the other strait; two ways, one broad and the other narrow; and two destinies, one destruction and the other life (Matt 7:13–14). This being so, the greatest benefit we can confer on any member of the human race is to introduce him to Jesus Christ. Jesus said as much when He asked: "What shall it profit a man, if he shall gain the whole world, and lose his own soul? Or what shall a man give in exchange for his soul?" (Mark 8:36–37, KJV). Man, the sinner, has many needs, but the greatest of all is his spiritual need. To meet his other needs but fail to meet this one is to mock him.

John Stott is on the right track when he asks: "Is anything so destructive of human dignity as alienation from God? How can we seriously maintain that political and economic liberation is just as important as eternal salvation?"[8] There is much talk these days about the need to liberate man from the demonic power structures and the dehumanizing influences of modern industrial society. Alienation and frustration are declared to be man's greatest problems. They are indeed pressing problems and somebody should be doing something about them, but what is overlooked in all the discussion is the fact that the worst form of alienation is alienation from God. With the vertical connection severed, all horizontal connections are at loose ends. The various forms of alienation—and Marx spoke of three—are but a reflection of man's alienation from God. What is needed, they tell us, is to get man out of the ghetto, or, better still, to destroy the demonic powers that built and maintain the ghetto, and thus to restore his authentic humanity. The ghetto is not the cause of man's alienation, however; it is the result of it. Man lost his authentic humanity in a garden; after that he went out and built himself a ghetto. His only hope of ever recovering his true humanity is to get back to the source of his humanity—God. This is why the evangelist believes that he is doing both God and man a service by preaching a personal rather than a social gospel.

8. Stott, *Mission in Modern World*, p. 35.

THE PURPOSE OF EVANGELISM

Evangelism has a twofold purpose, one immediate and the other remote.
The immediate purpose is the conversion of the individual and his incorporation into the Christian church. The remote purpose is the proclamation of
the Lordship of Christ over all creation and the extension of the Kingdom of
God throughout the earth. The first is emphasized in Mark's account of the
Great Commission. "Go ye into all the world, and preach the gospel to every
creature. He that believeth and is baptized shall be saved; but he that
believeth not shall be damned" (Mark 16:15-16, KJV). The second is found
in Matthew's version of the Great Commission. "All power is given unto me
in heaven and in earth. Go ye therefore, and teach [make disciples of] all
nations, baptizing them in the name of the Father, and of the Son, and of the
Holy Ghost" (Matt 28:18-19, KJV).

It is quite impossible to exaggerate the importance of conversion. One of
the strongest statements on the subject comes from Stanley Jones, who gave
sixty years to the evangelization of India.

> We divide humanity into many classes—white and colored, rich and
> poor, educated and uneducated, Americans and non-Americans, East
> and West. . . . But Jesus drew a line down through all these distinctions
> and divided humanity into just two classes—the unconverted and the
> converted, the once-born and the twice-born. All men live on one side or
> the other of that line. No other division matters—this is a division that
> divides; it is a division that runs through time and eternity. [9]

Unfortunately, "conversion" is a dirty word in some circles. It is
anathema among the Hindus of India. Gandhi inveighed against the missionaries for attempting to convert Hindus to the Christian faith. "If you
come to India to make us better Hindus, fine; but don't try to convert us to
Christianity." During the 1960s, two states in India passed anticonversion
laws; they were later repealed by the Supreme Court. Others in the Third
World regard conversion as an act of cultural imperialism; all right for the
nineteenth century but completely out of keeping with the more sophisticated mood of the twentieth century.

Even in the West we find an aversion to the idea of conversion. Some
theologians are embarrassed by the term and would like to get rid of it. J. G.
Davies says: "I would be glad if the term conversion could be dropped from
the Christian vocabulary."[10] Those who believe in baptismal regeneration
obviously have no need of conversion; baptism has already made them a
"child of God, a member of Christ, and an inheritor of the Kingdom of God."
Others regard conversion as a spiritual experience appropriate to skid row
but hardly acceptable in more refined circles.

Some equate conversion with proselytism, which has always been in

9. E. Stanley Jones, *Conversion* (New York: Abingdon Press, 1959), p. 5.
10. J. G. Davies, *Dialogue with the World* (London: SCM Press, 1967), p. 54.

disrepute in respectable circles. Missionaries in India, Uganda, and other places have been accused of "buying" converts by giving them money, famine relief, educational advantages, and medical services, or by according them other kinds of preferential treatment. Because of the humanitarian character of their work these charges seem to be substantiated. If a government wanted to press charges it could easily produce the required "evidence." Some governments have forbidden young people under the age of eighteen to accept Christian baptism.

In spite of the difficulties and dangers involved, however, the Christian missionary has no choice. His aim is to make converts, and if pressed to do so, he would have to acknowledge that such is the case, even in Muslim countries. At the same time he would vigorously deny that he engages in proselytizing. Such reprehensible conduct is beneath the dignity of the Christian missionary. He will not use force, nor will he offer inducements. He will present the claims of Christ and hope that the listener will voluntarily acknowledge Jesus Christ as his Savior. Beyond that he will not go; to do so would be to violate the freedom and integrity of the individual.

Conversion, to be genuine, must involve a complete change of heart and life. The root meaning of the word is "to turn." It was said of the Thessalonian believers that they "turned to God from idols" (1 Thess 1:9, KJV). It is therefore a threefold turning: *from* sin *to* righteousness, *from* death *to* life, *from* idols *to* God. It is morally impossible to embrace sin and righteousness at the same time. Paul asks: "What fellowship hath righteousness with unrighteousness? And what communion hath light with darkness? And what concord hath Christ with Belial?" (2 Cor 6:14–15, KJV). By conversion the person becomes a "new creature, old things are passed away; all things are become new" (2 Cor 5:17, KJV). The convert is then a "new man," with a new center of gravity, a new system of values, a new standard of morality, a new frame of reference, and a new purpose in life. The outstanding example of conversion in the New Testament is Zacchaeus in Luke 19. When this dishonest tax collector had a personal encounter with Jesus Christ, he was immediately and completely turned around. His confession is noteworthy. "Behold, Lord, the half of my goods I give to the poor; and if I have taken anything from any man by false accusation, I restore him fourfold." That is genuine conversion.

Following conversion, the convert does not remain in isolation. He becomes a member of the universal church, the Body of Christ, by the baptism of the Holy Spirit. By an act of his own he joins a local congregation and becomes part of its fellowship, work, and witness.

The second purpose of evangelism is the proclamation of the Lordship of Jesus Christ over all creation and the extension of the Kingdom into all parts of the world. The church's earliest creed was "Jesus Christ is Lord" (Phil 2:11, KJV). There is a direct connection between the Lordship of Christ and the world mission of the church. This comes out clearly in Matthew's account of the Great Commission. It is precisely because all authority in heaven and on earth has been given by God the Father to God the Son that the church has the responsibility to make disciples of all nations. The Kingdom of God becomes a reality only as the peoples of the world respond to the gospel and become part of that Kingdom (Acts 26:18; Col 1:13).

It is for this reason that Michael Cassidy declares the unashamed purpose of Christian evangelism to be conversion.[11]

VARIETIES OF EVANGELISM

There are three kinds of evangelism: presence evangelism, proclamation evangelism, and persuasion evangelism. The first is the kind most strongly advocated in ecumenical circles. The second is most widely practiced by evangelicals. The third has supporters and detractors in both camps.

1. **Presence evangelism.** In spite of widespread aversion to this kind of evangelism on the part of evangelicals, it is a valid, even a necessary, kind to use. We dare not preach a gospel that we are not prepared to live by. Bishop Azariah of Dornakal attributed the mass movement in the Telugu country to the quality of life manifested by the Christians.

> It is universally admitted by all missions and churches that the reason most often given by the converts for accepting the Christian way of life is the impression produced upon them by the changed lives of the Christian community.[12]

Not all Christians have this kind of testimony. Dr. Ambedkar was for many years the leader of the Untouchables in India. Realizing that Hinduism had nothing to offer his followers, Ambedkar decided to study the other religions with a view to joining one of them. After examining the claims of Christianity with Bishop Pickett, he remarked: "When I study the life of Christ in the Gospels I think that I and my people should become Christians; but when I see the lives of the Christians here in Bombay, I say to myself, 'No, Christianity is not for us.'" Some time later, at an open-air service in Nagpur, Dr. Ambedkar and 70,000 of his followers renounced Hinduism and became Buddhists. Let no one say that presence evangelism is not important. We have the same problem here in the West. It was the German philosopher Nietzsche who said: "I could more readily believe in your Savior if I could find more people who had been saved by Him."

If we insist on talking about the transforming power of the gospel, we had better be sure that we and our converts have really been transformed. Otherwise our words will have a hollow ring.

11. C. Rene Padilla, ed. *The New Face of Evangelism* (Downers Grove, IL: InterVarsity Press, 1976), p. 80.
12. *Evangelism, The Madras Series*, Vol. III (New York: International Missionary Council, 1939), p. 42.

2. Proclamation evangelism. In spite of its importance, presence evangelism is not enough to lead a person to saving faith in Christ. At best it can only create within him a desire to know more. To be really effective it must be accompanied by proclamation evangelism.

This is the form most frequently referred to in the New Testament. John the Baptist came "preaching." Jesus came "preaching." The apostles in the Book of Acts preached. Paul said: "Jesus Christ sent me not to baptize but to preach" (1 Cor 1:17, KJV). Again he said: "Woe is me if I preach not" (1 Cor 9:16, KJV). Certain things belong together. You ride a horse. You play a game. You preach the gospel. God has ordained that men should be saved through preaching (1 Cor 1:21).

The gospel contains certain propositional truths that must be understood before saving faith can be exercised. These include the truths concerning God, man, sin, and salvation, and the facts concerning the life, death, and resurrection of Christ. These truths must be preached with all the clarity we can muster.

It is rather strange that proclamation evangelism, which occupied such a large place in the preaching and teaching of the early church, should have fallen into disrepute. The Billy Graham type of evangelism, which is based on "the Bible says" and directed to the salvation of the individual, is totally unacceptable in certain quarters today. When Billy spoke to the National Council of Churches in Miami several years ago he was chided for his simplistic approach to the complex problems of present-day society. They said, "Billy, you'll have to give up this kind of preaching. You're taking us back to the nineteenth century." To which Billy replied, "I thought I was taking you back to the first century."

Alan Walker, a well-known Australian evangelist, does not share their point of view. He said: "I confess I cannot understand the current depreciation of the preaching ministry. Some protest against an over-verbalizing of the Gospel is justified, but the effectiveness of a man, a woman standing up to preach with conviction is undoubted."[13]

3. Persuasion evangelism. Persuasion goes one step beyond proclamation and tries to induce the hearer to *believe* the message for himself. There are those who repudiate this method, declaring that the evangelist is not responsible for results. He should be content to preach the gospel and leave the results with the Lord.

There is something to be said for both sides. It is possible to overstep the bounds of propriety and bring undue pressure to bear until the person accepts the gospel under duress. It should be categorically stated that this approach is both wrong and harmful. The results of such a method can be disastrous. It has no sanction in Scripture and should be studiously avoided.

On the other hand, the word "persuasion" is not foreign to the New

13. *International Review of Mission,* July 1975, p. 285.

Testament. Paul said: "Knowing therefore the terror of the Lord, we *persuade* men" (2 Cor 5:11, KJV). The New English Bible refers to Paul as "trying to *convince* Jews and Greeks" (Acts 18:4, NEB). In Ephesus, before moving over to the school of Tyrannus, Paul spent three months in the synagogue, "using argument and *persuasion* in his presentation of the gospel" (Acts 19:8, NEB). Preaching the gospel is serious business, fraught with eternal consequences for good or evil (2 Cor 2:16). Paul was never guilty of presenting the gospel on a take-it-or-leave-it basis. He pled with men to be reconciled to God (2 Cor 5:20). The apostles did not use force to win converts, but they did call for a response. Moreover, they expected results and when they did not get them they turned to other people more willing to receive the message (Acts 13:46).

METHODS OF EVANGELISM

The methods are almost endless, and they differ from country to country. Mass evangelism is not possible in the Muslim world. Saturation evangelism is not possible where the church does not yet exist. Tract and Scripture distribution is useless among illiterate people.

1. Personal evangelism. This is the most effective method known to the church. There are several reasons for this. It is natural and spontaneous. It requires no organization, no equipment, and no expense. It does not need special training or expertise. In the words of D. T. Niles, it is "one beggar telling another beggar where he can find bread."

This was the method used most widely in the early church. A cursory reading of the Acts of the Apostles might lead one to believe that all evangelistic work was done by the Apostles Peter and Paul and their traveling companions. A closer look will reveal the fact that the gospel spread from person to person in the ordinary course of daily life. So accustomed were they to "gossiping the gospel" that when they were chased out of Jerusalem on the martyrdom of Stephen they naturally "went everywhere preaching the word" (Acts 8:4, KJV). In Acts 11:19, Luke informs us that these people traveled as far as Phenice, Cyprus, and Antioch, and wherever they went, they "preached the word."

Harnack says: "The most numerous and successful missionaries of the Christian religion were not the regular teachers but Christians themselves in virtue of their loyalty and courage."[14] Kenneth Scott Latourette says much the same:

> *The chief agents in the expansion of Christianity appear not to have been those who made it a profession or a major part of their occupation, but men and women who earned their livelihood in some purely secular*

14. Adolph Harnack, *The Mission and Expansion of Christianity in the First Three Centuries,* Vol. I (New York: Putnam, 1908), p. 336.

manner, and spoke of their faith to those whom they met in this natural fashion. [15]

From the beginning, Christian converts should be encouraged to give their witness on a voluntary basis. No convert should be paid to share his faith. Rather, as John L. Nevius pointed out, he should remain in his secular calling and support himself by a legitimate trade, all the while acting as an "individual worker for Christ."

2. Organized evangelism. This may take many forms. John Sung was one of China's greatest evangelists. Wherever he went in China and later throughout Southeast Asia, he revived the churches and formed evangelistic bands which continued the work long after Sung had left. Each local church organized some kind of band. It required no money, no structure, and very little organization. On bicycle or on foot, the bands, with anywhere from two to twenty persons in each, went out once a week or once a month into the surrounding countryside preaching the gospel, selling Scripture Portions, and distributing tracts.

Tent evangelism is very effective. It usually requires one full-time person, preferably an evangelist, supported by many part-time workers who come and go during the weeks the tent is in their area. It remains in one place long enough to make a lasting impact on the community. During the morning the workers visit the shops and the bazaars, giving out literature and sharing the gospel on a one-to-one basis. In the afternoon new converts are gathered for instruction. In the evening an evangelistic meeting is held, with messages, slides, movies, etc. This is a good way to plant a new church in virgin territory.

There is also crusade evangelism. The larger crusades associated with Billy Graham, Leighton Ford, and Luis Palau are usually citywide affairs which have the cooperation of a majority of churches and missions. These call for a highly structured organization, a huge budget, and months of preparation. In the West this kind of evangelism seems to be running out of steam. Only Billy Graham has any real drawing power. In the Third World, where Christianity is relatively new and the churches are younger, it is different. There, citywide crusades are still popular, with such outstanding evangelists as Bakht Singh and Samuel Kamaleson (India), Akira Hatori and Koji Honda (Japan), Peter Octavianus (Indonesia), and Hermano Pablo (Latin America). Though not so well known as Billy Graham, these men have been mightily used by the Lord.

In all crusades, follow-up is the big problem. Not all converts end up in the church. Some denominations have been more active than others in this type of evangelism, among them the Southern Baptists and the Assemblies of God.

15. Kenneth Scott Latourette, *The History of the Expansion of Christianity*, Vol. I (New York: Harper & Row, 1937), pp. 116–117.

Saturation evangelism is another form. It began in 1960 in Nicaragua, where it was known as Evangelism-in-Depth. It was the brainchild of Dr. Kenneth Strachan, General Director at that time of the Latin America Mission. Altogether, ten crusades were held in various countries of Latin America. The genius of EID is in the total mobilization of all church members. The goal is to reach every family in a given country with an oral or written presentation of the gospel. In the smaller countries this is feasible, but not in the larger countries like Brazil. The idea spread to other countries around the world—Nigeria, Zaire, Japan, Philippines, etc. The statistical results were usually impressive. Actual results, however, differed from country to country. In Latin America the crusades resulted in rather meager church growth. In some parts of Africa, however, church membership doubled.

The Assemblies of God in Latin America have come to the conclusion that citywide cooperative efforts do not really pay off. Persons converted in the bull ring or the soccer stadium don't know what to do or where to go when the meetings are over. Consequently many of them are lost to the cause. Instead, an effort is now being made to make the local church the center of evangelistic outreach. Special weeklong meetings, led by a gifted evangelist, are proving to be much more productive. The converts automatically affiliate with the church in which they were converted. Evangelistic meetings in the local church have almost been forgotten in the U.S. It is exceedingly difficult to get outsiders into a church for such meetings; there is just too much indifference and competition. In the Third World, however, this kind of evangelistic effort is still possible.

There are other forms of evangelism—industrial evangelism, newspaper evangelism, radio evangelism, literature evangelism, to say nothing of evangelism by means of gospel records, cassettes, films, Bible correspondence courses, etc. The correspondence courses have been exceedingly well received in such Muslim countries as Bangladesh, Morocco, Tunisia, and Iran.

THE APPEAL OF EVANGELISM

A good deal has been said in recent years about "the whole gospel for the whole man." A full-orbed gospel should appeal to the three parts of the personality: intellect, emotions, and will. If the gospel is to have its full effect on the hearer and result in a genuine conversion it must make its appeal in all three areas.

1. The mind. Too often we have appealed only to the emotions and have invited people "to give their hearts to Christ" when they hardly knew what we meant by the expression. Before the heart can be warmed, the mind must be informed. The gospel must be *understood* in order to be believed. Philip's first words to the Ethiopian eunuch were not: "Do you *believe* what you are reading?" but "Do you *understand* what you are reading?" (Acts 8:30, RSV).

The gospel is based on the person and work of Christ. There are objective, historical facts about Christ to which the hearer must give honest intellectual assent. This he cannot do without a certain degree of understanding. If for any reason he cannot accept the biblical account of the crucifixion and the resurrection, there is no point in asking him to "believe."

2. The heart. We begin with the mind, but we do not stop there. Somewhere along the line the heart must become involved. The circumstances will differ from person to person, but sooner or later everyone must have his heart "strangely warmed," as did John Wesley at the Aldersgate Meeting in London in 1738. This is the great tragedy of American Christianity. On our church rolls are the names of millions of persons who consider themselves good Christians, but they have never had a definite, personal encounter with Jesus Christ. They "believe" the facts of the gospel; they celebrate His birth at Christmas and His death at Easter; but beyond that they know nothing experientially of the love of Christ or the power of the gospel. If they were to wake up tomorrow morning and discover that Jesus had never lived, it wouldn't make a bit of difference. They would eat breakfast and go off to work as if nothing unusual had happened. These are the ones Jesus had in mind when He lamented: "This people honoreth me with their lips, but their heart is far from me" (Mark 7:6, KJV). They know nothing of the sentiment expressed in the hymn:

> *Heaven above is softer blue,*
> *Earth around is sweeter green;*
> *Something lives in every hue*
> *Christless eyes have never seen.*
> *Birds with gladder songs overflow,*
> *Flowers with deeper beauties shine*
> *Since I know as now I know*
> *I am His and He is mine.*

3. The will. In the final analysis, conversion is an act of the will. Jesus said: "If any man's will is to do his will, he shall know whether the teaching is from God or whether I am speaking on my own authority" (John 7:17, RSV). This is why most evangelists give an invitation at the close of the service. In this way they hope to "close the deal." Alan Walker is one of them. He says:

> *Every Sunday night in the Church-in-a-Theatre in Sydney I extend an invitation for people to make an open commitment to God in Christ. Behind it lies the conviction that only by an act of the will, only by personal surrender can reconciliation with God be received. I continue to make this the goal of my preaching because over the years I have wit-*

nessed in countless lives the transformation which follows a conscious and deliberate acceptance of Jesus Christ. [16]

This method can be abused. The evangelist may prolong the service interminably just to get "one more convert." In doing so, he may alienate some sensitive persons who don't particularly appreciate high pressure methods. Not all who "go forward" have a genuine conversion experience. Like vaccination, it takes with some and not with others. But it is a good method and should be continued wherever solid results can be achieved without resorting to pressure or gimmicks.

THE RESPONSE TO EVANGELISM

Properly conducted, evangelism calls for a twofold response: repentance and faith.

The Greek word for repentance is *metanoia,* which means a "change of mind." The sinner has wrong thoughts about many things—God, man, sin, salvation, and others. In the days of Noah, God "saw that the wickedness of man was great in the earth, and that every imagination of the thoughts of his heart was only evil continually" (Gen 6:5, KJV). In Ephesians, Paul gives a fearful indictment of the unregenerate mind. He declares that "the Gentiles walk in the vanity of their mind, having the understanding darkened, being alienated from the life of God through the ignorance that is in them, because of the blindness of their hearts" (Eph 4:17-18, KJV). Paul himself had to acknowledge that at one time he *thought* he ought to do many things contrary to the name of Jesus of Nazareth (Acts 26:9).

Repentance involves a change of mind leading to a change of heart and life. There can be no salvation without forgiveness, and there can be no forgiveness without repentance. That is why John, Jesus, and the apostles all called upon their hearers to repent. The reason was moral rather than legal.

> So long as men cling to their sin, God cannot forgive. This is not because He is not forgiving, but because of the nature of forgiveness. For God's forgiveness is not release from the eternal consequences of sin, but the cleansing of the inner spirit and restoration to His fellowship. But He cannot cleanse from sin those who cling to their sin, and He cannot give fellowship to those who will have none of it. [17]

This great truth is not sufficiently known even in evangelical circles. It is largely missing in modern preaching.

Repentance does not stand alone. It is always accompanied by faith. These are not two separate and distinct experiences. They are two aspects of

16. *International Review of Mission,* July 1975, p. 287.
17. H. H. Rowley, *The Missionary Message of the Old Testament* (London: Carey Kingsgate Press, 1944), pp. 68–69.

one experience by which the sinner is reconciled to a holy, loving God. Repentance in the New Testament is always repentance towards God (Acts 26:20), for all sin is against Him (Ps 51:4; Luke 15:21); but faith is always faith in Jesus Christ (Acts 16:31; John 11:25–26; 14:1; 20:31). They are brought together by Paul in Acts 20:21, KJV, where he says he had testified "both to the Jews, and also to the Greeks, repentance toward God, and faith toward our Lord Jesus Christ." Sin must be renounced at the same time that faith is exercised. The command to repent comes through loud and clear in the preaching of the apostles (Acts 2:38; 3:19; 8:22, 17:30; 26:20). The exhortation to believe is equally clear (Acts 4:4; 10:43; 13:39; 16:31). The gospel is the power of God unto salvation only to those who repent (Luke 13:3) and believe (Rom 1:16).

THE CONTINUING NEED FOR EVANGELISM

At the height of the Student Volunteer Movement, John R. Mott, its leading light, called for the "evangelization of the world in this generation." This was never achieved, but even if it had been, the task would not be over, for each succeeding generation must be evangelized. The faith of the fathers will not save the sons. Christians are not born; they are born again, so evangelism must continue.

Another factor is the population explosion. The world's population is now growing at about two percent per year, which means that each year sees about eighty million additional people in the world. The great majority of these are in the non-Christian part of the world. It is a staggering fact that the population of China has increased by at least 400 million since the Communists took over in 1949. The population of India has, during the same period, increased by approximately 300 million. Both of these countries are overwhelmingly non-Christian.

About 28 percent of the world's 4.5 billion people are professing Christians. The remaining 72 percent are followers of other religions or profess no religion at all. This ratio has not changed appreciably in the past generation. Are those 1.3 billion Christians all genuine, practicing Christians? Many of them, alas, are Christian in name only. Their Christianity is a matter of culture, not conviction. Their names are on the church rolls, but they do not actively support the work and witness of the church. For all practical purposes they are non-Christians who need to be evangelized.

The older churches in the Third World also have their problems. Many of their members are second- and third-generation Christians who have followed in the steps of their parents but have never had a personal experience of salvation. They are nominal Christians, like so many in the West. After describing the remarkable ministry of Bishop Azariah of Dornakal, Stephen Neill goes on to say:

> *The work in Dornakal was very far from perfect. As we have already seen, at the end of his life Bishop Azariah was distressed to find in the*

second and third generations of Christians so much less zeal and devotion than he had hoped for.[18]

Hoekendijk makes the same observation: "It is sad but true that even in the younger churches the second generation of Christians becomes established and immobile. And for a next generation, Christian life has often already become an unexciting business routine."[19]

THE RESPONSIBILITY FOR EVANGELISM

Who is responsible for world evangelization, the Western mission or the national church?

During much of the 19th century when Protestant missions were getting under way, world evangelization was obviously the responsibility of Western missionaries, for the simple reason that there was no one else to do the job. If the gospel was to be given to the countries of Asia, Africa, and Latin America it would have to be introduced from the outside, and the missionaries were the agents used by God for this purpose. Ziegenbalg and Plutschau pioneered in India, Robert Morrison in China, and Adoniram Judson in Burma.

As indigenous churches emerged in all parts of the world, they began to assume responsibility for the evangelization of their own people. But this was a slow process and one that was not always encouraged and promoted by the missionary. By his very method of work he created the impression that world evangelization is the "white man's burden." Wherever he went he won converts, trained leaders, and organized a church. As soon as the church could stand on its own feet, the missionary moved on to another place to repeat the process. To be sure, he trained pastors and teachers and leaders of various kinds, but he did not train *missionaries*. They must come from the West. All forward movement work was done by the missionary. He was the pioneer, always on the go, always on the cutting edge of church expansion.

With or without intention he created the impression that pioneer evangelism (missionary work) is the responsibility of the mission, not the church. The churches founded in this way by the missionary were supposed to be self-governing, self-supporting, and self-propagating. The missions emphasized self-support. The churches demanded self-government. Neither church nor mission did much about self-propagation. By the second and third generation the churches were almost completely devoid of evangelistic zeal. They still continued to look to the missionary to take responsibility for that area of the work. That mentality has persisted to this day in many parts of the world. There are still mission leaders who continue to think and act in these terms. They are calling for more and more Western missionaries to

18. Stephen Neill, *The Unfinished Task* (London: Edinburgh House Press, 1957), p. 129.
19. J. C. Hoekendijk, "The Call to Evangelism," in *Eye of the Storm,* Donald McGavran, ed. (Waco, TX: Word Books, 1972), p. 42.

complete the task of world evangelization. There is no suggestion that this responsibility should be shared with the churches in the Third World. In this they are wrong.

At the Madras Conference of the International Missionary Council in 1938 the Bishop of Dornakal made this statement:

> *The task of filling the empty churches in the nominally Christian lands belongs to the churchgoing members of those lands; the task of bringing into the church those of the non-Christian faiths in other lands belongs to the Christians in these lands.... Evangelism is a necessary factor in growth in church life. Deprive the indigenous church of its God-given task—you will inevitably kill the divine life implanted in it.*[20]

Unfortunately the bishop was a voice crying in the wilderness. Few churches, East or West, took any notice of what he said.

In the last decade or two the indigenous churches have begun to show a lively interest in world evangelization. Today there are 15,250 Third World missionaries, but the overwhelming majority—some estimates run as high as 90 percent—are engaged in the evangelization of their own ethnic minorities overseas. They are moving in the right direction, but it is to be hoped that the day will come when they will manifest an equal concern for world evangelization without regard to cultural or ethnic groups.

The time has come for the indigenous churches to assume their full share of responsibility for world evangelization. They should begin with the total evangelization of their own communities and countries, then launch out and embrace the world in their plans. One thing is certain: the three billion non-Christians now in the world will *never* be evangelized by Western missionaries. As William Carey declared, India will be evangelized only by her own sons.

---

20. *Evangelism, The Madras Series,* Vol. III, pp. 39–40.

23

Educational Work

From the beginning education has been an important factor in the modern missionary movement. Even today, when educational missions are being phased out, 35 percent of all missionaries are engaged in educational work. Changes in the educational systems of the Third World and rapidly rising costs may reduce the number in the days ahead, but for the present the missionary movement is committed to educational work.

THE RATIONALE

How did the nineteenth-century missionaries get into educational work? Teaching played a large part in the ministry of Jesus and the apostles. In the Great Commission Jesus included the idea of teaching (Matt 28:19-20). The Apostle Paul spoke of "teaching every man in all wisdom" (Col 1:28, RSV) and instructed Timothy not only to engage in a teaching ministry but to train others to do the same (2 Tim 2:2). It is evident, however, that neither Jesus nor Paul had present-day teaching in mind. In the Great Commission the word "teach" is really "to disciple" or "to make disciples." Moreover, Jesus explicitly told them what the content of their teaching should be. They were to teach all that He had commanded. There is no reason to believe that Jesus or the apostles engaged in the teaching of what we today call "secular" subjects. They taught the truth concerning God, man, sin, and salvation, and this they called "the truth of the gospel" (Gal 2:5, RSV). Paul declared quite plainly that he did not teach the "wisdom of men" but the "wisdom of God"

(1 Cor 2:5,7, RSV). This being so, we must look elsewhere for the rationale for educational missions.

1. The situation in the 19th century. There is almost no comparison between the apostles of the first century and the missionaries of the 19th century. The activities of the apostles were confined almost entirely to the Roman Empire, whose advanced form of civilization, while not making education universal or compulsory, at least made it available to those who wanted it. The Greek Diaspora provided the Roman world with the Greek language and thus helped in the diffusion of Greek literature and institutions. The Jews, then as now a highly literate people, planted synagogues in all the major cities of the empire. Most of Paul's ministry was conducted in those synagogues, where he never failed to find an educated audience. There probably were illiterate people in the rural areas, but Paul ministered to the cities and presumably the other apostles did the same. The problem of illiteracy, therefore, did not occur. His converts had no need of further schooling. Immediately upon conversion they could be appointed elders (Acts 14:23).

Such favorable conditions did not exist on the mission field in the 19th century. In many parts of the world there were no schools, and in places such as India, China, Japan, and the Middle East only a tiny fraction of the people could read and write. As for women and girls, education was not for them. In such a situation the missionaries had no choice. They had to do something to meet the need.

2. The precedent in the homeland. In the West the churches have long been associated with higher education, especially in the U.S. Most of the colleges established during the colonial period were founded and maintained by the churches. During those early times the minister was usually the best educated person in the community. Later on, when the church-established colleges turned secular and failed to produce "Christian gentlemen for the Christian ministry," the churches began all over again and started seminaries in various parts of the country. In time, every large denomination had its own seminary, some of them more than one. The American churches have had a long history of supporting higher education, so it was natural that when the missionaries went abroad they engaged in educational work.

In addition, the missionaries themselves were usually college graduates. Some of them attended the prestigious schools on the eastern seaboard, now part of the Ivy League. Not a few of them went to seminary following college. This was another reason for their taking a special interest in education, especially when they discovered the appalling illiteracy then prevailing in the Third World.

3. The whole gospel for the whole man. The missionaries were not content simply to "save souls." They were determined to minister to the needs of the "whole man." Only by doing so could they fulfill their obligation to "make disciples of all nations." They argued that since the whole of man's being belongs to God they must be concerned with all aspects of his development. It is not enough to save the soul or even to nourish the body. If man is to realize his full potential as a child of God he must be given an opportunity to develop his mental faculties. This he cannot do as long as he remains illiterate. By establishing schools and teaching the students to read, write, and think in abstract terms the missionaries opened up to them a whole new world of ideas. Those who learned English or French were put in touch with the best thought in the Western world. They considered this to be a valid reason for engaging in educational work.

4. A strong indigenous church. The ultimate aim of the missionary movement was to establish a strong national church in the various countries of the Third World. This could not be accomplished unless the membership of the church received at least a modest education sufficient to enable them to read the Bible. In some parts of the world there were no written languages. The missionaries had to begin from scratch and invent a script for each linguistic group, then teach it to the church members. If competent leadership were to emerge, elementary education would not be enough. High schools, colleges, and eventually seminaries would have to be established. This was a long and laborious process that required much patience and ingenuity, but they persevered. Today the churches in the Third World have their share of dynamic, dedicated leaders who can hold their own with any in the West.

THE PURPOSE

The missionaries did not engage in education because they had nothing else to do. They had plenty to occupy their time and thought, but they soon came to realize that education was a necessity, not a luxury. They gave themselves wholeheartedly to the vast undertaking of educating their converts, with a four-fold purpose in mind.

1. To investigate the truth. Christianity is a revealed religion and therefore has a vested interest in truth. Jesus declared: "I am the way, the truth, and the life" (John 14:6, KJV). He also said: "Ye shall know the truth and the truth shall make you free" (John 8:32, KJV). The New Testament has a good deal to say about truth. The Holy Spirit is called the Spirit of Truth who was sent to guide us into all truth (John 16:13). Paul refers to the gospel as "the word of truth" (Eph 1:13, KJV) and describes the church as "the pillar and ground of the truth" (1 Tim 3:15, KJV).

The question of truth is of immense importance. Stephen Neill said: "The only reason for being a Christian is the overpowering conviction that the

Christian faith is true."[1] All truth is God's truth, whether it relates to science or religion, creation or redemption. The Christian convert must be taught to discriminate between what is false and what is true, what is right and what is wrong, what is good and what is bad. He will do this best if he is trained to think in logical categories. It is especially important that he learn the truth about the origin and destiny of man, the nature and reality of sin, the meaning of life, and the mystery of death.

2. To propagate the faith. Here in the U.S. we have the concept of the separation of church and state. In recent years this has come to mean that religion has no place whatsoever in the educational system. By decision of the Supreme Court, Bible reading and the Lord's Prayer have been banned from the classroom. This is not only a great mistake, it is also a violation of the real intent of the First Amendment. By no stretch of the imagination can teaching Christianity be construed as "establishing a religion." It is difficult to believe that our founding fathers intended to completely divorce religion from public affairs when they themselves resorted on more than one occasion to public prayer for divine guidance.

When the missionaries first established schools they did so with the purpose of making Christianity a required subject, using the Bible as a textbook. Some missionaries regarded mission schools as primarily an evangelistic tool, to be used not only to strengthen the faith of the converts but also to lead others to faith in Christ. In Africa, where there were thousands of "bush" schools, it was difficult to distinguish the church from the school, for both met in the same building and were led by the same person.

> *In Africa, perhaps more than anywhere else, education as a specific instrument of evangelism and also as a widely-recognized form of social service formed the spearhead of missionary policy. The "bush" school which was throughout Africa the main agency of primary education was also throughout Africa the main agency of evangelism. The teacher was also the evangelist. The school was also the church.*[2]

Today there is a tendency among Christians to be defensive about their faith and to remain silent on the question of religion lest they be accused of using the classroom as a podium from which to propagate their beliefs. Non-Christian professors have no such inhibitions. Many of our university professors are humanists, atheists, or agnostics, and they have no compunctions about spreading their beliefs.

The missionaries should not be faulted for using their educational institutions for the propagation of the Christian faith. It is a perfectly legitimate operation. It is interesting in this connection to remember that in many parts

1. Stephen Neill, *Call to Mission* (Philadelphia: Fortress Press, 1970), p. 10.
2. Max Warren, *Social History and Christian Mission* (London: SCM Press, 1967), pp. 113–114.

of the Third World religion is taught as a regular part of the curriculum from the elementary grades through high school. Islam is taught to Muslim students, Christianity to Christian students, Buddhism to Buddhist students. Only in the U.S. do we have a hangup about teaching religion in a pluralistic society.

3. To develop character. Among the outstanding features which gave mission schools such a fine reputation in the eyes of Christians and non-Christians alike were the moral tone and the kind of discipline which were maintained. Christian schools at home and overseas have always been noted for the dedication of their teachers and the discipline demanded of their students. Private Christian schools in the U.S. may have financial problems, but enrollment is rising so rapidly that they are bursting at the seams. The reason is obvious. The public school systems, especially in the large cities, are becoming virtual jungles where violence and drugs make study all but impossible for many students. By contrast, the Christian schools, while their academic standards and physical facilities may be inferior, offer a better education. The difference between the two systems is largely one of discipline. Without discipline there can be no real learning and no development of character.

Mission schools have always regarded character development as one of their prime objectives, and to achieve this they maintained discipline in the classroom, the dining room, the dormitories, the library, and even on the athletic field. It was this aspect of mission schools that proved so attractive to non-Christian parents. Hindus, Buddhists, and even Muslims preferred to send their children to Christian schools, even though they knew that by so doing they ran the risk of having them converted to the Christian faith. They took the risk in order to give their children the benefit of this kind of education. They wanted them to be good as well as educated.

4. To strengthen the church. The ultimate aim of all missionary work is the establishment of strong indigenous churches that can stand on their own feet, pay their own way, and make their own decisions. This cannot be achieved without strong leadership. Other things being equal, churches progress or regress according to the kind of leadership they have. The leadership need not be clerical in all cases, but lay or clerical, it must be educated. No church will last long without well educated, spiritual, dynamic leaders.

For this reason one of the first things the early missionaries did was to open schools and give their converts an elementary education. As the years came and went and the churches grew in strength and numbers, it became necessary to provide more advanced education until, after many decades, both high schools and colleges were included in the system.

One reason why the ecumenical churches in the Third World have more and better leaders than the interdenominational missions is that the mainline denominations had a head start. They had better educated missionaries and therefore made a much bigger investment in education. Very few colleges were established by the faith missions, and only now are they getting around to organizing seminaries. It will take several decades to catch up with the ecumenical missions, and in the meantime the indigenous leadership in their churches will remain weak.

HISTORICAL DEVELOPMENT

Educational missions have come a long way since the beginning of the modern missionary era 275 years ago, when the Danish-Halle Mission sent its first two members to India.

1. **Modest beginnings.** Few of the early missionaries were professional teachers. Many of them lacked a college degree. Nevertheless they felt the need for education and set themselves to the task of providing it. They began by inviting students into their homes. In the warmer climates they simply gathered under a nearby tree. Physical facilities were primitive in the extreme and textbooks were unavailable. Items such as pencils, paper, notebooks, and blackboards had to be imported or improvised.

The now famous Assuit College on the Nile River was founded by the American Presbyterians in 1865. Their original building was a rented, renovated donkey stable. When Dr. Ida Scudder opened her medical school for girls in Vellore, India, in 1918, she had two modest buildings: an old bungalow and a temporary shed erected for a dissecting room. One microscope, one or two books, and a few bones were the sum total of her equipment; but 14 of the first 18 students completed the course and successfully passed the presidency examinations.

2. **Initial opposition.** In the beginning, foreign education, like foreign medicine, was not readily accepted. In some places the nationals saw no practical use for education. To them it served no purpose; therefore they didn't want it. It was only in later years, after they had seen the material benefits of a good education in terms of government jobs, that they joined the schools in large numbers. Even then there were continuing problems. Parents took their children out of school during the height of the farming season. Some children wearied of study and dropped out after a year or two. It was a constant battle to keep them in school. In Africa the early converts were often detribalized and became outcasts. Other converts were often the scum of society, homeless and rootless. In many places the missionaries built resident stations where the converts and their children were in effect wards of the mission. They were given land, tools, seed, and plants. They were given an education and taught skills, all free of charge. In return they were expected to remain loyal and obedient to the mission. In this rather unusual way many of the early converts got an education.

In other parts of the world it was the education of girls that was difficult. Until the advent of the missionary, girls were not supposed to be educated. When the idea was introduced it met with strong opposition, but in the face of overwhelming odds the missionaries persevered and were richly rewarded for their efforts.

3. **Geographical differences.** Each of the major areas of the world— Asia, Africa, Latin America, Europe, and the Middle East—presented a different picture and posed special problems.

In some countries in the early years, education was the only method open to the missionaries. This was true in Japan, where the public edicts against Christianity were not removed until 1873. For the first fifteen years missionary work was confined largely to the education of the bright young *samurai* who had been disfranchised by the Meiji Restoration.

In India the young men wanted Western education in order to get good jobs with the colonial government. There were two schools of thought among the missionaries with regard to the use of English in mission schools. The Vernacularists, led by William Carey and Serampore College, were in favor of teaching English as a subject, but laid chief emphasis on the development of the vernaculars, the translation of books into these languages, and their use as the chief instrument of education. The Anglicists, headed by Alexander Duff, insisted that English be the chief medium of communication, especially at the higher levels. English, they said, would open to the students the whole world of Western thought. It would also serve as a unifying factor in India, where there were fourteen major languages and hundreds of dialects. After 1835, English became the language of government. Duff was so convinced that he was right that he said on one occasion: "Only use English as the medium and you will break the backbone of caste."[3]

Western education, entirely the work of missionaries, made a significant impact on China. In fact, Chinese nationalists accused the missionaries of destroying the social fabric of China by undermining the classical Confucian form of education. In the heyday of missions there were 340 middle schools and 13 universities. Christian education in China had three goals: (1) The conversion of the upper classes in the hope that their conversion would influence the masses. (2) Provision of a college education for the converts. (3) The gradual, progressive Christianization of the empire. The number of converts was disappointingly small, but the overall impact was immense. John Fairbank said:

> The influence of mission schools and hospitals, of missionary ideals and activities in seeking out the common man, translating Western literature, initiating women's education, assisting in the ancient tasks of charity and famine relief and in new tasks of modernization, was considera-

3. Robert E. Speer, *Some Great Leaders in the World Movement* (New York: Fleming H. Revell, 1911), p. 116.

ble. . . . The missionary movement, whatever its spiritual-doctrinal result in this period, was a profound stimulus to China's modernization. The riots against it seem to have been generally inspired less by the superstitious fears of the populace in the first instance than by the jealousy of the Chinese gentry, whose privileged status in society was directly threatened—socially, ideologically, and in the end politically— by the new class of privileged cultural invaders from abroad."[4]

The situation differed from country to country. In India mission schools were subsidized by the government; in China and Japan they were not. In India they were prestigious institutions and attracted the finest students. In Japan they were quite inferior to the government schools and ended up with their left-overs. In China the situation was somewhere between these two.

It was the missionaries who introduced Western education to Africa, and for many years they were its only proponents. It wasn't until the second and third decades of the 20th century that the colonial governments began to take education seriously. As late as 1961, 68 percent of all African students were in mission schools, most of them at the elementary level. High schools and colleges came later. Most of today's leaders in Africa received their education in a mission school. Not a few of them are practicing Christians.

In Latin America the Roman Catholics operated most of the schools. Protestant missions, therefore, saw no great need for educational missions. Some high schools—known as colleges—became outstanding institutions and achieved considerable fame.

In the 19th century three missions had large investments in the Middle East: the American Congregationalists, the American Presbyterians, and the Anglicans from Britain. All three missions engaged extensively in education, mostly because evangelistic work was difficult, if not impossible, in Muslim countries. Here also the missionaries were the first to introduce modern education. All over the Middle East—in Egypt, Jordan, Lebanon, Syria, and Turkey—they opened schools which are still in operation, though some of them have been nationalized and others are under secular auspices. The Congregationalists still maintain a boys' school in the home town of Saul of Tarsus. Until 1979, Iran was America's staunchest supporter in the Muslim world, due in large measure to the influence of mission schools. The prime minister of Iran, speaking before the Iranian Parliament in 1942, said:

The educational and medical service which the altruistic Americans have rendered in this country, and their assistance to the physical and intellectual development of our youth, are never to be forgotten. Their manifestations of love, free from any taint or design, have caused the people of Iran to have a feeling of attachment and love toward the United States of America and its peoples.[5]

4. John K. Fairbank, *The United States and China* (Cambridge: Harvard University Press, 1973), pp. 178-179.
5. James Batal, *Assignment: Near East* (New York: Friendship Press, 1950), p. 51.

In Europe the picture is entirely different. There was no need for missionaries to engage in educational missions. The same was true of medical missions. In that part of the world they have confined their efforts to evangelism, church planting, and theological education.

OUTSTANDING CHARACTERISTICS

Mission schools in the Third World were a unique institution, and wherever they were established, they made a name for themselves. Naturally they had some outstanding characteristics.

1. They opened their doors to everybody. There were schools in Asia long before the arrival of the missionaries, but for the most part, they catered to the children of the elite. Mission schools accepted all who applied, high and low, rich and poor, male and female. In India they welcomed even the untouchables who for thousands of years had been denied access to education. Though in the beginning they were designed to provide education for the converts and their children, in later years non-Christians were admitted and they soon outnumbered the Christians as much as ten to one. In some instances, modest fees were charged, but worthy students without funds were not denied entrance. The missionaries found a way to subsidize them, even if it meant digging into their own pockets.

2. They offered ethical and religious instruction. This was the prime reason for their existence. The missionaries saw in the schools a powerful evangelistic tool and were not slow to use it. The Christian faith, with the Bible as the textbook, was always part of the curriculum. Daily chapel services were conducted and all students were expected to attend. Discipline was maintained and rebellious students were expelled.

Preserving the spiritual atmosphere was always a problem. It became worse as more and more students came from a non-Christian background. Later on when nationalism became a factor and some schools were obliged by government order to drop the teaching of the Bible and to make attendance at chapel voluntary, the problem was greatly accentuated. The spiritual influence of many schools was further eroded when, for lack of Christian teachers, non-Christians were hired. As a result, some schools begun by missionaries now have little or no spiritual influence on the student body.

3. They included practical courses in the curriculum. This was especially true in the more primitive areas of the world, where cooking, sewing, knitting, and embroidery work were taught to the girls and carpentry, masonry, and mechanics to the boys. It is interesting to note in this connection that the schools in Africa, now nationalized and therefore under government control, are insisting that these courses be retained and even strengthened. Modern education in the Third World, especially at the lower levels, is designed to prepare the students to take their place in society and make their contribution to community development. Even here in the U.S. there has been an increasing emphasis on technical courses in addition to the usual offerings in liberal arts.

4. They pioneered in female education. Initially it was a hard, uphill fight, but the missionaries persevered and succeeded in introducing female education to those parts of the world where it had been completely unknown. Wherever Christianity has gone it has liberated and elevated womanhood, often in the face of entrenched opposition. This was especially true in India, China, Japan, Korea, and the Muslim world. One cannot but wonder where the Women's Liberation Movement in the Third World would be today had it not been for the influence and example of the missionaries. Women can never be liberated as long as they remain illiterate. They must be able to compete with the men, an accomplishment they cannot achieve without an adequate education. The women of the Third World owe a tremendous debt to the missionaries of the 19th century.

5. They produced a bourgeois class. When the missionaries began work in the 19th century there was no middle class to speak of in the Third World. The economy of most of the countries was agriculturally based and upwards of 80 percent of the people were peasants and workers. As Western education penetrated these societies, however, a bourgeois class emerged. Graduates of mission schools were able to get better jobs with higher pay in government, business, and the professions. In time they acquired land, capital, and economic and political power. They became the backbone of a new society with an increasing number of businessmen, merchants, traders, entrepreneurs, doctors, teachers, lawyers, and engineers. Though the new class was still a minority, its power and influence were out of all proportion to its numbers. They more than anyone else were responsible for the economic and social progress of the 20th century.

Max Warren has reminded us that the bourgeoisie is a Western phenomenon. It is

> ... that class which, being bent upon self-improvement, threw off apathy; cherished ambition; combined this ambition with sobriety and thrift; in pursuit of its ends sought political power; and historically combined all this with respect for certain Christian ethical insights, a respect which for many carried with it a deep commitment to the Christian Faith.[6]

Western scientific education, introduced to the Third World by the missionaries, has been the most potent single force in the development of the bourgeois class, especially in Africa.

6. Max Warren, *Social History and Christian Mission* (London: SCM Press, 1967), p. 118.

As far back as 1906, which is very early in terms of Zambia's modern history, an African 'white collar' class was beginning to appear, a direct result of missionary education. They were only a minority, and a very small minority at that, but they had lifted their sights. They were a vanguard of a new class, a new phenomenon in Africa, a bourgeoisie. And their immediate ambition was to imitate as closely as possible the only bourgeoisie they knew, the European, whether missionary, government official, trader or settler.[7]

It is popular in some circles to castigate the bourgeois class and hold it responsible for all the ills that afflict modern society, but the fact remains that the bourgeois class as defined by Warren is the only foundation on which a modern industrial state can be successfully built. The Communists would repudiate this idea, but even they are beginning to revert to type in many parts of the world and a "new class" has already emerged. This is true in the U.S.S.R., where the new class is known as the technocrats. The People's Republic of China has debunked Chairman Mao and his theory of perpetual revolution. Barely two years after his death the new strong man, Teng Hsiao-ping, has called for "four modernizations." After thirty years of self-reliance in almost total isolation from the rest of the world, China has decided to turn to the West for the credits and the technology she needs to make up for lost time. English is in great demand as the first foreign language, and its brightest students are being sent to the U.S. and Europe for advanced training. China must know that in doing this she is running the risk of being contaminated with the "decadent" bourgeois ideas and customs found in the West. Give China another 25 years and a bourgeois class will have reappeared.

6. They lent prestige to Christianity. Mission schools did much to enhance the image of Christianity, especially in Asia. China, Japan, and other countries of Asia have a rich and ancient culture of which they are justly proud. In some countries, notably China, the people had an inordinate veneration for learning. The scholar-gentry class was the most powerful group in the country. Many missionaries argued that if Christianity were ever to appeal to the masses it must first win the respect of the literati. Evangelistic endeavors were prohibited by law in Japan. Christianity therefore made its appeal to the *samurai*, the military elite who flocked to the schools in large numbers to take advantage of Western learning and languages, which were beginning to sweep the country. Even today the church in Japan is composed mostly of middle and upper class people, in contrast to other countries. In India the Christians came from a background of untouchability.

The same has been true of the Middle East where missionaries made a significant contribution to modern education, thus helping the cause of Arab nationalism.

7. Ibid., p. 122.

> *A very high tribute that can be paid to the contribution that American-sponsored education has made in the Eastern Mediterranean is the fact that among the ninety-two delegates and their advisors who represented the countries of the Near East in the drawing up of the United Nations Charter in the spring of 1945 in San Francisco, twenty-nine were graduates of Christian or Christian-inspired schools or colleges in the Near East.* [8]

THE PROBLEMS

Through the years missionary education has been plagued with its full share of problems.

1. Maintaining a Christian witness. If mission schools are to fulfill the purpose for which they were originally designed they must continue to bear a strong Christian witness. So great is this problem that, from a purely practical point of view, some mission leaders have questioned the value of mission schools. Have the results been commensurate with the vast amount of time and money invested? Almost to a man the educational missionaries have defended the system. Church-planting missionaries have grave doubts. Much depends on one's point of view. In China, 30 percent of all persons whose names appeared in China's *Who's Who* received part of their education in a mission school, but fewer than one percent of the populace ever embraced the Christian faith.

Increasingly, mission schools are being secularized. Sometimes this is the result of government action; in other instances it is the result of indifference or neglect on the part of the administration. They may be more concerned with nation building than with character development, more dedicated to social betterment than to personal conversion, more interested in humanization than in redemption. Some mission schools have become hotbeds of revolutionary fervor. In these institutions the distinctly spiritual impact has been reduced to a "spiritual emphasis week" once a year. Such schools are Christian in name only.

There are many factors that militate against a Christian witness. One is the presence of non-Christians on the faculty. Another is the ratio of Christians to non-Christians in the student body. Still another is government control. When a school registers with the government, it loses some of its freedom. Frequently, governments have prohibited the teaching of Christianity, or they have decided that chapel attendance must be on a voluntary basis. It becomes, therefore, a perennial struggle to maintain a strong Christian witness in these schools.

2. Securing qualified teachers. Teachers, both missionary and national, are difficult to get and equally difficult to keep. Some missionaries feel a

---

8. James Batal, *Assignment: Near East* (New York: Friendship Press, 1950), p. 44.

definite call to the teaching profession and go to the field with that end in view, but many of them never become career missionaries. Their vocation permits them to move about freely—three years here, five years there, two years somewhere else. Getting teachers for the Christian day school in the U.S. is difficult; it is much more so on the mission field.

The teacher who applies for overseas service has to raise his own passage and support for the period of his contract. This is an horrendous obstacle to some. He may also have to do double duty, assuming extra-curricular responsibilities made necessary by the fact that the institution is probably a boarding school. Saturdays and Sundays, therefore, are not "days off." It is likely, too, that he will have to teach one or two subjects for which he is not fully qualified. This is true of all educational institutions on the mission field.

Securing national teachers is an equally difficult problem. College graduates are in short supply so the choice is limited. Also, a person with a college degree is so rare in the Third World that he can just about write his own contract. He will be in great demand by government at all levels, provincial, municipal, and national. Most people prefer to go into government employ because the pay is much higher and because government service is usually a very safe and stable form of employment; the salary in a government school is often four or five times that in a Christian school. In Malaysia, Burma, Thailand, and perhaps some other countries, there are no Christian colleges. Where is the mission to get qualified Christian teachers? In some mission schools Buddhist, Hindu, and Muslim teachers outnumber the Christian teachers, which weakens the Christian climate of the institution.

Another contributing factor is the large number of Third World nationals who come to the U.S. for their higher education and then stay here.

> Recently one of our leading graduate schools in the Midwest conducted a survey of the number of Ph. D.'s it had conferred on foreign students between 1941 and 1961. It discovered that slightly more than half this group were still in the United States and, in all likelihood, would remain here permanently.... The American experience with a half-dozen so-called underdeveloped nations reveals disquieting evidence of substantial numbers of students who preferred to remain in the United States upon completion of their studies.... There are manifold reasons for their failure to go home. The phrase "cultural alienation" sums up the experience of many. Some of the students have become more American than the Americans.[9]

3. **Providing financial support.** Except in socialist countries, where public education is free from first grade through college, higher education is becoming increasingly costly. Private education is in even worse straits.

9. R. Pierce Beaver, *Christianity and African Education* (Grand Rapids: Eerdmans, 1966), p. 64.

Here in the U.S., to say nothing of the developing countries, private colleges are fighting with their backs to the financial wall; and every year some are forced to close their doors and go into liquidation. In the Roman Catholic diocese of Chicago, the largest in the world, several high schools are forced out of business every year simply because the diocesan budget is millions of dollars in the red. If this is true in affluent America, what must the situation be like in the developing countries?

Many mission schools were founded in the 19th century when land was cheap or, in some instances, given to the missions free of charge. The buildings erected then are now old and in need of repairs. The falling American dollar, coupled with rampant inflation in many of the host countries, makes it almost impossible for the schools to remain open, especially when they have to compete with newer schools built with tax money supplied by the government. To charge fees would help, but the income derived in this way would be insufficient to close the gap between income and expenditures. If the fees are too high, the students will be unable to pay. Most of the government schools are free and therefore offer keen competition. In the last years of the colonial era the governments began to subsidize mission schools and some of the newly independent governments have continued the practice, but the problem remains. In some countries the mission boards, seeing the handwriting on the wall, tried to turn the schools over to the churches, but this only aggravated the problem. In one or two cases they tried to get the government to take them over, but again they failed. In the meantime they are carrying on as best they can with inadequate finances, second-rate teachers, and students who feel they are being short changed.

4. Coping with student unrest. Student unrest is a recent phenomenon. In the 19th century, education was such a rare privilege that students walked for hours to get to school; and once they were there, they "hit the books" with such diligence that they had neither the time nor the inclination to go on the rampage for whatever cause. With the advent of nationalism in all parts of the Third World the situation has changed. Students are not as meek and docile as they used to be. They have had a taste of "student power" and they know what it can do. At the drop of a hat they will leave the classroom to demonstrate, expressing their displeasure either with conditions in the college or with the political or economic situation in the country. Students the world over are known for engaging in mass demonstrations to get what they want. They have given school administrators all kinds of trouble. They have even toppled governments in Korea, Japan, Turkey, Pakistan, and elsewhere. Quite frequently student unrest will develop anti-foreign overtones; this makes mission schools the first and most convenient object of attack. This was especially true in China in the 1920s when a wave of anti-foreign sentiment swept the country. From Peking to Canton, mission schools were attacked by students molesting teachers, destroying records, and even burning buildings.

It is exceedingly difficult for Western teachers and administrators to cope with student unrest because nationalism colors the thinking of the students. Students imbued with the spirit of nationalism cannot be expected to take a rational approach to the problems involved. The Western administrator because of his nationality suffers from guilt by association. Through no fault of his own he is part and parcel of the Western imperialism that overran Asia and Africa in the 19th century, and when tempers flare the specter of imperialism rises again. This is one good reason why all schools—and hospitals—should be in charge of nationals rather than foreigners.

RECENT TRENDS

Change is the order of the day in all parts of the Third World, but nowhere is this more apparent than in the area of education. Several trends are noticeable.

1. Education is on the increase. Everyone has heard about the astounding progress made by Communist China during the past thirty years. For the first time in history, education is universal, compulsory, and free. But China is not alone in this achievement. Other countries, including India, have made giant strides in education at all levels. Most of the developing countries have opted for socialism rather than capitalism, which means that most of the tax revenue is going into the public sector; and education, being part of the public sector, is getting its share of the national budget. Education is regarded as a panacea that will cure all the ills that afflict the "backward" countries. Some governments, therefore, are spending fifty percent of the national income on public education. Consequently there is not the same need for mission schools as there used to be, especially at the elementary level. There is still room for mission institutions at the secondary and tertiary levels, but even that is changing.

2. Governments are imposing higher standards. In the "good old days," when the only schools were mission schools, few questions were asked about quality. Both parents and students were delighted with what they offered, and even a fifth grade education placed the graduate in a class above most other people. This is no longer true. The government is not only dedicated to the proposition that every child has the right to an education, but it is also interested in the quality of the education made available. Their departments of education are staffed with nationals who have received their Ph. D. in Western education and have returned home determined to enhance the quality of education at all levels. The standards that are established are sometimes unrealistic, but nevertheless there is a universal determination to raise the educational standards right across the board, and all regulations apply to private as well as public schools. Just to read and digest all the government directives requires the efforts of a full-time administrator, and there are the usual records, reports, red tape, and bureaucratic control to contend with, all of which can be costly in time and money.

3. Private schools are on the way out. With government control on the increase, it will be only a matter of time until all private schools are taken over by the government. This is to be expected. Education is too potent an instrument for the forming of public opinion and the molding of the national character to be left in the hands of outsiders, no matter how noble and high-minded they might be. Such a powerful instrument belongs in the hands of their own leaders.

One of the first things a newly independent government does after designing a flag, choosing a national anthem, and drawing up a constitution, is to nationalize the private schools, including those run by the missionaries. This has been done in country after country so that today it is a rare thing to find an elementary school under mission control. For the time being, some high schools are exempt, but they too will be incorporated into the national school system as soon as possible.

Missions should not look with dismay on this development. The teaching of the three R's was never an integral part of the "teaching" referred to in the Great Commission. We got into the act by default and on the whole we did a good job while we were at it. Now the governments have the money, the personnel, and the expertise to run their own schools, and they should be applauded for doing so. Far from being a calamity, this new turn of events sets the missions free to concentrate their resources in areas where they alone have expertise. It is a good move.

It should be noted in passing that not all governments are meeting with the same measure of success. The government of Zaire nationalized all the schools in the early 1970s, but handed them back to the churches a few years later. They discovered that the educational standards were deteriorating, teacher morale was abysmally low, and discipline was completely out of hand. The churches were not keen to have the schools back under their control, and they acceded to the request only on certain conditions: (1) That the government continue to subsidize the schools, (2) that Christianity be put back into the curriculum, (3) that the school officials be given the authority to maintain discipline. Recalcitrant students, after sufficient counsel and warning, will be expelled and the government will back up the action. So desperate was the situation that the government was happy to agree to all three demands.

4. Mission schools are now church schools. Very few schools remain solely in the control of the missions except in very primitive parts of the world: Irian Jaya, Amazonia, and other frontiers where the churches are in their infancy. If the schools have not been nationalized by the government, they have long since passed under the control of the church, and at the elementary level all the teachers are nationals. Missionaries may be giving help in administrative areas, but the teaching is done exclusively by the nationals. These schools receive government subsidies and in that sense come under government control. For all practical purposes, however, they are now run by the churches, not the missions. High schools and colleges are in a different category. At that level there is still a need for expatriate teachers.

5. The curriculum is being indigenized. Under the colonial system the curriculum was almost completely Western in orientation. English, French, or some other Western language was the medium of communication. In British schools they were taught British history. In American schools they were taught American history. At the college level they were taught such dead languages as Latin and Greek and such modern languages as French and German. When they got through, they knew more about Western civilization than they did about their own. In many instances their own culture was all but ploughed under and they ended up being little Americans or little Britishers.

All this is changing. The people of the Third World are striving for authentic selfhood and nationhood. They want to understand and appreciate their own culture first. They want to know more about their own history, culture, and religion, not ours. They are no longer using the term "animism." Instead they refer to African Traditional Religion. The demand for moratorium had its roots precisely at this point; they wanted a cooling off period for reflection and reevaluation.

6. Education must serve a purpose. In the more sophisticated societies of the West a straight liberal arts education has had great appeal. The purpose of a college education is not to fit a person for any particular niche in society, but to provide a broad base to enable him to think critically as a rational human being and to act responsibly as a citizen in a democratic society. In this respect we have made a clear-cut distinction between education and training. The latter is a pejorative term in intellectual circles. You *train* laborers; you *educate* intellectuals. This is a valid concept in the West, though even here in the 1970s we have seen a shift in the direction of vocational training. Colleges that want to survive are including business administration in the curriculum to attract students. Students are asking: "What's the use of spending $30,000 on a college education if I can't land a job?" Their chief concern is with the bottom line: What financial returns do I get?

The needs and the goals of the Third World countries are different from those in the West. At this stage of the game they cannot afford to spend too much time and money on liberal arts. Nation building, community development, public health service, and other practical subjects are being given high priority, and the school systems are expected to contribute directly to the realization of these goals. China is a good example of this kind of approach to utilitarian education. Until recently all students had to spend three months each year "down on the farm," where they learned practical skills and were exposed to the peasants' point of view. In this way they learned to "identify with the people." More and more countries of the Third World are adopting this approach to education. What's the use of knowing Homer, Shakespeare, and Aristotle if you can't drive a tractor or repair a truck or harness a horse?

Educational missionaries are finding increasingly that it is necessary to consult the government, or at least the department of education, before going off on their own to build a curriculum which may or may not contribute to community development. In Nepal the educators, all of them non-professional missionaries, must work hand in glove with the department of education and a new contract is drawn up by the government every five years. This is the trend in most areas. Missionaries must be pre-pared to work closely with the governments of the newly independent countries that have such grandiose plans for their people.

7. **Increasing number of women students.** Prior to the coming of the missionary, women and girls were not allowed an education. Their chief responsibility in life was to bear children and care for the physical needs of the family; and for that, it was assumed, education was not necessary. It was the missionaries who first induced parents to educate their girls, and in the beginning it was a difficult, uphill battle. To this day male students out-number female students in the schools of the Third World, and the dropout figure is much higher for girls than for boys.

There are economic as well as social reasons for this. Parents see no sense in educating their daughters for the benefit of another family. Just about the time they become able to make a contribution to family life, they get married and are lost to their own family for good. Secondly, girls in the developing countries marry young, usually in their early teens, and are expected to leave school to make a home for their husbands, who, of course, continue in school.

This is changing, however. Governments are taking concrete steps to lower the high birth rate. One way of doing this is to discourage early teenage marriages. China has taken drastic action in this respect. Women must be 26 years old and men 28 before they are permitted to marry! This makes it possible for the girls to remain in school long enough to graduate before assuming the burdens of married life, and they are also beginning to see the value of a modern education which makes them less dependent on their husbands for their livelihood. In this they are, consciously or uncon-sciously, following the example of the women of the West.

PRESENT DAY OPPORTUNITIES

Conditions in the developing countries are changing so rapidly that it is difficult for an outsider to keep abreast. Some of the changes have robbed the churches and missions of privileges they once enjoyed, but other changes have worked in our favor and present us with opportunities undreamed of twenty or thirty years ago. Missions must be flexible enough to change with the changing times and to take advantage of new opportunities gained rather than bemoan the opportunities lost.

1. Teaching religion in secular government schools. This is one of the most exciting innovations in missionary work today. Formerly the missions had to own, support, teach, and administer their own schools, with all the financial burdens, disciplinary problems, and administrative chores involved. Now the schools have been taken over by the government and missionaries are hired to teach religion—a required course called Religious Knowledge.

This is in stark contrast to the U.S., where teaching Christianity is supposed to be a violation of the First Amendment which says that the government shall not establish a religion. Moreover, ours is a pluralistic society, they say, with Jews, Gentiles, Christians, and now a handful of Muslims, Hindus, Buddhists, and others; and this makes it impossible to teach religion. The U.S. is not nearly as pluralistic a society as some African countries where there are 250 tribal groups, each with its own language and culture. Yet in such countries as Nigeria, Ghana, Liberia, Kenya, etc., Religious knowledge is required of all students, each being taught the religion of his family. The system works well. Pluralism is no problem at all. These governments have the good sense to recognize that religion is a good, wholesome, and essential part of culture and should be taught in the public schools.

For many years the Sudan Interior Mission maintained a large education center at Kagoro in Nigeria, including a primary school, a secondary school, a teachers college, and a Bible college. The government has taken over everything except the Bible college. Six missionaries are teaching Religious Knowledge full time in the government schools—and are paid to do the job! Les Greer reported thirty-seven Bible classes a week in a government school in the predominantly Islamic city of Kano and more opportunities for personal witness than he could handle. In addition to teaching Religious Knowledge missionary teachers are often responsible for baptismal classes, leadership training courses, monthly Communion services, and the promotion of the Fellowship of Christian Students, which has branches in most of the high schools and colleges.

The Sudan Interior Mission in a January 31, 1977 news release reported: "Mission societies are besieged by requests from various State governments for qualified Bible Knowledge teachers. We can't begin to fill the requests. Right now we could use 30 couples just in six northern states. Similar requests are coming from all 12 states." To teach Bible Knowledge, missionaries should have a B.R.E., a B. Th., or a Masters degree in theology.

2. Opportunities for training teachers. More challenging than teaching courses in Religious Knowledge is the opportunity to train future teachers of the course. In an all-out effort to provide universal education the government of Nigeria is opening teacher training schools at an unprecedented rate. Universal Primary Education (UPE) is of such scope that Nigeria is appealing for 40,000 teachers. Thousands of new schools are under construction to accommodate an estimated 11.5 million primary students by 1980. It is predicted that this free education for all children through grade seven will bring about "the biggest social change in the history of the nation." Among the 40,000 teachers will be several thousand qualified to teach Religious Knowledge from the Christian point of view. This presents the Christian church with a unique opportunity. The impact of these Christian teachers could be extremely significant, and the opportunity is now, while the teacher training phase of UPE is developing. The government of Nigeria has asked the Sudan Interior Mission to act as a clearing-house for qualified teachers with the degrees already mentioned. What a glorious opportunity!

More strategic still is the opportunity some missionaries have had to actually write the entire curriculum for the course, from elementary through high school. This has occurred in Indonesia, South Africa, and other countries. In 1978 the Sudan Interior Mission was asked by the government of Liberia to help set up a curriculum for the teaching of Bible Knowledge and to supply as many teachers as possible. It would be difficult to imagine a more far-reaching ministry in the area of educational missions.

3. Teaching in government high schools. The big thrust is coming at the secondary level. Some years ago the government of Kenya asked the Africa Inland Mission to recruit 192 missionary teachers to staff 24 new high schools then on the drawing boards. They said they preferred missionaries, but if they could not get missionaries they would appeal to the Peace Corps. If the Peace Corps could not provide that number they would accept any qualified persons—Muslims, animists, non-Christians—anybody. When the 17-year civil war ended in Southern Sudan, the government there asked the ten missions of the Africa Committee for Rehabilitation of Southern Sudan to provide 19 missionary teachers for the new high school they were planning. Until the Military Council seized power in Ethiopia in 1974, one half of all the Peace Corps volunteers were teaching in high schools in that country. Missionary teachers can be full members of a mission seconded to the government or they can sign their own contract with the government. Either way they have an excellent opportunity to make a spiritual impact on the future leaders of these countries, and they do it all at government expense!

4. Teaching at secular universities. There are few Christian universities in the Third World, but state-supported universities are increasingly common in many countries. Dedicated Christians with advanced degrees and teacher certification are always welcome, as are Western students. Such teachers are accepted even in Muslim countries otherwise closed to the Christian message. They would not be able to "proselytize" in the classroom, but outside the school there are endless opportunities for personal friendship, Christian hospitality, weekend retreats, house parties, fellowship dinners, musical evenings, and other social gatherings which lend themselves to an informal but very effective Christian witness. Persons who serve in this capacity are generally known as nonprofessional missionaries, sometimes called "tent-making" missionaries. They have several advantages over the professional missionary. They are under government contract so their status in the country is secure. They are provided with a salary far in excess of what the average missionary gets. More important, they are recognized as full members of the academic community with all the prestige that attaches to professors in the non-Western world. R. Pierce Beaver is of the opinion that "the university is as much a mission field as any village or inner city or suburban area, but the missionaries must be appropriate to the academic world."[10]

5. **Teaching in schools for missionaries' children.** There are hundreds of these schools in Africa, Asia, Latin America, and Oceania, and every year the administrators have to make frantic appeals for qualified teachers. When they are not available other teachers have to do double duty. One school was so desperate for teachers that the administration called for a day of prayer, asking God to move the hearts of teachers at home who might be persuaded to go overseas. Some Christian teachers are retiring early to give five or ten years to teaching in a school for MKs and are finding the experience both exciting and rewarding.

This is one of the most difficult of all missionary posts to fill. Fully qualified teachers, if they go abroad, prefer to teach nationals. Somehow teaching a bunch of MKs doesn't seem like *missionary* work. The rewards, however, are great. MKs compare favorably with any peer group—sons and daughters of such professional people as doctors, lawyers, engineers, ministers, etc. They are usually above average in intelligence. When it comes to motivation they are well ahead of their peers in America. Discipline, an horrendous problem in stateside schools, seldom causes trouble. One of the greatest blessings is the absence of television, which has done more than any other one thing to demoralize the younger generation. As an invention it is one of the marvels of the 20th century. As an educational medium it has turned out to be a cultural wilderness. Without television, MKs are obliged to turn elsewhere for diversion, and usually they become inquisitive and innovative, organizing their own extra-curricular activities. Many of them become voracious readers. Teaching in a school for MKs is a rare privilege.

SUCCESS OR FAILURE?

Have educational missions been a success or a failure? There is no simple answer to that question. One could ask the same question about evangelistic

10. R. Pierce Beaver, *Christianity and African Education* (Grand Rapids: Eerdmans, 1966), p. 26.

and medical missions. Much depends on one's understanding of the purpose of educational missions. Before one can say a movement or an institution has been a failure, he must first decide what it was supposed to do in the first place. If Christian schools are to be regarded solely or even primarily as an evangelistic agency our success has been limited, for we have made comparatively few converts in the classroom. The same is true of medical missions. Only a handful who came for physical healing accepted spiritual healing as well.

Looking back over more than a century of educational missions we can say that on the whole they have been successful in a number of ways.

1. They made a significant contribution to man's intellectual development. By conducting educational missions and teaching the three Rs the missionary made possible the intellectual development of the human personality. Man is a tripartite being made up of body, mind, and soul, and if he is to achieve authentic personhood he must be given an opportunity to develop his mind along with his body. By teaching "the natives" to read and write the missionary opened to them a whole new world of ideas and made it possible for them to acquire a knowledge of the outside world. This is no mean accomplishment. The uneducated man who spends most of his time ministering to the elemental needs of the body is hardly living as God intended him to live. It is by the cultivation of the mind that man can fully develop all the powers of his God-given personality and take his place in, and make his contribution to, human society.

2. They introduced modern education. This included agriculture, mathematics, science, engineering, etc., on which the modern industrial state is built. They also gave to their students the best literature of the West, from Plato's *Republic* to Tolstoi's *War and Peace*, and the most explosive, most liberating book in the world, the Bible; in their own tongue. In this way they managed, by precept and example, to inculcate the ideas and ideals of democracy: the worth of the individual, the equality of the sexes, the dignity of labor, freedom of thought, and human rights.

3. They sowed the seeds of nationalism and helped promote independence. It was in the mission schools that the students got their first taste of liberation, and it turned out to be pretty heady stuff. It is a matter of record that it was the missionaries who sowed the seeds of nationalism in the hearts and minds of their students, and in nearly every colony it was the students who were in the vanguard of the independence movement. Speaking in 1920 Emir Feisal bore testimony to the influence of the Syrian Protestant College, which later became the American University of Beirut: "Dr. Daniel Bliss, the founder of the college, was the grandfather of Syria; his son, Dr. Howard Bliss, the present president, is the father of Syria. Without the education this college has given, the struggle for freedom would never have been won." Not a few heads of state in Africa were quick to acknowledge on Independence Day the contribution which the missionaries and their educational institutions had made toward the achievement of independence. It was the missionaries who introduced modern scientific education. Where would Africa be today had it not been for the thousands of schools of various levels maintained by the missionaries and their national colleagues? Without the contribution of educational missions few if any countries in Black Africa would be independent today.

4. They made English the *lingua franca* of the world. The majority of the Protestant missionaries were from the English-speaking countries. It was natural for them to teach English as the first foreign language in mission schools. At the secondary and tertiary levels English became the medium of communication. In a way this was part of the "cultural imperialism" that was characteristic of the missionary movement, and in that sense it was bad. When looked at from another point of view, however, it must be regarded as a blessing in disguise, for in time English became the *lingua franca* of the world. Even Communist China has reintroduced English as the first foreign language to be taught in the schools. When the Chinese Communists overran Tibet in 1953 and the Dalai Lama was forced to flee to India, he was met at the border by Prime Minister Nehru. They conversed in English! English is one of the unifying forces in India today. It is no longer the official language, which is now Hindi, but it is better known and more widely used than any of the fourteen regional languages. Most of the ex-British colonies still use English as the language of business and politics, and it is also used in the high schools and colleges. It is certainly the most widely used language in the United Nations.

5. They had a wholesome spiritual impact. The actual number of students converted to Christianity in the classroom was not large, but the overall impact of mission schools was wholesome. Though only a small number of students ever became committed Christians, those who did contributed to the defense of the faith and the building up of the church. Several of them became national leaders, some of them heads of state. What shall we say about the majority of students who never made any profession of personal faith in Christ? The time and effort spent on them was not lost. They may not have accepted Christ as Savior but they became friends of the West. Through the study of the life and teachings of Jesus Christ they got a good impression of Christianity as a way of life. They considered Him to be the greatest Person who ever lived. Even those who resented the tie-in between colonialism and Christianity and who rejected the latter because of the former, nevertheless speak well of Christianity. In Japan, for instance, fewer than one percent of the population are professing Christians and the students are almost all agnostics, but in a recent poll a surprising number of them said that if they had to choose a religion it would be Christianity.

Many students who completely rejected Christianity as a religion and turned out to be violently anti-Christian still had a high regard for the United States and the Christian principles for which it stands. Chou En-lai was the one man in Communist China who, almost single-handedly, turned China away from dependence on the U.S.S.R. and towards friendship with the U.S.A. What gave Premier Chou, a ruthless and dedicated Communist, a quiet, deep-seated appreciation, almost affection, for the U.S.? Was it the fact that he got part of his education in a Christian school and there developed an esteem for the American way of life which never really left him? The suggestion is an intriguing one.

Another well-known leader was Jomo Kenyatta, former president of Kenya. He too was educated in a mission school, but later he went to Moscow. He returned to Kenya to lead the bloody Mau Mau movement which vowed to kill every white man in Kenya. Yet when he became Prime Minister in 1963 he publicly thanked the missionaries for their contribution to Kenya's development and asked them to remain to help him build a new Kenya.

24

Medical Work

From the beginning, medical work has been an integral part of the missionary enterprise. Some of the most famous pioneers were medical personnel: Dr. John Scudder (India), Dr. Peter Parker (China), Dr. Paul Harrison (Arabia), Dr. Daniel Bradley (Thailand), Dr. Thomas A. Lambie (Ethiopia), Dr. David Livingstone (Africa). Two of the best known teaching hospitals in India are the Ludhiana Christian Medical College, founded by Edith Brown in 1894, and the Vellore Christian Medical College, founded by Ida Scudder in 1918. The most famous hospital in China was the Peking Union Medical College founded by Dr. Thomas Cochrane. Today there are 2,500 church and mission related hospitals on the mission fields of the world. There is hardly a country in the Third World which does not have a Christian medical institution of one kind or another. Indeed, modern scientific medicine was introduced into Africa, Asia, and Latin America by the missionaries.

THEOLOGICAL BASIS

The missionary, like his Master before him, cannot be indifferent to the physical needs of mankind. Jesus "went about all Galilee teaching... preaching... and healing all manner of disease among the people" (Matt 4:23, KJV). On several other occasions when Matthew records that the multitudes followed Jesus, he simply adds, "He healed them" (12:15; 15:30; 19:1,2; 21:14, KJV).

Thirty-five separate miracles are recorded in some detail in the four

Gospels. Most of them are miracles of healing. When Jesus sent out the Twelve (Matt 10:1), and later when He sent out the Seventy (Luke 10:1,9), He gave them authority to heal the sick.

Repeatedly Jesus asked: "Will you be made whole?" The word "whole" comes from an old Anglo-Saxon root, *hal,* from which we get our words "health" and "holiness." In order to be "whole" man needs both health and holiness. In his mundane existence man needs a body; in the resurrection he will have a glorified body. No religion places more honor on the body than does Christianity. Jesus cleansed the leper, healed the sick, fed the hungry, even raised the dead. Sickness, pain, weakness, and death are all part of the kingdom of Satan that Christ came to destroy.

It is true that only one of the five references to the Great Commission mentions healing, but Jesus did not intend by that to imply that the healing ministry would cease at the Ascension. He stated quite plainly that the apostles would continue the ministry He began. "He that believeth on me, the works that I do shall he do also; and greater works than these shall he do; because I go unto the Father" (John 14:12, KJV).

Peter's sermon on the day of Pentecost (Acts 2) and his healing of the lame man (Acts 3) set all Jerusalem in an uproar, so much so that the Council took measures to stop the new movement. It was the miracle more than the message that upset the Jewish leaders. They could deny the message; they could not deny the miracle (Acts 4:14). Not only did the apostles "fill Jerusalem with the doctrine" (Acts 5:28, KJV); they engaged in a healing ministry on a mammoth scale. "There came also multitudes out of the cities round about unto Jerusalem, bringing sick folks, and them which were vexed with unclean spirits; and they healed every one" (Acts 5:16, KJV).

The Acts of the Apostles does not give the impression that miracles played a large part in the ministry of Paul, but his own words, written towards the end of his third journey, prove that they did. "I will not dare to speak of any of those things which Christ hath not wrought by me, to make the Gentiles obedient, by word and deed, through mighty signs and wonders, by the power of the Spirit of God, so that from Jerusalem round about unto Illyricum, I have fully preached the gospel of Christ" (Rom 15:18,19, KJV). Harnack lists ten philanthropic works in which the early Christians engaged, one of which was "the care of the sick and infirm."[1] It is clear that healing played an important part in the life of the early church.

When the modern missionary took the gospel to the ends of the earth in the nineteenth century, he too engaged in a healing ministry. It is true that he did not perform many miracles, but he took with him the findings and facilities of modern medicine and shared them not only with his converts but with others as well. He used medicine and surgery to bring health and healing to bodies that had been racked with pain and deformed by disease.

---

1. Adolph Harnack, *The Mission and Expansion of Christianity* (New York: Harper and Brothers, 1962), p. 153.

In so doing he was in good company; he had the example of Christ and the practice of the early church to back him up.

THE GENERAL PURPOSE

There is nothing haphazard about medical missionary work. It has certain clearly defined objectives. All of these objectives have not been met to the same extent; we have been more successful in some than in others. But we have had objectives and these should be recognized for what they are.

1. **To alleviate human suffering.** In spite of all the advances made since World War II there is still an enormous amount of unrelieved sickness and suffering in many parts of the world. Half of the children die before reaching seven years of age, and those who survive often suffer from hunger, malnutrition, and disease. They go through life deformed, crippled, blind, infested with parasites, and covered with sores. Many of them never see a doctor, never visit a hospital, never own a toothbrush. Such common ailments as headaches, toothaches, and stomachaches are taken for granted and accepted with equanimity. They have nothing, not even aspirin, to relieve pain; and when they die, their relatives don't even have the satisfaction of knowing the cause of death.

It was said of Jesus that He "went about doing good, and healing all that were oppressed of the devil; for God was with him" (Acts 10:38, KJV). His miracles of healing were not performed only for the glory of God, though that was certainly true (John 17:15). They were acts of mercy designed to relieve suffering, remove pain, and restore health. The healing of the body was not simply a means to an end, namely, to save the soul. It was a good thing in and of itself. Jesus never said: "I have healed your body; now your soul belongs to me." He offered healing for body, mind, and soul, and men were free to make their choice. Not all accepted the healing of the soul. Most were content with physical healing; they were not interested in the Bread of Life but in the loaves and fishes. Jesus did not disqualify them on that account. His generosity was genuine. He offered healing with no strings attached. He had a deep desire to relieve human suffering.

2. **To combat ignorance and superstition.** In a world where germs were unknown and sickness was common, it was necessary to introduce modern scientific medicine with its emphasis on cleanliness. In many instances the sufferings of the people stem from ignorance as much as from poverty. They are totally unaware of the basic factors that contribute to sickness and disease: the existence of germs, the presence of parasites, contaminated food, impure water, etc.

The medical missionaries not only opened hospitals and clinics, they trained doctors and nurses, technicians and pharmacists. They also wrote and translated books and published medical journals. In hospitals, clinics, and schools they taught health courses, first aid, minor surgery, and other things. Many diseases that were formerly attributed to demons, witches, or other occult powers were seen to be natural rather than supernatural phenomena.

3. To dispel prejudice and create good will. In most mission fields the early missionaries were regarded with a mixture of suspicion and fear. Their very appearance was so strange as to strike fear into the hearts of the unsophisticated "natives." C. T. Studd, a pioneer missionary in China, wrote: "For five years we never went outside our doors without a volley of curses from our neighbors."

In the nineteenth century, China was one of the most difficult of all the mission fields. Most of its leaders were antiforeign and therefore antimissionary. Li Hung-chang, one of China's mighty men, was one of the few who befriended the missionaries and protected and promoted their work. The reason? His wife was cured through the medical skill of Dr. Mackenzie of the London Missionary Society. In the 1880s, the missionaries were in imminent danger of being expelled from Korea before they had even begun their work. The situation changed almost overnight in 1884 when Dr. Allen successfully treated the wounds of a member of the royal family.

4. To promote public health. Not only did missionaries minister to individual patients who came to their hospitals for surgery, but in many countries they pioneered in public health. During the nineteenth century Thailand's most prominent killers—tuberculosis, cholera, malaria, and smallpox—claimed the lives of thousands every year. Dr. Dan Bradley and his associates did not make much headway against the first three, but they were eminently successful in their fight against smallpox. He had the distinction of introducing smallpox vaccine into Thailand as early as 1836. He got his vaccine from America by way of the Cape of Good Hope, before the Suez Canal was opened and long before the days of refrigeration. Later, in the 1890s, Dr. James McKean developed his own vaccine from calves and manufactured his own quinine. He trained two hundred paramedical personnel and sent them into the surrounding countries to check the spread of smallpox and malaria. In a very short time he rid that part of northern Thailand of smallpox. The king decorated him with the Order of the Crown. This kind of preventive medicine was by no means confined to Thailand.

5. To demonstrate the love of God. Most of the people in the Third World are idolaters, and the gods they worship are not exactly gods of love. They are usually depicted as being cruel, powerful, vindictive, and capricious; they inspire fear rather than trust. Moreover, they are absentee gods, far removed from the sphere of earthly activity. They show little or no concern for the welfare of their devotees.

Into this situation comes the missionary doctor with his concern for human need, his sensitivity to pain, and his deep desire to help and heal. Like Jesus, he sees the multitudes as sheep without a shepherd and is unwilling to send them away without help "lest they faint in the way" (Matt 15:32, KJV). His heart goes out to the unfortunate sufferers, many of whom have been cast off by their own society. He usually charges no fees for his services, only for the medicines used. He does all this because he himself has been reached and reclaimed by the love of God and he wants to share that love with others. Patients in mission hospitals are usually impressed by two things: the professional skill of the surgeon, and the care and compassion shown by the entire staff. Patients have been known to pass government hospitals and walk an extra day's journey to reach a mission hospital because they know they will get this kind of care.

6. To point the patient to Christ. Every patient who enters a mission hospital has two kinds of disease: physical and spiritual. He is aware only of the physical, but the missionary doctor knows that his patient is also suffering from soul sickness. Of the two, the latter is the more important in the long run. For this reason mission hospitals do their best to give a Christian witness. In Muslim countries, where a verbal witness is often prohibited, the hospital staff must be content with a non-verbal witness. This is accomplished by serving the patients in the name and spirit of Christ, hoping that they may be moved to ask questions about the Christian faith. For a patient to spend a week or longer in a mission hospital without hearing the gospel is an unmitigated tragedy.

THE PAUCITY OF MEDICAL PERSONNEL

One of the biggest problems in medical missions is the lack of qualified personnel, both Western and national. In both cases the reasons are the same: the arduous period of training, and the lure of the huge salaries they can command when they get into private practice.

In the U.S. it is exceedingly difficult to get into medical school. Two years ago a friend with a good college record applied to seven medical schools and was turned down by all of them. Each year 40,000 students apply for 13,000 openings.

Their problems are by no means over once they are accepted. In state universities the total cost of tuition and living for four years is about $30,000. In the private schools the bill may run as high as $50,000. If the student has to borrow that money he will graduate with a sizable debt which may take him four or five years to liquidate. By that time he will be over thirty and will probably have a family and an established practice. To pull up roots at that stage and move the family to the mission field is a big undertaking. Even if he wants to go, his wife may have other ideas. If he does go abroad he will take a large cut in salary. Surgeons in our larger cities have incomes that run into six figures, but a missionary doctor does well to be able to maintain a decent standard of living in the host country. For this reason, missionary doctors are all too few. Forty percent of the mission hospitals have only one doctor, another twenty-seven percent have two, and thirteen percent have three. Most of the hospitals are small and very few have more than 200 beds. Two or even three doctors to a hospital is a far cry from the fabulous facilities we enjoy in the U.S., where hospitals of comparable size may have over a hundred physicians and surgeons on the staff.

Through the years mission hospitals have given a good deal of attention to the training of medical personnel including doctors, nurses, and technicians. To do an adequate job it is necessary to have a medical school and/or a teaching hospital, and there are not many of these in existence. The training of practical nurses and midwives is a much simpler proposition. Here the hospitals have done yeoman service. A survey taken by the Medical Assistance Program in Wheaton, Illinois, reveals the fact that 73 percent of the 158 mission hospitals responding have a training program for nationals, but only 44 percent of these are recognized by the government. Many nationals go overseas for their medical training, especially those who want to be doctors and surgeons. The majority of them do not return to their home country. There are several reasons for this. First, they are willing to accept the jobs that American doctors don't like such as resident doctors, anesthesiologists, radiologists, etc. Second, the political situation in their homelands may be highly explosive and they prefer the security of the U.S. Third, they can make much more money here than at home. Even those who do return home don't want to serve in a mission hospital when they can work for the government and make five or ten times greater salary.

As a result of all this, most mission hospitals are woefully understaffed. This means that the doctors and nurses work long hours, treating outpatients in the morning, performing surgery in the afternoon, and visiting the wards in the evening. It is a dawn to dark operation six days a week.

ADMINISTRATIVE PROBLEMS

Mission hospitals have all the administrative problems of an American hospital with a few more thrown in for good measure.

1. **Financial support.** Inflation and rising standards of living are playing havoc with mission finances. The price of land is so high that mission boards have almost given up the idea of trying to acquire land for building purposes. In some cities today, an acre of land costs well over $100,000, in contrast to the nineteenth century when land was cheap and in many cases was donated by the colonial government to be used for humanitarian purposes.

Hospitals built in the nineteenth century now need constant upkeep and repair. These bills are often beyond the ability of the mission to pay. Modern equipment, which has sent the cost of health care soaring in the U.S., is out of the question. Mission hospitals are therefore finding it increasingly difficult to compete with government hospitals supported by tax money. To make matters worse, 47 percent of the mission hospitals in Asia have to pay taxes to the government. In other continents the figure is lower: 8.3 percent in Latin America and 6.3 percent in Africa. Apparently no preferential treatment is afforded to non-profit organizations.

In the nineteenth century, mission hospitals seldom charged for their services; if they did the fees were nominal. In some places no currency existed in which the bills could be paid! More recently they have been forced to charge for their services in the hope of ultimately becoming self-supporting. This is an important consideration in the event that the missionaries are asked to leave by the host countries. At present, 25 percent of the hospitals in the Missionary Assistance Program survey are completely self-supporting and 16 percent are almost as independent. Another 25 percent raise half of their support and a further 15 percent report that they are partially self-supporting. They are moving in the right direction, but in so doing they may be making it impossible for the poor people to come for treatment because they can't afford to pay. One criticism leveled at mission hospitals is that they have tended to become "elitist," ministering primarily to the middle and upper-middle classes.

2. Government restrictions. In the "good old days" of colonialism hospital administrators were on their own. They were free to do as they pleased. With the advent of independence following World War II, however, the entire picture has changed. Local governments are now establishing policies, setting standards, and requiring reports. The fact that most governments in the developing countries have opted for socialism means that socialized medicine will soon be common in most places. In that case it will not be long before a huge bureaucracy is established with all the difficulties, delays, and frustrations that are an inevitable part of such a structure.

In many instances the standards set by the government are higher than those previously maintained by the missions. These have to do largely with buildings and equipment rather than with professional competence, though the latter is by no means overlooked. In an increasing number of countries missionary doctors are obliged to take a full set of medical examinations *in the vernacular* before being allowed to practice. This is done in spite of the fact that their services are desperately needed. Some older doctors who were evacuated from China in the early fifties were unable to pass such exams in the countries to which they were deployed, because they were not completely familiar with the vernacular. As a result, they were not allowed to function in a medical role regardless of their medical knowledge and years of experience. Why do countries in such great need of medical personnel act like this? The answer is simple: It is a tit-for-tat gesture. Our government requires this of their doctors wanting to practice in America. They retaliate by making the same demand of our doctors. Such is the nature of nationalism.

3. Discipline and morale. In recent years, when young people the world over have been fighting for their rights and thumbing their noses at the Establishment, institutional discipline and morale have become major problems. Labor unions, which are becoming a formidable force in the developing countries, are urging their members to make unreasonable demands of their employers. Sit-down strikes, work stoppages, and other disruptive tactics unknown in former times are becoming increasingly common. Since the Marxist regime came to power in Ethiopia in 1974 mission administrators have been subjected to an almost incessant barrage of pillory and propaganda. One field superintendent spent two years fighting and losing lawsuits all over the country.

The employees of the internationally famous Vellore Christian Medical College in South India joined a union in 1968. Since then, organized labor has used strikes, harrassment, and violence to block all management measures to exercise discipline. When several employees were dismissed in 1975 for corrupt practices, 37 percent of the hospital's total work force walked out. The strike lasted seventy days and was terminated only when the Chief Minister of Madras State abandoned pressure on the hospital to reinstate the discharged employees.

4. Nationalization. Many people think that the evangelistic missionary is the first to suffer when nationalists with an anti missionary bias come to power. This is not the case. It is true that the governments of these countries are vitally interested in community development and nation building and they want only those expatriates who can contribute directly or indirectly to those worthy ends. The fact remains that medical and educational missionaries are the first ones in danger of losing their jobs. The elementary schools in Black Africa have all been nationalized and only a handful of missionaries remain in those schools. The governments are beginning to show signs of nationalizing medical institutions as well. The government of Nigeria has plans to nationalize all hospitals in the country as soon as they have the qualified personnel to operate them. The Sudan Interior Mission has "lost" several hospitals in this way, and more are slated for nationalization in the future. Other missions are having the same experience.

This is not all bad. In fact it is, in my opinion, a good trend. The Western missions have limited resources of men and money. In the past these were divided among three major areas: evangelistic, medical, and educational work. The missions offered free education and free medical care when no one else was able to. Now that the governments have the ability to manage these institutions they should by all means do so. This will set the missions free to concentrate their meager resources in the area of their expertise, evangelism and church planting. No government is likely to move into that area.

When mission schools and hospitals are nationalized, the governments involved seldom discuss compensation. They say that these institutions were established for the benefit of the poor people in the Third World. By "giving" their facilities to the government, the institutions will continue to serve those people, thus fulfilling the original purpose for which they were founded.

5. Ecological conditions. We have heard a great deal in recent years about the ecological problems here in the U.S., but they are nothing compared with similar problems in the undeveloped countries of the world. A missionary doctor working in one of these countries has given us an account of the appalling conditions faced by missionary doctors in primitive areas. In a prayer letter dated March 21, 1974 he described the little town near which he and his wife live. It has a population of 5,000. This is what he says:

> It is a source of little amazement that hardly a trace of modern civilization can be detected here. To set foot in the town is to step back a thousand years, about the only hint of the twentieth century discoverable being cigarette wrappers, an occasional kerosene lamp, and Secret Agent 007 belt buckles. In distinction to the capital, where at least the sewage flows along open gutters along each street, here there are no gutters. In a more jaundiced moment, the entire town could be likened to one great toilet for goats, pigs, chickens, cows, and humans; and your nose would not belie it. The houses are joined one to another, separated here and there by foul narrow alleys. Inside there is virtually no illumination except that afforded by the fire, the smoke from which in due time imparts to the interior of the house along with its occupants a characteristic coating of black soot. In fact you can't remain standing inside lest the smoke burn your eyes and together with the general darkness prevent you from seeing at all, which, however, is a distinct advantage when it comes to eating what's on your plate at mealtime.

> You would think that a town so burdened with sickness and suffering of all kinds that has never seen a doctor or nurse until recent years would cry out for medical help and welcome us with open arms and tears of gratitude. . . . In their eyes we've merely come to take their money in exchange for some trifling medicine of untested worth and very likely with an ulterior motive besides. It's a healthy thing for a doctor or nurse to encounter a reception like that, because it recalls to us once more how easy it is in the medical profession to be propelled and sustained by the dramatic needs and tears of gratitude instead of by God. We need to remember that there is nothing intrinsically holy or good about the field of medicine that entitles us to be welcomed everywhere as heavenly angels of mercy.

In another letter dated March 9, 1976, he wrote:

> Behind the romantic facade of peaceful villages, exotic temples, rhododendron forest, and majestic mountains, an ecologic and human catastrophe is inexorably taking shape. . . . As the population increases,

the demand for farmland and firewood will intensify, thus accelerating the destruction of the once magnificent forests. . . . Floods, famines, and droughts are well known to the people; what is new is that after centuries of living in relative balance with their environment, that balance has finally been upset, and rapid and relentless deterioration of the environment is under way.

The fields even now can support the population only in a bumper year, and the year before last the village experienced a severe famine; and worse is coming. Families have been forced to go south in search of food, leaving cattle and fields untended, thus jeopardizing next year's harvest. Men have to travel a full day's journey to cut firewood in the receding forests, generally spending a couple of weeks procuring the year's supply at one time. They take their livestock up to a day away just to find fodder, and as a consequence spend a third to a half of their lives out in the fields with their animals. Short of fodder, short of fuel, short of food, and half the population youngsters running around getting set to reproduce in a few years; and where will they go then?

THE SPIRITUAL IMPACT

A great deal of time, thought, energy, and money has been invested in medical missions. It is fair to ask: From a spiritual point of view has the investment paid off? Reliable statistics are difficult to obtain, but we may assume that hundreds, if not thousands, of persons have found healing for the soul while they sought healing of the body.[2]

We might begin by asking: What is the prime purpose of a mission hospital? We would have to answer that it is the healing of the body. The patient will hear the gospel during his stay in the hospital and in some cases he will accept it. Thus he will get a double blessing. That is the *total* purpose, however, not the *prime* purpose, of the hospital. We dare not use our medical facilities as bait to get the populace to accept the gospel. That would be utterly unworthy of a follower of Jesus Christ. No form of subterfuge should ever be used in the service of the gospel.

On the other hand we should question the findings of the Laymen's Foreign Mission Inquiry in the 1930s which stated that "ministry to the secular needs of men in the spirit of Christ *is* evangelism in the right sense of the word." Out of this came a recommendation that "direct and conscious evangelism be divorced from medical and educational work."[3] The rationale for this was based on the fact that in a hospital ward the missionary has a "captive" audience. Under such conditions all attempts at conversion are "subtly coercive and improper."[4]

2. Rosalind Goforth's book, *Chinese Diamonds for the King of Kings*, is an account of individuals who found Christ in a Presbyterian hospital in Changteh.
3. William Ernest Hocking, *Re-Thinking Missions: A Laymen's Inquiry After One Hundred Years* (New York: Harper, 1932), p. 326.
4. Ibid., p. 201.

Coercion is never proper in evangelistic work. We must always respect the integrity of the other person lest we be guilty of the old charge that missionaries "ram religion down the throats of the people."

Missionary doctors should not be expected to be evangelists in the full sense of the term. They don't have time to talk with each patient about Christ, much as they might like to. How then is a mission hospital to have a spiritual ministry? It should have on its staff a full-time evangelist and/or Biblewoman who can give full time and thought to the spiritual and emotional needs of the patients. To do this effectively they must take the time to sit by the bedside, to listen as well as speak, to pray as well as preach. In this way enough Christian instruction can be given to enable the patient to make an intelligent response to the gospel.

Every effort should be made to maintain an effective follow-up program. Without this, many converts will return to their non-Christian communities only to lose interest in their new-found faith and fall away. If there is a church in his town or village the convert should be put in touch with it. If there is no church someone from the mission should contact him as soon as possible after his return home. This will require time and planning, but the results will justify the investment.

Some have questioned the ethics of preaching to outpatients while they are waiting to see the doctor. This, they say, is a subtle form of coercion inasmuch as they are really part of a "captive" audience in that they have paid their registration fee and are on their way to see the doctor. They can't very well leave without losing their fee so they must listen to what the evangelist has to say whether they want to or not. Some mission hospitals have discontinued the practice because of such criticism.

The following observations are in order at this point, however. First, absolutely no attempt is made to force the patient to accept the gospel. Second, most patients know before they arrive that the hospital is a Christian institution and that they will probably be exposed to a presentation of the Christian faith. Third, even the medical profession is now talking about a "holistic" approach to the problems of general health care and is arranging to have psychiatrists and chaplains on hospital staffs. The health of the mind, they say, is just as important as the health of the body; the one has a direct bearing on the other. In other words, they are beginning to realize that man does not live by bread alone. He has mental, emotional, and social needs as well as physical needs; these must be met if the "whole person" is to receive any benefit. Missionary doctors have always believed this. Why should they have a change of mind at this stage? In a recent declaration they said: "Our ultimate goal is the whole man, not X number of souls saved and bones healed."[5]

Mention should also be made of the fact that people are always more open to the "comforts of religion" when they are in distress. Somehow

5. *Evangelical Missions Information Service*, Vol. VIII, No. 4, September 1977, p. 5.

suffering and pain drive them to look for help outside of themselves. Jesus acknowledged this when He said: "They that are whole need not a physician, but they that are sick" (Luke 5:31, KJV). He also said: "Come unto me, all ye that labor and are heavy laden, and I will give you rest" (Matt 11:28, KJV). There is nothing unethical about offering rest for the soul as well as health for the body.

Nowadays hospital administrators have to reckon with government rules and regulations. Some governments are beginning to restrict what they call the "proselytizing" activities of missionary medical institutions. In most Muslim countries such restrictions have always been very stringent. What should be done when a government prohibits any kind of religious propaganda in a mission hospital? Should the order be obeyed or ignored? If it is ignored the hospital runs the risk of being closed by the government or taken over by the department of health. If it is obeyed the hospital must be prepared to operate on a purely humanitarian basis.

Mission boards are divided in their response to this dilemma. Some boards prefer to close their medical institutions if they are deprived of the privilege of sharing the gospel with the patients. That is the purpose for which the Christians back home have supported medical missions through the years. Other hospitals remain open in the hope that the situation will change and that they will once again have the freedom they desire. In the meantime they are grateful for the non-verbal witness they are able to give. Still others take the attitude that as Christians we are called upon to "do good to all men" (Gal 6:10, KJV), regardless of their response. Good works are an end in themselves, not just a means to an end. They bring their own reward. They also have the sanction of Scripture. They formed a large part of the ministry of Christ (Luke 4:18; Acts 10:38). They were enjoined by the apostle Paul (Tit 3:8) and practiced by the early church (Acts 6:1; 11:29), and they are glorifying to God (Matt 5:16).

RECENT DEVELOPMENTS

Changes in health care are taking place in all parts of the world, especially in the developing countries where poverty, illiteracy, malnutrition, and other problems exist on a mammoth scale.

So pressing are these problems that thirty medical and administrative personnel from the Interdenominational Foreign Mission Association and the Evangelical Foreign Missions Association met in a Medical Consultation at Missionary Internship in Farmington, Michigan, in March 1977.[6] They focused their attention on five areas: Government and medical missions, the national church and medical missions, the philosophy of medical missions, interchurch cooperation in medical missions, and the future role of medical

6. For a report of this Consultation see *Emissary*, Vol. VIII, No. 4, September 1977, published by Evangelical Missions Information Service, Box 794, Wheaton, Illinois 60187.

missions. They came to the conclusion that if medical missions are to have a future they will have to make some drastic changes in their practices.

1. **Shift from urban to rural areas.** A study made by the World Health Organization revealed the fact that in Africa, Christian missions allocated 95 percent of their available resources to hospitals and clinics, with little attention being given to disease prevention and health promotion. Quite often, location was determined not by health needs and priorities but by the location of church or mission-owned property. This meant that most mission hospitals were located in the larger cities and the clinics in the smaller cities and towns.

Very little has been done about the health needs of the rural areas, which in many countries constitute almost 80 percent of the population. China has done more than any other country to deliver health care to the peasants at the village level. The government has trained thousands of paramedical personnel, known as "barefoot doctors," who have set up clinics in every commune. As a result, everyone in China today has access to basic medical care.

Mission boards are now giving attention to this kind of health care. As mission hospitals in the cities are taken over by the government, the missions are opening clinics in the rural areas. The Latin America Mission has organized Goodwill Caravans which are made up of medical and dental personnel, social workers, and evangelists. They make periodic visits to the country areas which do not have any kind of modern health care. Drs. Rex and Jeanne Blumhagen of the Bible and Medical Missionary Fellowship spent two years in mobile medical work in the hinterland of Afghanistan, an area where medical facilities are unknown.

A concrete example is furnished by Dr. Tom Hale in Nepal:

I can only speak about personnel needs in Nepal; but here the greatest opportunity lies in the recruitment of community-health oriented nurses—that is, nurses willing to work in villages. Preferably they should have special community health training and/or midwifery training. Many kinds of practical training are better obtained informally on the mission field; many courses offered at home are largely impractical for the mission field, and the missionary still has to learn how to do his or her job almost from scratch. This would be particularly true of community health and nurse practitioner training. However, as a general rule, if a suitable course can be found at home, it is advisable to take advantage of it; the host government is more likely to recognize the value of such a worker, and also it gives the workers some additional security in case he or she has to leave the mission field.

Within the field of medicine itself there is a growing tendency nowadays to place more importance on community or preventive medicine and less on hospital medicine. Actually, in my opinion, the pendulum has swung a little too far away from hospitals. Community medicine is clearly more

important in benefiting the largest numbers of patients for the least
amount of money and for raising health standards in general; but it is
also true that you cannot have an effective community health program
without a base hospital. Therefore both are necessary.

2. Shift from curative to preventive medicine. Generally speaking the
medical profession in the West has tended to view health care in negative
terms. If a person isn't actually ill, then he is healthy and doesn't need
attention. The World Health Organization, founded in 1948, has defined
health as follows: "Health is a state of complete physical, mental, and social
well-being and not merely the absence of disease or infirmity."

Much of the illness experienced in the Third World is not due to the
presence of germs or some organic malfunction, but to poverty, malnutrition, ignorance, and other abnormal conditions prevalent in the developing
countries. Most of the patients coming to mission hospitals are cases of this
kind. Personal hygiene and public sanitation are unknown. Infant mortality
is extremely high and life expectancy is distressingly low. Communicable
diseases are a major cause of the high mortality rate.

It is not enough to heal the sick; it is more important to prevent people
from getting sick in the first place. For this reason more attention is now
being given to nutrition, immunization, vaccination, and other devices designed to prevent rather than cure disease. A tremendous amount of work
must be done in this area in the years to come.

3. Shift from individual health to community development. In the past,
medical missions have been almost completely preoccupied with ministering
to the physical needs of the individual. The patient came to the hospital, had
his tonsils removed, and went back home happy. No attempt was made to
provide health care on a wider, more comprehensive basis to meet the needs
of the community.

If the health care delivery system is ever to meet the rapidly growing
needs of the rural populations in developing countries, a concerted effort
must be made to establish community services. Good health depends on a
plentiful supply of wholesome food and pure water, but these are precisely
the ingredients which are missing in many communities. To provide them on
anything like an adequate scale will demand community action.

Improving the quality of life in these communities will require the expansion of medical and social services. The quantity and quality of food will
have to be increased by the introduction of better seed, deeper ploughing,
kitchen gardens, fish ponds, chicken and rabbit rearing, and the use of
fertilizer and insecticides. A sufficient supply of germ-free water will necessi-
tate the digging of wells, irrigation and fluoridation, storage tanks, etc. The
health and well-being of the community will be enhanced when the people
are taught the rudiments of personal hygiene, public sanitation, germs,
parasites, infection, family planning, and birth control.

Dr. Hale wrote:

> One major development is a decreased emphasis on the old-time pioneer
> missionary doctor who went out and built his hospital and built up a local
> practice and following, often isolated from other missionary efforts.
> Today the "in" word is integration, which means that medical work
> should ideally be closely connected with other fields of endeavor, such as
> education, technical and agricultural development, getting communities
> to help themselves, etc. This implies a team approach on the mission
> field—not only within each respective mission agency, but equally
> important—between the different agencies.

There can be no doubt about it—the health of the individual is bound up
with the social and economic life of the community. It is no longer enough to
cure the individual of his aches and pains; we must somehow remove the
conditions that are responsible for the spread of sickness and disease. To do
the one without the other is a waste of time and money. It is like sweeping
away the cobwebs instead of killing the spider.

Unfortunately the word "development" is suspect in some mission quarters. Wade T. Coggins, Executive Director of the World Evangelical Fellowship, says:

> Evangelical missions tho' actively engaged in education, medical service,
> and emergency relief, may, at the same time, be uneasy with the word
> "development." The ingredients encompassed within its meaning (it is
> feared by some) may not be compatible with evangelical goals. Yet more
> and more these agencies are involved in activities which are clearly a part
> of the larger area known as "development," "community development,"
> or "socio-economic development."[7]

Whether we like it or not, community development must become a vital part
of our medical strategy in the days ahead.

4. Government-mission cooperation on the increase. Since most of the
newly independent countries prefer socialism, which includes socialized
medicine, huge amounts of money are being allocated to education and
health care. Specialized medicine requires central planning on a wide scale;
consequently, more and more governments are demanding that medical
missions bring their plans into line with those of the department of health.

Two examples are Nepal and Afghanistan. In both countries all mission
agencies are obliged to work under the umbrella of one organization. In
Nepal it is the United Mission to Nepal, and in Afghanistan it is the International Afghan Mission. In both countries it is the government that controls
every action. In Nepal the overall health care system is reviewed every five
years. At the beginning of each period the United Mission signs a contract

7. *Latin America Pulse,* August 1978.

with the government which spells out in minute detail what the United Mission will undertake during the following five years.

Not all governments have gone that far; but the trend has begun, and sooner or later there will be more and more government control. This is both good and bad. It is good in the sense that the government is growing to realize the total needs of its own people, and it also has the means to implement and, if necessary, to enforce its plans and policies. The bad aspect is that it entails a vast amount of paper work. Government policy differs from country to country and changes occur from year to year within a given country. Some governments take over a medical facility one year only to hand it back the next. This makes planning difficult for the mission boards.

Be that as it may, the precedent has been set and more and more governments are demanding a say in the medical work of Christian missions. It would be wise for the missions to take the initiative and consult with the government, inviting its input and enlisting its support in the early stages before relations deteriorate.

Medical Assistance Program (MAP International), Wheaton, Illinois, lists five areas of basic human needs to which Christian medical missions must give attention. 1) People need freedom from spiritual bondage in order to enjoy abundant life. 2) People need access at the local level to health services which care for the daily health needs of the community. 3) People need access to higher-level medical services to deal with more severe health disorders. 4) People need to understand basic health care principles, which can be learned through community education programs. 5) People need a safe and protected environment that will support healthful living.

DO MEDICAL MISSIONS PAY?

The cost of medical work is high, not simply in terms of dollars and cents but in terms of blood, sweat, toil, tears, and prayer. For the missionary doctor and nurse the hours are long, the work is hard, the risks are great, the difficulties are many, and the problems are staggering.

The prospective medical missionary should know beforehand something of the conditions under which he will have to work, especially in the undeveloped countries of the world. There is no way for the American doctor to fully appreciate the incredible conditions under which he will have to ply his trade on the mission field. The following description of a 10-day medical safari in Zaire in the spring of 1978 will convey some idea of what it is like:

> We're so thankful for theMAF transportation. Two flights took us and all our "stuff" and only an hour's time from Tandala to Badja. Hilda and I were concerned about our load that was limited to 900 pounds each trip. Hilda had figured down to the pound each carton of supplies, medicines, big pressure cooker for sterilizing, lamp for the operating room, battery for the radio transmitter, etc. etc. (We never did get the generator to work and were concerned about the heat in the small operating room—

"but God"—sent just the right kind of weather—not too hot, rain at night and bright sunshine for the day so we had natural lighting and good "clothes dryer." One day a dirty dust storm blew through the whole building—it was just the beginning of rainy season for them up north and we had to light the kerosene pressure lamp and also had to finish up some night jobs by kerosene light.)

Our day started at 5 a.m. Breakfast at 6. Most mornings Dr. Bill and Hilda were at "hospital" by 6:30. I stayed at the house for radio transmission at 6:45 and to help Kosipangu know what to fix for our noon meal (between 2 and 3 p.m.). There was a wood-burning stove in which we had to place red coals in the oven to get rolls baked to tide over our bread situation since we had no fridge. Most of our time at the dispensary-hospital was just a race to keep up with the operating room team. They did 6 major surgery cases each day. We had 8 sets of packs and 4 sets of instruments; so as soon as one case was carried back to the post-operative building the linens and instruments were "thrown" at the laundry boy. He did his washing in 2 tubs under the mango trees, cold water, bar soap, with White Cross bandages for clothes line and no clothes pins. We managed to keep up supplies. We were grateful to discover that charcoal was the most excellent fuel for these 2 big pressure cookers.

Bed linens were not a problem. Each patient brought his own bamboo bed. The bottom sheet was a grass mat. A few brought blankets. The top sheet was a piece of native cloth, often the skirt of the man's wife! The one piece of "new" linen they did have was a nice "White Cross shirt." One of the patients made his payment by giving Sorbea a goat. So the last evening there we had a feast together with some of the station personnel.

We were really tired each night but a "good tired." What was accomplished for eternity in just caring for these physical needs? We leave that with the Lord. One evening Dr. Bill met with some of the church leaders to explain the concepts of church growth from a book by Vergil Gerber just recently translated in resume into Lingala by Dr. Tom. The book encouraged correct reports and the importance of evaluating numerical as well as spiritual growth. This was gratefully received.[8]

NECESSITY OF CONTINUING EDUCATION

Of particular interest to missionary nurses are the laws that have been passed recently in some state legislatures regarding continuing education. The Organization of Continuing Education for American Nurses, Inc. (OCEAN) in *Emissary*, Vol. IX, No. 5, November 1978, informs us that most R.N.s must renew their licenses at least every two years. Until recently renewing a license was a simple matter of sending the required fee to the Board of Nursing Registration. Mandatory education has changed that. Many states are now requiring each nurse to take 10 to 15 hours of continu-

8. Contained in a prayer letter written by Hilda Stenstadvolt and Ruth Brown.

ing education every year in order to qualify for renewal. Missionary nurses, though serving overseas, are not exempt from the laws of the states in which they are licensed. It is imperative, therefore, that each nurse find out what her state requires and act accordingly. OCEAN, Inc. exists for the specific purpose of providing continuing education to missionary nurses to enable them to gain the necessary credit to maintain their licenses. It conducts week-long workshops and seminars in the developing countries and offers courses at Bible colleges and Christian liberal arts colleges in the U.S. It also helps nurses set up their own workshops overseas, thus enabling them to receive credit through OCEAN. In order to take advantage of OCEAN's help, mission boards are now being asked to pay a fee of $25.00 for each practicing nurse. The services rendered by OCEAN are well worth the modest fee. The same services provided elsewhere would cost five times as much.

Already laws have been passed by the states of Florida, Colorado, California, and New Mexico. Others are bound to follow suit. To obtain OCEAN's services, write to:

> Eleanor L. Rowe, R.N., Ed. D.
> OCEAN, Inc.
> P.O. Box 21276
> Columbia, SC   29221

25

Theological Education

The greatest weakness of the missionary movement has been the failure to train and educate leaders for the national churches. The former moderator of the Church of South India told me that each of his ordained pastors is responsible for ten to twenty congregations. In Indonesia the situation is desperate. A Lutheran Church in North Sumatra has only eleven trained pastors for 337,000 church members. The Protestant Church of West Indonesia has one pastor for every eighty-eight congregations. In Taiwan there are reported to be 300 congregations without a pastor. Japan and Korea, it seems, are the only countries where the churches are well supplied with capable leadership. A 1978 government survey indicated that in Korea there were 169 theological schools with 1,600 students and 39 Bible schools with 6,500 students. Sixteen of these schools have graduate level programs. Ninety percent of the graduates go into full-time Christian service.

THE PURPOSE OF THEOLOGICAL EDUCATION

1. **To provide pastors for the national churches.** It is not certain that every congregation in the Third World should have its own full-time pastor, but there should be at least one for every five or six churches. If the churches are to grow spiritually as well as numerically they will need the ministry and oversight of a person with theological training. In the early years when the congregation is small it may be able to get along with local lay leaders. The time will come, however, when stronger leadership is needed.

2. To teach the prospective pastor how to cultivate his own spiritual life. Many Christians, including some seminarians, do not know how to minister to their own spiritual growth. Over the years they have come to depend on external props—meetings, conferences, seminars, workshops, etc. When these crutches are suddenly removed, however, they find themselves unable to cope with the situation. Many missionaries, especially those in their first term, have the same problem. They have depended too long on the fellowship of others, church services, prayer meetings, and other forms of "body life." Suddenly they are alone and they find they do not know how to meet their own spiritual needs.

Every seminary should make a point of dealing with this crucial issue, for if the pastor is not a man of God, a man of faith, and a man of prayer, able to do battle with the powers of darkness, he will not be of much use in the pulpit. Each day may include a chapel service and each class may open with prayer but more is needed. Every incoming freshman should be required to take a course in spiritual development designed to teach him how to cultivate his own spiritual life. This could be the most important course he will ever take.

3. To inculcate in the prospective pastor a deep commitment to evangelism. Every pastor and every missionary should be an evangelist at heart. This is the most important factor in terms of church growth. It is not enough to generate an "evangelistic atmosphere" in the institution. One of the requirements should be that every student take at least one course in evangelism. He should also be obliged to engage in evangelistic work while in seminary. Of course, it would be most helpful if the professors themselves are men with a passion for evangelism.

4. To train the prospective pastor to make the gospel relevant to his people and culture. In all too many seminaries this aspect has been sorely neglected if not completely overlooked. The missionary instructors have been teaching the same courses they themselves took at home. The tendency has been to make the seminaries in the Third World replicas of those in the U.S. Pastors and evangelists in India, however, must know how to make the gospel attractive and meaningful to Hindus whose life and religious views are totally different from those in the West. In Southeast Asia the missionaries will be teaching Buddhists. Those in the Far East will have Shinto and Confucianism to deal with. In the Middle East there are the Muslims. This will be no easy task. Unfortunately it is one for which the average seminary makes almost no provision. It is absolutely essential that pastors and evangelists in the non-Christian world be able to articulate the Christian faith in a manner intelligible to their non-Christian compatriots. A great deal of work needs to be done in this area.

5. To produce a small number of theologians. The primary task of the mission seminary is to prepare men and women for the Christian ministry within the context of the local church. There is nothing wrong, however, with producing a graduate now and then who will go on to graduate school and become a first-class theologian. This will have two immediate benefits. First, it will help meet the need for national professors in the seminaries. Second, it will produce men and women who will be in a position to engage in that most important of all tasks—the contextualization of theology. This can best be done by indigenous theologians, not Westerners. Nationals are in a much better position than expatriates to handle this difficult assignment.

PROBLEMS OF THEOLOGICAL EDUCATION

There are seminaries in various parts of the Third World that are large and strong and compare favorably with those in the West, but these are few in number. There are hundreds of others that are sadly below standard. The fault lies not with the institutions themselves, but with the long history of neglect on the part of the supporting missions. Bruce J. Nicholls writes: "Theological education has been the Cinderella of missionary aid in terms of personnel and finance."[1] Norman A. Horner has said the same thing:

> With notable exceptions, seminaries have long been the weakest link in the entire chain of educational work in the Protestant missionary outreach. Bishop Stephen Neill, Charles Ranson, Yorke Allen, Jr., and others who have made recent studies of the training of the ministry in Africa, Asia, and Latin America bear eloquent testimony to the fact that this is still widely the case. By and large the seminaries are small, ill-equipped, understaffed "stepchildren" of the churches.[2]

We have made some progress in the last fifteen years, but we still fall far short of the West in this matter of theological education.

1. **Proliferation of schools.** Mention has already been made of the theological schools in Korea. Fortunately in that instance the great number of schools has paid off so that church growth there has been described as "wildfire." In 1976 there were reported to be 640,000 Christian converts and over 2,000 new churches were begun.

In other countries, however, it has been a different story. Evangelism seems to be the area in which inter-mission cooperation is most easily achieved while theological education is the one in which it is most difficult. Each mission must have its own Bible school or seminary in each country in which it has worked for any length of time. This is especially true of Asia. In countries with a dozen or more major languages and scores of dialects there is conceivably some justification for proliferation. India and Indonesia are good examples of this. Even taking that factor into consideration, however,

1. Bruce J. Nicholls, "Toward an Asian Theology of Mission," *Evangelical Missions Quarterly*, Winter 1970, p. 65.
2. Norman A. Horner, *Cross and Crucifix in Mission* (New York: Abingdon Press, 1965), p. 105.

there is still a good deal of unwarranted duplication of effort. It is an established fact that the largest, strongest, and best known seminaries are union institutions, founded and supported by half a dozen or more missions and serving an equal number of churches. Most of these institutions are ecumenical in character. Conservative evangelicals have been slow to follow suit. One shining exception is Union Biblical Seminary in Yatvamal, India. It was founded in 1953 when eleven missions and churches pooled their resources to create a school on the graduate level. Today, Union is supported by twenty churches and missions. With 180 students it is one of the largest seminaries in India. Another example of evangelical cooperation is the Bangui Evangelical Theological Seminary in the Central African Republic. One wishes that evangelical mission leaders would see the value of this kind of cooperation. What is needed is fewer Bible colleges and seminaries with a higher quality of education.

2. **Small enrollment.** This problem stems from the same roots as the previous one—too many schools. If the number of schools were reduced by fifty percent, enrollment in those remaining would double. As it is, there are hundreds of mission seminaries and several thousand Bible schools and colleges in foreign countries. The average enrollment per seminary is about twenty-five. That makes for a good faculty-student ratio, but it is very costly in terms of men and money. There are several factors that contribute to the problem: (1) In most Asian countries the Christian community is very small, perhaps less than five percent of the population. (2) Most national parents, including Christians, are reluctant to see their children go into a vocation that carries little or no prestige and which will not permit them to care for their parents when they get old. (3) Not many young men are attracted to the ministry when it has so little to offer in the way of worldly rewards. (4) As long as each mission insists on having its own seminary there will not be enough students to go around.

3. **Low academic standards.** Many of the mission seminaries would not be considered as such in the West; they are actually Bible colleges. Only a handful are graduate-level schools. Most of them operate on two, some on three, levels. This is not by choice but of necessity. In most countries there are few college graduates, and not many of them feel called into full-time Christian service. In order to give the institution some financial stability, therefore, it is necessary to operate on more than one level. This is not always bad; but it does tend to lower the academic standards, and therefore the reputation, of the institution. Very few of the schools are accredited. In fact, accrediting associations are only now beginning to function in some parts of the mission field. This is especially true of the evangelicals.

4. **Paucity of qualified teachers.** In order to teach in a Bible college one should have at least an M.A. in Bible or Theology. In order to teach in a

seminary one should have a Ph. D. Evangelical seminaries in North America are bulging at the seams. Why then should we continue to have a shortage of qualified teachers on the mission field? The answer is simple. When a person has had a great deal of education it is easy for him to consider himself "too good" for the mission field. He prefers to remain in this country where he can teach in a well-known school with excellent facilities and resources for research and writing. As a result, the seminaries are not turning out many missionaries. Most missionaries are graduates of the Bible colleges.

What about national teachers? There are several reasons for their small numbers. One is that nationals with a Ph. D. in Biblical Studies are not common. Most nationals who go into full-time service enter the pastorate. Few of them go on to get the advanced education that would permit them to teach in a seminary. Then there is a second factor—the brain drain. An abnormal number of national Christian workers, especially from Eastern Asia, are to be found in the U.S. They come here for advanced studies, but they stay so long and become so accustomed to the American way of life that they remain year after year and finally become citizens. Dr. Bong Rin Ro, Executive Secretary of the Asia Theological Association, informs us that in Los Angeles alone there are 100 Korean churches but approximately 150-200 pastors. In Chicago there are thirty-eight Korean churches. One Filipino church in Chicago has seven Filipino pastors sitting in its pews. There are fifty Filipino pastors in the Los Angeles area selling insurance.

5. Inadequate library facilities. A school is no better than its library. Even a strong faculty is no substitute for a well stocked and comprehensive library. A recent study of Chinese schools in Asia reported:

> The greatest need felt by the schools was for Chinese libraries. Of the 181,000 books held by 16 schools responding to the question, the ratio of languages was English 53%, Chinese 44%, and Others 3%.... The largest library has 33,000 volumes, the smallest 4,665 volumes, with the average being 11,325 volumes. The average number of library staff workers is 2.75; but only half have had training for library work.[3]

It is not uncommon for a pastor in the U.S. to have at least 1,000 books in his personal library. The average pastor on the mission field can usually put all his books on an 18-inch shelf.

6. Placement. With so many churches and so few trained pastors, why should placement be a problem? Several questions are pertinent at this point: (1) Will the seminary graduate with his advanced education be willing to go where he is needed, or will he insist on a large church in a big city? Three or four years in the academic atmosphere of an urban institution may incapacitate a man for the very work to which he was originally

3. *Asia Theological News,* January 1978, p. 17.

called. He may find it difficult to go back to his own town, where life is simple and where the people are unsophisticated. To retain his services the denomination may have to create a special administrative or ecclesiastical position for him. (2) Will the church that invites him be able to pay him a salary commensurate with his training? With the same amount of education he could command a handsome salary in business or government, where he would enjoy a far greater degree of prestige. (3) Will he be accepted by the older pastors with more experience but with much less education? This is an acute problem in Africa, where the faithful older pastors with only three or four years of education but twenty or thirty years of experience are reluctant to welcome the younger, better educated men. They feel threatened by them.

MISTAKES IN THEOLOGICAL EDUCATION

Mistakes have been made here as in other areas of missions, and once they were made it was difficult to correct them. Some of them have not been corrected yet. Faculty members as a class tend to be reactionary. They do not react well to change, especially if it involves what they consider to be an "encroachment" upon their discipline or department. They seem to have a vested interest in the status quo. He is a rare professor who will volunteer to give up one of his courses in order to make room for a general course required of all students. The various mistakes made are outlined as follows:

1. **No discretion in the choice of students.** Students were accepted without an inquiry as to whether or not they had spiritual gifts to be cultivated. Some of the greatest and most solid church growth is occurring among the Pentecostal churches in South America, particularly Chile and Brazil. Their Christian workers are chosen not on the basis of how much schooling they have had but on what they have been able to accomplish with the help of the Holy Spirit. In the Chilean Pentecostal Church for a man to graduate as a "worker" he must have led a specific number of people to Christ; to graduate as a "pastor" he must have led people to Christ and brought them together to form a missionary church; to graduate as a "reverend", he must have started five or six churches. In addition, students and workers were often taken out of their cultural milieu and kept in a "hothouse" for three or four years, during which time they acquired a taste for the amenities of modern civilization and found it hard to give them up. In many cases their education was subsidized to the point where they expected to be supported by mission funds after graduation.

2. **Choice of program.** The entire program, based largely on Western practice, emphasized leadership to the exclusion of discipleship. The emphasis was on class lectures, note-taking, examinations, papers, grades, etc. There was a big gap between the teacher and his students. No connection

was made between classroom instruction and field education. Seminary professors at home and overseas have forgotten, if they ever learned, the five principles laid down by Alvin C. Erich: (1) Whatever a student learns, he must learn for himself—no one can learn it for him. (2) Each student learns at his own rate, and for any age group, the variation in the rate of learning is considerable. (3) A student learns more when each step he takes is immediately reinforced. (4) A full, rather than a partial, mastery of each step makes total learning more meaningful. (5) When given the responsibility for his own learning the student is more highly motivated; he learns and retains more.

Few seminaries or Bible colleges have structured their curriculum in terms of these principles. There have been exceptions, but they have been few in number. One outstanding exception is the Discipleship Training Center in Singapore, where the student body is kept small and the contact between teacher and student is very close. They have adopted a communal lifestyle, teachers and students living and eating together. In this way the students are in almost constant contact with the teachers and the resulting intimacy provides much greater student-teacher communication. This conforms to the Eastern idea of discipleship.

Another successful example was the *Ling Kung T'uan*—Spiritual Work Team—which operated in China in the 1930s and 1940s. In that Bible school, run by Yang Shao-t'ang, the student year was divided into two almost equal parts. Half was spent in the classroom and the other half in evangelistic and church work in company with the teachers. It proved to be a successful method of producing evangelists.

3. Too much Westernization. To begin with, the schools were almost always run by the missions, not the churches. The missions hired the teachers who were mostly Westerners, paid the bills, and ran the show. Only in recent years have the churches become involved in the schools; progress along this line has been very slow. As recently as 1975 Dr. Bong Rin Ro said in a paper which he presented to American missiologists at Wheaton Graduate School:

> *On the mission field now the emphasis is on what the missionary can accomplish and do. However, the emphasis should be on what the national can do with the assistance of the missionary. Mission policy should fit into the national church pattern rather than national churches fitting into mission policy. The urgent need now is to train the national and build up the church by giving the national the place of responsibility and leadership. Our Asia Theological Association sent out a questionnaire to the theological schools in Asia. We received back 64 replies. More than 50% of these schools still had foreign missionaries as presidents. In one country the ten main theological schools all had foreign presidents. In my travels to theological schools throughout Asia, I noticed that the conservative schools are still mainly controlled by Westerners. Their liberal*

> *counterparts have already indigenized. It is fine to retain our conserva-*
> *tive theology; but must we also retain traditional practices of the past*
> *century?*

This particular problem is highly complex and there are many contributing factors. Missionaries in positions of leadership tend to hold on to their
power too long. On the other hand, qualified nationals who could fill leadership positions often prefer to teach in the U.S. where the salaries and benefits are much greater. There is also the economic problem. While the missionary retains his teaching post his salary is paid by the mission but if he
retires or resigns and a national takes his place the mission subsidy ceases. In
other words, Western funds are used to support the person, not the position.
Some missions have used Western funds too freely to the impoverish-
ment of the church. Other more conservative missions have erred in the
opposite direction, and in many cases they have hindered desirable growth.
The time has come to give serious consideration to supporting important,
strategic offices in the church and/or school on the mission field. This does
not include giving financial support to pay the expenses of the local church.
By this time local churches should be entirely self-supporting.

4. Choice of Curriculum. The curriculum of the average seminary in the
Third World is almost identical with that in the West. The early missionaries
simply took the seminary courses they had had in the U.S., translated them
into the vernacular (sometimes didn't even bother to do that), and passed
them on to the students virtually unchanged.

Peter Savage of Latin America, speaking of this problem, made the following statement:

> *The classic curriculum found in most seminaries and Bible colleges has*
> *followed the patterns that have existed for the last two hundred years,*
> *where emphasis has been placed on the digestion of packets of knowledge*
> *rather than on bringing each student to spiritual maturity and effective*
> *ministry. It is but natural that the teacher who concentrates on the*
> *content and feels his primary responsibility is to communicate this con-*
> *tent will tend to overlook the educative and pastoral responsibility he has*
> *towards his student-brother in the Lord. It is sad to see the frequent*
> *chasm that exists between teacher and student—the teacher hides him-*
> *self behind his lectern giving out his knowledge "paternalistically," while*
> *the tensions, frustrations, identity crises, depressions, etc., of his stu-*
> *dents are unknown to him. His flurries of Greek and Hebrew may im-*
> *press the student but do not answer the crucial questions that are burn-*
> *ing in his students' hearts.* [4]

It is questionable that Greek and Hebrew should be required of all
students. Many of them will never use these languages after graduation.
Apologetics, a very important course, is usually taught from a purely West-

4. *Evangelical Missions Quarterly,* Fall 1972, pp. 30-31.

ern point of view, with a heavy emphasis on reason and logic and the law of self-contradiction. Much is said of truth; little reference is made to power. Western homiletics is excellent for the homeside pastor but of doubtful value to the pastor on the mission field, where truth is not usually presented in the abstract but in concrete terms—in stories, folk lore, drama, poetry, etc. The traditional story-teller, with his dramatics and his gestures, facial as well as physical, and his two wooden clappers, has an enormous advantage over the seminary student who knows only Western homiletics. And what shall we say about Church History? Where is there a textbook in Church History, outside of Latourette, that gives "equal time" to the history of the church in the Third World? Church History as *we* know it is really the history of the church in the West. The history of the great missionary movement of the past 275 years is barely mentioned. Thus, when a student in India finishes his seminary training he knows all about the Renaissance and the Reformation but nothing about the church in Japan, Nigeria, or Brazil. He is well acquainted with Martin Luther, John Calvin, and John Wesley but has never heard of William Carey, Hudson Taylor, Adoniram Judson, or even David Livingstone. What kind of church history is that?

There are other areas of neglect. One is Systematic Theology. The missionary will have studied the usual major divisions: the doctrines of God, Christ, Man, Sin, Salvation, Ecclesiology, and Eschatology. He will have been duly indoctrinated in the inspiration and inerrancy of Scripture, but will he have confronted the uniqueness of the Christian revelation or the finality of Jesus Christ? What about ancestor worship in China and emperor worship in Japan, or polygamy, demon possession, and witchcraft in Africa? Will any of these crucial issues be discussed? Not likely.

When the seminarian gets into the Indian church he will not be asked what he knows about Brunner, Bultmann, or Barth; he will be asked how the incarnation of Jesus Christ differs from an avatar of Krishna. He will be expected to know something about Eastern Mysticism and Transcendental Meditation. The average seminary graduate, however, knows nothing about Transcendental Meditation or any other kind of meditation. It is not included in the seminary curriculum. What about such exotic subjects as exorcism, dreams, visions, miracles, etc.? Will he be able to cope with these questions?

The seminary curriculum in the Third World needs to be totally revamped. Some courses will have to be removed, or at least reduced, to make room for others which should be added.

CONTEXTUALIZATION OF THEOLOGY

The purpose of contextualization is to make Christianity as intelligible as possible to the non-Western mind and as relevant as possible to non-Christian culture. This is the most important and the most difficult task of the Christian mission.

It is quite impossible to do justice to a subject as broad as this in a page or two but certain guidelines might be helpful.

1. Some elements of Christianity are absolute and therefore must not be altered in any way. Paul made this quite clear in Galatians chapter one verses 6–8 (KJV) when he said: "I marvel that ye are so soon removed from him that called you into the grace of Christ unto another gospel; which is not another; but there be some that trouble you, and would pervert the gospel of Christ. But though we, or an angel from heaven, preach any other gospel unto you than that which we have preached, let him be accursed." Paul and his fellow apostles believed with all their hearts that in the gospel of Christ they possessed the truth about God, man, sin, and salvation. Nothing could be added to it; nothing should be taken away from it. To alter it in any way would be to pervert it.

These essential elements include: the doctrine of the inspiration and authority of the Holy Scriptures, the doctrine of the Trinity, the finality of Jesus Christ, the lostness of man, salvation by grace through faith alone, the unique ministry of the Holy Spirit in the regeneration of the sinner and the sanctification of the saint, the love and holiness of God, the reality of the Kingdom of God, and the consummation of all things in Christ. These are clearly set out in the Scriptures. They constitute the heart of the Christian message and are not subject to change.

2. Some elements are relative and may be changed. These include kinds of liturgy, modes of worship, methods of evangelism, varieties of music, and many other things. They are matters of form and style and may change from place to place. There is nothing particularly sacred about the 11 o'clock hour for worship on Sunday morning. The time could be altered, even the day could be changed, without any great loss. In a predominantly Muslim culture the church might worship on Friday as the Muslims do, or in Israel on Saturday as the Israelis do.

Our evangelistic methods are not immutable; they, too, can be changed. Even baptism may be administered in a number of ways, as the church in the West has been doing for centuries. *When* we worship and *where* we worship are not important. Only one thing is important: *how* we worship. Jesus said we must worship in spirit and in truth (John 4:24). No other requirements are laid down. In this area we have full freedom, and the churches in the Third World should be allowed to develop their own style of worship, the only criterion being that it must be pleasing to God.

3. All cultures have both good and bad elements. Culture is man-made, not God-given. Like its creator it has become corrupt. Some elements are patently sinful. Others are obviously pure, healthful, and moral and should be retained. Most, however, are neither good nor bad but represent a grey area where wisdom and caution are required. There is much that is good and wholesome in the non-Christian cultures. All of this should be preserved.

Only what is contrary to the clear teaching of Scripture should be rejected. Idolatry is *always* wrong. Murder is *always* wrong. Adultery is *always* wrong. Polygamy, however, is not regarded in either the Old Testament or the New as adultery and should be handled differently, with patience, compassion, and understanding. It may have to be accepted in the first generation as the lesser of two evils, but it should be made clear that it will not be tolerated in the second generation. Christian maturity should take care of it. Lying, cheating, stealing—these are always wrong and should never be accepted.

4. **Who is to decide what is good and what is bad?** The missionaries? The national leaders? Or both? The missionaries have a better understanding of Christianity. The nationals have a better understanding of their own culture. The missionary, therefore, should not take it upon himself to state categorically what is good and what is bad, especially in the grey areas where most of the problems lie. The nationals are often harder on their own than the missionary is. They know, as he can never know, all the ramifications of so-called "heathen" practices. Missionaries and national leaders should work together under the authority of Scripture and the guidance of the Holy Spirit to solve the problem. The missionary will have to exercise patience and give the Holy Spirit time to apply the truth of Scripture to the hearts and minds of the converts. He should remember that there were serious problems even in the church at Corinth.

5. **All culture, Christian and non-Christian, comes under the judgment of Holy Scripture.** A custom is wrong only if the Bible says it is wrong, not because Western Christian experience has declared it to be wrong. Likewise, a custom is not necessarily wholesome simply because it has been part of Western Christian culture for hundreds of years. We need to have our consciences awakened and our hearts stirred on many matters.

6. **We may be charged with "cultural imperialism."** There is such a thing as "the offense of the cross" as Paul called it (Gal 5:11, KJV). There are some aspects of the gospel that can never be made palatable to the unbeliever; he will reject them every time. When this happens in a non-Christian culture the consequences can be serious. We shall be subject to the ever-present charge of "cultural imperialism." It is a cross we shall have to bear if we are to remain true to Jesus Christ and His gospel. We will have to choose between pleasing men and pleasing God. In a similar situation Paul decided that he would rather please God (Gal 1:10).

THE MATTER OF ACCREDITATION

The Bible schools and seminaries in the Third World developed without plan, preparation, or supervision. They began in a very humble way—a missionary and a few students in his home, on his verandah, or under a tree in his garden. Short-term schools soon led to long-term schools. Bible institutes raised their academic standards and became Bible colleges. More recently seminaries have come into existence. Today there are thousands of these institutions all over the world.

The ecumenical institutions were established much earlier and have already developed their own accrediting apparatus. In the evangelical camp the progress in this direction has been slow. The needs were so obvious and pressing and the problems were so great that nobody thought to inquire about quality. As for accreditation, nobody ever heard of it.

All that is changing now. In Asia, Africa, and Latin America there are evangelical accrediting associations working long and hard to raise the standards of the many schools in their regions. It will be some time before they measure up to the standards in the West, but that is to be expected, and the accrediting associations will be wise to take it into account when they establish their criteria for accreditation. They will have to be particularly patient with regard to physical facilities and library holdings. Perhaps there should be two kinds of accreditation, full and partial, to coincide with two kinds of membership, full and associate.

The theological schools in the Third World should be encouraged to establish a relationship with similar institutions in the West. There could be exchange of faculty and students in both directions, to the enrichment of both institutions. It would do faculty members in our American schools a great deal of good to teach in the Third World for a year, or even for a semester. Our Western institutions would be greatly blessed by having Third World professors spend a similar time with us. They would bring to our schools a world view of the Christian church which is sadly lacking in Western circles.

THEOLOGICAL EDUCATION BY EXTENSION

This new and rapidly growing program came out of the Evangelical Seminary in Guatemala in the early 1960s. Ralph D. Winter did more than anyone else to promote the concept in the beginning, and it was largely through his efforts that it became so popular.

TEE was never intended to take the place of the traditional seminary or Bible college. It was designed to meet the special need for leadership training in those parts of the world where the churches are growing so fast that thousands of congregations are without a pastor and other thousands have a pastor with little or no theological training.

TEE was not a new gimmick thought up by the missionaries. It grew out of the existential situation in Latin America where, according to Peter Savage, only 15,000 of the 75,000 pastors have had adequate theological training. Growth was so fast and the needs were so great that something different, something drastic, had to be done to solve the problem.

In many cases the pastors were older men with dependent families. In middle life, they could not leave their farms, shops, and families for any extended period of time in order to attend seminary. If they were to get any kind of training at all, the seminary would have to go to them.

To be successful, TEE should be associated with a seminary or a Bible college. The pastor-students study on their own. Once a month or once a quarter they gather in some central place to spend a week or so with the seminary professor, who comes for the express purpose of meeting with them. These are not study periods; the studying must be done before they gather for the seminar. The time is used for testing, interaction with the professor, fellowship, and prayer.

TEE is conducted on several academic levels, depending on the educational background of the students. In a few cases they have all the qualifications for seminary work. In others they must settle for Bible college or Bible school work. In any event, the program is planned, structured, and supervised. Extensive use is made of programmed instruction materials. This enables the students to arrange their own study times and to proceed at their own pace, at the same time continuing to conduct their business, support their families, and engage in church work. It is an ideal way of providing solid theological training for those who have never had the opportunity to go to Bible college or seminary.

The response to TEE has been most encouraging and progress has been exceptionally good. Excellent leadership has been given in Africa by Dr. Fred Holland and Dr. Marjorie Shelley and in Brazil by Dr. Lois McKinney, Coordinator of the Committee to Assist Ministry Education Overseas, which has given a good deal of moral and material support to the program, arranging and conducting TEE workshops at home and abroad. The most recent report indicates that nearly 60,000 students were involved in early 1980. These students have affiliated with some 300 institutions or programs in sixty countries of the world. Latin America accounts for 52.1 percent of the students, Africa 19.7 percent, Asia 12.1 percent, and North America 9.8 percent. The other three regions—Caribbean, Europe, and Oceania—together account for 6.3 percent. The program operates on four levels: certificate, diploma, baccalaureate, and licentiate. It has the enthusiastic backing of the Asia Theological Association and the Theological Commission of the Association of Evangelicals of Africa and Madagascar. Its monthly letter is *Extension*. Dr. Fred Holland is the present editor.

CHRISTIAN EDUCATION

The Christian Education Movement began in the U.S. in the early 1930s. Dr. Clarence Benson of Moody Bible Institute was one of the leading pioneers. Besides writing several books on the subject, he founded the Evangelical Teacher Training Association, the National Sunday School Association, and the Scripture Press. For many years his book, *The Sunday*

School in Action, was a classic text for the study of Christian Education in the local church. He more than anyone else helped to popularize the graded Sunday school lessons.

Beginning in the 1960s Chrisitan Education was exported to the mission field. The pioneer in this area was the Reverend Clate Risley, for ten years the Executive Secretary of the National Sunday School Association. Following his resignation from the NSSA he founded the Worldwide Christian Education Ministries, which for a time was loosely affiliated with the National Association of Evangelicals. As the leader of WCEM Risley made many trips to Africa and Asia, where he conducted workshops arranged for him by the various mission leaders. He did more than any other person to promote Christian Education on the mission fields of the world. Unfortunately, his work was abruptly ended when he was shot on the streets of Chicago in 1974.

In recent years three evangelical publishers have made a large contribution to Christian Education in the Third World: Gospel Light, Scripture Press, and David C. Cook. They are now publishing Sunday school materials in more than fifty languages. Drs. Lois and Mary LeBar, professors emeritus of Christian Education at Wheaton Graduate School, have in the last two or three years made several trips to Africa and Asia to conduct workshops in Christian Education. As a result of all this activity the churches in the Third World are beginning to see the immense value of Christian Education in the Sunday school curriculum. In the past, Sunday schools have not been very successful, particularly among the adults. They feel that Sunday school is for the children. This attitude is changing, thanks to the efforts of the Christian Education specialists who have visited the mission fields.

In Asia several countries including India, the Philippines, and Korea, have formed their own national Association of Christian Education. The Christian Education Evangelical Fellowship of India is publishing Sunday school courses in twenty-nine languages. It has regional committees, each with its own secretary, in twenty-six areas of India. Every year it conducts Christian Education workshops in various parts of the country. A national conference on Christian Education is held every three years. In November 1978 the Asia Theological Association sponsored the first Pan Asia Christian Education Seminar in Singapore.

According to a questionnaire prepared by the Asia Theological Association, the churches of Asia identified three areas of need: the need for teacher training, the need for suitable Sunday school literature, and the need for pastors and seminarians to promote the concept of Christian Education. A large part of the Christian Education materials now in use are translations or adaptations from English. Most of them come from the U.S. and are produced by the three publishing houses already mentioned. These organizations are to be congratulated on the vision and vigor with which they are helping the churches of the Third World.

Christian Education was born and bred in the U.S. and it carries a "Made in the U.S.A." label. The entire operation is so closely identified with the

American church and culture that it is not easy to use it on the mission field without a good deal of adaptation. American churches have the facilities and trained personnel necessary to use this type of material, and Sunday school attendance in the evangelical churches continues to grow. In the Third World, however, the churches have neither the money nor the facilities that we have.

Third World nationals coming to this country to study Christian Education should understand this fact and not return to their own countries expecting to use this "Made in the U.S.A." material unchanged. One returnee, after speaking at a Christian Education workshop in the Philippines, was asked when she finished, "Do you realize that you are now back in the Philippines?" Her presentation, apparently, had been too American in its approach.

Real progress is being made and Christian Education is now accepted and respected in the Third World churches. Western missionaries should bear this in mind and be prepared to make whatever contribution they can. Missions majors should by all means take some Christian Education courses as electives in Bible college or seminary and Christian Education majors should also take a few missions courses. In the past there has been little cooperation between these two departments in our educational institutions.

26

Radio Work

Radio is still the most important medium for the dissemination of information on a worldwide scale. Even here in the West, where every home has a television set, radio is by no means dead. In New York, Chicago, and other large cities there are scores of radio stations, all of them doing a good job in reaching their particular segment of the listening audience.

Dr. S. G. Franklin Mack of the National Council of Churches says:

> *Radio presents the Christian Church with the greatest opportunity of the century. The printing press made the Bible and the whole range of culture available to all who could read. Pictures and radio make them available to every man, woman, and child who can see and hear. To use these media rightly and to the fullest extent—both at home and abroad—is the biggest challenge the church has ever faced.*[1]

Governments regard radio as the most effective means of communicating their message. The world still listens to the British Broadcasting Corporation for the widest and most accurate coverage of news. All the major countries of the world have powerful short-wave broadcasting facilities. These include Radio Moscow, Radio Peking, Radio Cairo, the Voice of America, and Radio Vatican.

The Christian church, especially the conservative wing, has made extensive use of radio in the past forty to fifty years. Paul Rader, pastor of Chicago Gospel Tabernacle, led the way in June 1922. He was followed by John

1. Frank W. Price, *Occasional Bulletin*, September 25, 1969, p. 2.

Roach Straton, pastor of Calvary Baptist Church in New York. Then came Charles E. Fuller and his *Old Fashioned Revival Hour* in May 1924, Moody Bible Institute in July 1926, and *The Lutheran Hour* in October 1930. *The Radio Bible Class,* and the *Back to God Hour* of the Christian Reformed Church, both began in 1939. Billy Graham's *Hour of Decision* first went on the air in 1950.

Many of these broadcasts are evangelistic in content. Billy Graham and Oswald Hoffman are concerned primarily with reaching the unsaved. The *Radio School of the Bible* and the *Back to the Bible Broadcast* are designed to minister to the spiritual needs of believers. Far from dying out, Christian radio stations are increasing at the rate of one every two weeks. There are over 800 in the U.S. at the present time. It is difficult to assess the value of radio broadcasting, but it can be said that it has played an important part in the resurgence of religion in this country in the 1970s.

Some of these programs are heard by tens of millions every week. *The Lutheran Hour* is released over more than 900 stations in the U.S. and Canada and over 700 stations around the world in more than forty langauges. Oswald Hoffmann and Billy Graham speak to more people in one broadcast than the apostle Paul preached to in his entire lifetime. Such is the power of radio.

MISSIONARY RADIO OVERSEAS

Known as The Voice of the Andes, the first missionary radio station was HCJB in Quito, Ecuador. It was the brainchild of Clarence Jones and Reuben Larsen. Its first program was aired on Christmas Day, 1931. It was a modest beginning with a 200-watt transmitter designed and built by Larsen, and it barely covered the city of Quito. Today, HCJB is one of the most powerful stations on earth. It has a total of one million watts of power. It beams the gospel to all parts of the world, including the U.S.S.R. It has a staff of more than 500, an annual budget of $3,000,000, two hospitals, and a Bible Institute of the Air in which tens of thousands have enrolled through the years.

The Far East Broadcasting Company, organized in 1948, is another very powerful agency. Located in Radio City twelve miles outside of Manila, it has twenty-seven transmitters broadcasting the gospel 1,496 program hours each week.

Trans World Radio has powerful broadcasting facilities in Monte Carlo, Cyprus, Swaziland, Bonaire, Guam, and Sri Lanka. Some of its transmitters have 600,000 watts of power. The two largest, with 1.2 million watts and two million watts, are in Monte Carlo. Trans World Radio does most of its broadcasting on medium wave, thus reaching millions of people who don't have short-wave sets.

Several faith missions operate radio stations in addition to their other work. These include TEAM in Korea and the Sudan Interior Mission in

Liberia. The Canadian Baptists' station, The Southern Cross, is in Bolivia. Altogether there are more than seventy radio stations owned and operated by church and missionary organizations in the Third World.

There is probably more ongoing inter-mission cooperation in radio than in any other type of work, including evangelism. The large, powerful stations cannot possibly produce all the programs which they broadcast every week. For that they are dependent upon the missions in the different countries to produce tapes and send them to the central station for broadcasting back to the country of origin. For instance, ELWA in Liberia beams the gospel to five language groups in Guinea. These programs are all prepared by the Christian and Missionary Alliance missionaries and pastors in Guinea.

In Japan the Pacific Broadcasting Association, supported by twenty missions, makes programs that are aired over many of the commercial stations. TEAM provides tapes for a network of commercial stations in Taiwan. The Christian and Missionary Alliance in Colombia reports that in 1977 the Spanish language program, *Alianca en Marcha,* had seventy-seven weekly broadcasts, most of them over local commercial stations.

Christian programs are accepted by more than 400 commercial stations in Brazil. The Brazilian Association of Evangelical Radio Stations includes six commercial stations which provide time for evangelical programs at low cost. The Roman Catholic Church is active in radio work and owns more than 120 stations.

It is impossible to exaggerate the influence of radio in our day. According to the British Broadcasting Corporation's report of June 1978 the total number of radio receivers now stands at 1,076,500,000. It is estimated that one-third of those receivers have some short-wave capability.

Gospel broadcasters are presenting the message of Jesus Christ in over 100 of the principal languages of the world. Powerful international stations are operating in at least seventeen key locations around the globe. Recording studios for Christian programs now total at least 250 in Latin America, Asia, Europe, and Africa. There are hundreds more in North America. In the Third World, Latin America and Asia have the largest number of stations, with forty in Latin America and thirty in the Far East. In Central America a short-wave listener can tune in seven Christian radio stations in Spanish, and in the U.S. there are three short-wave stations and 1000 long-wave and FM stations, with more being added every week. The following languages have the largest amount of Christian programming: English, German, Russian, Japanese, French, and the Nordic languages. In addition there are many programs in Chinese, Arabic, Portuguese, and Quechua.

Much of the credit for these achievements must go to the International Christian Broadcasters, organized in 1954. Its leaders, more than anyone else, have helped to promote Christian broadcasting at home and overseas. Acting as a service agency, its basic operational principle has been sharing. It has shared ideas and contacts. It has helped find personnel, equipment, and programs. It has consulted with those who were building new stations, often undertaking considerable research, travel, and expense. It regularly brought together hundreds of missionary broadcasters from all over the world. The triennial International Communications Congresses in such cities as Chicago, Washington, London, and Tokyo were strategic in developing many ministries. Special conferences included the Communications Conference for Educators, the Conference on Media Use to Reach Muslims, and the Children's Television Round Table. The Satellite Symposiums were used to launch television programs via satellite and to initiate what has now become Project Lookup. Among its published works is the *World Directory of Religious Radio and Television Broadcasting*.[2]

THE ADVANTAGES

The electronic media can never take the place of the missionary, but there are enough advantages to make them abundantly worthwhile.

1. Transistor radios are plentiful. Since World War II, Japan has become an industrial giant with trade and business interests in all parts of the world. The Japanese economy depends almost entirely on overseas trade, and as a result its exports are huge. Among them are transistor radios. They are small, cheap, and within the reach of the most backward peoples. Today they can be found in the most remote parts of the earth. Taxi drivers in the cities, peasants in the paddy fields, workers in the factories, women in their homes, children in the schools—all have transistor radios and listen to them most of the day. In this way the most primitive peoples keep in touch with the modern world. W. Pius Wakatama, himself an African, made the following statement:

> *Most Africans can now afford transistor radios. Many of them are being assembled in Africa and are inexpensive. All one has to do, if he lives in the village, is to sell one or two of his goats, and he will have the price of a transistor radio. He may also need to sell a chicken for the batteries. On many grass-thatched African roofs today are one or two reeds joined together as antennae for transistor radios.*[3]

2. Illiteracy is no problem. The illiteracy rate continues to be high in the developing countries, especially in the rural areas. These people are beyond the reach of Christian literature, but they are not beyond the reach of Christian radio. It is because they are illiterate that they make full use of the radio. It is one of the first things they buy when they get enough money together.

2. The information in the above two paragraphs was taken, with permission, from the *International Christian Broadcasters Bulletin*, Fourth Quarter, 1978.
3. Pius Wakatama, *Independence for the Third World Church* (Downers Grove, IL: InterVarsity Press, 1976), p. 62.

3. Radio is a cheap and effective medium for gospel preaching. The larger, more powerful stations cost a great deal to install, but once the initial expenses are paid the programming is fairly reasonable. When one compares the number of people reached every day by a single gospel program and the number contacted by a missionary, it can easily be seen that radio is an economical way to evangelize the world. The world's population, now at 4.5 billion, will never be completely reached by the missionaries. If they are reached at all it will be by means of radio.

In some countries the government is placing a radio in every village, hoping thereby to bring their rural peoples into the 20th century. Usually these radios are in use almost around the clock; there is always somebody listening. The Far East Broadcasting Company has what it calls Portable Missionaries, which they place free of charge in certain strategic villages. These PMs are small receiving sets pre-tuned to station DZAS in Manila. In this way the village people hear all the programs aired by DZAS.

It will be only a matter of time until such small receiving sets will be recharged with solar power. Already Portable Recordings Ministries in Holland, Michigan, has invented cassette players that operate on solar power. When the Solar Pack runs down all that it needs is a little sunshine! It will operate the average cassette machine for over 30 hours with one charge. The sun will completely recharge the battery in a little over 30 hours. If the Solar Pack is recharged a few hours each day it may never run down. Its estimated life is 5,000 hours.

Compared with radio time in America, broadcasting over commercial stations is exceedingly cheap in most countries. In Taiwan a 15-minute program costs only 50 cents! In Thailand, a 15-minute daily program during prime time costs $25.00 a month. In Japan 15 minutes of time costs $1.00, and that dollar beams the gospel to 7,500 people.

4. There are no "closed" countries. There are today an increasing number of countries closed to the Christian missionary. Included in this list are China, Tibet, Vietnam, Laos, Burma, North Korea, Cambodia, Libya, Iraq, Syria, South Yemen, Saudi Arabia, and others. But there is no way to keep the people in these countries from hearing the gospel by means of radio. The air waves carry the gospel message across the boundaries, geographical and ideological, into countries closed by government action. Letters received from these countries indicate that the Word of God is being heard by millions of people otherwise cut off from all contact with the Christian gospel.

5. Radio programs carry no stigma. In many countries Christianity is not exactly popular, but in some it labors under a definite stigma. The problem has political as well as religious overtones. To be a patriot in Thailand one must be a Buddhist. In India to be a loyal citizen one must be a Hindu. In every Muslim country it is necessary to be a Muslim. To be anything else is to be a traitor to one's country. In all of these countries it takes a certain amount of courage even to attend a church service. Friends and neighbors immediately begin to ask questions. If it looks as if a person is showing a real interest in the gospel he might be subjected to pressure or persecution. For these reasons many people never darken a church door; it causes too much trouble. But these same people are not averse to listening to Christian programs on the radio. This can be done in the privacy of their own homes without exciting suspicion. This one fact makes Christian broadcasting extremely valuable.

Church-planting missionaries find Christian radio an excellent ally in the propagation of the gospel. A missionary in Argentina writes: "Radio breaks down the barriers, prejudices and hatreds which 400 years of teaching has built up against evangelicals. Our programs give us a platform from which to introduce Christ in conversations. We depend heavily on our broadcasts."

From Africa comes this word:

> Multitudes across Senegal listen to The Voice of the Gospel. Our program is effective preparation for other gospel contacts. The hostility of Muslim villagers has changed to demands for Bibles when they identify themselves with the broadcast. To our surprise this Christian broadcast in Muslim Senegal has drawn only one negative remark. We hear dozens of positive comments.

6. Government stations often grant free time to the churches. In some countries of the Third World there is only one powerful radio station and it is owned and operated by the government. In many instances the station managers are glad to have outside organizations provide them with enough programs to round out a sixteen- or eighteen-hour day. Religious programs are usually well received, especially in Africa. The 100,000-watt government-owned Voice of Kenya devotes thirty hours a week to religious broadcasts that can be heard all over East Africa. This time is offered free of charge to the churches in Kenya that are willing to produce religious and cultural programs. In Zambia President Kaunda has offered the churches as much free time on government radio as they can profitably use.

7. The popularity of the radio. In the West, radio has had to take a back seat to television, but not in the Third World. There, radio is king. One missionary in Zaire wrote: "The radio fever rages in Africa. Everyone who can afford it has a radio. Those who can't, listen to their neighbor's." In much of the world radio is still new and the novelty has not yet worn off. It will be several decades before television takes over. In the meantime, missions and church groups are capitalizing on the popularity of this marvelous invention.

> In some of the remote and traditional areas of Africa, people literally live in the fields to protect their crop from wild animals. They build tree outlooks where someone sits all day and night to protect their pro-

duce. . . . If we go together to Africa, we will probably see a man sitting on such a lookout platform. Next to his drum or gong we will also see a transistor radio. If we ask him to come down, he will graciously oblige. This man, who has never been to school a day in his life, who has never been outside his immediate area and who has never put a pair of shoes on his feet, will come down. He will come down and discuss with us the latest international news. [4]

THE PROBLEMS

Radio, in spite of its immense popularity, has problems peculiar to itself. Some of them are more formidable than others.

1. Radio to a marked degree is government controlled. A mission cannot decide entirely on its own to erect a broadcasting station in a foreign country. It must first get the approval of the government. Its place on the band, its call letters, and other important features all require government approval. A good deal of red tape is involved in the negotiations and it may take months, even years, to get the necessary permission.

2. Some governments have a monopoly on radio. In many countries the government has yet to consolidate its hold on the people, which makes it very reluctant to grant broadcasting privileges to individual persons or groups. In these countries even commercial stations are not allowed. Under these conditions it is impossible for a mission to get permission to erect a radio station, and if there are no commercial stations it is difficult to break into broadcasting unless the government gives time on its stations. Religious broadcasting such as we have in the U.S. is unknown in Europe.

3. Some governments do not permit Christian broadcasting. India is an example. India, with 680 million people, does not have a single Christian broadcasting station. Buying time on local commercial stations is equally difficult. The gospel has to be beamed into India from Manila, the Seychelles Islands, and Sri Lanka. This is true also in almost all of Europe. Apart from Trans World Radio in Monaco there isn't one Christian broadcasting station in Europe. It is possible to buy time on Radio Luxembourg, but the hours are not convenient and the cost is prohibitive. Even in the United Kingdom the British Broadcasting Corporation is in sole control and there is very little Christian broadcasting.

In Muslim countries, with the exception of Indonesia, Christian broadcasting is not permitted. Several radio studios have been built in Beirut. It was hoped that the government of Lebanon would grant permission for the establishment of a Christian radio station, especially when half of the population used to be Christian. As of today the figure is only 40 percent. The

4. Pius Wakatama, *Independence*, p. 62.

best that could be done was to build studios in Beirut. The tapes made in these studios are sent to Trans World Radio in Monte Carlo, ELWA in Liberia, and the Far East Broadcasting Company in the Seychelles Islands. In late 1979, a small Christian radio station in southern Lebanon began broadcasting the gospel.

4. Christian radio stations are vulnerable to political change. It is one thing to get the good will of the government; it is another to keep it. Governments in the Third World are notoriously unstable. In choosing a site for a powerful station great caution and wisdom must be exercised or the whole project is likely to end in failure. FEBC had a 100,000 watt station on Okinawa from which it beamed the gospel into China. When Okinawa reverted to Japan in 1974 the entire station had to be dismantled and shipped to Cheju Island in Korea. That was a costly move.

Station HCJB in Quito, Ecuador, recently signed a 25-year contract with the government of that country. There had been some concern as to whether the government would renew the contract for that length of time. The leaders of HCJB go out of their way to keep the favor of the government officials, especially those responsible for negotiations. This can be done in a number of friendly ways without compromising the integrity of the gospel. Nevertheless it points up the delicacy of the situation where a government could close down a station at will if it felt like doing so. In 1966 the HCJB staff honored the 406th anniversary of Quito's founding with a bilingual concert in National Opera House. This was deeply appreciated by the government and well accepted by the people.

FEBC in Manila has maintained good relations with the government of the Philippines for over a quarter of a century. When President Marcos declared martial law in September 1972, newspapers and radio and television stations were closed down. On the second day, however, FEBC was permitted to resume broadcasting, an eloquent testimony to the good relations between FEBC and the government trying to stave off chaos occasioned by the "Communist threat."

The only way for these Christian stations to retain the favor and cooperation of the governments is to scrupulously avoid any mention of politics on the air. They must maintain a neutral stance, usually one that leans in the direction of the government. That is the price they have to pay for the privilege of broadcasting in a foreign country.

In addition these stations are placed at the service of the government in times of natural disasters—typhoons, floods, earthquakes, etc. In this capacity they do useful service which the government appreciates. In November 1972 FEBC in Manila reported: "The floods in the Philippines affected 500,000 people! Our staff coordinated evangelical relief efforts. . . . Our radio stations made appeals for help from the listeners. We were able to feed 16,500 families. Even the Communists praised the FEBC staff for a good job!"

Not all the Christian stations have survived the political upheaval of our times. When the Marxist Military Council seized power in Ethiopia in 1977 it commandeered the Lutheran station, The Radio Voice of the Gospel, in Addis Ababa. The same thing happened to Radio CORDAC in Burundi when a change of government occurred. Trans World Radio moved from Morocco to Monaco in 1960 because the Moroccan government outlawed all private stations. The move turned out to be a happy one, for the political situation in the tiny kingdom of Monaco is not likely to change in the foreseeable future. It was the part of wisdom for that same mission to recently erect a powerful station on Guam in the Pacific. Its station on Bonaire is equally safe. It remains to be seen how safe the newly opened station in Sri Lanka is.

5. **In hostile countries jamming is always a possibility.** Both China and the U.S.S.R. have been known to jam incoming short-wave broadcasts. This is costly, and it is difficult to achieve one hundred percent effectiveness. China has never bothered to jam Christian broadcasts. They were probably not considered important enough for that kind of reaction. Christian programs beamed into the U.S.S.R. have been jammed from time to time, but that is no longer the case. However, the broadcasts have been sufficiently effective to attract the adverse attention of *Pravda*.

6. **Indigenization is a perennial problem.** Programs produced by local churches and aired over commercial stations are nearly always completely indigenous. The same cannot be said of the stations owned and operated by the mission boards. Most of the funding comes from the West. Almost all of the top administrators are missionaries. Pastors and other local leaders are used extensively as speakers for the programs, but they have little or no voice in the administration. Much of the correspondence is carried on by national staff members. Bible correspondence courses are translated or prepared and graded by nationals.

Sooner or later the governments will demand that nationals be included in the decision-making process and have a place in the upper echelons of power. It may be that the time will come when these stations, if they wish to continue their ministry, will have to be administered by nationals rather than by missionaries. It is not too early for mission executives to give serious thought to this problem.

7. **Followup is difficult.** All Christian stations make some effort to get a response from the listening audience, and some of them are surprised at the result. FEBC in Manila receives 18,000 letters a month, coming from sixty countries. It is quite impossible to arrange for anything like an adequate followup scheme when the audience is so gigantic and so diverse. Where the broadcasts are local in extent it is a good deal easier to get in touch with listeners and refer them to nearby local churches. The followup then de-

pends on the local church and the facilities it has for such an outreach. Not all churches are so equipped.

Every letter should be answered, and most Christian radio stations do their best to answer all the letters they receive. Many stations offer a Bible correspondence course to those who write. HCJB has a Bible Institute of the Air, with thousands enrolled in their courses, which are offered in four languages. This is one of the most effective methods of followup. It keeps the listener in touch with the station and studying the Bible at the same time. Some stations do not have the staff to handle this huge amount of correspondence, however.

The most effective radio ministry is that carried over local commercial stations by medium wave. In country after country polls show that almost invariably the people keep their radios tuned to the local station. A poll taken in Thailand in 1971 revealed the fact that 90 percent of the letters received in response to the Christian programs came from Buddhists replying to the local stations. Only ten to fifteen replies out of 11,000 a year were received in answer to short-wave programs.

David Michell (Japan) in an article on evangelism suggested that "we stress the need for Radio and TV evangelistic ministry that is integrated with the church-planting programme and followed up effectively." Ralph Toliver (Philippines) made this comment: "For radio to be effective in the growth of a local church, the listeners to a Christian broadcast must be able to connect that broadcast with a local church. The voice in the box must be related to the church on the corner."[5]

8. Programming. This poses all kinds of problems. Stations which are on the air 12 to 15 hours a day have gigantic problems in this area: for those which use twenty or thirty languages the problems are compounded many times over.

Imagine the logistical problems faced by FEBC in Manila, which broadcasts the gospel in ninety-one languages and dialects, mostly of Asia. Most of the programs are recorded in studios located elsewhere. Besides its own studios in Tokyo, New Delhi, Bangalore, Bangkok, Jakarta, Hong Kong, and Singapore, it cooperates with thirty-five additional studios belonging to other missions. As we have already said, tapes are made by nationals in these studios and mailed to Manila for airing. To keep the tapes flowing into Manila on time is a big project, to say nothing of checking them and making arrangements to broadcast them at the proper time and in the proper sequence.

How does a remote tribe hear the message in its own language? One example will suffice. Before Laos fell to the Communists, every two months two missionaries took a group of Laotian Christians to the recording studio at

5. *O.M.F. Bulletin*, January 1972, p. 8.

Korat, Thailand—a hot and trying trip through the jungle. There they recorded 50 programs in four days. The tapes were then mailed to Manila and broadcast to Laos by means of a complicated antenna system. Thus, the Meo tribespeople heard the gospel in their own tongue.

Another problem pertaining to programming is variety. If all the programs are religious the interest of the audience will soon be lost. There must be variety in order to hold the listeners. Radio Station HLKY in Seoul, Korea, is on the air fifteen hours each day with 380 programs a week. Five hours weekly are broadcast in English, one hundred hours in Korean. Program breakdown is as follows: 15 drama programs, 115 music, 65 news, 86 worship, 14 meditation, 38 educational, 47 cultural. It is estimated that with 250,000 receivers in the area the number of listeners is approximately one million. Obviously the people like this format, otherwise the response would not be so good.

Experience has shown that if too many of the programs are religious the broadcasts become self-defeating. People turn to other stations for variety. Some Christian broadcasters prefer to keep the religious element down to about 25 percent of the total offerings, with music, news, drama, plays, etc. making up the remainder of the time. If a station is ministering exclusively to the Christian population a much higher percentage of religious programming would be in order. If the aim is to evangelize the population as well as to edify the Christians, religion should not preempt more than fifty percent of the time.

Missionary radio is largely a work of faith. The broadcasters never see the audience to whom they minister. Day after day they talk into a microphone, hoping that there is someone "out there" listening. Those who respond with a letter are only a small fraction of the total number of listeners, especially in areas where the illiteracy rate is high. Prior to 1979, few letters were received from Communist China. There is no personal contact, and often the speaker does not see the letters that come in. They are usually taken care of by other members of the staff.

It takes a lot of faith to keep at this kind of work week after week without seeing any tangible results, but perhaps one should not expect immediate results. The measure of success, however, cannot be gauged merely by statistics.

> When anyone is called upon to become directly involved in missionary broadcasting, he or she must be willing to accept the limitations which are inherent in this type of ministry. The important question is not: How successful am I? The crucial question is: Am I truly preaching Jesus Christ and Him crucified in such a way that I feel I am discharging my calling in the way Paul and Peter and the rest of the apostles did?[6]

6. Bassam Madany, *Follow Up*. An address delivered at the International Convention of the International Broadcasters, London, April, 1967.

CHRISTIAN TELEVISION

Christian television is still in its infancy. Even here in the U.S. few churches or organizations can afford the high cost of TV production. Several times a year Billy Graham and Oral Roberts have specials on TV. The Lutheran Church-Missouri Synod and the Southern Baptists have continuing programs which are well received. Smaller evangelical denominations have neither the funds nor the personnel for such an operation.

On the mission field Christian television is beginning to make its appearance. Station HCJB in Quito pioneered in this medium, but they found the costs so high that they had to change their plans and be content with producing programs and making them available to commercial stations.

Commercial television in most of the Third World is just getting into stride and station managers often have a difficult time securing enough programs to round out a full day's schedule. Consequently they are delighted when Christian organizations undertake to provide them with religious programs. These are especially appreciated at Christmas and Easter, when the station may want to devote the entire day to live religious programs. This is especially true in Latin America.

West Africa's first Christian television studio is now in preparation. It is an outgrowth of New Life For All, started some years ago by the Sudan Interior Mission. Already evangelicals in Nigeria have assumed leadership in Christian TV programming. For the past seven years they have provided programs for government-owned stations. Presently they have a daily prime-time program on NTV Jos, called "The Christian Half Hour"; they also have 40-minute programs three Sundays a month. NTV Jos is seen in parts of four Nigerian states. It is expected that within two years, all 19 state capitals will have their own TV stations linked to a network by satellite transmission. Ninety-five percent of the TV scripting is now done by Nigerian Christians.

This is a developing trend and mission leaders should be giving top priority to radio and television as a chief means of world evangelization. It will be costly in money and personnel and for some time to come the churches may need special funding to help in this effort. In many instances the government-owned stations are so keen to get the programs that they air them free of charge even during prime time. How long this will last is anyone's guess, but for the time being it presents a splendid opportunity for church and mission leaders to get the message of the gospel into the hearts and homes of the world.

The Evangelical Mass Communications Consortium for Asia organized by ECCE (Encouraging Contemporary Communications Enterprises) is a good idea. Operating on a continent-wide basis ECCE is an inter-mission service organization to initiate, encourage, and assist the greater development and wider diversification of the Christian use of mass media.

27

Bible Work

God has given the world two inestimable gifts: the Written Word, the Bible; and the Living Word, Jesus Christ. The supreme task of the Christian missionary is to share these gifts with the world for whom they were intended.

Bible work has traditionally been accomplished in three phases: translation, publication, and distribution.

TRANSLATION

It is difficult to imagine that for the first 2500 years the world had no Bible, not even the Book of Genesis. The production of the Bible was the work of some forty human authors over a period of 1500 years, beginning with Moses and ending with the apostle John around A.D. 90. It is equally difficult to believe that for almost 1500 years the Roman Catholic Church kept the Bible from its own people and therefore from the world. The Latin Vulgate was translated by Jerome about A.D. 400 and for approximately 1500 years was the authorized version of the Roman Catholic Church, but it was only the church leaders who were able to read Latin so the Bible remained a closed book.

In the 14th century, Wycliffe made an attempt to give the Bible to the people of England in their own language. He was followed by Tyndale in the 16th century. Both of them paid dearly for their efforts to give the Bible to the common man. Luther gave the Bible to the Germans. It was not until the modern Protestant missionary era, which began in 1705, that any concerted

329

effort was made to make the Word of God available to the peoples of the world in their own tongue.

The first was the translation of the New Testament into Tamil by Ziegenbalg in 1715. Since then, Protestant missionaries the world over have devoted endless time, thought, and energy to the translation of the Bible. Today, the Scriptures have been translated into 1750 languages and dialects. Ninety percent of the world's peoples now have the complete Bible in their own language. The New Testament is available to another five percent. At least one book, usually called a Portion, is available to a further three percent. This leaves only two percent of the population of the world with no part of the Bible; Wycliffe Bible Translators, with its 4200 missionaries, is dedicated to the task of giving the New Testament to these remaining 80 million people scattered among several thousand tribes in all the remote parts of the world. They hope to have it completed by the end of the century.

Until Vatican II almost all Bible translation was done by Protestant missionaries. Since that historic event, the Roman Catholic Church has decided to give the Bible to its people in the vernacular, and their missionaries are now engaging in Bible translation with the blessing of the pope. Actually, the present policy for the United Bible Societies is to produce union Bibles acceptable to both Catholics and Protestants, and Catholic scholars are now members of most translation teams.

In 1946, several national Bible societies joined to form the United Bible Societies with headquarters in London. Today there are 66 national agencies in the UBS. There are three thousand translators now working on more than 500 projects, many of which involve revisions rather than original translations. To aid these translators the UBS in 1966 published a new edition of the Greek New Testament based on contemporary studies and edited by an internationally renowned group of New Testament experts. The edition served a twofold purpose: (1) to provide scholars with a new text and a more representative and exhaustive selection of variant readings: and (2) to provide students and Bible translators, especially missionaries and nationals of the younger churches, with a new tool with which to do their work more accurately. A similar edition of the Hebrew Old Testament is now in preparation.[1]

Whenever Bible translation is mentioned we naturally think of first-time translations. These are very important, but they are not the whole story. Languages change, and when they change significantly a new translation of the Scriptures is needed. This is called revision rather than translation and it is a never-ending task.

Most of the Bible translation being done in the world today, except that undertaken by Wycliffe Bible Translators, is done under the auspices of the United Bible Societies. It decides on the basis of its annual budget which translations and revisions can be undertaken in a given year.

1. *American Bible Society Record,* January 1978, pp. 11–12.

Bible translation is a highly technical occupation and requires special linguistic skills. The pioneer missionaries were at a great disadvantage in this respect. They had none of the benefits of the modern science of linguistics—phonetics, phonemics, morphology—and had to develop their own tools as they went along. Each translator was a law unto himself and used symbols of his own. Today the linguists have a written symbol for every sound that can be produced by the human voice. Students of linguistics are taught to detect these sounds and to scientifically record them. This is a tremendous advantage over the early days.

In many instances the language of the more primitive peoples of the world had no written form. The missionary had to learn to speak the language and then invent a script for it, after which it was his job to translate the Scriptures and teach the converts to read the script he had invented for them.

In translating the Scriptures certain books are preferred before others. Usually the first to be translated is the Gospel of Mark. It is the shortest of the four Gospels. It is a book of action rather than contemplation. It contains fewer abstract terms and is generally best suited for young semi-literate converts. Other books follow, in some such order as this: John, Psalms, Acts, and others until the New Testament is completed, followed by the entire Bible. The New Testament takes at least ten years, the Old Testament even longer. It often takes thirty or forty years to translate and publish the whole Bible.

Not all missionaries are qualified to do this kind of exacting work. Certain rigid qualifications are necessary. First, the translator should have a thorough understanding of the original languages of Hebrew and Greek. Second, he should have a working knowledge of the language into which the translation is to be made. Third, he must have been in the country long enough to immerse himself in its culture; otherwise his best efforts will have a Western flavor. Fourth, he should have completed his first term of service on the field before even considering translation work. Some of the pioneers did not wait that long. Some of them completed the translation of the New Testament in four or five years, but their work suffered from haste, which was one reason why revisions had to be made in later years. Fifth, he should have linguistic training before undertaking the work. The best place to get such training is at the Summer Institute of Linguistics conducted each year in various universities in the U.S. and abroad.

The best translation is done by committees rather than by individuals. It is true here as in other areas that there is wisdom in a multitude of counselors. In addition, nationals should always be full members of the committee. Only they can ensure an accurate, idiomatic translation. Clarity of expression rather than elegance of style should be the first objective. The translator must remember that the end product is designed for the masses, not for scholars. In the case of China the translators had no choice; they had to translate the Bible into the ancient classical language, Wenli, understood only by the scholar-gentry class. This was because there was at that time no other written form of Chinese. In the 1920s Hu Shih brought about a cultural revolution by introducing a popular form of Chinese known as Kueh Ü, into which the Bible was then translated. The Communists in our day have further simplified the written form and it is now called the new Communist script. Already the New Testament has been translated into this new script by a committee in Hong Kong.

Bible translation abounds in problems, one of which is securing the services of a qualified national informant. Preferably he should be a mature Christian with some understanding of Christian doctrine. Another problem is the lack of suitable terms for biblical words. How does the translator deal with such words as sheep, snow, rock, temple, and numerous others when these things do not exist in the culture? And if concrete terms are difficult, what about abstract ideas like sin, grace, love, forgiveness, trust, etc.? It has sometimes taken missionaries years to find the word they were looking for. Bible translation is a long, laborious, and tedious operation and requires an inexhaustible supply of patience and perseverance.

Even the term for God, by far the most important word in the Bible, is often a problem. If there is no equivalent for our word God, then one has to be invented, but if it is an invention who will understand its connotation? If an existing term is available it may or may not convey the full force of the meaning. Chinese is an example of this. The missionaries had no reason to invent a new term. Three were already in wide use: *T'ien, Shen,* and *Shang-ti.* The first was used extensively in the ancient Chinese classics. It means "Heaven" or "Providence." The second has a very broad connotation and might be translated as gods, spirits, ghosts, etc. Technically speaking it is the closest to our term God, but its broader connotation made it unacceptable to many. The third means Supreme Ruler. The human emperor of China was *Hwang-ti;* the Creator and Ruler of the Universe was called *Shang-ti.*

Missionaries could not agree which term to use, so they ended up using all three! The Roman Catholics settled for *T'ien-chu* (Heavenly Lord) and the Protestants were divided into two schools of thought, one preferring *Shen* and the other *Shang-ti.* The China Bible House published two kinds of Bibles, each using one of these terms. In our church in Fowyang the church leaders used both terms: *Shang-ti* when preaching in the street chapel to outsiders, and *Shen* when preaching in the church to believers!

Missionaries in the Middle East have run into another kind of problem. Classical Arabic is the language of the Koran. It is regarded as sacred. Some Arabs believe that God speaks classical Arabic in heaven. The Bible and all Christian literature, to be acceptable to the educated Arab, must be in classical Arabic. Even sermons are better received if they are preached in classical rather than spoken Arabic. In recent years attempts have been made to translate the Bible into common Arabic, the language used by newspapers and radio. It will be some time before this kind of Bible gains acceptance with the educated class.

Another problem stems from government interference. One of the greatest of all problems in Third World countries is how to unify a country made up of hundreds of different language groups. Clearly it is in the interest of political stability to have one language spoken by all. This is difficult to achieve; nevertheless many countries have settled for one language and are requiring all citizens, especially school children, to learn it. In India it is Hindi. In Taiwan it is Mandarin. In Malaysia it is Malay. In Liberia it is English. In Ethiopia it was Amharic until the Communists took over.

This poses dire problems for Bible translators who are eager to give the Bible to the people in their own tongue—what they call their "heart" language. In some countries the government has confiscated Scriptures in tribal languages. In others they have forbidden the missionaries to proceed with tribal translations. This has been particularly hard on Wycliffe Bible Translators, who are involved exclusively in Bible translation for the hundreds of tribes who have no Bibles in their native tongues. Some of the governments in Latin America would like to "civilize" the Indian tribes and bring them into the mainstream of Latin culture, including the speaking of Spanish. In all these countries those involved in Bible translation for tribal language groups are regarded with a certain degree of suspicion, or at least disapproval, by the government. Bible translation is at best a difficult operation without the nagging impression that the whole undertaking is "illegal" by government definition.

The Bible societies have from the beginning adhered to two sound principles. First, the Scriptures were to be published "without note or comment," thus making them nonsectarian. In this way they were able to avoid the theological hassles so common in ecclesiastical circles. Second, the Scriptures were to be made available at a price the common people could afford. To make this possible all Scriptures have to be subsidized by the Bible societies.

In my day in China the Bible came in three sizes. They sold for thirty cents, sixty cents, and ninety cents, even though it cost a good deal more to produce them. Nevertheless, they were dear by local standards, for a skilled carpenter's daily wage was only 26 cents!

PUBLICATION

Through the years most of the translations have been published either by the British and Foreign Bible Society or the American Bible Society. Before they undertake publication their experts check the translation for accuracy. They proceed with publication only when they are satisfied that it is a good translation.

In the early days most of the publishing was done in London or New York, but more recently it has become cheaper and more practical to publish the Scriptures in the countries to which they belong. This has long been true in India, China, and Japan. In the 1930s more Scriptures were published in Shanghai than in New York or London.

Publication also has its problems. Sometimes it is lack of type; other times it may be lack of paper. Most Bibles are printed on special thin paper which is not available in all countries. In the Communist countries paper is rationed by the government and it is often difficult for the Bible societies to get their share. If the government wants to hinder the publication of the Bible, all it has to do is withhold the paper. This has been done many times in Eastern Europe.

The publication of the Scriptures in the Eastern European countries is subject to a variety of limitations and restrictions. First of all, permission is always needed from the authorities before Scriptures can be produced. Second, the technical problems are often considerable. At both the printing and the binding stages special knowledge and equipment are required because the Bible is a large book printed on special paper. For these and other reasons it is necessary for the United Bible Societies to give help. The UBS production manager for Europe makes periodic visits to Eastern Europe to offer advice. Printing equipment, including presses, is sometimes supplied by the UBS, which also makes paper available from the West free of charge, since only a few of the Eastern European countries produce Bible paper themselves.[2]

It is difficult to get exact figures for the total local production in Eastern Europe during the postwar years; but Scripture production there during 1973, 1974, and 1975 amounted to approximately 1,950,000 Scriptures, including 500,000 Bibles, 350,000 New Testaments, 500,000 Portions, and 600,000 Selections, which is far more local production than before World War II.

The Czechoslovak Ministry of Culture, which allocates printing paper, has given approval for the publication in 1979 of 120,000 copies of the new Czech ecumenical version of the Bible. The new Bible, a project supported by the Czech Bible Work, will mark the 400th anniversary of the greatly revered and still used Kralice Bible.

For many years the Bible societies produced Bibles, New Testaments, and individual books, or Portions. In recent years they have greatly increased their publication figure by producing certain parts of the Scriptures called Selections: the Beatitudes, the Sermon on the Mount, and special selections for Christmas, Easter, Pentecost, and other Christian festivals.

More recently still the American Bible Society has decided to raise $63 million over a 12-year period to help newly literate peoples around the world improve their reading ability. *Good News for New Readers* will involve the production of 725 million Bible stories in multi-colored four-page leaflet form. It is by far the most ambitious program ever undertaken by the Bible Society in its 165-year history. By the end of 1978 these had been made available in 358 languages of the world. This is a very significant undertaking in that it provides new readers in the Third World, of whom there are tens of

2. *American Bible Society Record*, April 1977, p. 4.

millions each year, with simple, clearly printed, and well illustrated reading material. And they get the gospel in the bargain!

DISTRIBUTION

On the mission field nearly all Scriptures are produced and distributed by the national Bible societies with the help of the United Bible Societies. Distribution is left pretty much to the local Bible society in the individual country. It takes many forms. The Bible societies have agencies and depots in the larger cities and many of the Scriptures are distributed through them.

Colporteurs are often hired, sometimes by the Bible societies and sometimes by the missions or the churches. These are men who give their entire time to traveling throughout the countryside selling the Scriptures. They almost never give them away free. If they did, the Scriptures would not be appreciated. Experience has proved it to be much wiser to charge a small amount, thus making sure that the buyer will prize the book and read it rather than use the paper to roll cigarets or package peanuts!

In addition to the Bible societies, there are other agencies that specialize in Scripture distribution: Gideons International, Scripture Gift Mission, Bibles for the World, World Home Bible League, and the Pocket Testament League. Among them they have distributed hundreds of millions of copies of the Scriptures in the last 20 years. The Gideons place Bibles in hotels, motels, schools, and prisons. The Pocket Testament League has concentrated on military personnel in such places as China, Taiwan, Vietnam, Korea, etc.

Bibles for the World, with headquarters in Wheaton, Illinois, is engaged in a unique operation. It sends Scriptures, mostly New Testaments, through the international mails to persons whose names and addresses it gleans from the telephone directories. It has already mailed almost 4 million copies to 14 countries, including India and the U.S.S.R. Where English is a well known language, as in India, they send the Scriptures in English. The New Testaments sent to India bore the title, *Love Is the Greatest*, and on the cover there was a picture of the Taj Mahal. They were well received.

The Scriptures destined for the Soviet Union are in the Russian language and are mailed from New Delhi, India. Over 410,000 copies of the New Testament and the Psalms have been sent. Nor have the Chinese been left out. Two hundred thousand copies have gone to Hong Kong and 560,000 to Taiwan. Thirty thousand copies of the New Testament in the new Communist script printed in Hong Kong, have been mailed to Communist China from Japan. Before getting into full swing in any country a test consignment of 5,000 copies is sent. If they are received without interference the full operation proceeds. The greatest problem is in Russia, where all 24 telephone directories in the country are kept in government offices and not made available to the public. The most recent venture is in Kenya, where the response has been phenomenal.

Unlike the U.S., where the Bible is kept out of the school system, many countries in Africa have requested that Bibles and New Testaments be furnished for the school children. The largest order ever placed with the British and Foreign Bible Society, for 500,000 Bibles, half in English and half in 5 main dialects, was received from the Department of Education in Ghana. In 1977 the schools in Zaire were returned to the churches, and immediately they set about teaching the Bible in the school system again. In these schools there are some 2.6 million children. Within the past year the Bible Society has been working on a program to reach every pupil in the primary schools, grades one through three with a Scripture Portion and grades four through six with a diglot Gospel of Mark in French and his own language. In the secondary schools the Society hopes to supply a New Testament for every pupil in grades one through three and a complete Bible for each student in grades four through six. Even in predominantly Muslim Bangladesh, government schools were visited by Bible Society distribution teams who were allowed to enter the classrooms and personally present thousands of Scriptures to the children.

One shipment of Bibles has recently been received in Cuba, where 2500 Bibles and 2500 Spanish common-language New Testaments were distributed among forty-four denominations—not nearly enough to go around but certainly better than nothing.

Today there are some sixty-six national societies in the United Bible Societies. Those in the West are fully self-supporting and are able to contribute to the budget of the UBS, the American Bible Society providing about half of the total budget. Most of the Bible societies in the Third World are not yet self-supporting and therefore have to be subsidized by the UBS.

From all parts of the world come reports of increased sales. In 1977 Scripture distribution in Asia increased by 42 percent. In 1978 the UBS distributed a record 505,252,066 Scriptures in 158 countries and territories, an increase of 23 percent over 1977.

The American Bible Society is the largest and most active of them all. Its distribution system here in the U.S. is unbelievably comprehensive. It is cooperating with schools, prisons, rescue missions, store-front churches in the inner cities, affluent churches in the suburbs, army camps, and state conventions of the various denominations. Bibles, New Testaments, Portions, and Selections in many languages are distributed every year by the tens of thousands to seamen in the ports of the country, everywhere from San Francisco to Boston.

It provides Scriptures free of charge to migrant workers, prisoners, victims of earthquakes and airplane crashes, immigrants, refugees, hospitals, nursing homes, senior citizens homes, and medical centers. For the blind it provides Bibles in Braille and on cassettes.

28

Literature Work

Napoleon is reported to have said that the pen is mightier than the sword. From the beginning, Christian missions have stressed the importance of literature, both in the spread of the gospel and in the building up of the church. In almost every instance the first task of the pioneer missionary was the translation of the Scriptures and the setting up of a printing press.

Time and again we have been told that the missionaries taught the people to read but it was the Communists who gave them literature. This is one of those half-truths that can be so misleading to the uninformed. Missionaries have always placed a high priority on the printed page. Writing to William Ward, a printer, in 1793, William Carey said: "If the Lord bless us we shall want a person of your business to enable us to print the Scriptures."[1] Ward soon joined Carey and established the first mission press in North India. The first thing the American missionaries did when they arrived in the Middle East in the early 1820s was to write home for a printing press. Robert Moffatt arrived in Africa in 1817. Writing to a friend he said: "You cannot conceive what a threefold cord it requires to drag me from the work of translation."[2] When the first press arrived in 1823 no time was lost in getting it into working order. "Arriving at Chumie on 16th of December, the press was got in order on the 17th; on the 18th the alphabet was set up; on the 19th fifty copies were thrown off; and on the 20th Mr. Dennis recorded that a new era had commenced in the history of the Bantu people."[3]

1. H. H. Holcomb, *Men of Might in Indian Missions* (New York: Revell, 1901), p. 77.
2. John S. Moffatt, *Lives of Robert and Mary Moffatt* (London: T. Fisher Unwin, 1885), p. 288.
3. R. H. W. Shepherd, *Lovedale and Literature for the Bantu* (Lovedale: Lovedale Press, 1945), p. 3.

From that day to this, missionaries all over the world have been engaged in literature work on a massive scale. In the early 1920s Arthur J. Brown reported: "Today one hundred and sixty presses are conducted by the Protestant mission boards in various parts of the world, and they issue annually about four hundred million pages of Christian literature."[4]

China can serve as an example of the extent to which Christian literature was used by mission agencies. Almost three decades before China opened in 1842, William Milne set up a printing press in Malacca for the publication of Christian literature in the Chinese language. In the 1830s, when China was still closed to resident missionaries, Karl Gützlaff, a free-lance missionary, made three journeys up and down the coast of China, selling Bibles and Christian literature printed in Malacca. Forty years after China began to admit foreigners, there were eleven presses and an equal number of tract societies in operation. The presses were mission owned and operated; the tract societies were undenominational.

By the time the Communists came to power in 1949, catalogs issued by the various publishing houses revealed the fact that the Chinese church was well supplied with literature of all kinds: tracts, posters, hymnbooks, primers, catechisms, commentaries, dictionaries, and a host of books dealing with Bible exposition, church history, theology, philosophy, biography, hygiene, home economics, and many other subjects. There were 136 Christian periodicals, including weekly and monthly magazines for children and adults.

A number of favorable factors contributed to this achievement. Among them were China's rich and ancient culture, a veneration for scholarship and the printed page, a highly developed and unified written language, a large scholarly class, some of whom became Christians, and an unusual number of brilliant linguists among the early missionaries.

Today, practically every mission of any size maintains its own literature work. In addition there are several organizations, operating mostly on an interdenominational basis, that engage solely in the production and distribution of Christian literature: United Society for the Promotion of Christian Knowledge, Society for Christian Literature, Christian Literature Development, Christian Literature Crusade, Evangelical Literature Overseas, Literature Crusades, Operation Mobilization, World Literary Crusade, and Moody Literature Ministries. MLM is now producing and distributing gospel literature in 184 languages in over 100 countries. In addition, Moody Institute of Science has made its science films available in twenty-one languages to missionaries in 120 countries.

Evangelical Literature Overseas is working with ninety missions and thirty national church agencies in fifty-six countries. It is also cooperating with 380 bookstores. Of these, 196 are self-supporting or are working toward

4. Arthur J. Brown, *The Why and How of Foreign Missions* (New York: Missionary Education Movement, 1921), p. 127.

it. Emphasis is on business management and self-support programs. ELO facilitates the development of bookstores and publication centers. It serves all aspects of literature development—writing, editing, production, and distribution.

Many of the larger countries have their own Christian Literature Society, Sunday School Union, and Religious Tract Society or their equivalent. Nobody acquainted with the facts can accuse the missions of neglecting the promotion of Christian literature.

Some Christian literature is produced for non-Christians, some for Christians. The former consists mostly of tracts, pamphlets, booklets, and posters presenting the simple truths of the gospel. More advanced literature for students and intellectuals includes books on various topics of interest—apologetics, ethics, science and religion, evolution, atheism, comparative religion, etc. Recently several missions have produced popular magazines designed to be sold on the newsstands. They contain articles dealing with world news, current events, outstanding personalities, sports, economics, politics, and at least one article on some aspect of the Christian life. The Sudan Interior Mission pioneered with *African Challenge,* first in English and then in Yoruba. Later on, when they ran into labor difficulties, *African Challenge* was dropped and in its place the mission published ads in the local newspapers. They found this to be much cheaper, less bothersome, and even more effective, since they offered Bible correspondence courses to those who wrote for them. The Overseas Missionary Fellowship began, and for ten years supported and subsidized, a beautiful Chinese-language monthly called *Dengta* (Lighthouse). Published in Hong Kong, it was sold to Chinese-speaking people all over Southeast Asia. It was discontinued when the government of Indonesia barred Chinese-language literature published outside the country. Another contributing factor was money. The magazine never became self-supporting, but while it lasted it was a successful literary endeavor.

It must be said that for the most part, missions have concentrated more on literature for non-Christians than for Christians. This means that the church members don't have nearly as much helpful literature as they should have. One reason for this is the fact that in most countries Christians represent a tiny minority of the total population; therefore emphasis is on evangelism and church growth.

Compared with the churches in the West, those on the mission field still have a long way to go when it comes to the production of Christian literature. The average church member considers himself well off if he owns a complete Bible and a hymnbook. There is still a vast market for suitable literature in the Christian church.

World Christian Books, with headquarters in London, is an agency devoted to the production of books on basic Christian themes: the Christian home, stewardship, witnessing, evangelism, church history, ethics, etc. They are designed for new believers, many of whom are semi-literate. They are written in basic English, using simple words and short sentences such as would be readily understood by a fifth or sixth grader. They are then translated into the various languages of the world. In this way new converts can be introduced to elementary Christian teaching. The program has been eminently successful. Already it has produced hundreds of titles in scores of languages.

KINDS OF LITERATURE

1. **Bible correspondence courses.** These are available for Christians and non-Christians and have been widely used throughout the world. Tens of thousands of persons who would like to attend Bible school but can't, find the correspondence course a good substitute. One of the earliest courses was *Light of Life*, written by Dr. Don Hillis in India back in the 1940s. It began with one course in the Gospel of John in Marathi. Today it has five courses (John, Acts, Galatians, Mark, and Luke) available in 70 languages. More than three and a half million persons have enrolled and 650,000 have completed one or more courses. The Emmaus Bible Correspondence School has produced sixty courses which have been translated into 120 languages; over six million persons have enrolled.

Bible correspondence courses are particularly effective in Muslim countries, where people are reluctant to identify with the Christian church. In the seclusion of their homes, however, they can study the Word of God without fear. Over 20,000 Muslims in Tunisia and an equal number in Morocco have signed up for courses sponsored by the North Africa Mission and the Gospel Missionary Union. Bangladesh is another Muslim country where Bible correspondence courses have been well received. In the last twenty-five years almost 50,000 persons, half of them Muslims, have enrolled in such courses.

Bible correspondence courses are divided into several categories: book studies, salvation courses, children's courses, Christian life series, Bible prophecy, Bible survey, doctrine, witnessing, teacher's certificate courses, etc. Those designed for beginners are short and simple. Others intended for serious, more mature Christians are longer, more advanced, and demand much deeper commitment and study.

2. **Sunday school material.** Sunday school in the Third World churches is a pathetic undertaking. Teachers are hard to get, and those who do teach have little or no training. Very little preparation goes into the teaching of the lesson. One reason for this is the lack of suitable materials for Sunday school use. Some countries have a Sunday School Union which produces such materials, but not all churches subscribe to it. Of those who do, not many make the best use of it when they get it. Few churches have teacher training sessions, so the teachers are pretty much on their own.

3. **Gospel tracts.** These are produced in prolific quantities and quality is often sacrificed for quantity. It is essential that the tracts be attractive, readable, and within the means of those for whom they are intended. They should be prepared with the utmost care, and each one should be written with a particular group in mind. Tracts for semi-literate peasants are not likely to impress the high school student, much less the college graduate. Gospel literature prepared for Hindus or Buddhists will not be very helpful to Muslims. Hindus, Buddhists, Muslims—each should have his own kind of gospel tract, geared to his particular needs and expressed in religious terms he can understand. Other major groups in the Far East—Confucianists, Shintoists, etc.—require something different again. Gospel literature is best produced by the nationals themselves. Few missionaries have the linguistic ability or the cultural expertise to write acceptable literature for non-Christians.

One of the most effective pieces of literature in China was the Human Heart Poster, which I understand is now being widely used throughout Southeast Asia. It is in flip-chart form and has seven or eight pages. The first page depicts the depraved human heart, which is full of darkness and all kinds of sins and vices, each one represented by an evil beast. Each succeeding page shows the light of the Gospel penetrating the heart and the Holy Spirit in the form of a dove chasing out the evil beasts. The last page of the poster presents the new heart of the Christian, washed and made clean by the blood of Christ. The evil beasts have all fled and the Holy Spirit is in control. This poster has been used more extensively than any other gospel poster and always with good effect.

4. **Flannelgraph.** Flannelgraph is used in many places and has proved to be an effective teaching tool. The material is cheap to buy and the sets are easy to make. Nearly every Biblewoman and evangelist has his or her own set. The advantage with flannelgraph is that the characters are movable which causes the interest to grow as the story unfolds. They don't see the whole picture at once.

5. **Cassettes.** During the last decade cassettes have become popular on the mission field. They have several advantages. First, they can penetrate the inaccessible regions where missionaries seldom go. Second, the message comes through loud and clear because the voice is that of a national. The audience, therefore, however illiterate, can fully understand what is being said. Third, the fact that the message comes out of a "box" is a source of complete bewilderment and thus attracts great attention. People who wouldn't bother to listen to an evangelist in the bazaar will listen for hours to the voice coming from the box. Fourth, the cassette remains in the village and can be played over and over again long after the missionary or the evangelist has gone. Using a cassette with a solar pack solves the problem of running out of batteries in remote areas where they can't be replaced.

6. Gospel Records. Scripture portions, Bible talks, and other gospel messages are now available on records produced by Gospel Recordings. Millions of records in over 4000 languages have been made and sent free of charge to missionaries in almost every country of the world. More recently they have invented a simple record player that can be operated by hand. The rural folks will keep on winding the recorder as long as the words continue to come out.

7. Hymnbooks. From time immemorial the church has been a singing institution. Many a revival has been accompanied by the singing of the great historic hymns of the church. The first hymnbooks on the mission field were produced by the missionaries, using Western words and Western tunes, and the translations weren't always as correct as they might have been. It is difficult enough to translate prose; it is much more difficult to translate poetry. It is true that the churches of the Third World should be aware of these great hymns which have been translated from one European language to another until the whole Western church is familiar with them. But when all is said and done it must be recognized that they have not always been as meaningful to our brethren in the Third World as they are to us, for obvious reasons.

In the part of China in which I served, it was almost impossible to find any stone larger than a pebble, which made "Rock of Ages, cleft for me" seem a trifle out of place. "Jesus, Savior, pilot me over life's tempestuous sea" didn't make much sense either to people who had never seen a body of water larger than the Hsia River flowing slowly through the North China plain.

Western tunes are also a problem. The Chinese have a pentatonic scale with no half-notes. I remember my first assignment after our arrival in Fowyang. The annual Bible school was in session and I was assigned to teach music. I tried in vain to teach the simplest hymns in the book, for every time they came to a *fa* or *ti* they dropped half a note. By the time we reached the end of the fourth stanza they were in the basement! I never did succeed in getting them to sing the hymns "properly." Later when I visited the country churches, I discovered that they had come up with their own hymns— actually short choruses—written in their own words and set to their own pentatonic tunes. They had no trouble memorizing the words, for they dealt with themes out of their own rustic, agricultural background. As for the tunes, they were already familiar with them. They knew the words and tunes by heart so they needed no books, and they sang them with great gusto and delight. Each annual Bible conference they introduced a new chorus and sang it over and over, not only during the meetings but far into the night and even after they returned to their homes. I learned that when I visited the country churches I didn't need to take my hymnbook along; it was never used.

While on the subject of music let it be said that the national churches should be free to use their own musical instruments. They don't *have* to use a piano or an organ; they can use whatever instruments they are accustomed to. The fact that they sound strange to our ears is not important. The purpose of music in the church is to make a joyful noise to the Lord, and I don't think He has any of the hangups that bother us. If the music comes from the heart the instruments on which it is played make little difference.

8. Newspaper evangelism. This form of evangelism has been widely used and has proved to be very effective in Japan, where the literacy rate is almost 100 percent and where good newspapers with large circulations are found in all the cities. The plan was to use paid space in the daily press for presenting Christian truth through a series of expositions of Scripture. The articles were short, pithy, and to the point. Those wishing for additional help were invited to write. Their questions were answered by mail or by a personal interview. The same method has been used elsewhere, especially in Ghana, with good results. It is both direct and cheap and can be used to supplement radio ministry, which serves much the same purpose.

9. Literature for children. As more and more children are learning to read, it is imperative that suitable materials be provided for them. In this area, the gap between the affluence of the West and the poverty of the East is embarrassing. In the U.S. we have a superabundance of all kinds of Christian literature designed for all ages. We even have some books especially for boys and some especially for girls! In the larger countries such as India, Japan, the Philipppines, Nigeria, etc., they are beginning to make a dent in this problem, but in other countries almost nothing is available along this line. Perhaps missions should lead the way in the promotion, if not the actual production, of Christian literature for children.

10. Helps for preachers. The majority of national pastors are under-trained, underpaid, and overworked. To make matters worse they have large families to feed, clothe, and educate. For the most part their own education has been neglected. This is especially true in Africa and Latin America, where thousands of pastors have had little or no formal theological training. Even in other countries where the educational levels are fairly high the pastors have very few tools with which to do their work. Many of them know little about homiletics and less about hermeneutics. Very few of them possess a Bible dictionary, much less a Bible encyclopedia. They don't even have a concordance. As for expository books, there aren't any. As a result, the average pastor has to make his bricks without straw. The pastors who are fortunate enough to have been to Bible school or seminary usually have only the books they acquired at school. They seldom have money to invest in books later on, even if the books were available.

The church in the U.S.S.R. is particularly hard hit when it comes to suitable literature. Peter Deyneka, Jr., in a form letter dated January 2,

1979, deplores the "stark contrast" between the U.S. and the Soviet Union so far as the availability of Christian books and Bibles is concerned. He goes on to say: "When I asked one Russian pastor what books he needed he responded, 'The single, most valuable book of all would be a Bible study concordance. If you could get such a book to me, I would pay two months salary for it!'"

In Russia the problem stems from government interference. In other countries it has nothing to do with persecution. Production, or the lack of it, is the culprit. Such books are simply not available in the vernacular, and where they are available the price is often out of reach of the average pastor. So we have a twofold problem.

Both problems could be solved if some organization or foundation would provide the funds for the production of Bible helps for church leaders and make them available free of charge. No pastor would abuse the privilege of receiving free books. It is seldom a good idea to make outright gifts on the mission field, for by doing so we often undermine their desire to become self-supporting. Making Bible helps available, however, is one instance where an outright gift would be a godsend to the pastors and evangelists. It would in no way interfere with their obligation to become, or to remain, self-supporting. We have a precedent for this kind of operation here in the U.S. In colonial days the Society for Promoting Christian Knowledge (London) regarded it as one of its chief projects to stock the meager libraries of pastors in the American colonies, who greatly appreciated the service.

It is time to do something about this problem. Too many pastors are working without proper tools and their ministry is hampered thereby. It would be an excellent idea if each mission board were to set aside some funds every year for the purchase of books for the pastors and other church leaders in the Third World. We see to it that our missionaries are well supplied with everything they need, including the material things of life. Why should we not make sure that the national pastors are supplied with the helps they so desperately need. Imagine how our pastors at home, even those with seminary training, would get along without the many helps they have in their libraries. There is no greater need on the mission field today. Funds invested in this way will pay the highest dividends not only for time but also for eternity.

11. Literature for students. In the West the largest item in the national budget is often for military expenditures. In the Third World the largest item is for welfare and education. Since independence the number of college students has multiplied many times. In Mexico City, Tokyo, and some other large cities, there are well over 100,000 university students and the number is still rising. We used to say that students are the leaders of tomorrow, but in some cases they are the leaders of today. They have immense power as a body and have toppled one government after another in Africa, Asia, and Latin America.

For the most part, students are open to new ideas and eagerly read anything put into their hands. Tens of thousands of them, for lack of Christian literature, are reading material put out by the Marxists and are turning in ever increasing numbers to the Marxist view of history and society. This is especially true in Europe and Latin America. In those continents, to be a university student *is* to be a Marxist.

Both the Western missions and the national churches have been woefully negligent of this important sector of society. Few books have been written with the bright young students in mind. Many of them are frustrated with the status quo, fed up with the church, and completely dissatisfied as they face an uncertain future which holds little hope for the betterment of mankind. Christian books dealing with personal ethics, economics, politics, public morality, history, philosophy, and religion, are desperately needed. The work done along this line by InterVarsity Press in the U.S. must be duplicated on the mission field. IVP books should be translated into scores of languages and made available to the students of the Third World. Even if they were supplied in English, it would serve the purpose, since many students know English well enough to read books of this kind. It takes money and vision, however, and we seem to lack both at the moment. It would be even better if the young Christian scholars in the Third World were to write their own books; then they would not have to depend on translations. To accomplish this they also would need money and vision. We could easily supply the money; it would be more difficult to impart the vision.

Marxism purports to be the coming world philosophy and China and the U.S.S.R. are flooding the world with their propaganda in attractive book, pamphlet, and newspaper form. I daresay the students of the Third World are better acquainted with Marxism than with any other current ideology. Marxism, with its philosophical world view, its "scientific" interpretation of history, its land reform program, and its promise of a better life for the poor and the oppressed, is making converts among the intelligentsia faster than we Christians are making converts to Christ. Very few Christian students have an adequate understanding of the strengths and weaknesses of Marxism, for the simple reason that they have never examined it from a Christian point of view, nor can they hold their own with Communist agitators on the university campuses. The need for suitable Christian literature in this area is staggering.

12. Missionary literature. The aim of the Western-based missionary movement was to establish self-supporting, self-governing, and self-propagating churches, but the road to self-sufficiency is not an easy one. Until recently, these churches have been chiefly preoccupied with their own survival in a hostile environment. In the last ten or fifteen years, however, many of them have begun to show a definite interest in world missions.

Why did the national churches take so long to get the vision for world missions? Because the missionaries in the Bible schools taught everything *except* world missions. Western missionaries were responsible for world evangelization. The national churches did well if they paid their own pastors and maintained a strong local witness. World missions was neither taught in the Bible schools nor expected of the churches.

Books on world missions have yet to be produced in the Third World, and only a handful of Western books have been translated. *The Progress of Worldwide Missions* was translated into Chinese and Korean. *A Global View of Christian Missions* has also been translated into Chinese; *Christian Missions in Biblical Perspective* has been translated into Japanese and Chinese and doubtless other missions books have been translated into other languages, but they are not nearly enough.

Some missions courses should be included in the curriculum of the Bible colleges and seminaries of the Third World. These basic courses include History of Missions, Cross-Cultural Communication, Missionary Principles and Practice, Non-Christian Religions, and Area Studies. Non-Caucasian scholars should be writing texts for these courses, texts that will be culturally relevant to their own particular part of the world.

National leaders from the Third World who have taken missions courses at Fuller, Trinity, and other seminaries are now returning to their own countries. Some of them are pastors, but others are teaching missions in various Bible colleges. They should be writing the books that are so sorely needed. Hopefully, another ten or twenty years will show great advance in this area. There is no reason under the sun why world evangelization should continue to be "the white man's burden." It is every Christian's burden.

SLOW PROGRESS

The churches in Africa, through no fault of their own, are at least twenty years behind those in Asia. It will take time for them to produce the caliber of writer required for the new day. This is especially true in evangelical circles. Pius Wakatama, who has an M.A. in journalism, has already given us one fine book, *Independence for the Third World Church*. We can hope for others from his pen in the future. Wakatama himself bemoans the fact that much of the Christian literature in Africa was written by missionaries. Some of it was written in, or translated from, English by Africans who had rather limited training. Most of it is elementary and deals with such mundane subjects as smoking, drinking, dancing, and the evils of having more than one wife. Wakatama goes on to say:

> *Only African Christians can write books for our young people on courtship and marriage which also take into account the social change that we are undergoing due to Western influences without outraging our traditional customs. Unfortunately we have too many missionaries who insist on writing Christian literature for Africans. Some missionaries,*

*today, instead of training nationals in creative writing, do the writing
themselves and then ask the nationals to translate.*[5]

African Christian Press in Ghana is doing much to inspire and encourage
new African authors. A good number of their titles are relevant to the needs
of African Christians. Joyce Chaplin, in her book, *Adventures with a Pen*,
reprinted in paperback by ACP, challenges would-be writers on all continents to take advantage of the many opportunities for creative writing. From
her wide experience in Africa she gives step-by-step practical advice on how
to write books that will have an impact on both Christians and non-
Christians. Though written with special reference to Africa, this book is
exceedingly helpful for all Christians who would like to develop their writing
skills.[6]

Daystar is a research and communications center in Nairobi. Each summer it conducts an International Institute that attracts people from various
countries of the world as well as from all parts of Africa. Its purpose is to
encourage research in different forms of Christian communication. It has a
loose affiliation with Wheaton Graduate School whereby its graduates can
obtain a degree in communications.

DISTRIBUTION

This remains a bottleneck in the dissemination of Christian literature. It
is one thing to produce a book; it is another to get it into the hands of the
people for whom it was intended. The Christian presses in the U.S. have a
built-in distribution system that is the envy of the world. Christian
bookstores abound in every city of any size. Every Christian college and
seminary has its own bookstore. Thousands of professors in these institutions
get a catalog of books from the major publishers at least once a year. In the
catalogs, old and new books are listed under various categories: philosophy,
sociology, psychology, history, religion, missions, etc. In many instances
examination copies of new books are sent to professors free.

Every large denomination has its own publishing house and its churches
are furnished annually with a catalog. If a Sunday school superintendent or a
director of Christian Education needs material all he has to do is drop a
postcard into the mail on Monday and he will have it in time for the following
Sunday.

In the Third World it is entirely different. To begin with, Christian
literature is still a trickle compared with the enormous quantities we have in
this country. There are few Christian bookstores and mails are very uncer-

5. Pius Wakatama, *Independence for the Third World Church* (Downers Grove, IL: InterVarsity Press, 1976), p. 61.
6. The book can be obtained from David C. Cook Foundation, Elgin, Illinois 60120, or from
African Christian Press, P.O. Box 30, Achimota, Ghana.

tain. Pastors are not deluged with the second-class mail so plentiful here. Moreover, even if they had money to spend on books, there is no way to safely send money through the mail. How can these obstacles be overcome?

Missions should be encouraged to open bookstores in the larger foreign cities and, if necessary, to subsidize them until they become self-supporting. To attract a larger clientele and sell more books, they should stock non-religious books, magazines, and other literature. The profit from the non-religious merchandise will help defray the total cost of the operation. In time they will become self-supporting. From the beginning nationals should be trained to manage them, and they should take over as soon as possible so that the bookstores become an ongoing operation independent of the mission.

In the smaller cities the churches should be encouraged to keep on hand a good supply of Christian literature for the rural churches in their own district. In our city of Fowyang (China) I started such a bookstore. It was a modest affair occupying one small room in the church. The stock was limited to Bibles, hymnbooks, posters, and not more than a dozen other books. It soon became self-supporting with a full-time manager. It ministered to the needs of more than one hundred satellite churches in the rural areas. Every time an outstation leader came to town he would visit the bookstore and take home a supply of Bibles, hymnals, and posters. It was a small but effective operation. Without it those country churches would have been unable to get the materials they needed.

In the "good old days" the colporteur went from village to village selling Bibles. Perhaps in some areas there is still a need for such an approach, but we should be thinking, however, in terms of a larger enterprise. Missions could invest in bookmobiles which could carry thousands of books and travel far and wide, selling their wares door to door during the day and in the evenings holding evangelistic meetings and showing Christian films. In small towns films never fail to attract huge crowds, who are sometimes drawn for no other reason than the novelty. In many parts of the world the ministry of a bookmobile, if it remained in one place for a week, would almost certainly result in the establishment of new churches. In early 1979 the Sudan Interior Mission sent the first cinema van to Ghana. With a potential audience of 60,000 a month it is expected to be a powerful tool for evangelism.

29

Community Development

Dr. Paul Hiebert, speaking to the leaders of World Vision in 1978, said that in his opinion ten years from now only the missionary societies which combine development activities with their church growth concerns will be permitted to function in much of the non-Western world. Whether or not this actually comes to pass, one thing is clear: evangelical mission leaders must begin to make room in their church-planting program for community development.

Missions have always engaged in educational, medical, and sometimes agricultural work, but little of this was tied in with community development. Each mission carried out its own work without reference to government priorities or even to inter-mission cooperation. Today there is ample evidence that things are changing and evangelical missions are giving more attention to community development.

In December 1978 representatives of ten evangelical relief and development agencies met in Chicago and announced the formation of the Association of Evangelical Relief and Development Organizations (AERDO). The organization grew out of a series of informal meetings over the preceding two years and brought these agencies together for the purpose of addressing common concerns and needs.

Member organizations of AERDO are: Compassion International, Compassion/Canada, Development Assistance Services, Food for the Hungry, Food for the Hungry/Canada, Institute of International Development, Inc., MAP International, World Concern, World Relief Commission of NAE, and World Vision International.

Speaking of the goals of AERDO, President Arthur Beals said: "We are seeking better integration with the programs of evangelical mission organizations and local churches so that our services to communities in the developing world might be more coordinated. We are also anxious to maintain professional standards in our programs, staffs, and finances."[1]

While this is a good move the new organization includes only those agencies already engaged in relief and development, and the cooperation envisaged is cooperation among the agencies rather than with the groups on the receiving end—Third World governments and communities. It doesn't include the run-of-the-mill missions, denominational and interdenominational, that traditionally have engaged only in evangelistic, medical, and educational work. Hiebert's remark was really directed to them.

The ecumenical groups have long been engaged in community development. At the Conference on World Cooperation for Development in Beirut in April 1968, both the Roman Catholic and the Protestant churches called on the nations in the West to devote two percent of their Gross National Product to relief and development in the developing countries. A similar note was sounded at the Uppsala Assembly of the World Council of Churches in August of the same year. As a matter of fact the ecumenical groups today are chiefly interested in the social and economic betterment of mankind. Little is said about the appalling spiritual needs of the non-Christian world, where almost three billion persons are totally without any knowledge of Jesus Christ.

But Hiebert is telling us that the evangelical missions must engage in community development or they will find themselves barred from many countries. If this is true—and it may well be—it is the part of wisdom for the evangelicals to heed the warning and do what they can to help the developing nations in their struggle for social and economic justice. By doing so, they will have an open door to minister to the nation's spiritual needs as well.

WHAT IS MEANT BY DEVELOPMENT?

For centuries peoples in various parts of the world have tried to cope with the problems of famine, floods, pestilence, poverty, and hunger, but it is only in these post-war years that the problems of development have taken on global significance. With the founding of the United Nations in 1945 and the emergence of the newly independent countries beginning with India in 1947, the world has suddenly become conscious of the fact that it is divided into two parts: the "have" nations and the "have nots". With the help of the many agencies and missions of the United Nations the developing countries are determined to close the gap between these two groups, but this can be achieved only if development takes place on a massive scale.

Development, as the word is used today, involves all aspects of national

1. *Missionary News Service*, January 15, 1979, p. 2.

life: transportation, communications, education, health care, agriculture, flood and famine control, irrigation, industry, technology, and a host of other activities, all designed to raise the standard of living and assure the people of their full share of the "good life." Great strides have been made in some of these areas, particularly transportation and communication, but in others, progress has been all too slow. In addition, the growth in population in many countries has just about wiped out the economic progress achieved by the various five-year plans that have been devised. India has had five or six of these plans and all have been moderately successful, but the increase in population, which has doubled since independence, has left the peasants (80 percent of the population) just about where they were at that time.

Family planning obviously plays a role in the development process. Birth control, however, is exceedingly difficult to maintain in an agricultural economy where illiteracy runs high and where the children are expected to help their parents in the fields and on the farms, to say nothing of providing them with economic security in their old age. Only in China and Singapore has family planning been really successful.

LIMITATIONS OF DEVELOPMENT

Joseph Parker in his commentary on John 1:23 says: "It is a good thing when a man knows the limitations of his own calling." Mission leaders should realize that with their limited resources in men and money their contribution to community development will of necessity be on a very modest scale compared with what others can do. Missions have neither the manpower nor the funds to compete with the United Nations Development Program, or the World Bank, or the International Monetary Fund, or even the Ford and Rockefeller Foundations. Moreover, much of the poverty in the developing countries is caused by political and economic structures that are not susceptible to peaceful change. Land reform is an excellent idea which would go a long way towards solving the economic problems of the poverty-stricken peasants, but who can persuade the wealthy absentee landlords to voluntarily give up their land? Thus far, only the Communists and the totalitarian governments have succeeded in land reform. High tariffs, government restrictions, religious and cultural taboos, and unreasonable quotas often stand in the way of social and economic reforms, and there is little that the missionary can do to correct these. They are quite beyond his control.

This means that if missions in the future are to engage in community development they will have to be satisfied with modest plans and correspondingly meager results. They will not be able to build power plants or four-lane highways or international airports, but they will be able to make an important contribution to community development at the grassroots level. Agriculture will probably be their most fruitful field of endeavor. If it is true that two-thirds of the world's population go to bed hungry every night, agriculture is clearly a good area in which to begin. The worst poverty is found in the villages. It can be alleviated, or at least ameliorated, by new techniques and tools introduced by the missionary. A missionary with a degree in agriculture, working alongside the church-planting missionary, can do much for both the development of the country and the evangelization of the people.

People in the rural areas need a more adequate and more healthful water supply. In many places there are no wells, so they depend on polluted streams and stagnant pools for their drinking water. This results in sickness and generally poor health. The land is overworked and exhausted of all nutrients. Thus the food produced has little nutritional value. They don't need us to give them food. They need fertilizer in large quantities and they need to be taught how to use it.

The peasants in many areas depend on one crop—rice or wheat or sorghum or sweet potatoes—and they eat that staple 365 days a year. It is not quantity they need so much as quality and variety that will provide minerals, proteins, and vitamins. The agricultural missionary can work wonders by introducing new and better seeds, plants, vegetables, fruit trees, etc. Peanuts and soybeans are excellent sources of protein.

Instead of giving them clothes it is much better to provide a sewing machine and enough money to invest in several bolts of cloth. In this way they can make a decent living by sewing. Chicken farms can be set up in the same way. Better livestock can be introduced so that cows and goats will give more and better milk in addition to providing meat. With seed funds all kinds of small industries can be started; once started, they will pay for themselves and yield a profit for further development.

One of the most exciting examples of this kind of grassroots development is United Action, under the leadership of a Colombian pastor, Gregorio Landero. Working closely with the churches it shows Christians how to care for their health and how to farm productively. It helps them begin small industries to achieve economic well-being for their families in a region where most people, including Christians, are incredibly poor. United Action has started a 200-acre demonstration farm to aid in teaching the Christian farmers, and in the process has given opportunity to ten Christian families for a new start in life. It has also helped families get started with flocks of laying hens, supplying them with hybrid birds, feeds, medicines, and technical instruction. The eggs that are produced help provide needed protein as well as income.

Pastor Landero persuaded an extremely needy farmer about to migrate to the city to plant pineapples instead. The farmer took out a loan of 2000 pesos (about $100), bought some seed, and planted half a hectare. At harvest time he took the first 100 pineapples into Puerto Libertador and sold them all the first day for four pesos apiece. In no time at all he recovered his initial investment, paid off his debts, and went on to become a successful pineapple grower. This kind of simple yet effective operation can be duplicated a thousand times over in all parts of the world. This is development on a modest scale, but it is effective, costs very little, and renders a family independent for life. It is much better than handing out food or money.[2]

The peoples of the developing nations, even when the food supply is fairly adequate, seldom have enough meat and protein. Take Ghana as an example. Though the country now produces all of its own rice and nearly enough corn to meet the requirements of its almost ten million people, there is still a chronic shortage of meat. When animal products do find their way to market they are priced far beyond the reach of the majority of the people.

To meet this pressing need the government has launched a National Rabbit Program which promotes backyard rabbit breeding as a means of increasing meat supplies at low cost and with a minimum of effort. The rabbit has several characteristics which make it an ideal source of meat. Most significant is the short gestation period of only 31 days. A healthy female can produce 20 to 30 offspring in a year. Starting with a buck and a doe, a backyard breeder can obtain a quantity of meat over the course of a year equal to the weight of a cow. The byproducts of the rabbit are also of benefit to developing countries. Rabbit fur is a main ingredient of felt, and pelts can be used to make hats and coats. The brain is used in making a blood-clotting agent widely used in hospitals.

This is the kind of project that missions could undertake with a minimum of funds and effort. Once it is launched and the people get a taste for the meat it will become self-perpetuating. Only people who have lived in the Third World can possibly appreciate the full significance of such a modest development project.

LEVELS AT WHICH DEVELOPMENT OCCURS

There are four levels at which the missions can undertake this kind of work.

1. **The government.** It is always desirable to work in cooperation with local officials. In some countries the missionaries have no choice. They are required to submit all their projects to the government for its approval. This is the case in Nepal and to a lesser extent in Afghanistan. The United Mission to Nepal, comprising some 30 mission agencies and almost 200 missionaries, is working in three major areas: education, medicine, and community development. Religious work is forbidden; it is against Nepalese law to change one's religion. Every Nepali Christian who accepts baptism faces a one-year prison term, and the person who administers baptism may get seven years in prison. In spite of this, after 30 years of work in Nepal there are 6,000 Christians in 200 communities throughout the country. Not all of these are the result of work done by the UMN, but the non-verbal witness of this dedicated group of missionaries has reaped great rewards.

2. Landero's story can be found in *Latin American Evangelist*, November-December 1972. January-February 1974.

More and more governments, especially in the smaller countries, are demanding that the non-religious activities of mission agencies be coordinated with the development plans of the government, which is perfectly reasonable. Christian missionaries can be grateful that the governments are showing a concern for the physical and material needs of the people. It was not always so.

Let no one imagine, however, that working in cooperation with government agencies is always a pleasant experience. Inevitably there are difficulties, delays, misunderstandings, inefficiencies, and the usual amount of red tape, all of which can be frustrating to the Western missionary who would much prefer to "get on with the job" without having to consult anybody. We are living in a new day and the new day makes new demands on all of us.

A missionary in Nepal writes:

> *There is more and more emphasis being placed on cooperation with the host government. Previously missions could go into an unserviced area and start up a medical work largely independent of the government's plans. That is no longer advisable and often not possible in today's developing world. Missions more and more are signing agreements with governments and making determined efforts to mesh with and support government programs rather than to do their own thing. It's much more fun and self-satisfying to do your own thing. Much less frustrating. Many missionary personnel are being seconded to government agencies where they must work under orders of the agency in question. That's the toughest kind of missionary work going now, in my opinion. That's really getting out of the "mission compound." And it is a good trend, and opens up tremendous new opportunities for witness.* [3]

2. The community. Even where the government doesn't demand coordination it is still wise to work in cooperation with the leaders of the local community. Too often in the past relief work has been done by mission agencies working on their own without consulting the local leaders.

The Peace Corps can teach us a lesson at this point. All Peace Corps projects *must* be carried out with the consent and cooperation of the local community. Indeed, the government or the community must supply both the funds and the materials. No Peace Corps volunteer is authorized to begin a project on his own. Even if it takes him six months, he *must* get the consent and cooperation of the populace. This ensures that the people will consider the project as theirs and thus will continue it even after the Peace Corps has withdrawn.

Both the Peace Corps and the Christian mission have encountered three formidable obstacles: ignorance, superstition, and indifference, and the greatest of these is indifference. A missionary engaged in medical work wrote to his friends:

3. Letter from Dr. Tom Hale, September 23, 1978.

It is a humbling experience to come into an area of half a million people served by one other missionary doctor and realize that 90 percent of the inhabitants couldn't have cared less whether we came or not. Most of the people here still have not come to appreciate any particular advantage in modern medicine. In their view we are simply another kind of peddler selling our wares. They regard us with a natural distrust and suspicion, not being able to comprehend our motive for coming to their land. . . . Many of our patients have no sense of gratitude for our services; rather they expect that we be grateful to them for providing us with an opportunity to gain merit for ourselves by treating their illnesses.

Perhaps the greatest obstacle to improving health care in an area such as ours occurs in the field of preventive medicine. Centuries of customs and superstitions militate against any hope of significantly improved health standards until widespread and effective health education can be made available to the younger generation. We are looked upon with amusement when we fuss about all sorts of invisible creatures like bacteria and tiny worms. Nepalis prepare and serve their meals on mud floors and eat with their hands. The water supply is usually contaminated, and they resist boiling their water because it flattens the taste and uses up their already limited firewood. Latrines and outhouses are a curiosity, and the progressive citizen who ventures to construct such a facility usually abandons the whole project after a week because the place stinks so badly. [4]

Such a predicament points up the necessity of working with the community leaders, getting their support, and integrating all efforts at relief and development. The schools must begin to teach the basic principles of personal hygiene and public sanitation. Otherwise the missionary labors in vain. Preventive medicine is really what is needed. In many respects it is more important than therapeutic medicine, but it is much more difficult to promote. A surgical operation may be performed in an hour or two and within ten days the patient is able to leave the hospital and return home, to the delight of himself and his relatives. But to persuade that same community to improve its health standards to *prevent* disease is an entirely different matter. It takes a whole generation of educational effort *plus* the support and cooperation of the community leaders. This is why working at this level is so important.

3. The church. The ultimate goal of every mission is to establish self-supporting, self-governing, self-propagating churches, and in most countries we have almost achieved this goal. One thing we have not done, however, is to secure the active cooperation of the church in the matter of community development. If such development is taking place at all it is being accomplished largely without the church. Too often the missions are content to go it alone without getting the churches involved.

4. Ibid.

Even in medical work this is often the case. The hospital or the clinic is in charge of the doctors, most of whom are missionaries. There are national staff members, but they are hired by the hospital as individuals, not as church members. The church feels no responsibility for the medical institution. They are quite willing to have the mission carry this responsibility.

Some of this is due to the poverty of the people, which also accounts for the reluctance of the church to assume additional financial responsibilities. It is difficult enough, they say, to pay their own bills without having to help defray the expenses of a hospital. This, however, is not the whole story. The missions have always had a tendency to operate their medical institutions without any reference to the churches. As a result, the churches have felt no great desire to become involved. This state of affairs must be changed. The churches, however small and weak they may be, should be encouraged to participate in the operation of the hospital. It should be understood that it is *their* hospital and as such should have their help and support. Even if they can't make any financial contribution there are other ways in which they can be identified with it. The pastor and several of the church leaders should be active members of the board that runs the hospital.

Working with the church is much easier and more satisfying than working with either the government or the community. Church people are usually more dependable, more dedicated, and have more reasons than others to support community development. Christianity seldom fails to inspire its devotees to greater effort at self-improvement. Christian parents want their children to have an education even if they themselves had none. Where there is no school the church should be guided in starting one with the help of the missionaries. If the children cannot pay for tuition, the mission should encourage the church to start some business enterprises that will render the school self-supporting. This should also be done with Bible schools. The students could study half time and work half time to put themselves through. Thus, if the missionaries were ever to be withdrawn the school would not fold.

The churches should urge their members to work together to start their own small businesses, family industries, credit unions, etc. In this way the standard of living among the Christians could be raised, not only enabling them to enjoy a better life for themselves but also giving them the opportunity to contribute more to the needs of the church. Assistance offered by the Rural Development Department of the Evangelical Churches of West Africa enabled Christian farmers to increase their annual harvest offering tenfold between 1975 and 1979.

Even community development involving non-Christians should be a concern of the church. This is one way in which the church can show its compassion for the poor and its desire to enhance the welfare of the entire community. Too often the church has left community development to the mission and in so doing has overlooked an occasion to manifest the love of Christ to the needy.

It is estimated that 60 percent of the Christians in India come from a background of untouchability, and their lot in life has not been greatly improved since they became Christians. J. Singarayar asserts: "Conversion to Christianity has not really changed their culture and their caste, nor their status in social and economic life. They remain on the last rung of the social ladder."[5]

As a result many Christians of Scheduled Caste origin, as they are known, have reconverted to Hinduism to receive the preferential treatment the government is now giving them to compensate for its past unfair treatment. In society they have been treated as untouchables, and in the Christian church they are often regarded as second-class citizens. They must sit in a separate place in the church, their weddings are performed not at the main altar but at a side altar, and their dead are buried in separate cemeteries.

Singarayar concludes with a plea to end discrimination in the church and a request for united effort to pressure the government to stop its discrimination. But the real problem is one of economics. The church in India, with the help of Christian missions, should be able to give economic aid to these people. If suitable jobs which pay a living wage cannot be found, they should be made. Here is a glorious opportunity for missions and churches to work together for the development of a large sector of the Christian community. If this problem could be solved the image of the church in India would be greatly enhanced, the gospel would become more attractive, and church growth would be advanced.

4. The individual. In every society there are enterprising individuals who, given an opportunity, will rise to the top and become not only productive citizens but community leaders. All they lack is an economic base from which to work. If they could somehow raise the necessary capital they would start their own business and in a few years become employers of labor.

These individuals may or may not be Christians. That is not the important thing. They should be given a chance to see what they can do for themselves and their families. Who knows? In the process they may become Christians.

Most missionaries, not without good reason, think the free enterprise system is better than socialism. This is the time for them to put their convictions into action.

WHERE CAN FUNDS BE FOUND?

Community development even on a small scale requires seed money. Where can the missions get the money that is needed when they are having such a difficult time just keeping ahead of the devaluation of the U.S. dollar at home and inflation abroad?

5. *National Christian Council Review*, August 1978.

It is a little-known fact that in the various government agencies in Washington there are tens of millions of dollars waiting to be allocated to any available projects. Government leaders prefer to make these funds available to mission agencies who already have the personnel, the programs, and the expertise to handle them. They know that if money is channeled through religious organizations it is more likely to end up where it belongs—in the hands of the poor. Missions have an excellent record when it comes to relief and rehabilitation in the Third World, and the U.S. government knows this. This explains its willingness to make these funds available for the asking. It is too bad that so few mission leaders are aware of these possibilities.

Such funds should as much as possible be given as seed money on a revolving basis. Then when the individual has established himself he can pay back the loan, thus making it available to a second person and a third, on down the line.

One Christian organization, the Institute for International Development, is working exclusively in this area and it has access to this money. It needs dedicated laymen with various skills and expertise to spend a year or two overseas setting up a small business enterprise, teaching the nationals to run it, and then withdrawing when they have achieved their purpose. When the business begins to make a fair profit the seed money is returned and made available to help another business to get started.

If Christians participate in these business ventures the entire church gains. The family income is doubled or tripled in a few years and increased giving to the church becomes possible. This enables the church to become self-supporting, to expand its ministry, and to pay its pastor a living wage.

A CONCRETE EXAMPLE

Concord, Inc., of Fargo, N.D., is a new organization established by a former student of mine at Trinity Evangelical Divinity School. Its purpose is to help facilitate the growth of Third World countries, a growth to be reflected physically, intellectually, and spiritually. The name Concord was chosen because it symbolizes the company's goal of reaching mutual agreement with the national leadership and local populace in a country before a project is begun.

Concord, Inc., has outlined five basic objectives: 1. To achieve a sympathetic understanding of Third World problems relating to agricultural conditions, the socio-political framework, and the potential for technology appropriate to the milieu. 2. To develop liaison with Third World leaders to plan cooperative projects for selected agricultural mechanization. 3. To design and produce agricultural machinery at prices that are realistic for farmers in developing countries; to begin production of a small 4-wheel drive, hydrostatically driven tractor with optional auxiliary equipment. 4. To market and help finance such machinery, chiefly in the Third World; also to manufacture locally where possible. 5. To institute training, marketing, and maintenance centers around the supply depots developed for the tractor. There would be an effort to staff these centers with nationals as soon as possible.

Four models of a small tractor have already been produced and are now being tested at several agricultural centers in the U.S. before they are exported. Each piece of machinery must have five characteristics: (1) Simplicity—easy to operate; (2) Durability—long life; (3) Serviceability—easy to repair; (4) Performance—does many jobs well; (5) Value—at the most reasonable price.

If agricultural machinery is to function effectively in the developing countries where technology is almost unknown, it must have these characteristics. Too often Western organizations have engaged in ambitious projects in Third World countries only to have them fail completely. The machinery would break down in the first month, and without spare parts or skilled mechanics to take care of the repairs the project would come to a screeching halt. The machinery was left to rust in the field.

ONE EVANGELICAL MISSION

There is growing evidence that evangelical missions are catching the vision of an integrated ministry not only to the whole person but also to the entire community. The following paragraphs are taken from a brochure published by the BMMF International.

> As the compassionate Christ engaged in a ministry of healing, so we are pledged to deal with disease, debility, and deformity in His name. Christian medical service, however, should be considered an integral part of over-all community development, which involves assisting communities to achieve physical, mental, social, and spiritual well-being; motivating them to self-reliance, and encouraging them to attain social justice and vital necessities, for the realization of the dignity of the individual as a creature made in the image of God.
>
> In cooperation with other agencies, we are committed to community development programs which include health care (curative, preventive, and promotive); economic development (community dynamics, functional literacy, vocational education, agriculture, and appropriate technology); training nationals at every level of medical and economic development work; pastoral and evangelistic ministry among medical, nursing, and paramedical staff/students, as opportunity is providentially given.
>
> Such a comprehensive ideal is like the North Star. Although it may not be reached, it is useful to steer by. The realization of the vision may be limited by our resources of money and manpower, as well as national openness and political stability abroad. But the pursuit of this program should not distract us from our ultimate goal: the making of disciples, in obedience to His mandate.

EPILOGUE

Missionary work is hard but missionary life is both rewarding and exciting. To have even a small part in the evangelization of the world is the highest honor that can be conferred on any member of the Christian church.

A large American firm in Japan was looking for a person who could fill a top post in the company. He would have to be fairly young, bright, honest, aggressive, and absolutely dependable. Moreover, he would need to have administrative ability. Above all, he must be able to speak Japanese fluently. The search went on for some time without success. At last they thought they had their man—a missionary.

They forthwith made him a generous offer with all kinds of fringe benefits which he proceeded to turn down. Later they came back with another offer, bigger and better than the first. Again, he said no. They contacted him a third time with an offer so tempting they were sure he would accept. But again he said, "No, thanks."

Finally they asked him: "What's the problem? Is the salary not big enough?" He replied, "The salary is big enough; it's the job that's too small."

Select Bibliography

Adeney, David H. *The Unchanging Commission*. Chicago: InterVarsity Press, 1955.
Adolph, Paul E. *Missionary Health Manual*. Chicago: Moody, 1970.
Allen, Roland. *The Ministry of the Spirit*. Grand Rapids: Eerdmans, 1962.
————. *Missionary Methods: St. Paul's or Ours*. Grand Rapids: Eerdmans, 1962.
————. *The Spontaneous Expansion of the Church*. Grand Rapids: Eerdmans, 1962.
Almquist, Arden. *Missionary, Come Back*. New York: World, 1970.
Beaver, R. Pierce, ed. *To Advance the Gospel: Selections from the Writings of Rufus Anderson*. Grand Rapids: Eerdmans, 1967.
Beck, James R. *Parental Preparation of Missionary Children For Boarding School*. Taipei, Taiwan: Mei Ya Publications, 1968.
Brewster, E. Thomas and Elizabeth S. *Language Acquisition Made Practical*. Colorado Springs, CO: Lingua House, 1976.
Broomhall, A. J. *Time for Action*. London: Inter-Varsity Christian Fellowship, 1965.
Brown, Arthur J. *The Foreign Missionary*. New York: Revell, 1950.
Brown, Ina C. *Understanding Other Cultures*. Englewood Cliffs, NJ: Prentice-Hall, 1963.
Bryant, David. *In the Gap: What It Means to be a World Christian*. Downers Grove, IL: InterVarsity Press, 1979.
Cable, Mildred and Francesca French. *Ambassadors for Christ*. Chicago: Moody, 1935.
Cannon, Joseph L. *For Missionaries Only*. Grand Rapids: Baker, 1969.
Cervin, Russell A. *Mission in Ferment*. Chicago: Covenant Press, 1977.
Chambers, Oswald. *So Send I You*. Fort Washington, PA: Christian Literature Crusades (Reprint), 1975.
Clark, Dennis E. *The Third World and Mission*. Waco, TX: Word Books, 1971.
Cleveland, Harlan et al. *The Overseas Americans*. New York: McGraw-Hill, 1960.
Coggins, Wade T. *So That's What Missions Is All About*. Chicago: Moody, 1975.
———— and E. L. Frizen. *Evangelical Missions Tomorrow*. S. Pasadena, CA: Wm. Carey Library, 1977.

Collins, Majorie A. *Manual for Accepted Candidates*. S. Pasadena, CA: Wm. Carey Library, 1973.

———. *Manual for Missionaries on Furlough*. S. Pasadena, CA: Wm. Carey Library, 1972.

———. *Who Cares About the Missionary?* Chicago: Moody, 1974.

Cook, Harold R. *An Introduction to the Study of Christian Missions*. Chicago: Moody, 1954.

———. *Missionary Life and Work*. Chicago: Moody, 1959.

Cornell, D. L. *The Role of Single Women in Present Day Missions*. Fort Washington, PA: Worldwide Evangelization Crusade, 1965.

Corwin, Charles. *East to Eden? Religion and the Dynamics of Social Change*. Grand Rapids: Eerdmans, 1972.

Cotterell, Peter. *Language and the Christian: A Guide to Communication and Understanding*. London: Bagster, 1978.

Cousins, Peter and Pamela. *The Power of the Air*. London: Hodder and Stoughton, 1978.

Darkes, Anna Sue. *How to Make and Use Overhead Transparencies*. Chicago: Moody, 1978.

Dayton, Edward R., ed. *Medicine and Missions: A Survey of Medical Missions*. Wheaton, IL: Medical Assistance Program, 1969.

———. *That Everyone May Hear*. Monrovia, CA: Missions Advanced Research and Communication Center, 1979.

———. *You Can So Get There from Here*. Monrovia, CA: Missions Advanced Research and Communication Center, 1979.

DiGangi, Mariano. *I Believe in Mission*. Phillipsburg, NJ: Presbyterian and Reformed Published Company, 1979.

Dodge, Ralph E. *The Unpopular Missionary*. Westwood, NJ: Revell, 1964.

Douglas, J. D., ed. *Let the Earth Hear His Voice: International Congress on World Evangelization, Lausanne*. Minneapolis: World Wide Publications, 1975.

Engstrom, Ted W. *What in the World Is God Doing?* Waco, TX: Word Books, 1978.

Exley, Helen and Richard. *In Search of the Missionary*. London: Highway Press, 1970.

Fenton, Horace L. *Myths About Missions*. Downers Grove, IL: InterVarsity Press, 1973.

Fife, Eric S. *Man's Peace God's Glory*. Chicago: Inter-Varsity Christian Fellowship, 1961.

Fleming, Daniel Johnson. *Living as Comrades*. New York: Agricultural Missions, 1950.

———. *What Would You Do?* New York: Friendship, 1949.

Fuller, W. Harold. *Mission Church Dynamics*. S. Pasadena, CA: Wm. Carey Library, 1980.

Glasser, Arthur F. et al. *Crucial Dimensions in World Evangelization*. S. Pasadena, CA: Wm. Carey Library, 1976.

Goldsmith, Martin. *Just Don't Stand There*. Downers Grove, IL: InterVarsity Press, 1976.

Gray, Bryce, H. *Buying Print*. Wheaton, IL: Evangelical Literature Overseas, n.d.

Griffiths, Michael M. *Give Up Your Small Ambitions*. London: InterVarsity Press, 1976.

———. *Who Really Sends the Missionary?* Chicago: Moody, 1974.

Grunlan, Stephan A. and Marvin K. Mayers. *Cultural Anthropology: A Christian Perspective*. Grand Rapids: Zondervan, 1978.

Hancock, Robert L. *The Ministry of Development in Evangelical Perspective*. S. Pasadena, CA: Wm. Carey Library, 1979.

Hardin, Daniel C. *Mission: A Practical Approach to Church-Sponsored Mission World*. S. Pasadena, CA: Wm. Carey Library, 1977.

Healey, Alan. *Language Learner's Field Guide*. Huntington Beach, CA: Summer Institute of Linguistics, 1975.

Henderson, W. Guy. *Passport to Missions*. Nashville, TN: Broadman Press, 1979.

Hesselgrave, David J. *Communicating Christ Cross-Culturally*. Grand Rapids: Zondervan, 1978.

Hillis, Don. *I Don't Feel Called (Thank the Lord!)*. Wheaton, IL: Tyndale, 1973.

Hodges, Melvin L. *The Indigenous Church and the Missionary*. S. Pasadena, CA: Wm. Carey Library, 1978.

Hogben, Rowland. *In Training*. Chicago: Inter-Varsity Christian Fellowship, 1946.

Houghton, A. T. *Preparing to Be a Missionary*. London: Inter-Varsity Christian Fellowship, 1956.

Howard, David M. *Student Power in World Evangelism*. Downers Grove, IL: Inter-Varsity Press, 1970.

Isais, Juan. *The Other Side of the Coin*. Grand Rapids: Eerdmans, 1966.

Kane, J. Herbert. *The Making of a Missionary*. Grand Rapids: Baker, 1975.

‗‗‗‗‗‗. *Understanding Christian Missions*. Grand Rapids: Baker, 1974.

‗‗‗‗‗‗. *Winds of Change in the Christian Mission*. Chicago: Moody, 1973.

Keidel, Levi O. *Stop Treating Me Like God*. Carol Stream, IL: Creation House, 1971.

Kiser, Wayne. *From Manuscript to Printed Piece*. Wheaton, IL: Evangelical Literature Overseas, n.d.

Kitagawa, Daisuke. *Race Relations and Christian Mission*. New York: Friendship, 1964.

Kraft, Charles H. *Christianity in Culture*. Maryknoll, NY: Orbis, 1979.

Lamott, Willis C. *Revolution in Missions*. New York: Macmillan, 1954.

Larsen, Donald and William Smalley. *Becoming Bilingual: A Guide to Language Learning*. S. Pasadena, CA: Wm. Carey Library, 1972.

Ledyard, Gleason H. *Sky Waves: The Incredible Far East Broadcasting Company Story*. Chicago: Moody, 1963.

Lindsell, Harold, ed. *The Church's Worldwide Mission*. Waco, TX: Word Books, 1966.

‗‗‗‗‗‗. *Missionary Principles and Practice*. Westwood, NJ: Revell, 1955.

Lockerbie, D. Bruce. *Education of Missionaries' Children: The Neglected Dimension of World Mission*. S. Pasadena, CA: Wm. Carey Library, 1976.

Luzbetak, Louis J. *The Church and Cultures*. Techny, IL: Divine Word Press, 1963.

McCurry, Don M., ed. *The Gospel and Islam*. Monrovia, CA: Missions Advanced Research and Communication Center, 1979.

McGavran, Donald. *The Clash Between Christianity and Cultures*. Grand Rapids: Baker, 1974.

‗‗‗‗‗‗. *Crucial Issues in Missions Tomorrow*. Chicago: Moody, 1972.

‗‗‗‗‗‗. *Eye of the Storm*. Waco, TX: Word Books, 1972.

Mickelsen, Alvera. *How to Write Missionary Letters*. Wheaton, IL: Evangelical Literature Overseas, n.d.

Miller, Sheila. *Pigtails, Petticoats and the Old School Tie*. Robesonia, PA: Overseas Missionary Fellowship, 1981.

Moore, Raymond and Dorothy. *Home Grown Kids: A Practical Handbook for Teaching your Children at Home*. Waco, TX: Word, 1981.

Morgan, G. Helen. *Who'd Stay a Missionary?* Fort Washington, PA: Christian Literature Crusade, 1971.

‗‗‗‗‗‗. *Who'd Stay a Missionary?* Fort Washington, PA: Christian Literature Crusade, 1971.

Murray, Andrew. *Key to the Missionary Problem*. Fort Washington, PA: Christian Literature Crusade, 1979.

Nelson, Marlin L. *The How and Why of Third World Missions*. S. Pasadena, CA: Wm. Carey Library, 1976.

———. *Readings in Third World Missions*. S. Pasadena, CA: Wm. Carey Library, 1976.

Nida, Eugene A. *Customs and Culture: Anthropology for Christian Missions*. S. Pasadena, CA: Wm. Carey Library, Reprint, 1975.

———. *Religion Across Cultures*. New York: Harper and Row, 1968.

———. *Understanding Latin Americans*. S. Pasadena, CA: Wm. Carey Library, 1974.

Phillips, J. B. *The Church Under the Cross*. New York: Macmillan, 1956.

Preheim, Marion K. *Overseas Service Manual*. Scottdale, PA: Herald Press, 1969.

Richardson, Don. *Peace Child*. Glendale, CA: Regal, 1974.

Rosengrant, John et al. *Assignment: Overseas*. New York: Thomas Y. Crowell, 1955.

Rutledge, Don. *The Missionary Photographer*. Wheaton, IL: Evangelical Literature Overseas, n.d.

Sargent, Douglas N. *The Making of a Missionary*. London: Hodder and Stoughton, 1960.

Scherer, James A. *Global Living Here and Now*. New York: Friendship, 1974.

———. *Missionary Go Home: A Reappraisal of the Christian World Mission*. Englewood Cliffs, NJ: Prentice-Hall, 1964.

Schroetenboer, Paul B. *Training for Missions*. Grand Rapids: Reformed Ecumenical Synod, 1976.

Seel, David J. *Challenge and Crisis in Missionary Medicine*. S. Pasadena, CA: Wm. Carey Library, 1979.

Soltau, T. Stanley. *Facing the Field*. Grand Rapids: Baker, 1959.

Stone, Clara. *Library Manual for Missionaries*. Watertown, MN: Christian Librarians' Fellowship, 1979.

Stott, John and Robert T. Coote, eds. *Gospel and Culture*. Pasadena, CA: Wm. Carey Library, 1979.

Street, Harold B. *Distributing Christian Literature*. Wheaton, IL: Evangelical Literature Overseas, n.d.

Subbamma, B. V. *New Patterns for Discipling Hindus*. S. Pasadena, CA: Wm. Carey Library, 1970.

Taylor, Rhena. *Rough Edges: Christians Abroad in Today's World*. Leicester: Inter-Varsity Press and London: Patmos Press, 1978.

Troutman, Charles. *Everything You Want to Know About the Mission Field*. Downers Grove, IL: InterVarsity Press, 1976.

Tuggy, Joy T. *The Missionary Wife and Her Work*. Chicago: Moody, 1966.

Wagner, C. Peter, ed. *Church/Mission Tensions Today*. Chicago: Moody, 1972.

———. *Frontiers in Missionary Strategy*. Chicago: Moody, 1972.

———. *Stop the World I Want to Get On*. Glendale, CA: Regal, 1973.

Wakatama, Pius. *Independence for the Third World Church: An African's Perspective on Missionary Work*. Downers Grove, IL: InterVarsity Press, 1976.

Warren, Max, ed. *To Apply the Gospel: Selections from the Writings of Henry Venn*. Grand Rapids: Eerdmans, 1971.

Webster, Douglas. *Yes to Mission*. New York: Seabury, 1966.

Williamson, Mabel. *Have We No Right?* Chicago: Moody, 1957.

Wilson, J. Christy. *Today's Tentmakers*. Wheaton, IL: Tyndale House, 1979.